The Giant Encyclopedia of Kindergarten Activities

Over 600 Activities
Created by Teachers for Teachers

Edited by Kathy Charner,
Maureen Murphy, and
Jennifer Ford

Illustrated by Kathi Whelan Dery

Dedication

This book is dedicated to all the wonderful, curious, and enthusiastic five-year-olds and wonderful, curious, and enthusiastic adults who teach them.

The GIANT Encyclopedia of Kindergarten Activities

Over 600 Activities
Created by Teachers for Teachers

Edited by Kathy Charner,
Maureen Murphy, and Jennifer Ford

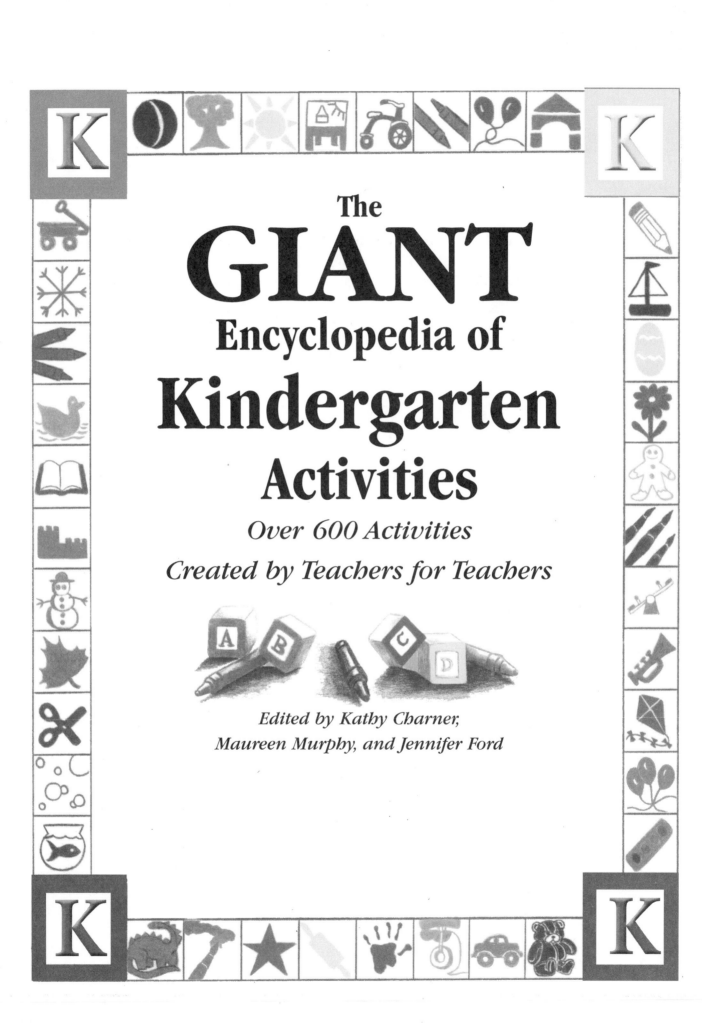

Bulk purchase

Gryphon House books are available for special premiums and sales promotions as well as for fund-raising use. Special editions or book excerpts also can be created to specification. For details, contact the Director of Marketing at Gryphon House.

Disclaimer

Gryphon House, Inc. and the authors cannot be held responsible for damage, mishap, or injury incurred during the use of or because of activities in this book. Appropriate and reasonable caution and adult supervision of children involved in activities and corresponding to the age and capability of each child involved, is recommended at all times. Do not leave children unattended at any time. Observe safety and caution at all times.

Copyright

© 2004 Gryphon House, Inc.
Published by Gryphon House, Inc.
10726 Tucker Street, Beltsville, MD 20705
800.638.0928; 301.595.9500; 301.595.0051 (fax)

Visit us on the web at www.gryphonhouse.com

Illustrations: Kathi Whelan Dery
Cover Art: Beverly Hightshoe

Library of Congress Cataloging-in-Publication Data

The giant encyclopedia of kindergarten activities / edited by Kathy Charner, Maureen Murphy, and Jennifer Ford ; [illustrations, Kathi Whelan Dery].
    p. cm.
Includes index.
  ISBN 13: 978-0-87659-285-4
  ISBN 10: 0-87659-285-X
  1. Kindergarten--Activity programs--Encyclopedias.
I. Charner, Kathy. II. Murphy, Maureen. III. Ford, Jennifer, 1980-
  LB1169.G52 2004
  372.21'8--dc22

200302571

Table of Contents

Introduction 15

    How to Use This Book 17

Art

My Own Art Apron 19

Artistic Autograph 20

Personalized Name Plates 21

USA Rugs 21

Homemade Sidewalk Chalk 22

Silly Putty 23

Grass Playdough 23

Bag Wrappers 24

Wallpaper Artwork 25

Salad Spinner Art 26

Incredible Shrinking Art 26

Aluminum Foil Crinkle Art 27

Dried Glue Ornaments 28

Plastic Wrap Art 29

Baby Footprint 29

A Piece of Beach 30

Water Roll 31

Scented Pictures 31

Butterfly Feet 32

Talented Toes 33

Magic Opposites 33

Evaporating Painting 34

Fish Kite 35

Tissue Paper Corsage 37

A Cutting Mosaic 37

My Kindergarten Quilt 38

Patchwork Colors 38

My Jeans Picture 39

Paper Bag Birds 40

Portraits 41

Razzle Dazzle Raindrops 42

Pressed Flower Placemats 43

Crunchy Leaf Creatures 44

Leaf Rubbing Wreath 45

Autumn Leaf Ornaments 46

Autumn All Around 47

Clay Leaf Roll-Outs 48

ClayPressions 48

Snazzy Sunflowers 49

Snow-Painted Pictures 51

Coffee Filter Snowflakes 51

Ball Bounce Art 52

Marble Spider Webs 52

Spider Web Weaving 53

Stamp Printing Helper 54

Rainbow Blend 54

Strips of Color 55

Bug Headband 55

Memory Shirt 57

Blocks

First Day of School Sculpture 58

Labeling Blocks 58

Block Beach Party 59

Building the Great Wall of China 60

Cardboard Cityscapes 61

The Letter Bb 62

Special Block Play People 63

Books

Caring for Books 64
Book Buckets 64
Author Study 65
The Bookworm 66
Chocolate Kiss Bookmarks 67
Stage Debut 67
Bring a Storybook Character to Life . . . 68
Stick Puppet of a Book Character 69
Stuffed Animal Collection 70
Food Riddle Book 70
Bear-shaped Big Book 71
Alphabet Photo Book 72
What Do You See? 74
Personalized Classroom
    "Brown Bear" Book 74
Curious George Hunt 76
Children's Book Week 77
Alligator Purse 78
"Old Lady in the Shoe" Shoelaces 80
Our Tribute to Eric Carle 80
Alphabet Caterpillar 81
Our Own Secret Message 82
Book Character Introductions 83
Flannel Board
    Chicka Chicka Boom Boom 83
Chicken Soup With Rice Poems 84
Colorful Bears 85
Corduroy's Pocket 85
"Gingerbread Boy" Marionette 86
Horton Hears a Who Obstacle Course . 88
I Have a Family 88
If I Were President... 89
Glittery Leaves 90
Planting a Beanstalk 90
Rhyming Words 91
The Houses of the Three Little Pigs 92

A Variety of Three Little Pigs 93
The Three Bears Go to Bed 94
Mixing Colors Like Mice 95
Movin' in the Grass 95
Nature and Creative Movement 96
Owling 96
Making an Insect 97
Tadpoles and Frogs 99
Polar Express Day 100
It Looked Like... 100
It Looked Like Spilt Milk Paint Blots . . 101
Sponge-Painted Swimmy 102
A Bunny and a Duck 104
Where Do I Live? 105

Circle Time

Carpet Squares 109
Friendship Flag for Circle Time 109
Circle Time by Month 110
Holiday Circle Time Helpers 111
Whose Is It? 112
Star of the Day 112
Hobbies and Collections 113
Class Weather Forecaster 113
Dress-Up Song 114
Colors, Colors, Colors 115
Pet Store 115
Safety School 116
Chicka Chicka Boom Boom These
    Are the Letters I've Learned
    in My Room 117
Are You Game? 118

Dramatic Play

Let's Pretend 119
Jester Hat 119
Blast Off Into Space 120
Delivering the Mail 121
Dinosaur Dig 121

The Circus Comes to Town 122
Dramatic Play Circus 124
Flying Carpet 124
Funky Fashion Show 125
Grow an Indoor Garden 125
Learning to Count 126
Let's Camp Out 126
Dramatic Play Library 127
Ocean Life 128
Puppet House 129
Sledding and Winter Fun 130
A Snowman That Won't Melt 131
Study the Arctic 132
Indoor Shanties 132
Play Restaurant 134
Taking Restaurant Orders 134
Wagons Ho! 135

Fine Motor

Button Buzzers 137
Candy Cane Ornaments 138
Hopping Origami 138
Make a Quilt 140
Cereal Box Puzzles 140
Name Puzzles 141
Photo Puzzles 141
Paper Pizzas 142
The Scissors Store 142
See-Through Pockets 143
Sew Fun 144
Scented Seaside Playdough 145
Scented Playdough 145
Squiggle Pen Mazes 146
Sad Little Rabbit Story 146
Teach Me to Tie 147

Fingerplays, Songs, and Poems

Calendar Snowmen 148
Dame Cinco, Give Me Five 151

Buenos Dias Greeting Song 151
Cinco Vaqueros 152
Call a Friend 153
Silly Songs 154
Craft Stick Count 155
Did You Ever Hear a...? 155
Flag Salute Song 156
"Green Frog" 157
"Little White Duck" 157
My Ears 158
My Eyes 159
My Nose 160
My Skin 160
My Tongue 161
Bubble Game 161
Rainbow Bubbles 162
"Five Brown Teddies" 162
Funtime Fair Time 163
"Little Bunny" 164
Effie Lee Newsome 165
"Mice Are Nice" 166
Phyllis Wheatley 168
Scarecrow Fun 169
Sister Sky 170
Flower Poems 171
"Sounds at Night" Poem 172
Summer Sun 173
"Visiting the Farm" Poem 174
Weather Moves 175

Games

Changing Old to New 176
Learning Mats 176
Alphabet Hopscotch 177
Dart Balls 178
Doggie, Doggie, Where's Your Bone? . 179
Wrapping Paper Dominoes 180
Button Math Game 181
Insect Match Card Game 181

Listening Game 182
Action Words for Sight Words 183
Matching Body Parts to Actions 184
Monkey, Monkey Game 185
Mystery Box 185
Mystery Clothes Box 186
Secret Items Bag 186
Name and Toss 187
Tablecloth Fun 188
Nursery Rhyme Game 188
Old Maid Sequence 189
On the Road Again 190
Part of the Whole 191
Photo Memory Game 191
Photo Name Match 192
Play the Game 192
Roll a Collage 193
Spin Art 194
Spinner Board Games 195
The Busy Month of February 196
Valentine's Heart Game 197
"Who Goes First?" Box 198

Take-Home Games 211
Observation Sticky Notes 212
Assigned Seats for Snack 213
Days-of-the-Week Seating 213
Where Will I Sit? 214
Magic Scrap 215
Cleaning Tip 215
Iron Unstuck Lamination 216
Remove Crayon Markings 216
Substitute or Volunteer Roll Sheet 217
For the Substitute 217
Substitute Plans Box 218
A Place for Everything 219
Covered Boxes 219
Big Book Box 220
Recycle Book Boxes 220
Monthly Sacks 221
Paper Collection Tray 222
Quick Solution for Storage Containers 222
Table Set Up 223
Art Sorting Box 223
Art Area Set Up 224
Classroom Display Index 225
Lesson Plans Made Simple 226
Materials List 226
Make Your Own Page Protectors 227
Windowed File Jackets 227
Color Words Songbook 228
Game Booklet 229
Hang It Up! 230
Long Reach Stapler 231
Time-Saving Tip for a Book Cover . . . 231
Our Book of Poems and Songs 232
Poem and Song Cards 232
Stories on Tape 233
Children's Favorite Poems on Tape . . . 233
Laundry Bag for Flannel Board Storage 234
Build a Large Library of Flannel Board
  Stories 234

General Tips

Social Development of Five-Year-Olds . 199
"Kinder" Garden 200
Teachable Moments 201
Tips and Techniques for Working With
  Five-Year-Olds 202
Bear Hugs 204
Community Adventure 205
Lining Up 206
"Off to Kindergarten" Button 207
Welcome Board 208
Swap Day 208
Cinco Vaqueros to Centers: "Colores" . 209
Class Photo Album 209
A Tip for Saving Work Samples 210
Weekly Parent Note 210

Reading on a Bench 235
Build a Reading List for
   Character Education 236
Literature List 239
Blindfold 262
Make Your Own Bubbles 263
Stress Jars 263
Science Jars 264
Treasure Box 264

Gross Motor

Balloon Fun 266
Crawl Under Smoke 266
Butterfly Hunt 267
Clothespin Drop 268
Gross Motor Fun With Colors and
   Shapes 268
Paper Bubble Catch 269
Party Bowl 270
Pumpkin Patch 270
Beanbag Toss 271
Airplane Toss 272
Snowman Toss 273
Texture Balance Beam 274
Styrofoam and Saw 275

Holidays and Special Days

Any-Holiday Lacing Cards 276
All-Occasion Hats 276
Albuquerque Turkey and Song 278
Edible Hanukah Menorahs 279
Horn O' Plenty 280
Thankfulness Cornucopia 282
Hanukah Handprint Menorahs 282
Tree of Hands 283
Tissue Christmas Tree 284
Toilet Roll Santa 284
Holiday Treat Container 285
Home for the Holidays 286

New Year's Hat 286
National Soup Month (January) 287
George Washington Carver 288
Groundhog and Its Cave 289
Groundhog Looks for His Shadow . . . 290
Chinese Dragon for the New Year 291
Chinese Dragon and Feast 292
Five Little Valentines 293
Valentine Fun Candy Making 294
Edible Peppermint Valentine Hearts . . 295
Paul Revere Williams 296
President's Day Hats 297
Harriet Tubman 297
Shamrock Ladder 298
St. Patrick's Day Tic Tac Toe 299
Clue Finder 300
Bunny Easter Egg Basket 300
Duck Easter Bag 301
Basket of Mother Goose Books 302
May Baskets 303
Mother's Day Tea 304
Father's Day Footprints 304
Silvery Star Banner 305
Making a Flag 306
Yankee Doodle Hat 306
Mary McLeod Bethune 308

Language

Felt Theme Boxes 309
The Art Critic 309
Bare Bear 310
Little Red Riding Hood (Left and Right) 313
Word Card Flash 315
Categories Toll Booth 315
Character Cubes 317
Fairy Tale Dice 318
Cows Out to Pasture 320
Do You See What I See? 321
Growth Flowers 321

Kinder Chatter 322
Monster Moods 323
People in Motion Collage 324
Riddle Me This 325
Riddle Rhymes 326
Spanish Days of the Week 327
Prop Storytelling 327
Rhyming Objects 328
Story Box 329

Literacy

All Through the Week 330
Adjectives 331
A Is for Apple and Ads 331
ABC Names 332
Alphabet Art Book 333
Alphabet Fun 334
Alphabet Sorting Case 335
Egyptian Cartouche 336
Bunnie's Bunches of B's 337
Animal Alphabet Parade: Walrus 338
Animal Name Game 340
Class ABC's Book 341
Grocery Bag Books 341
Leaf Baggie Books 342
Bookmaking Center 343
How to Fetch a Rainbow 344
I Can Read This Book! 344
If I Were a Dinosaur or Me as a
  Dinosaur 345
My Me Book 346
My Opposite Book 348
Our Stories 349
Dictated Story Day 350
Snowman Big Book 351
Rainy Day Big Book 352
Christmas Cards for Book Illustrations . 353
Silly Salad 353
Unscramble 354

The Magic Letter Game 355
Letter Carrier Game 356
Letter Hunts 357
Magnetic Names 357
Texture Book 358
Sandpaper Letters 359
Reading With Your Hands 359
Solomon Grundy 360
Rebus Rhymes 361
Rhyming Words 362
Signing Letters/Signing Words 362
Visit the Local Library Frequently 363

Manipulatives

Counting Cards 364
Creating Games Using Old CDs 364
Picket Puzzles 365
Pipe Cleaner Bead Rings 366

Math

Math Every Day 367
Adding Box 367
Sticker Counting 368
Bear Counting 368
Let's Learn About Money (Coins) 369
Money Activity 370
$100 371
Zero the Hero 371
Book of 100 372
The Count to 100 Game 372
Build Your Own Pizza 373
Finding Numbers in the Environment . 375
Sorting It Out 375
Fun With Sorting 376
One Leaf, Two Leaf, Red Leaf,
  Green Leaf 377
Grab a Handful! 377
Guess My Number 378
Guessing Jar 379

How Many Feet? 379

These Belong Together 380

Woodland Animals 381

Mitten Matching 382

AB Patterning Using Wallpaper 383

Wallpaper Shape Match 383

Fingerpaint Math Chart 384

Graphing Apples 385

Our Favorite Apple 386

Question Charting 386

What's a Minute? 387

Morning Greeting

Attendance Garden 388

Roll Call Responses 389

Greeting Rap 390

Waving Song 390

Welcome Song 391

Welcome Song 392

Music and Movement

Can You Do This? 393

Character Tags 393

Container Shaker-Wands 394

Creative Ideas for Carpet Squares
    Everywhere 395

Cylinder Band 396

Dance-a-Word 397

Foot Dance T-Shirt 397

Balloon Dance 398

Colorful Scarf Dancing 399

Waving, Wrapping, and Folding Fabric
    Pieces... For the Fun of It! 399

Freely Fluttering 400

Hula-Hooping 401

Movin' and Groovin' and Goin'
    Down the Aisle 401

Music! Music! Music! 402

Musical Parents 403

Musical Walk of Colors 404

Rhythm Band 404

Rhythm Sticks 405

Rhythm Train 406

Singing "Bingo" and Beyond 406

Sound Magic 407

Clapping Patterns 408

Syncopated Names 408

Rubber Bands Can Be Instrumental . . 409

Funky One-String Fiddle 409

You Can Make Music 410

Outdoor Play

100 Days Activity: Outside 411

ABC Hopscotch 412

Outdoor Sharing House 413

Blowing Bubbles 413

Box Kites 414

ExerDice 415

Washing Chairs 416

Mud Party 416

Soaring Birds 417

Outdoor Animal Safari 418

Ice Castle, A Winter Activity:
    Study of Russia 418

Painting in the Snow 420

Red String Maze 420

Good Luck Pet Rocks 421

Rock Garden 422

Shadow Chasers 422

Koosh Ball Painting 423

Sheet Spray Painting 424

Color Races 424

Slide Races 425

Tricycle, Bicycle, or Wagon
    License Plates 426

Playground Sculptures 427

Playground Excavations 429

Rest or Nap Time

Learning to Relax 431

My Favorite Musician 431

Nap Buddies 432

Naptime Activity Bags 433

My Naptime Sheet 433

Rest Time 434

Nifty Nap Mats 435

Rest Time Buddies 436

Someone to Watch Over Me 436

Winter Has Come 437

Sand and Water

What Can Be Found
   Under the Leaves? 438

Finding ABCs 438

Fruit Sorting 439

Ice Cube Hockey 439

More Than Sand and Water 440

Recycled Materials 440

Seasonal "Sand" 441

Sink or Float- With a Dash of Salt 442

Water Day 443

Science and Nature

Science Kits 445

3-D Deep Sea Porthole 445

Shark Hat 447

Tropical Fish Striper 448

Seal Show 449

Animal Alphabet Parade:
   Little Lobster 450

Frog Eatery 451

Animal Alphabet Parade:
   Pretty Peacock 452

Bird Silhouettes 453

Birdfeeding Garlands 454

Animal Habitat Game 454

Animal Habitats Interactive
   Bulletin Board 455

Making Fossils 455

Apple Star 456

Apples and Pumpkins 457

Food Facts 458

Color Nappers 459

Dancing Colors 460

Roy G. Biv 460

Double Celery Color 462

Glycerin Leaves 462

Leaf Rubbings and Categorizing 463

Leaf Skeleton 463

Adopt a Tree 464

Designer Insects 465

Worms 466

Ladybug Life Cycle 467

Circle of Life 467

Big, Medium, and Small 468

Light and Darkness 469

Guess Drop 469

Marble Raceway 470

Balance Bears 470

The Mirror and Me 471

The Recycling Game 471

Shadow Guessing Game 472

Colored Ice Cubes 473

Icy Picture 473

Frost Formations 474

Snowflake Exam 474

Snowman Soup 475

Physical Science Experience:
   Oobleck, Liquid, or Solid? 475

A Sticky Experiment 476

Balloon Greenhouse 477

Get Growing 478

Watch Us Grow 478

Water, Water, Everywhere 479

Dry Finger Surprise 480
The Surprising Wet Finger 481
Oil and Ice 481
Raisin Elevators 482

Snack and Cooking

Cooking Aprons 483
My Tea Party 483
Stargazing Party 484
100 Day Celebration 484
Eat a Letter 485
Alphabet Soup 485
Bag Ice Cream 486
Brown Leafy Toast 487
Cheerio Necklaces 487
Chummy Chive 488
Cinnamon Hearts 488
Edible Quilt Squares 489
Edible Rocks 490
Aquarium Snack 490
A Fish Mix 491
Fish in the Ocean 491
Easy Banana Treat 492
Sun Fruit Roll-Ups 492
Fruit Salad Fun 493
Fun Ice Cubes 493
"Gingerbread" Houses 494
Hot Dog Butterflies 495
Making Lavender Smoothies 495
Pizza Crackers 496
Apple Pizza 496
Mini Apple Pies 497
Pumpkin Pie 498
Quesadillas 499
Shape Pancakes 499
Shape Snacks 500

Stoplight Snack 501
Tooth Candy 501
Vegetables in a Pan Pocket 502

Social Development

Cooperation Puzzle 504
Ka-Choo Bulletin Board 504
My House 505
Dragon's Rules 506
Problem-Solving Puppet 507
All About Me Flowers 508
An Evening at Home 509
Bulletin Board Children 510
Hand Wreath 511
Moving Day 512
The People in My School 512
Tricycling for Cancer 513
Voting and Ballots 514
You Have Two Hands 515

Transitions

Cinco Vaqueros Circle Time 516
Play That Tune! 516
Train Whistle Station 517
Transition Time 517
Wild Cards 518
Animal Movements 518
Funny Bone Ticklers 519
Language Lineup 519
The Quiet Game 520
Shapes and Colors 520

Patterns 522
Index 525

Introduction

Kindergarten teachers look forward to the rewards and challenges of working with five-year-olds. At age five, children are friendly and outgoing and are learning to be confident, responsible, and reliable. Their world is growing to include more than just their homes and schools or childcare centers, and they are eager to learn about each other. It is not surprising that friends and group activities are very important to kindergartners.

Children in this age group will constantly work on mastering developmental skills. They are growing quickly both cognitively and physically. However, their eagerness and energy for learning can lead to mishaps. They often do not foresee dangerous consequences to their actions, and, therefore, teachers must strike a delicate balance between maintaining safety and preserving the children's confidence and self-esteem.

To help kindergartners develop the many skills they are mastering, teachers need tools and resources that are appropriate to their classrooms. *The Giant Encyclopedia of Kindergarten Activities* is a compilation of activities submitted by teachers of five-year-olds that are effective, appealing, and interesting for kindergartners. It is a resource book filled with ideas to help children learn and grow.

Use the following milestones for five-year-olds to select activities for your classroom.

Physical milestones:
- ☆ Take responsibility for toileting, although they may have occasional accidents
- ☆ Walk unassisted up and down stairs, alternating feet
- ☆ Dress completely on their own
- ☆ Walk a balance beam
- ☆ Catch a ball from three feet away
- ☆ Cut on lines with scissors (not perfectly)
- ☆ Establish hand dominance

Cognitive milestones:

☆ Sort objects by shape, size, color, and form

☆ Count to 20 and above, sometimes to 100

☆ Relate times on a clock to daily schedules

☆ Identify the letters of the alphabet, sometimes all lower- and uppercase

☆ Recognize the values of coins and bills

Speech and language milestones:

☆ Tell familiar stories while looking at a book

☆ Recognize humor and make up jokes and riddles

☆ Create sentences with five to seven or more words

☆ Use past-tense verbs

Personal and social development milestones:

☆ Share toys, take turns, play cooperatively, and be generous

☆ Enjoy many friends and a few special playmates, but might crowd out a third

☆ Help with family and school chores

☆ Demonstrate caring and affection with other children

☆ Learn to control their emotions but still need adult assistance and reassurance

How to Use This Book

We asked teachers to send us their favorite activities for five-year-olds. We carefully selected the most appropriate entries and, as a result, this book is full of over 600 child-friendly, teacher-approved activities. The contributing teachers have used these activities successfully in their own classrooms. We believe that you and the kindergartners in your classroom will greatly benefit from the many years of experience that are reflected in these useful and fun activities!

Each activity in this book contains some or all of the following elements:

Materials

Each activity lists readily available materials. Investigate all possible resources for donated and free materials in your community. Look into gifts from paper stores, framing shops, woodworking shops, other teachers, lumberyards, and, of course, parents.

What to do

The directions for each activity are presented in an easy-to-follow numbered list. Patterns and illustrations are included where necessary to enhance the usability of each activity.

More to do

Some activities include additional ideas for extending the activity into other curriculum areas. Many of the activities will expand into areas such as Science, Math, and Literacy.

Related books

Books are listed in this section. A list of well-known children's books that are related to the topic of the activity can enhance the teaching value of the activities.

Related songs and poems

This section includes familiar songs and poems as well as original poems written by teachers.

Above all, enjoy the spirit of fun and passion for learning that are reflected in these pages. Learn and laugh with the children, enjoy their presence and their youthful energy, and use the activities in this book to help guide them to discovery.

My Own Art Apron

Materials

Small, adult-size sweatshirts, one for each child • several pieces of sturdy cardboard • fabric paints • sponges and small paintbrushes • fabric scissors • fabric glue

What to do

1. Ask each child to bring in a small, adult-size sweatshirt.
2. Insert a piece of sturdy cardboard inside the shirts.
3. Encourage the children to use fabric paints, sponges, and brushes to make designs on the front of the shirt. Make sure the children include their name somewhere on the shirt.
4. If the children want to put handprints on their shirts, offer assistance as needed.
5. Let the shirts dry and remove the cardboard.
6. Use fabric scissors to cut the back of the shirt in half (adult only). This creates an opening in the back. Also, cut off the sleeves of the shirt.
7. Cut two 6" fabric strips from the leftover sleeves. Attach one strip to each side of the back opening using fabric glue. These become the tie to keep the apron on the child.
8. Let the children use their own art aprons when they are painting at the easel or at the tables. They can also use these wonderful creations for any messy activity. The fabric paints are washable, so cleanup is as simple as throwing the shirts into the washing machine.

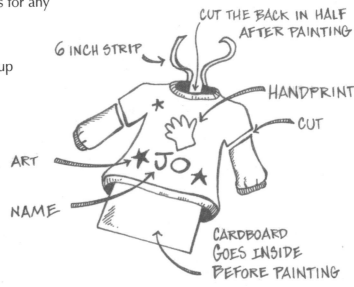

(continued on the next page)

Related books

Anna's Art Adventure by Bjorn Sortland
Art Dog by Thacher Hurd
Art Lesson (La Clase de Dibujo) by Tomie dePaola
Ma Dear's Aprons by Patricia C. McKissack
Matthew's Dream by Leo Lionni
Willy's Pictures by Anthony Browne

☆ Virginia Jean Herrod, Columbia, SC

Artistic Autograph

Materials

Markers or pencils • large feathers, twigs, empty spools, ribbon, and yarn • basting brushes • paint • glue • paper

What to do

1. Encourage the children to use art materials to write their names in a creative way. Put out a variety of materials and let them create a unique autograph. For example, they could paint it using a feather, glue ribbons in the shape of the letters in their names, paint their name using glue and twigs, and so on.
2. For children who cannot write their names yet and do not want to try, write their name on a piece of paper and let them use it to paint or glue over. Give them several choices when writing their name, such as picking the color of the paper, asking them how big to write their name, and so on.

 Ann Kelly, Johnstown, PA

Personalized Name Plates

Materials

8 ½" x 11" sheets of white card stock • wide-tip black marker • markers and crayons

What to do

1. Give each child a sheet of card stock. Ask them to fold their paper lengthwise.
2. Ask the children to print their name on their card. Help them as needed.
3. Encourage the children to decorate their name using markers and crayons. Encourage them to be creative. For example, a name with several circular letters could become the faces of each family member. A child who likes to skate may turn an "A" into a skater. A child who likes ice cream may turn a "V" into an ice cream cone.
4. The children can use their name plates to mark their desk, table, or storage unit.

Related books

How I Named the Baby by Linda Shute
Mommy Doesn't Know My Name by Suzanne Williams
What's Your Name? by Eve Sanders

 Wanda Pelton, Lafayette, IN

USA Rugs

Materials

Carpet squares, one for each child • red, white, and blue permanent paints • star-shaped sponges • paintbrushes

What to do

1. Give each child a carpet square. (Most carpet stores will donate enough samples for each child in your class if you explain what you are doing with them.)

(continued on the next page)

2. Ask the children to paint their square white.

3. After the rugs have dried, help each child square off a section and paint it dark blue.

4. Show them where to paint red stripes.

5. After the blue section has dried, encourage the children to sponge paint white stars.

6. These make great welcome mats for 4th of July, or sit-upons in the classroom.

 Lisa Chichester, Parkersburg, WV

Homemade Sidewalk Chalk

Materials

Plaster of Paris • water • tempera paint • empty toilet tissue tubes • duct tape

What to do

1. Mix the plaster of Paris with water until it is runny.

2. Add tempera paint until it is the desired color.

3. Tape the bottom of the cardboard tube.

4. Pour the plaster of Paris in the toilet tissue tube and let it dry.

5. Remove the toilet tissue tube and use the sidewalk chalk.

Tip: Find small boxes such as gift boxes and make different shapes of sidewalk chalk.

 Jean Potter, Charleston, WV

Silly Putty

Materials

Large bowl • white glue • measuring cup • food coloring, optional • liquid starch • large spoon • zipper-closure baggie or container with airtight lid

What to do

1. Pour one cup of glue into a bowl. If using food coloring, add it to the glue.
2. Add one cup of liquid starch to the glue.
3. Encourage the children to use a large spoon to stir the mixture. Keep mixing until it congeals, and then pour off the extra liquid.
4. The silly putty should be used in a sand and water table or on a table. It is best to use in a tiled-floor area—it can be difficult to remove from carpeting and clothing.
5. This is a great activity for strengthening fine motor skills and sensory exploration. As the putty becomes drier, it becomes more taut. It can be fun for children to use child-safe scissors to cut it.
6. Store in an airtight container. It can last up to a couple of weeks.

☆ Sandra L. Nagel, White Lake, MI

Grass Playdough

Materials

Homemade playdough (see recipe below) • small containers • scissors • grass clippings

What to do

1. Let the children help make playdough according to the recipe on the next page.
2. Give the children scissors and a small container. Take them outdoors and let them use the scissors to clip some grass and put it into their containers. Encourage them to clip the grass and not pull it up by the roots.

(continued on the next page)

3. Show them how to use the scissors to shred the grass they have collected.

4. Encourage the children to add the grass to the playdough and knead firmly to mix. Enjoy your grass playdough! Challenge the children to use the playdough to create colorful sculptures.

5. If desired, change the playdough add-ins with the seasons. For example, use flower cuttings in the summer and collect colorful leaves and shred them with scissors in the fall.

Homemade Playdough

1 cup cold water

1 cup salt

2 teaspoons vegetable oil

Tempera paint or food coloring

3 cups flour

2 tablespoons cornstarch

Mix water, salt, oil, and enough paint to make bright colors. Gradually work in flour and cornstarch. Knead to consistency of bread dough.

More to do

Encourage the children to collect small rocks, pebbles, and sand. Add these to the playdough for an interesting texture. Brainstorm with the children about other things that can be added to playdough. Give each safe and reasonable suggestion a try.

☆ Virginia Jean Herrod, Columbia, SC

Bag Wrappers

Materials

Large 1"-thick sponge • scissors • shallow containers such as jar lids or Styrofoam trays • poster paint • paper bags • tissue or easel paper • raffia or stick-on bows

What to do

1. Draw simple shapes such as circles, triangles, and squares on the dry sponge and cut them out.

2. Pour paint into the shallow containers.

3. Wet the sponge shapes and squeeze out most of the water.

4. Demonstrate how to dip the shapes into the paint and press them onto one side of an unopened paper bag. Stamp one side of the bag at a time. Do not paint the other side until the bag dries.

5. When dry on both sides, open the bags. If desired, let the children use pens to embellish the shapes after the paint dries.

6. Encourage the children to wrap presents in tissue or easel paper and place them into the bags.

7. Tie the bags with raffia or staple the tops closed and stick bows on them.

8. If desired, make cards to match the bags. Cut out small rectangles and fold them in half. Print one shape on the outside and write the names on the inside.

9. Let the sponges dry and save them for re-use.

Tip: Instead of paper bags, use the sponges to stamp butcher or brown craft paper.

⭐ Barbara Saul, Eureka, CA

Wallpaper Artwork

Materials

Sample wallpaper books • scissors • templates of shapes or ruler • glue or paste • large sheets of construction paper • markers, crayons, or watercolor paints

What to do

1. Cut out a variety of medium and large shapes from a wallpaper book using templates, a ruler, or freehand.

2. Ask the children to choose a shape, glue it to a large piece of construction paper, and use it as a base for an art project. For example, circles can become faces or flowers; ovals can become airplanes, rockets, or spaceships; rectangles can become buses; squares can become houses or buildings, and so on.

More to do

Fine Motor: Wallpaper is a different consistency and can offer a new experience to improve cutting skills. Make available a variety of sheets of wallpaper and ask the children to cut and paste their own "abstract" artwork.

 Mary Volkman, Ottawa, IL

Salad Spinner Art

Materials

Paper • scissors • salad spinner • paint • squeeze bottle or large eyedroppers

What to do

1. Cut the paper into circles that will fit inside the salad spinner.
2. Put a paper circle into the salad spinner. Add paint by squeezing from a bottle or eyedropper (red, blue, and yellow work well). Dribble it around the paper.
3. Close the salad spinner and spin! The colors twirl and blend.
4. Let each child have a turn with his own paper circle. Discuss how the colors blended and made new colors.

 Audrey Kanoff, Allentown, PA

Incredible Shrinking Art

Materials

Clear plastic #6 deli and bakery containers • scissors • fine-tip permanent markers in assorted colors • hole punch • cookie sheet • oven • spatula • small towel • thin cord, thread, or wire

What to do

1. Cut off the flat bottoms and tops of clear plastic deli and bakery containers. Encourage the children to draw and write on the plastic with markers.
2. With a hole punch, make a hole at the top of each piece.
3. Bake them on a cookie sheet at 350° for 2-3 minutes. The plastic will shrink, and the artwork will be miniaturized.
4. Remove from oven (adult only). If necessary, flatten them with a spatula while still warm. Place them on a small towel to cool.
5. Use the pieces for necklace pendants, key chains, or sun catchers by attaching thin cord, thread, or wire through the hole.
6. If desired, demonstrate how to thread a piece on a cord and string beads on both sides of the piece to make necklaces.

More to do

Science and Nature: Talk about how heat changes things. Leave a crayon in the sun to melt. Discuss what happens to a burning candle.

 Sandra Gratias, Perkasie, PA

Aluminum Foil Crinkle Art

Materials

Aprons or art smocks • aluminum foil, one large sheet for each child • colorful permanent markers • glitter • small colorful craft items such as confetti, beads, and sequins • glue • 3" x 5" note cards, one for each child

What to do

1. Make sure each child wears an apron or art smock for this messy activity.
2. Give each child a large sheet of aluminum foil.
3. Let the children mark all over their aluminum foil with permanent markers. (Water-based markers will not work; the ink will not adhere to the foil.) Encourage the children to draw pictures or fancy designs and color them in.
4. After the children have colored to their satisfaction, ask them to roll and crinkle the foil.
5. Help them unroll and straighten out the foil. Wrinkles and crinkled areas should remain.
6. Put out glitter, confetti, small beads, sequins, and glue. Encourage the children to embellish their foil artwork as desired. Comment positively on the children's works of art as they take shape. Notice the colors the children are using, the shapes they are making on the paper, and their use of positive and negative space on the foil. Encourage children to talk with each other as they work on their individual art.
7. Lay the foil designs flat to dry.
8. Encourage the children to dictate a description of their artwork. Ask leading questions such as, "What were you thinking when you added confetti to your artwork?" Let the children tell you any special meaning they have put into their artwork. Print their statements on a note card.

(continued on the next page)

9. Encourage the children to notice what happens when two or three colors intersect on the foil. Talk about primary, secondary, and tertiary colors.

10. Post the artwork and descriptive statements for all to see and enjoy.

Related books

Anna's Art Adventure by Bjorn Sortland
If You Take a Mouse to the Movies by Laura Numeroff
The Lion and the Little Red Bird by Elisa Kleven
The Little Painter of Sabana Grande by Patricia Maloney Markun
Mouse Paint by Ellen Stoll Walsh
Painted Dreams by Karen Lynn Williams
Willy's Pictures by Anthony Brown

☆ Virginia Jean Herrod, Columbia, SC

Dried Glue Ornaments

Materials

Flat Styrofoam meat trays • felt-tipped markers (water-based) • white glue • scissors • hole punch • fishing line

What to do

1. Give each child a flat Styrofoam meat tray. Encourage them to make designs or pictures on the meat trays using felt-tipped markers.

2. Tell the children to pour enough glue on their tray to cover the design. Let them stand overnight.

Tip: Use different colors of glue or add glitter to the wet glue.

3. When the glue is completely dry, peel the edges of the glue and let it dry another day.

4. The second day, peel off the glue from the tray completely.

5. Encourage the children to cut out a design from the dried, peeled glue.

6. Punch a hole into the dried glue design and hang it by a fishing line.

☆ Jean Potter, Charleston, WV

Plastic Wrap Art

Materials

Tempera paint in a variety of colors • plastic spoons • white construction or fingerpaint paper • roll of plastic wrap • tape

What to do

1. Ask each child to spoon two to four colors of paint onto a large sheet of paper.
2. Help them cover the sheet of paper with a larger piece of plastic wrap and secure on four sides with tape.
3. Encourage the children to smooth and pat the plastic wrap to mix the colors together. The children can use a finger to draw on top of the plastic wrap.
4. Remove the plastic wrap and dispose of it.
5. Allow the art project to dry.
6. This project is great for children who do not like to get their hands dirty! It is also great for teaching what happens when colors blend together.

Tips: Blending different shades of blue makes a great sky background for a picture; blending different shades of green makes a great grass background for a picture.

 Mary Volkman, Ottawa, IL

Baby Footprint

Materials

Newspaper • smocks or art shirts • fingerpaint • paint tray • paper

What to do

1. Cover the table with newspaper and help the children put on smocks or art shirts. Pour a small amount of paint into trays.
2. Show the children how to bend their fingers so they touch the inside of their hands. Encourage them to dip the side of their hand (pinky side) into paint and then press it onto the paper.

(continued on the next page)

3. Then, encourage them to dip their finger in the paint and then press it over their other print (these will be the toes). They have just made baby footprints!

PAINT (PINKY SIDE)

FINGERS TOUCHING INSIDE OF HAND

PAINT TRAY

⭐ Darleen A. Schaible, Stroudsburg, PA

A Piece of Beach

Materials

Sand • white glue • bowl • small shells

What to do

1. Mix the sand and glue together in a bowl until it has a syrup-like texture.
2. Push shells into the mixture to form a sculpture.
3. Allow this to dry for a couple of days.

⭐ Jean Potter, Charleston, WV

Water Roll

Materials

Water bottles filled with water • playdough • glitter, food coloring, and plastic, optional

What to do

1. Let the children use the water bottles as rolling pins for playdough.
2. If desired, decorate the inside of the water bottles by adding glitter, food coloring, and little pieces of plastic to the water.

 Jean Potter, Charleston, WV

Scented Pictures

Materials

Paper • glue • blue Jell-O

What to do

1. This is a great activity to do when studying the sense of smell or the color blue.
2. Ask the children to spread glue on their paper.
3. Then they sprinkle blue Jell-O on the glue.
4. Shake off any excess Jell-O and let it dry.
5. The Jell-O makes a great design and also smells good.

 Sandy L. Scott, Vancouver, WA

Butterfly Feet

Materials

Marker • brightly-colored construction paper • scissors • narrow strips of black paper • glue • scrap materials (yarn, small pieces of paper, glitter, sequins, and so on)

What to do

1. Trace around each child's feet on construction paper to make butterfly wing shapes.
2. Encourage the children to draw a body shape between the two butterfly wings.
3. Cut out the butterflies.
4. Help the children paste narrow strips of black paper in place for the antennae.
5. Encourage the children to decorate their butterflies with scrap materials.
6. Hang the butterflies in your room.

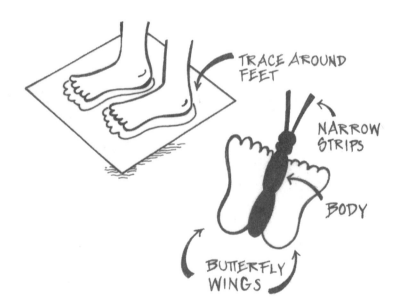

TRACE AROUND FEET

NARROW STRIPS

BODY

BUTTERFLY WINGS

☆ Jean Potter, Charleston, WV

Talented Toes

Materials

Paper • tape • dishpan filled with soapy water • towels • chair • paper plates • paint

What to do

1. Tape a large piece of paper to the floor.
2. Place the pan of water, chair, and towel near the piece of paper.
3. Put three or four dabs of different-colored paint onto a paper plate and put it on the floor next to the paper and chair.
4. Invite a child to take off his shoes and paint a picture with his toes.
5. When he is done, use the water and towel to wash the paint off his feet.

More to do

Fine Motor: Encourage the children to write their names on their paper using their toes.

☆ Ann Kelly, Johnstown, PA

Magic Opposites

Materials

Black and white 9" x 12" construction paper, one piece of each for each child • carbon paper • paper clips • white colored pencils • cardboard shapes

What to do

1. Give each child a sheet of white and black construction paper. Show them how to place a piece of carbon paper between the black paper and white paper. Paper clip the papers together with the black sheet on top.
2. Encourage the children to use a white colored pencil to trace shapes on the black paper. (Shapes can overlap.) Tell them to press hard or trace over several times. (See the illustration on the next page.)
3. Remove the paper clips and the carbon paper. There will be two copies of the same pictures: one light and one dark—opposites!

(continued on the next page)

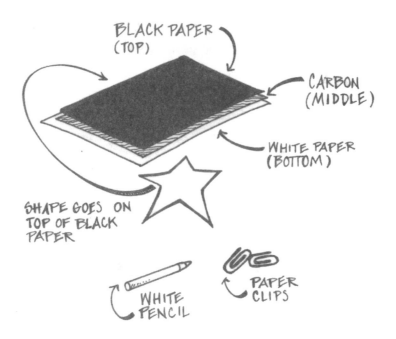

BLACK PAPER (TOP)

CARBON (MIDDLE)

WHITE PAPER (BOTTOM)

SHAPE GOES ON TOP OF BLACK PAPER

WHITE PENCIL

PAPER CLIPS

More to do

Print big and little pictures. Use 9" x 12" and 12" x 18" paper of the same colors. Gather assorted objects, one large and one small (Legos, blocks, measuring cups, and so on). Use them to make prints—large objects on large sheets and corresponding small objects on small sheets.

Movement: Model an action and have the children do the opposite (for example, clap slow/fast, raise/lower arms, open/close mouth, and so on).

Related books

The Opposites by Monique Felix
That's Good, That's Bad by Margery Cuylen
Tops and Bottoms by Janet Stevens

 Sandra Gratias, Perkasie, PA

Evaporating Painting

Materials

¼ cup salt • ¼ cup warm water • bowl • food coloring • painting paper • paintbrushes

What to do

1. Pour salt into a bowl and add warm water.
2. Add several drops of food coloring to the mixture.
3. Let the children use the mixture to paint a picture.
4. Let the paintings dry overnight. The water will evaporate from the painting, but the colored salt will remain on the paper.

 Jean Potter, Charleston, WV

Fish Kite

Materials

Pastel colored construction paper • pencils • markers • scissors • stapler • hole punch • 25-mm wiggly eyes • white glue • paper towels or tissue paper • ¼" dowel rod, pencil, or tongue depressor • string

What to do

1. Copy the fish pattern on the following page and cut it out. Cut out enough so that each child gets one.
2. Encourage the children to trace the fish on two pieces of pastel paper and then cut them out.
3. Help the children staple the two fish together, leaving the mouth area open. Then punch one hole in the mouth through both sides.
4. Let the children use markers to draw a large eye on both sides of the fish, and then glue wiggly eyes in the center of the colored eye.
5. Encourage the children to use a variety of colored markers to draw scales and lines on the fish and to color the mouth.
6. Show the children how to stuff the fish with paper towels.
7. Tie string around a small dowel or pencil and through the punched holes on the fish.

More to do

Outdoor Play: Encourage the children to hold the sticks of their kites and run around outside, allowing the kites to blow in the wind.
Science and Nature: Learn about the carp fish. Compare it with other types of fish.

 Mary Brehm, Aurora, OH

(CUT TWO)

Tissue Paper Corsage

Materials

Tissue paper in pastel colors • scissors • small doilies • glue

What to do

1. Cut the tissue paper into 2" squares.
2. Give each child a small doily. Show them how to squish the paper and glue it to the center of the doily.
3. Let the glue dry. The children now have a unique corsage to give to their grandmother or other special person.
4. Let the children invite their grandmothers (or other special adults) to an event at school to present the corsages.

 Sandy L. Scott, Vancouver, WA

A Cutting Mosaic

Materials

Pictures of mosaics • sheets of paper in a variety of colors • scissors • glue • white paper

What to do

1. Show the children pictures of mosaics to give them an idea of how to use pieces of paper to make a picture. Discuss what the various colors could be used for, such as blue pieces for water or the sky, green for leaves or grass, yellow for flowers, a car, or the sun, and so on.
2. Ask the children to cut the colored paper into strips. Then, ask them to cut the strips into smaller pieces.
3. After the children have cut a number of small pieces, they can glue the pieces onto white paper to create a picture.

Note: At first, it may be challenging for the children to cut with scissors. This activity provides an opportunity for the children to cut without having to stay on lines.

 Sandra L. Nagle, White Lake, MI

My Kindergarten Quilt

Materials

Different colored construction paper including black • scissors • glue stick • 9" x 9" poster board squares, one for each child • black marker • hole punch • string or yarn

What to do

1. Cut an ample supply of 3" x 3" squares of different colored construction paper including black. Place the colored squares on the table for the children to choose.
2. Glue three black squares randomly on each 9" x 9" poster board square so the children have an idea of where to place the other squares.
3. Give each child a poster board square. Begin by asking the following questions: What color are your eyes? Your hair? What is your favorite color? What color is your pet?
4. Encourage the children to select the corresponding colors using the 3" x 3" squares and glue them to the poster board.
5. Ask the children to write their name in a blank square.
6. Punch a hole into the paper quilts and attach string to hang them.
7. If desired, ask the children to write what each color represents on the reverse side.

 Ingelore Mix, Gainesville, VA

Patchwork Colors

Materials

5" squares of laminate, one for each child • red, blue, and yellow watercolor paint • paintbrushes

What to do

1. Give each child a laminate square.
2. Ask them to put all three colors of paint on their laminate. Encourage them to swirl some of the colors together or blend them as desired.

3. Leave the paintings flat to dry.

4. Adhere the painted laminate squares to a window. Place them so that they form a larger square, similar to a patchwork quilt.

5. When the sunlight shines through the paint, encourage the children to comment on the colors they made.

More to do

Punch a hole into a corner of each laminate square and thread string through it. Tie the strings on the end of chopsticks to make mobiles. Use different interlocking shapes of laminate, such as squares and diamonds or triangles.

☆ Elizabeth Bezant, Quinn's Rock, WA, Australia

My Jeans Picture

Materials

One or more pairs of used clean jeans (adult size) • scissors • paper • glue • markers or crayons

What to do

1. Cut the jeans at the seams so that you have one layer of denim. Use the denim to cut out small 2" to 4" pairs of jeans. Vary the sizes and styles of the jeans for interest. Make sure there are enough for each child to choose at least one pair for the art project.

2. Give each child a piece of blank paper. Ask them to pick a pair of jeans and glue them on their paper.

3. Encourage them to use crayons or markers to fill in the head and body for the jeans.

4. Ask the children to title their pictures (Sally's Jeans) or have them write a story or answer a question ("Where are Sally's jeans going?").

5. Display the works of art!

☆ Gail Morris, Kemah, TX

JEANS GLUED ON PAPER

ART

Bob

Paper Bag Birds

Materials

Newspaper • paper lunch bags • paintbrushes • washable paint in a variety of colors • glitter (optional) • rubber bands, thick yarn, or ribbon • scissors • yellow pipe cleaners and other assorted colors • hot glue gun (adult only) • craft eyes • thick craft glue • burlap sheets

What to do

1. Cover the work surface with newspaper—this is a messy activity! Give each child a paper bag. Ask them to lay their bags flat and paint each side using whatever color paint they desire. Let the paint dry a bit and then ask the children to unfold their bag and place it over one hand so they can paint the areas previously hidden (under flaps, and so on). If using glitter, let the children sprinkle it on the bags now. Dry them on a puppet stand, if available. **Author Note:** I use washable paint, place each bag on newspaper, and prop them against a wall.

2. When the bags are dry, demonstrate how to ball up a piece of newspaper and stuff it into one corner of the bottom of the bag. Smooth the rounded end and twist at the "neck." Secure with a rubber band, thick yarn, or ribbon.

3. Fan the back of the paper bag. With scissors, cut the back end into strips up to ½" from the neck. This will resemble feathers. Help the children, if needed.

4. Show them how to lay two yellow pipe cleaners flat on the table to resemble a "T." Bend all four ends downward; join the bottom tips and twist. Bow a little at the middle. This creates a somewhat three-dimensional beak.

5. With a pencil or pen, poke a small hole in the middle of the head. Insert the

PAINTED BAG

NEWSPAPER INSIDE

GOOGLE EYES

PIPE CLEANERS

SECURE AT NECK

BURLAP WINGS (PIPE CLEANERS GLUED ON BACK SIDE)

joined ends of the beak and attach it with hot glue (adult only).

6. Above the beak, glue two craft "googly" eyes (adult only).

7. Next, show the children how to cut out two wings from burlap sheets to resemble a triangle shape.

8. Cut two pipe cleaners (any color) into six 2" pieces. Glue three pieces on the back of each wing to make them sturdy.

9. Using thick craft glue or hot glue, help the children glue each wing behind the head on either side. Ta da! You have made a bird!

10. If desired, tie yarn around the necks and hang them from the ceiling.

Author Note: My class worked on this project as spring arrived. We created a spring-theme bulletin board and hung the birds from the ceiling above it. We also discussed how animal babies, like birds, are usually born in the spring. We looked for nests, tried to catch signs of birds making nests or collecting material to build them, sang spring- and bird-related songs and fingerplays, and read books pertaining to birds and springtime.

 Stacy Edwards, Jermyn, PA

Portraits

Materials

Portrait art print • mirror • paper • pencils • crayons or pens

What to do

1. Show the children a portrait art print. Explain that a portrait is a picture of a person that represents something special about him or her. Encourage them to talk about it. Point out different features such as the hair, eyes, nose, mouth, and ears.

2. Encourage the children to look into the mirror and see what they look like.

3. Ask them to draw a self-portrait and color it.

4. If desired, ask the children to draw pictures of a partner.

 Barbara Saul, Eureka, CA

Razzle Dazzle Raindrops

Materials

Pencil • cardboard • scissors • light blue construction paper • glue • small cups • paintbrushes • silver glitter • dark blue washable paint • plastic wrap • masking tape • yarn and paper clips, optional

What to do

1. Trace or draw a raindrop on cardboard and cut it out. Then, trace the raindrop on the construction paper and cut it out (outside the line to make it slightly larger than cardboard piece). Make one for each child.

2. In a cup, mix some glue with a little bit of water. Encourage the children to use a paintbrush to lightly brush the mixture over the paper raindrop (this gives it a light sheen). Sprinkle on the glitter while the raindrop is still wet. Set aside to dry and then shake off excess.

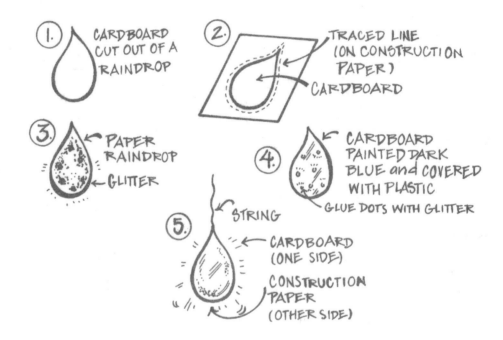

3. Ask the children to paint the cardboard raindrop dark blue on one side (only one coat is necessary) and let it dry.

4. Once the paint is dry, help the children wrap their raindrop tightly in plastic wrap, securing in the back with masking tape. The plastic on the blue side should be smooth and even, and the plastic on the back side should be bunched in spots, with each bunched spot taped down.

5. Ask the children to use glue to make dots over the surface of the blue side. Sprinkle on glitter, let it dry or get firm, and shake off excess.

6. Once the raindrops are dry, ask the children to glue them together back-to-back. Now they have a Razzle Dazzle Raindrop!

7. If desired, hang the raindrops from the ceiling. Before gluing both sides together, tape the tip of a strand of yarn to the back of the cardboard raindrop, at the pointed tip. Then glue them back-to-back and tie the other end to an unfolded paper clip.

More to do

Science and Nature: Use this project as part of a unit on spring. Discuss what the saying "April showers bring May flowers" means. Discuss the importance of rain. Ask the children what they use water for.

 Stacy Edwards, Jermyn, PA

Pressed Flower Placemats

Materials

Fresh flowers (If possible, let the children collect these: buttercups, violets, mock orange blossoms, pansies, or any blossoms with delicate petals. Don't use daffodils, roses, or other bulky flowers.) • paper napkins • old telephone books • wax paper • pads of old newspapers • electric iron • paper cutter

What to do

This activity is done in two stages, a week or more apart.

Stage one:

1. Collect flowers with the children.
2. Demonstrate how to open a napkin halfway and place the flower face down, spreading the petals.
3. Replace the other half of the napkin.
4. Carefully place the napkin inside the telephone book.
5. When all the flowers have been prepared, stack the books (extra weight will help press the flowers) and leave them for a week to dry.

(continued on the next page)

Stage two:

1. Before beginning this stage, test to see how much heat your iron needs to fuse two pieces of waxed paper. Then pre-heat the iron to that setting. Supervise this part of the activity carefully and use caution! Assist the children when pressing and be certain the iron is safely out of reach when not in use.

2. Carefully remove the dried flowers from the telephone books and open the napkins so the children can select which ones they want.

3. Tear off sheets of wax paper, about 28", and fold in half. Open a folded sheet of wax paper and place it on the pad of newspapers.

4. Arrange several of the dried flowers and cover with the other half of the waxed paper.

5. Help the children press the paper with the hot iron to fuse the two sheets of paper.

6. Trim the finished product to desired size, using a paper cutter so the edges will be straight.

7. Use the finished product as a placemat or sun catcher. These make great gifts for Mother's Day.

Tip: In the fall, use this idea to make placemats with autumn leaves.

 Mary Jo Shannon, Roanoke, VA

Crunchy Leaf Creatures

Materials

Colorful autumn leaves • leaf presses or heavy books • construction paper • markers or pencils • lamination sheets • glue

What to do

1. Explain to the children that they are going to do an activity that focuses on colorful autumn leaves and forest animals that they see in the fall.

2. Discuss with the children the types of animals that they might see in the forest in the fall. Also, discuss the different colors of leaves and why leaves change colors.

3. If you have access to a wooded area, take the children for a walk to collect autumn leaves. If not, ask the children to collect leaves at home and bring them to school. Ask the children to collect between 10 and 20 large, colorful leaves. If they choose to collect smaller leaves, ask them to collect more.

4. Demonstrate how to use the leaf presses to flatten and dry the leaves. If you don't have access to leaf presses, use several heavy books instead.

5. It will take several days to a week for the leaves to completely dry. During this period, remind the children to think about their favorite forest animal.

6. Once the leaves are completely dry, remove them from the leaf presses. **Note:** If the leaves are not completely dry, they will leave moisture marks when laminated.

7. Encourage the children to draw a large picture of their favorite animal that they can see in the fall.

8. Next, tell the children to completely cover their animal with a thin layer of glue.

9. Encourage the children to crunch up the various colors of dried leaves and make several different colored piles of "leaf litter."

10. The children can sprinkle the leaf litter over their drawing to serve as the color.

11. Allow the project to completely dry. Then, laminate it to make the colors come alive. The children will be thrilled with how colorful their projects turn out.

☆ Mike Krestar, White Oak, PA

Leaf Rubbing Wreath

Materials

Fresh leaves • double-sided tape • copy paper or newsprint in pale colors • unwrapped crayons • scissors • construction paper in fall colors • newspaper • paint in fall colors • paintbrushes

What to do

1. About two hours prior to doing the activity, gather fresh leaves from outside. Using double-sided tape, tape the leaves vein-side up in a 9" diameter wreath design on a flat surface.

Note: Leaves gathered too early may dry out and crumble.

2. Tape a sheet of copy paper over the wreath design, making sure not to tape the leaves. Show the children how to use the sides of unwrapped crayons to rub gently over the leaf wreath to create the design on the copy paper.

3. Let the children choose a sheet of copy paper or newsprint and encourage them to make their own leaf wreath rubbings.

4. Cut out 3" to 4" circles and 12" squares from fall-colored construction paper.

(continued on the next page)

5. Ask the children to bring their copy paper rubbings to another surface covered with newspaper. Put out a variety of leaves, paint in fall colors, and paintbrushes. Demonstrate how to paint the underside of a leaf and carefully press it onto a paper circle. Let them dry.

6. Encourage the children to glue their leaf print paper circle in the center of their leaf wreath. Ask them to cut around the wreath shape to eliminate the corners of the copy paper.

7. Show the children how to glue the wreath onto a 12" square of fall-colored paper.

 Susan Oldham Hill, Lakeland, FL

Autumn Leaf Ornaments

Materials

Autumn leaves • contact paper • scissors • pen • hole punch • string

What to do

1. Collect leaves from trees around your school or in a nearby park. Choose a variety of bright colors, but remember that leaves with a crisp texture (such as maple and oak) will retain their color longer than leaves with a soft texture (such as poplar and sassafras).

2. Cut out two 5" x 7" pieces of contact paper per child. Peel the paper backing from one piece and lay the contact paper on a flat surface, sticky side up.

3. Ask the children to place a leaf or leaves on their contact paper. Encourage them to be creative (for instance, if you put two maple leaves bottom to bottom, you make a shape like a butterfly).

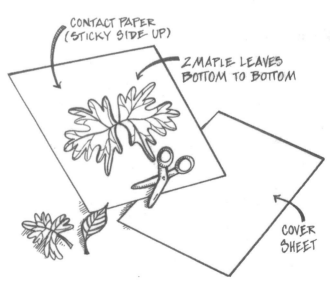

CONTACT PAPER (STICKY SIDE UP)

2 MAPLE LEAVES BOTTOM TO BOTTOM

COVER SHEET

4. Once the leaves are in place, peel the backing from the second piece of contact paper and place it, sticky side down, over the leaves. Show the children how to iron out any air bubbles using their hands, a ruler, or a book.

5. Ask the children to draw a line around the outer shape of the leaves, leaving about ¼" of contact paper all the way around the leaves. Then they can cut away the excess paper, following the lines they have drawn.

6. Use a hole punch to punch a hole into each child's ornament. Help them thread a piece of string through the hole. Hang the ornaments in a sunny spot.

Related books

Use a tree/leaf identification guide to learn more about the trees in your back yard or park.

National Audubon Society Field Guide to North American Trees: Eastern Region Trees: Trees Identified by Leaf, Bark, and Seed (Fandex Family Field Guides) by Stephen M.L. Aronson

 Melissa O. Markham, Huddleston, VA

Autumn All Around

Materials

Small paper plates • scissors • construction paper in fall colors • glue • hole punch • yarn

What to do

1. Cut out the centers from small paper plates, one for each child. Cut out a variety of fall-colored leaves from construction paper.

2. Show the children how to create leaf wreaths by gluing a variety of construction paper leaves around the perimeter of the plate.

3. Help them punch a hole into the top of their wreaths and attach a piece of yarn for hanging.

 Joan Bowman, Langhorne, PA

Clay Leaf Roll-Outs

Materials

Self-drying clay • rolling pin • leaves • paint and brushes

What to do

1. Flatten a lump of clay.
2. Use a rolling pin to roll out the clay about ¼" thick.
3. Place a leaf on the clay and roll over it with the rolling pin.
4. Remove the leaf and let the clay dry.
5. Paint the clay with tempera paint.

☆ Jean Potter, Charleston, WV

ClayPressions

Materials

Polymer clay (Sculpey or Primo) in a variety of colors or white • nature items • old cookie sheets • parchment paper (used for baking)

What to do

1. Condition the clay according to the package directions. This step needs to be done by an adult. The clay is very hard to manipulate at first and small hands will find the task too difficult.

Tip: If buying clay is out of your budget, you can do this activity using homemade clay. However, the result will not be as durable or as long-lasting as polymer clay.

2. Let each child choose a block of clay. Encourage the children to roll and squeeze the clay between their hands to keep it soft.
3. Let the children explore outdoors to find objects that interest them. Encourage the children to investigate the trees, grass, woody plants, large flowers, or even the ground itself.
4. When they find something interesting, show the children how to shape their block of clay into a thick oval and press it over the object.

5. Help the child to peel the clay off the object, taking care not to ruin the impression.

6. Carefully turn the piece over in your hand and use a toothpick to put the child's initials on the back.

7. Place the clay on a cookie sheet that has been covered with a piece of parchment paper.

8. When all of the children have made their ClayPressions, bake them according to the package directions.

9. Allow the ClayPressions to cool thoroughly before handling.

10. If using white clay, let the children paint their baked clay impressions.

11. If desired, use leftover clay to make impressions of other interesting objects such as keys, combs, buttons, or toys. Just about any object you find would make an interesting impression.

More to do

More Art: Create a tile mosaic with the ClayPressions. When the children make their impressions, help them form their clay into uniform rectangular shapes. Bake according to directions. Alternate laying the ClayPressions and random rectangular craft tile pieces on craft board. Glue the pieces to the board.

Fine Motor: Make ClayPression pendants by poking a straw through the clay before baking. Let the children use leftover clay to make round beads. Ask them to thread the beads onto a wooden skewer and bake along with the ClayPressions. The children can use the beads and pendant to make a necklace.

☆ Virginia Jean Herrod, Columbia, SC

Snazzy Sunflowers

Materials

Print of Van Gogh's Sunflowers and real or silk sunflowers • pencils • 11" x 17" blue card stock • oil pastels or poster paint • paintbrushes • glue

What to do

1. Show the children the sunflower print. Discuss the colors and the different angles at which the sunflowers are painted. Some flowers are facing up, some droop down, and some stand straight. If available, also show real or silk sunflowers.

(continued on the next page)

2. Demonstrate how to draw the center of a sunflower by making a circle about three or four inches in diameter on the card stock.

3. Draw petals outward from the center. Emphasize that the petals should be very big.

4. Using oil pastels or paint, encourage the children to color the petals and make stems and large leaves.

5. When the colors are painted, ask them to spread glue in the center of the flower and attach the sunflower seeds.

6. Save some seeds for the children to taste. Ask them to describe what they taste like.

Related books

Camille and the Sunflowers by Laurence Anholt
Painting the Wind by Michelle Dionetti

⭐ Barbara Saul, Eureka, CA

BLUE CARD STOCK 11 X 17

Snow-Painted Pictures

Materials

Container • 2 tablespoons powdered tempera paint • 1 tablespoon warm water • 1 teaspoon dishwashing liquid (Joy works best) • window • vinegar

What to do

1. Pour 2 tablespoons of powdered paint into a container.
2. Mix in about a tablespoon of water to achieve a smooth paste.
3. Add in a teaspoon of Joy, mixing well, but gently, to avoid making the paint too sudsy.
4. Encourage the children to paint the mixture on a window in your room. The mixture dries on windows in 5 to 10 minutes.
5. Wash the paint off the windows using a mixture of water and vinegar.

 Jean Potter, Charleston, WV

Coffee Filter Snowflakes

Materials

Coffee filters • scissors • paintbrush • glue • glitter

What to do

1. Give each child a coffee filter. Help them fold their coffee filter in half, then in half again, and half again.
2. Show them how to cut little pieces from their coffee filter.
3. After they have made several cuts, ask them to open their snowflake.
4. Ask them to carefully paint their snowflake with glue and sprinkle glitter on top of the glue.
5. Hang in the classroom.

 Sandy L. Scott, Vancouver, WA

Ball Bounce Art

Materials

Large box • large paper • 2 bouncing balls • plates • paint

What to do

1. Put a large piece of paper into the bottom of the box.
2. Ask the child to roll the ball in a plate of paint.
3. Encourage the child to drop the ball into the box. It bounces and leaves a print each time. Take the ball out and repeat the process.
4. Give each child a turn using another sheet of paper. This makes a really great poster for children to take home.

 Susan M. Myhre, Bremerton, WA

Marble Spider Webs

Materials

Black paper • scissors • box with low edge • marbles • white paint • spoon • tacky glue

What to do

1. Cut out a large circle from a piece of black paper and place it in the box.
2. Soak a couple of marbles in white paint. Encourage the child to use a spoon to remove the marbles from the paint and add them to the box.
3. Show the child how to tilt the box so the marbles roll around the paper.
4. After the marbles have rolled around the paper, allow the paint to dry.
5. Let each child have a turn with different sheets of paper.
6. Once dry, the children can add a spider to their web using tacky glue.

Related song

"The Itsy-Bitsy Spider"

 Sandy L. Scott, Vancouver, WA

Spider Web Weaving

Materials

Rectangular piece of heavy cardboard • craft knife (adult only) • yarn • pipe cleaners • large buttons with 4 holes • thick string

What to do

1. Slice notches around the piece of cardboard using a craft knife (adult only). Weave yarn across the cardboard and back, creating a web.
2. Cut two pipe cleaners in half and thread them through the buttonholes to create the spider's legs.
3. Thread a piece of string through the buttonhole and knot it onto the button, then attach it to the web.

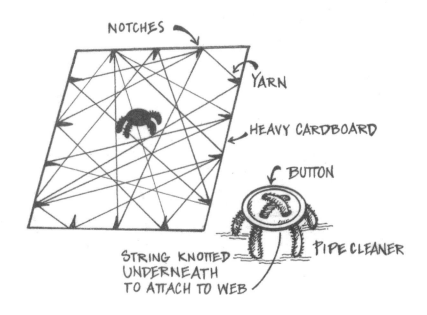

NOTCHES
YARN
HEAVY CARDBOARD
BUTTON
PIPE CLEANER
STRING KNOTTED UNDERNEATH TO ATTACH TO WEB

Related books

The Eensy Weensy Spider by Mary Ann Hoberman
The Itsy Bitsy Spider by Iza Trapani
Miss Spider's Tea Party by Kirk
The Very Busy Spider by Eric Carle

 Kaethe Lewandowski, Centreville, VA

Stamp Printing Helper

Materials

Heart-shaped piece of wood (from a craft supply store) • wooden bead or spool • hot glue gun (adult only) • paint • paper

What to do

1. Make your own inexpensive heart-shaped stamp. Use hot glue to attach a wooden lacing bead or wooden spool on the back of a thin piece of heart-shaped wood (adult only).
2. Encourage the children to dip the stamp into paint, then onto paper to create a pretty print.

Related book

Four Valentines in a Rainstorm by Felicia Bond

 Jackie Wright, Enid, OK

Rainbow Blend

Materials

Light blue construction paper • thick tempera paint or fingerpaint (red, orange, yellow, green, blue, indigo, and violet) • small dishes • wax paper

What to do

1. Give each child a sheet of blue construction paper. Pour each color of paint into a small dish.
2. Encourage the children to drop a small spoonful of each color of paint closely together on the paper in a rainbow-shaped arch.
3. Show the children how to cover the paint with wax paper and press down and rub to mix the paint together.
4. Peel away the wax paper to see the rainbow.

Jean Potter, Charleston, WV

Strips of Color

Materials

Paper towels • scissors • shallow tray of water • different colored water-based markers, one for each child

What to do

1. Cut paper towels into 1"-wide strips. Give one strip to each child.
2. Ask the children to use their marker to draw a wide stripe across the narrow width of their paper towel strip. The stripe should be approximately 1" from one end of the paper towel.
3. Ask the children what primary colors they think make up their color. (The primary colors are red, yellow, and blue.)
4. Making sure the ink part stays out of the water, place the drawn end of the paper towels in the tray. Lay the other end of the towels outside the tray.
5. As the water travels along the paper towel, it will dilute the ink and separate the primary colors. Wait and see which colors split and which don't.

More to do

Using paper towels and food coloring, reverse the experiment. Place drops of different colors of food coloring close together on the paper towel. Watch to see which colors they make when they merge.

 Elizabeth Bezant, Quinn's Rock, WA, Australia

Bug Headband

Materials

Tape measure • construction paper cut into 2"-thick strips • scissors • stapler, glue, or tape • marker • pipe cleaners, 2 for each child • pompoms, 2 for each child

(continued on the next page)

What to do

1. Use the tape measure to measure the circumference of each child's head.
2. Make a headband for each child by cutting the paper strips the same length as the measurements. You may need to staple or glue two strips of paper together.

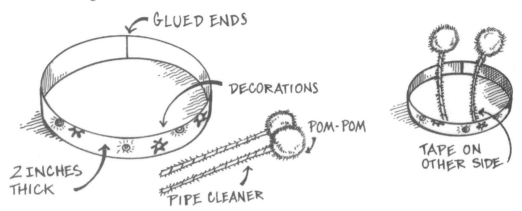

GLUED ENDS

DECORATIONS

POM-POM

2 INCHES THICK

PIPE CLEANER

TAPE ON OTHER SIDE

3. Encourage the children to draw bugs or anything else they desire on their headbands.
4. Let the children glue a pompom to one end of each pipe cleaner. Let the glue dry. These will be used for the antennae of the bug.
5. Attach the pipe cleaners several inches apart to the undecorated side of the strip of paper. Staple, glue, or tape them in place.
6. Staple or tape the ends of the strip together to fit snuggly around each child's head.

⭐ Jean Potter, Charleston, WV

Memory Shirt

Materials

Pre-washed T-shirts, one per child • stencils and sponge shapes • cardboard or paper • fabric paints • paper plates

What to do

This is a great activity to do at the end of the school year.

1. Brainstorm with the children about what they learned throughout the year (for example, letters, numbers, themes, dinosaurs, bears, and so on).
2. Then, make or buy stencils and sponge stamps in the needed shapes.
3. Let the children work in very small groups (with an adult in each group) to make their T-shirts.
4. Give each child a pre-washed T-shirt. Put paper or cardboard inside the shirt so the paint won't soak through to the back.
5. Pour fabric paint on paper plates. Encourage the children to dip the sponge shape into the paint and then onto the shirt. If using stencils, demonstrate how to put the stencil on the shirt where desired, dab a small piece of sponge in the paint, and then all around the area inside the stencil.
6. Allow the shirts to dry before removing the cardboard.

Author Note: I use fabric paint to write "Mrs. Cagney's Kindergarten 2001-2002" (write the correct year) at the bottom of each shirt. I have had parents come back years later and tell me they still have their memory shirt! I suggest that the parents make it into a pillow when the child outgrows the shirt.

⭐Lynn Cagney, Lutz, FL

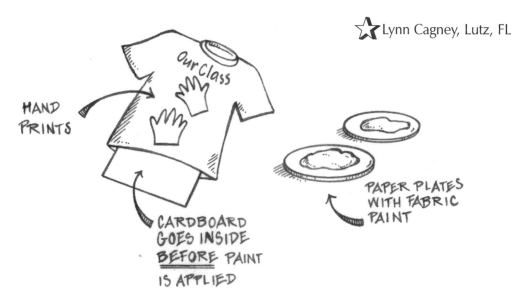

HAND PRINTS

Our Class

CARDBOARD GOES INSIDE BEFORE PAINT IS APPLIED

PAPER PLATES WITH FABRIC PAINT

First Day of School Sculpture

Materials

Blocks

What to do

1. As each child enters the room on the first day of school, give her a few blocks and tell her she is going to help create a First Day of School sculpture.
2. Encourage the children to arrange the blocks as they wish in the Block Center.
3. After all the children have arrived, stand back and enjoy the creation!

 Lisa Chichester, Parkersburg, WV

Labeling Blocks

Materials

Wood blocks • construction paper • markers • scissors • clear adhesive paper

What to do

1. Ask the children to find one block of each type in the Block Center.
2. Encourage them to trace the blocks on construction paper and cut out the shapes.
3. Encourage the children to compare the actual wood block and the tracing. Talk about the shape and size of the block and the tracing. Brainstorm to decide what descriptive words should be printed on the block tracing. For example, large squares, small squares, large rectangles, triangles, short circular columns, and so on.
4. Print the descriptive words on each block tracing.
5. Let the children choose where each type of block will be stored on the shelves in the Block Center. Place the block tracings in the appropriate places and cover them with clear adhesive paper to attach them to the shelf.

6. Encourage the children to use the labels to help them sort the blocks as they put them away after use. Occasionally read the descriptive words with them to remind them of what they say.

More to do

Math: With the children, use a ruler to measure the dimensions of each block. Print these measurements on the tracing along with the descriptive words.
More Math: If you measure the blocks and include those measurements on the block label, use the blocks to discover the measurements of other things in the room. For example, how long is the block area shelf? How tall is it? How big is the block area?

 Virginia Jean Herrod, Columbia, SC

Block Beach Party

Materials

Blocks • sand buckets and shovels • beach props • ribbons, optional

What to do

1. Plan ahead of time and let parents and children know you will be having a "beach day" in the Block Center.

(continued on the next page)

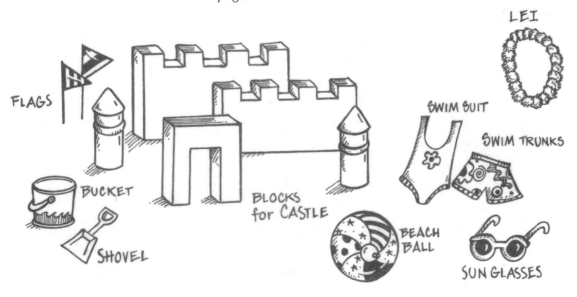

2. Ask parents to dress their children in beach clothing on the big day: swim trunks, swimsuits, sunglasses, flip flops, hats, and so on.

3. Hand out flower leis made from tissue paper.

4. Encourage the children to build block sandcastles while listening to beach music, such as "Wipe Out."

5. If desired, hand out ribbons for different categories, such as prettiest sandcastle, tallest sandcastle, and so on.

☆ Lisa Chichester, Parkersburg, WV

Building the Great Wall of China

Materials

Pictures of the Great Wall of China • blocks

What to do

1. Talk about the Great Wall of China. Show the children pictures and talk about how it was constructed.

2. Hang the pictures in the Block Center.

3. Encourage the children to work together to build their own version of the Great Wall of China.

4. When it's finished, celebrate by sitting in the middle of the creation and eating fortune cookies!

☆ Lisa Chichester, Parkersburg, WV

Cardboard Cityscapes

Materials

Pieces of cardboard • scissors • pictures of cities and city skylines • 9″ x 12″ construction paper • glue • markers, paint, or crayons • aluminum foil

What to do

1. Ahead of time, cut cardboard into building shapes, about 4 ½″ x 12″. Cut a variety of roof designs such as gabled, flat, and so on. Vary the heights of the cardboard buildings by cutting ½″, 1″, or 1 ½″ from the base of the building.

2. Show the children pictures of cities and city skylines.

3. Ask each child to choose three buildings from the cardboard cutouts. Show them how to line up the buildings and glue a 9″ x 3″ strip of paper to hinge two buildings together, leaving a ¼″ space to move the buildings back and forth. Glue another paper hinge on the back and repeat with the last building so that all three are joined.

4. To decorate the buildings, ask the children to trace each building separately on a piece of construction paper, cut it out, and glue the paper on the cardboard cutout (covering the hinges). Weight the buildings with heavy books as they dry to prevent wrinkling.

(continued on the next page)

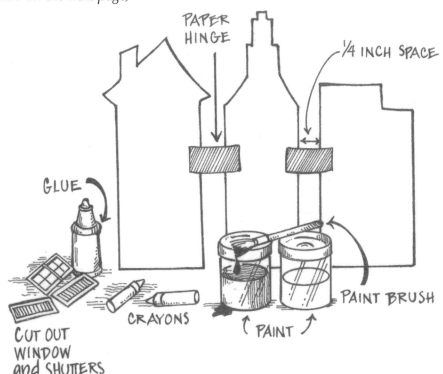

5. Invite the children to add doors, windows, shingles, and other architectural features. Glue on aluminum foil windows, if desired.
6. Stand the building threesomes together on a large flat surface for a big-city look.

Related books

The Little House by Virginia Lee Burton
Richard Scarry's Busy Town by Richard Scarry

 Susan Oldham Hill, Lakeland, FL

The Letter Bb

Materials

Large blocks • blue and black balloons

What to do

1. Encourage the children to use blocks to build a square house with no roof and 18"-high sides.
2. Help the children fill the house with balloons.
3. The children will have a fun time trying to keep all the balloons in the house!

SUPER BLOCKS ↗

Related books

Balloons: And Other Poems by Deborah Chandra
Block City by Robert Louis Stevenson
Circles, Triangles, and Squares by Tana Hoban
Harvey Potter's Balloon Farm by Jerdine Harold
How a House Is Built by Gail Gibbons
So Many Circles, So Many Squares by Tana Hoban

Elizabeth Thomas, Hobart, IN

Special Block Play People

Materials

Empty toilet paper rolls • glue • photos of the children

What to do

1. Glue photos of the children around the toilet paper rolls so that when standing up on end, the faces will be right side up.
2. Add these special block play people to your Block Center.

More to do

Ask children to bring in or take photos of other significant people in their lives (family members, principal, bus drivers, cafeteria workers) and turn them into Special Block Play People.

 Ann Kelly, Johnstown, PA

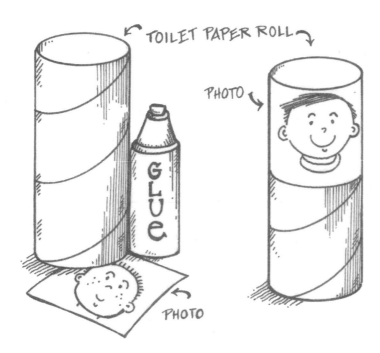

Caring for Books

Materials

I Love Going Through This Book by Robert Burleigh

What to do

1. Read *I Love Going Through This Book* to the children. Talk about the care of books. Discuss the following book responsibilities:
   - ☆ Protect your books from babies (babies like to scribble with crayons).
   - ☆ Protect your books from pets (pets sometimes chew or eat books).
   - ☆ Protect your books from the rain.
   - ☆ Turn pages carefully so that the pages do not tear.
   - ☆ Keep your hands clean when looking at books so that the pages don't get dirty.
   - ☆ When not reading your books, put them in their proper places such as a shelf.
   - ☆ Use a bookmark to mark your place in the book.
   - ☆ Try not to break the book's back (spine).

Related books

Book by George Ella Lyon
The Library Card by Jerry Spinelli

 Liz Thomas, Hobart, IN

Book Buckets

Materials

Two or three large buckets with handles • classroom books • white construction paper • markers

What to do

1. If you have trouble keeping your classroom books in order or if your bookshelves are not big enough, create some handy Book Buckets.
2. Buy two or three large buckets. The plastic kind with simulated rope handles are great to use.

3. Store extra books in the buckets or fill them according to a certain theme. For example, you could have a "Dr. Seuss Bucket" or a "Clifford Bucket."

4. Use white construction paper and markers to label the book buckets. Remember to change the label when the theme changes.

5. Let the children carry the book buckets around the room as they play. Also encourage them to read the books in the buckets.

6. Take empty book buckets with you on field trips to the library. They make carrying all those great books back to school a snap!

Tip: If you truly do have too many books, help the children decide which ones they want to keep and then let them donate the rest to a needy early childhood program.

More to do

Art: Let the children create their own mini book buckets. Purchase a sand bucket for each child. Provide permanent colorful markers, colorful adhesive paper, and stickers so the children can decorate their own buckets. Let them take these great little buckets home for use in their rooms.

Related book

Clara and the Bookwagon by Nancy Smiler Levinson

 Virginia Jean Herrod, Columbia, SC

Author Study

Materials

Books by selected author • basket

What to do

1. Every month, choose an author on whom to focus. Instead of just reading books by that author, extend the activity by making the author more real to the children.

2. Gather all your books (classroom books and borrowed books) by the author and put them in a special basket labeled "Author Study" along with the

(continued on the next page)

author's name. Gather any stuffed or plastic characters that are included in the story and put them in or near the basket.

3. In a special place on the bulletin board, hang a photo of the author (check the Internet or the book jacket). When you read the stories, share information about the author. Encourage the children to look for similarities in the author's books.

4. Send home a list of books by that author so the parents can also participate.
    Author Note: The children in my class really enjoy this activity. For example, they love pointing out that all Eric Carle books have a similar sun, the special way he signs his name, and how he has changed through the years in the photos on his book jackets. They love finding where Donald Crews has drawn himself into the story and seeing the photo of when he was a little boy going to "Big Mama's" house.

 Tracie O'Hara, Charlotte, NC

The Bookworm

Materials

Small paper plates, about 2 dozen • black pen • tape • books

What to do

1. Draw the face of a worm on a paper plate and attach it to the wall.
2. Select a picture book and read it to the children.
3. After you have finished reading the story, mark the title on another paper plate and ask a child to tape it to the first plate.
4. Every time you read a book to the children, write the title on a paper plate to add to the "bookworm."
5. Watch the bookworm grow and encourage the children to count all the books that have been read. Mark favorite stories with a big red circle in the middle of the paper plate.

 Ingelore Mix, Gainesville, VA

Chocolate Kiss Bookmarks

Materials

Cardboard • pencil • scissors • foil • glue • markers and crayons • hole punch • yarn

What to do

1. Draw chocolate kiss shapes onto small pieces of cardboard, one for each child. Cut out bookmarks from cardboard, one for each child.
2. Ask the children to cut out their kiss shape and cover it with foil.
3. Encourage the children to glue the foil-covered kisses to their bookmarks. Let them decorate the bookmarks as desired.
4. Help each child punch a hole into the top of his bookmark and string yarn though it.
5. During book time, let each child pick two books to enjoy.
6. Pass out real chocolate kisses to the children as they read.
7. When book time is over, ask the children to mark their place in the book with their kiss bookmark.

 Lisa Chichester, Parkersburg, WV

Stage Debut

Materials

Any appropriate book, such as *Ask Mr. Bear* by Marjorie Flack • classroom materials to make simple props, optional

What to do

1. This activity incorporates reading a story and giving children an opportunity to role play the tale. It enables children to take small parts, work cooperatively, and then see it all come together. It helps develop their listening and speaking skills, and their imagination.
2. Read any appropriate book to the children. *Ask Mr. Bear* by Marjorie Flack is a good one to use for this activity.

(continued on the next page)

3. Assemble the children into small groups and let them choose roles. If you are doing *Ask Mr. Bear*, you need a boy (or girl or both) and various animals such as a chicken, goose, goat, sheep, cow, and bear.

4. Go through the story with the children, repeating the lines in the book or a simple variation of them. (I am not advocating memorization!) Once they get the general idea, they usually use the lines in the book or their own words. Do not "rehearse" more than two or three times or it will become less exciting to the children.

5. If desired, work with the children to make costumes and props for acting out the story.

 Maxine Della Fave, Raleigh, NC

Bring a Storybook Character to Life

Materials

Mrs. Gigglebelly Is Coming for Tea by Donna Guthrie • lampshade • shawl • long skirt • teapot, teacup, and saucer • costumes and props for other story characters

What to do

1. Inspire children to read by bringing to life one or more storybook characters as you read to the children. A good example is to dress up like the character in the book *Mrs. Gigglebelly Is Coming for Tea* by Donna Guthrie. Dress like Mrs. Gigglebelly by putting a lampshade on your head and wear a shawl and long skirt. Carry a teapot, teacup, and saucer.

2. Read the story to the children in costume. Try expressing the type of personality you think the character might have in the story.

3. Dress like storybook characters when you read other books to children.

Related books

I'm a Little Teapot by Iza Trapani
Just Me and My Mom by Mercer Mayer

Miss Spider's Tea Party by David Kirk
Raggedy Ann's Tea Party Book by Elizabeth Silbaugh
Tea Party Today Poems to Sip and Savor by Eileen Spinelli
Teatime With Emma Buttersnap by Lindsey Tate

 Cookie Zingarelli, Columbus, OH

Stick Puppet of a Book Character

Materials

Book with a favorite character, such as *Miss Bindergarten Gets Ready for Kindergarten* by Joseph Slate • color copier • oak tag • scissors • laminate • craft stick • hot glue gun

What to do

1. Introduce a book by first showing the children a stick puppet of the main character. Make a stick puppet of any main character in any book you choose to read.
2. Before reading the book aloud (for example, *Miss Bindergarten Gets Ready for Kindergarten*), use a stick puppet to discuss what activities and experiences Miss Bindergarten's students might encounter at school.
3. To make the stick puppet, enlarge a picture of the character using a color copier.
4. Cut out the picture and glue it to oak tag or poster board.
5. Laminate for durability.
6. Attach a craft stick to the back of the picture using a hot glue gun (adult only).
7. This idea really gets the children involved in the story. Place the book and stick puppet in the Dramatic Play area or Reading area for repeated use. Watch this favorite book character come to life with this imagination-inspiring technique.

 Jackie Wright, Enid, OK

Stuffed Animal Collection

Materials

Inexpensive stuffed animals

What to do

1. Look for stuffed animals that correlate with your themes and book titles at yard sales, consignment stores, and on sale at retail stores. When you see good bargains that relate to your curriculum, snatch them up!
2. Feature a book and stuffed animal in a special display in the classroom. Change the display regularly to keep interest alive. Possible suggestions are:
   - ☆ A mallard duck for *Make Way for Ducklings* by Robert McCloskey
   - ☆ A penguin for *Cinderella Penguin* by Janet Perlman, *Tacky the Penguin* by Helen Lester, or *Little Penguin's Tale* by Audrey Wood
   - ☆ A dolphin for *What's Under the Ocean?* by Janet Craig
   - ☆ A teddy bear for *Sleepy Bear* by Lydia Dabcovich, *Where's My Teddy?* by Jez Alborough, or *Little Bear* by Else Holmelund Minarik
   - ☆ A lion for *Dandelion* by Don Freeman
   - ☆ A whale for *The Whale's Song* by Dyan Sheldon
   - ☆ A dinosaur for *The Dinosaur Who Lived in My Backyard* by B.G. Hennessy

Tip: When buying used stuffed animals, make sure they are in good condition with no holes in the fur, loose buttons, and so on. Also make sure to wash them before letting the children play with them. Most are machine washable; check the label to be sure.

 Jackie Wright, Enid, OK

Food Riddle Book

Materials

6 ½" x 3 ⅝" envelopes • crayons • markers • colored pencils • 3" x 5" cards • laminate, optional • hole punch • metal rings

What to do

1. This is great to do after finishing a unit on food. Discuss what a riddle is and do a few with the children.

2. On the front of an envelope, write "My Food Riddle" at the top. Then write three things describing the food without telling what it is. For example, the envelope could look like this:

   My Food Riddle
   I am juicy.
   I am red.
   I have skin on me.
   What am I?
   By _____

3. Encourage the children to guess what the food is. Then give the children envelopes to make their own riddles, helping them as needed.

4. Give each child a plain index card to color a picture of the food. Help the child write what the food is (for example, "I am an apple"). The children place it inside the envelope.

5. Laminate the envelopes (if desired). Punch a hole in the corner of each envelope and place a metal ring through it.

6. Combine the class riddle envelopes to make a food riddle book. Read the book to the class. The children have a great time guessing the food riddles.

 Debbie Barbuch, Sheboygan, WI

Bear-shaped Big Book

Materials

Deep in the Forest by Brinton Turkle • 11" x 17" white copy paper • scissors • crayons • binding machine or hole punch and yarn

What to do

1. After reading *Deep in the Forest*, tell the children they will be making a wordless big book.

2. Cut out the desired number of sheets of paper in the shape of a bear.

3. Give each child crayons and a bear-shaped sheet on which to draw a scene from the traditional story of the three bears.

4. Let the children help you arrange the pages in sequence.

5. Cut out a bear-shaped front cover and back cover. Bind the pages together using a binding machine or a hole punch and yarn.

(continued on the next page)

6. The children will enjoy revisiting their creation and telling the story in their own words.

Tip: Encourage the children to act out the story.

 Jackie Wright, Enid, OK

Alphabet Photo Book

Materials

A Helpful Alphabet of Friendly Objects by John Updike • chart paper and marker • objects commonly found in the classroom or playground • camera • glue or paste • 29 pieces of construction paper of varying colors • sentence strips, optional • markers • hole punch • three-ring binder, metal rings, or thick yarn

What to do

Phase One

1. Read the book *A Helpful Alphabet of Friendly Objects* to the children. Explain that they are going to work together to make an alphabet book.

2. Survey the first name of each child in the class to see how many share a common first letter. Determine how many alphabet letters are and are not represented by the first names of the children in the class. Create a chart of the results.

3. Ask children whose names begin with the letter "A" to work together to find small- or medium-size objects that also begin with the letter "A". For example, Alex, Angela, and Andrew would work together to find a plastic apple from the Housekeeping Center, an apron from the Art Center, an abacus, and so on.

4. Seat the letter "A" children at a table and arrange their objects on the table in front of them. Take a photo of the children with their found objects. Make sure the objects show clearly in the photo.

5. Repeat step 3 until you have worked your way through all the letters represented by the first letters of the names of the children in your classroom.

6. As you progress, mark off each letter on the chart (created in step 2). This will help you keep track of which letters are done and which letters need to be done.

7. After doing all the letters represented by the children's names, begin working on the remaining letters. Refer to the chart (step 2) to see which letters

remain. Ask the children to form groups to find objects for the remaining letters. If there are children whose names contain, but do not start with, the remaining letters, point this out and ask if they want to volunteer. For example, Angela Pizzi could help find objects for the letters "A" and "Z."

8. Have the children work together to find objects for each remaining letter. You may have to remind them that they are now looking for objects that begin with a letter that is not the same as the first letter of their names.

9. Remember to take photos of the children with the objects they find.

10. When all the photos are taken and developed, you are ready to begin making your book.

Phase Two

1. On the back of each photo, write the letter that the photo represents. This might seem unnecessary, but things can get confusing after a while!

2. Paste each photo in the middle right side of a piece of construction paper. Leave room on the left for border and binding.

3. On a sentence strip, print a descriptive statement about the photo. For example, "Alex, Angela, and Andrew found an apple, an apron, and an abacus." (Or just print the words directly on the construction paper.)

4. Continue until you have mounted each photo and printed a descriptive sentence for each. When printing sentences for the remaining letters, remember to show the connection between the children in the photo and the letter. For example, "Carl, Ralph, and Angela PiZZi found a zebra."

5. If there is no connection between the children in the photo and the letter, you can leave out the children's names in the descriptive sentence. For example, "These friends found a xylophone."

6. Encourage the children to create decorative borders and artwork on the borders of each page. Encourage creativity, but also ask them to relate objects they draw to the letter represented in the photo.

7. At the same time, have several children work together to create a front cover and a back cover for the book. Brainstorm together to create a catchy title and print it on the front cover.

8. Use a three-hole punch on the left edge of each page.

9. Put the pages in order in a three-ring binder, use metal rings, or sew the pages together with thick yarn. (Because this book is large, it's best to use a three-ring binder.)

 Virginia Jean Herrod, Columbia, SC

What Do You See?

Materials

Brown Bear, Brown Bear, What Do You See? by Bill Martin, Jr. • paper • pencils • crayons or markers • stapler

What to do

1. Read *Brown Bear, Brown Bear, What Do You See?* to the class several times before attempting this activity so the children are very familiar with the story and the flow.
2. Give each child a few pieces of paper. On the first page, ask the child to write "Bobby, Bobby (child's name), what do you see?" Each child writes his own name on his page.
3. Then ask the children to draw a picture of themselves on the page and write, "I see a _____ looking at me." The child then draws whatever he writes.
4. This continues for each animal or person that the child sees.
5. This can be done over several days, with the children making one page each day.
6. Help the children put their pages together and staple them to make a book.
7. When finished, the children will have their own book that they will be able to read without adult help.

 Phyllis Esch, Export, PA

Personalized Classroom "Brown Bear" Book

Materials

Brown Bear, Brown Bear, What Do You See? by Bill Martin, Jr. • mirrors • black medium-point markers • white paper • copy machine • crayons • stapler • colored construction paper for covers

What to do

1. For several days, read *Brown Bear, Brown Bear, What Do You See?* with the children so that they are all very familiar with the story. Encourage them to read it to each other in the book corner, and suggest that parents check out a copy from the library.

2. Discuss making self-portraits. Provide mirrors for the children to examine their hair and eye color and other features. Ask each child to use a black marker to draw a self-portrait so that it looks like a drawing in a coloring book. Remind them not to fill in any areas of the drawings; instead, ask them to draw just the outlines of their hair, eyes, and other features.

3. On the copy machine, make duplicates of each drawing. Return the first picture to each child to color in the areas, providing the mirrors again. Encourage them to color their features exactly the way they really look.

4. The next day, distribute the duplicates to the children and ask them to color the second picture. Encourage them to match the colors they used for the first picture so the two pictures will be the same.

5. Plan to make one book for every group of eight to ten children. Put the drawings in order (keeping the duplicates with the original). On the lower part of the first picture, write the child's name in this way:

   Andrew, Andrew,
   What do you see?

   On the second drawing of Andrew, write:

   I see Talitha looking at me.

6. Continue adding text in this way with until all have been written on except the last duplicate drawing for the last child. For this last picture, ask the children to name a favorite book character, such as Curious George.

   I see Curious George looking at me.
   That's what I see.

7. Add covers and staple the pages together. Continue making books for each group of eight or ten children.

8. If desired, laminate the pages for durability. You can also make enough copies so that each child gets a book to bring home.

9. To enjoy the stories even more, read the book as a class and have each child pop up to answer the question asked of him in the story.

 Susan Oldham Hill, Lakeland, FL

Curious George Hunt

Materials

Stuffed Curious George monkey • any *Curious George* book by H.A. and Margret Rey • several bananas • stuffed monkey

What to do

1. This is a great activity to do at the beginning of the school year to help the children become acquainted with the new environment. The children will go on a hunt around the building for George, allowing them to see the entire school and meet different people.

2. Before the children arrive, hide bananas throughout the building.

3. Introduce Curious George (the monkey) to the children in the morning. Read any *Curious George* book by H.A. and Margret Rey.

4. While the children are busy with activities, hide George and leave a note that he went on an adventure. Leave one banana on the chair where George was sitting.

5. When someone notices that George is missing, talk about having to search for him and the fact that he may have left clues.

6. Take the children throughout the building to look for all the bananas (the clues).

7. While you and the children are out of the room, have another adult put George back in the classroom in his seat.

   Tip: This can be done with different characters such as Peter Rabbit (using carrots for clues).

 Sandy L. Scott, Vancouver, WA

Children's Book Week

Materials

Tagboard • pencils • scissors • *I Took My Frog to the Library* by Eric Kimmel •
paper lunch bags • green, red, black, and white construction paper • glue

What to do

1. Ahead of time, use tagboard to make patterns for bulging frog eyes. Cut
   tagboard into strips that are rounded on the bottom (see illustration). Then
   cut tagboard into three different sizes of circles for the eyes and spots.
2. Make your own paper bag frog puppet ahead of time (see following
   directions) and use it to introduce Children's Book Week.
3. Read *I Took My Frog to the Library* to the children.
4. Explain to the children that they are going to make their own frog puppets.
5. Give each child a piece of green, red, black, and white paper. Let them take
   turns tracing the tagboard pattern (rounded strip) on the green paper. Ask
   them to trace the rounded strip twice and cut them out.

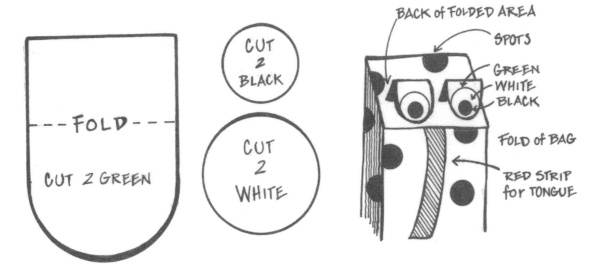

TAG BOARD PATTERNS

FOLD
CUT 2 GREEN

CUT 2 BLACK

CUT 2 WHITE

BACK of FOLDED AREA
SPOTS
GREEN
WHITE
BLACK
FOLD of BAG
RED STRIP for TONGUE

6. Then let them take turns tracing the larger circles on white paper and the
   smaller circles on black paper (two of each). Cut them out.
7. Help the children make bulging eyes by folding the straight end under the
   rounded part of the green paper strips.

(continued on the next page)

8. Encourage the children to glue the white circles on each eye, and then the black circles onto the white circles (see illustration).

9. Give each child a paper lunch bag. Ask them to lay them flat with the folded bottom facing up. The flap made by the bottom fold will be the mouth.

10. Show the children where to glue the eyes onto the folded base of the bag.

11. Help them carefully cut out a long piece of red paper for the tongue.

12. Ask the children to glue the red tongue inside the flap.

13. Encourage them to cut out small green spots to glue on the bag to decorate the frog's body.

Related books

Library Dragon by Carmen Deedy
Library Lil by Suzanne Williams
Too Many Books by Caroline Feller Bauer

 Liz Thomas, Hobart, IN

Alligator Purse

Materials

12" x 18" green construction paper • pencil • *The Lady With the Alligator Purse* by Nadine Bernard Westcott • scissors • markers • tape • glue

What to do

1. Enlarge the alligator purse pattern (on the next page) so that it will fill most of a 12" x 18" piece of paper. Trace a purse for each child on the green construction paper. Each child should get two copies (front and back).

2. Read the book *The Lady With the Alligator Purse* and tell the children that they are going to make an alligator purse.

3. Help the children cut out the purse (using the solid lines as a guide).

4. Encourage them to use markers to decorate their purse.

5. Instruct the children to tape the purse together, leaving the top open.

6. Ask the children to take their purses home and bring them back filled with a treat to have an Alligator Purse Party!

 Quazonia J. Quarles, Newark, DE

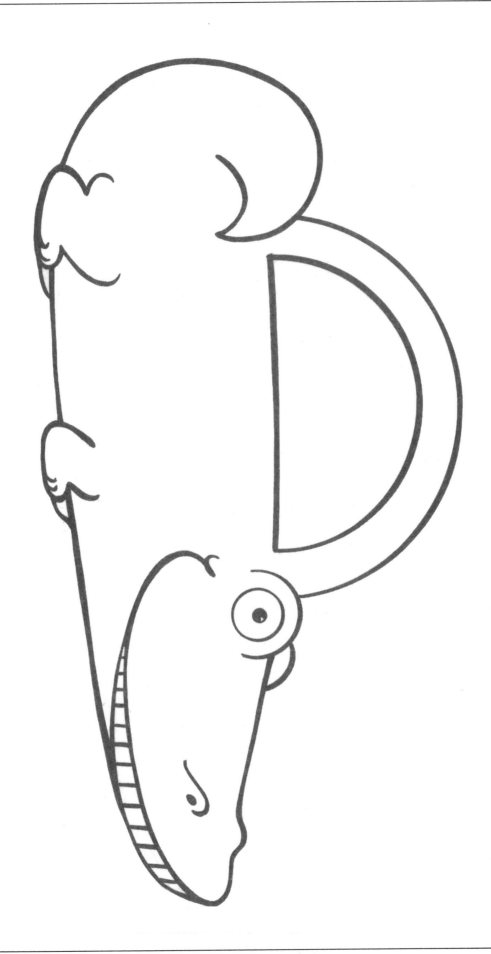

"Old Lady in the Shoe" Shoelaces

Materials

"There Was an Old Lady Who Lived in a Shoe" nursery rhyme • card stock • hole punch • markers • shoelaces

What to do

1. Beforehand, draw an outline of a pair of shoes (from the top view) and cut it out. Trace the shoe pattern on card stock, one for each child. Pre-punch shoelace holes in each shoe.
2. Read the nursery rhyme aloud. Brainstorm what it would be like to live in a shoe. Ask the children to think of other unusual houses to live in.
3. Give each child a shoe outline. Ask the children to color them.
4. Pass out the shoelaces. Working with a few children at a time, show them how to lace and tie the shoes.

Tip: Keep some of the shoes in a learning center for the children to practice on.

 Barbara Saul, Eureka, CA

Our Tribute to Eric Carle

Materials

Variety of books by Eric Carle • paint • variety of art materials to make textures • assorted brushes, such as kitchen, bottle, large, small, roller, scrubber, and so on • recyclable material, such as bubble wrap or other packing material, corrugated cardboard, egg cartons (cut into small sections) • flowers (real or artificial) • sponges, koosh ball, plastic fork or spoon, and so on • paper • die-cut machine, optional

What to do

1. Start by reading a variety of books by Eric Carle.
2. After reading the books, look back over the pages and point out how Eric Carle uses collage art with many different textures.

3. Talk about texture and experiment with it in your Art Center before getting started.

4. Let the children pick a theme for your tribute to Eric Carle.

5. Put out art materials and paint in various colors. If possible, try to have each child pick a different item to paint with so you have many different textures.

6. Ask each child to paint an entire page with texture. Show them how they can stamp with the item to get the best prints, but let them experiment. When they have covered the entire page, let the paintings dry completely.

7. Take all the sheets to the die-cut machine (if available) and die cut each page with something that relates to the chosen theme. For example, if the theme is Zoo Animals, die cut all kinds of zoo animals.

8. Make sure to put the child's name on each texture page and on one shape and set it aside (you will be able to get many shapes from each page) so each child will have at least one textured shape on the completed project.

9. After all the pages have been die cut, let the children pick from the selection of shapes and glue them onto a blank piece of paper. Then encourage them to add scenes to the paper such as cages for the zoo animals.

10. If you do not have access to a die-cut machine, help the children cut out or tear the sheets into different shapes. This is more true to Mr. Carle's technique.

☆ Gail Morris, Kemah, TX

Alphabet Caterpillar

Materials

The Very Hungry Caterpillar by Eric Carle • paper plates • markers • hole punch • scissors • string • thick marker or pre-cut letters and glue • cards with upper- and lowercase letters

What to do

1. Read *The Very Hungry Caterpillar* to the children.

2. Help the children make a caterpillar by decorating the paper plates to make the body and head.

3. Punch holes on each side of the plates and tie them in a row, beginning with the head. Use a very thick marker to write the letters of the alphabet on the plates, or glue on pre-cut letters. Write one letter per plate.

(continued on the next page)

4. Tell a hungry caterpillar story where the caterpillar eats the letters of the

alphabet. Sing the "Alphabet Song."

5. Put cards with matching letters into a box or bag. Encourage the children to draw them out, one at a time, and match them to the letters on the caterpillar.

Tip: The children can use the caterpillar and letter cards to practice matching lowercase letters to uppercase letters and words to their beginning sounds.

 Sandra L. Nagel, White Lake, MI

Our Own Secret Message

Materials

The Secret Birthday Message by Eric Carle • construction paper • stapler • glue • scissors • magazines • markers and pencils

What to do

1. Read the book *The Secret Birthday Message*.
2. Staple together a few pieces of construction paper to make a book. Make one for each child in the class.
3. Encourage the children to cut out shapes to use as part of their secret messages. They can choose to make the surprise at the end a birthday present or something else.
4. Help each child write a note at the beginning of the book that will lead the reader to a surprise.

Tip: The class can make one book, or groups of children can work on a book. It may be helpful to have volunteer helpers from the upper grades or parents to help the children make the books.

 Sandra L. Nagel, White Lake, MI

Book Character Introductions

Materials

Come to Our House: Meet Our Family by Ulises Wensell • color copier • scissors • 8 ½" x 11" tagboard • glue stick • clear contact paper or laminate, optional • felt • rubber cement • flannel board

What to do

1. The characters in the book *Come to Our House: Meet Our Family* are illustrated on the book's endpaper.
2. Enlarge a copy of the characters on a color copy machine.
3. Cut out the pictures and glue them to a piece of tagboard. After the glue has dried, cut out the pictures (so they are now attached to tagboard).
4. Cover them with clear contact paper or laminate them for durability, if desired.
5. Glue felt to the back of the characters using rubber cement.
6. Use the pictures on the flannel board to introduce the characters in the book or retell the story.

 Jackie Wright, Enid, OK

Flannel Board Chicka Chicka Boom Boom

Materials

Chicka Chicka Boom Boom by Bill Martin Jr. • brown and green felt • scissors • *Chicka Chicka Sticka Sticka an ABC Sticker Book* by Bill Martin Jr. • construction paper • rubber cement • flannel board • cassette tape to accompany book

What to do

1. Read the book *Chicka Chicka Boom Boom* to the children.
2. Make a coconut tree using brown and green felt.

(continued on the next page)

3. Cut out the letters of the alphabet from construction paper or use the brightly colored letters found in *Chicka Chicka Sticka Sticka an ABC Sticker Book*. Add felt to the back of the letters using rubber cement (adult only).

4. Put the tree, letters, and a flannel board in the Book Center along with a recording of the book so the children can sing along and recreate the rush of the letters up the coconut tree.

 Jackie Wright, Enid, OK

Chicken Soup With Rice Poems

Materials

Large tagboard • marker • *Chicken Soup With Rice* by Maurice Sendak • clear contact paper or laminate

What to do

1. On each piece of tagboard, copy a poem from the story *Chicken Soup With Rice*.
2. Laminate each of the cards for durability.
3. For each month of the school year, read one poem to the children.
4. Choose a child each day to circle the letters. Write the upper- and lowercase letters on the chalkboard so the children can notice whether they are the same or not. Then, brainstorm a list of words that start with that letter sound and use it as the letter for the day.

 Melissa Browning, Milwaukee, WI

Colorful Bears

Materials

Bear die cuts of each color • zipper-closure bags • *Red Bear* by Bodel Rikys • bear counters

What to do

1. Ahead of time, punch out bear die cuts from assorted laminated construction paper for each child.
2. Put one color of each bear into zipper-closure bags, one for each child.
3. During circle time, hand out the bags of bears.
4. As you read *Red Bear*, show the illustrations and encourage the children to match the correct die-cut bear on the page.
5. Afterwards, provide colorful bear counters and let the children sort them by color.

 Quazonia J. Quarles, Newark, DE

Corduroy's Pocket

Materials

Scissors • glue • construction paper • *A Pocket for Corduroy* by Don Freeman • markers • 1 ½" flocked bears from a craft store

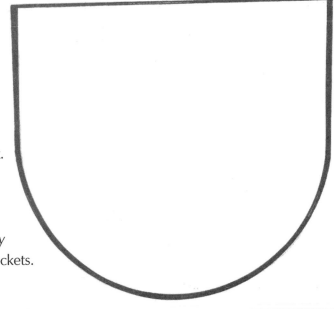

What to do

1. Ahead of time, copy the pocket pattern (see illustration) and cut it out. Glue two pocket shapes together, leaving the top open. Make one for each child. Let dry.
2. Read the book *A Pocket for Corduroy* several times and discuss uses for pockets.

(continued on the next page)

Ask the children wearing clothing with pockets to stand; count the number of pockets each child has. Discuss phrases such as "pocket watch" and "pocket change."

DECORATED POCKET

3. Give each child a paper pocket and a small flocked bear.

4. Encourage the children to decorate their pockets using markers. Then they can stick their bears into the pocket and re-read the story.

 Susan Oldham Hill, Lakeland, FL

"Gingerbread Boy" Marionette

Materials

Brown construction paper • marker • drinking straws • yarn • scissors • brass fasteners, 2 per child • white crayons • 1" squares of black tissue paper • gummed reinforcements

What to do

1. Beforehand, prepare the following for each child:
   ☆ Trace the gingerbread man silhouette (see pattern on the next page) onto brown construction paper (one for each child). Cut them out and mark them with dots at the top of the head and shoulders.
   ☆ Tie a 4" piece of yarn at the center of a straw and a 6" piece one inch from each end.
   ☆ Trace two arms per child onto brown construction paper and mark them with dots at each end.
2. Read the story of the Gingerbread Boy. Encourage the children to chant the Gingerbread Boy's repeated refrain.
3. Discuss the ending and whether or not the children like the fact that the boy is eaten at the end.
4. Encourage the children to suggest new endings, such as ways he could escape or a new character that could save him.

5. Help the children make puppets using the prepared materials.

6. The children cut out the arms and punch holes in all marked dots.

7. Show them how to attach the arms to the boy's shoulders with brass fasteners.

8. Encourage them to crumble black tissue paper to make "raisins" to glue on the puppet. They can use the crayon to draw on white "icing" squiggles.

9. Attach reinforcements to the back of the puppet at the head hole and the holes in the arms. Tie yarn through the holes.

10. Show the children how to make the puppet move by holding the straw at the center and wiggling the ends up and down.

 Sandra Gratias, Perkasie, PA

Horton Hears a Who Obstacle Course

Materials

Horton Hears a Who by Dr. Seuss • tunnel (or something to crawl through) • jump rope or piece of rope • balance beam • chairs • small stuffed elephant • plastic eggs • bowl for stuffed elephant

What to do

1. Read *Horton Hears a Who*. Set up an obstacle course before reading the story, or have another adult set it up while you read the story.
2. Explain to the children that they are going to go through the obstacle course to bring an egg to Horton.
3. They go through a forest (the chairs), jump over a log (the rope), cross a bridge (the balance beam), and crawl through a cave (the tunnel). As you explain, model the different obstacles. At the end of the obstacle course, encourage the children to put the egg with Horton in his nest (the bowl).
4. If desired, change the course using other obstacles.

 Darleen A. Schaible, Stroudsburg, PA

I Have a Family

Materials

Are You My Mother? by P.D. Eastman • manila paper • paste • scissors • red, yellow, orange, and green construction paper

What to do

1. Read *Are You My Mother?* and encourage each child to tell something fun that his family does.
2. Make family trees. Give each child a piece of manila paper, scissors, paste, crayons, and colored paper.

3. Help the children trace their hand and forearm on the paper. The forearm represents the trunk and the fingers depict branches. Ask the children to draw themselves and write their names at the base of the tree.
4. Ask the children to draw or trace one leaf for every family member on the colored paper.
5. Encourage them to cut out the leaves and paste them on the tree. Then they can draw pictures on each leaf representing the family members.
6. Help the children write the names on the leaves.

Related books

Amelia Bedelia's Family Album by Peggy Parish
Christina Katerina and the Time She Quit the Family by Patricia Lee Gauch
Daddy Makes the Best Spaghetti by Anna Grossnickle Hines
Nobody Asked Me If I Wanted a Baby Sister by Martha Alexander

 Wendy Pfeffer, Pennington, NJ

If I Were President...

Materials

So You Want to Be President? by Judith St. George • paper • pen or computer

What to do

1. Read the story *So You Want to Be President?* to the children. Have a discussion about what the president might do in his job.
2. Ask the children, individually and away from the other children, to dictate what they would do if they were the president.
3. It is nice to write the dictations on a computer and make a copy for each child.

 Sandy L. Scott, Vancouver, WA

Glittery Leaves

Materials

Why Do Leaves Change Color? by Betsy Maestro • real leaves • magnifying glasses • leaf pattern enlarged to 200% • red, orange, green, and yellow construction paper • glue squirt bottle • glitter (red, gold, orange, copper, green) • scissors

What to do

1. Read *Why Do Leaves Change Color?* Afterwards, discuss how leaves produce sugar for the tree. Point out the veins and holes on a real leaf.
2. Let the children examine leaves with magnifying glasses.
3. Encourage the children to trace enlarged leaf patterns onto the construction paper color of their choice. Then ask them to cut out the leaves.
4. Using the glue bottles, show the children how to dribble and squirt vein patterns onto their leaves.
5. Encourage the children to sprinkle glitter onto glued areas.
6. Let leaves dry and place them on a bulletin board to display this beautiful foliage.

 Quazonia J. Quarles, Newark, DE

Planting a Beanstalk

Materials

Jack and the Beanstalk • green bean seeds • small pots for planting (3–6") • potting soil • photocopies of Jack and the castle, one for each child • crayons or markers • scissors • clear contact paper or laminate sheets • oak tag or heavy paper • garden stakes cut 12–15" long

What to do

1. Read *Jack and the Beanstalk*. Pass around a few bean seeds. Explain to the children that they are going to plant their own "Magic Seeds."
2. Give each child a small pot. Ask them to fill their pots ¾ full with potting soil. Ask them to make three small holes, place one seed in each hole, and cover with more soil. Water.

3. Encourage the children to color and cut out the pictures of Jack and the castle.
4. Cover the front and back of the pictures with clear contact paper.
5. Give each child a garden stake. Help the children tape their picture of Jack about 4" from the bottom of the stake and tape the castle to the top.
6. Ask the children to place the garden stakes into their pots.
7. As the vines grow, wrap them around the garden stake to encourage climbing.

More to do

Science: Gather five small cotton balls, one clear plastic glove, five bean seeds, and an eyedropper. Place a cotton ball in the tip of each finger on the glove. Place one bean seed on top of the cotton. Taping just the back top of the glove, hang it in a window. Using the eyedropper, moisten the cotton balls (be sure to keep them moist).

Author Note: We could not "see" our beans growing in the soil so we did this extension. We were then able to observe all the changes that our seeds were going through. As the beans began to sprout on the cotton, our vine sprouts began popping out of the soil.

 Kim St. George, Derry, NH

Rhyming Words

Materials

One Duck Stuck by Phyllis Root • objects from around the room • basket or tray • bag

What to do

1. Read *One Duck Stuck*. Talk about the rhyming words.
2. Collect pairs of rhyming objects. Place one of the pair in a bag and the other in a basket or on a tray. At circle time, let the children pull out an object and find the match in the basket or tray.
3. When lining up, give each child a word and ask him to tell you a word that rhymes with it.

 Sandra Gratias, Perkasie, PA

The Houses of the Three Little Pigs

Materials

Three old twin-size sheets • red, yellow, brown, and black paint • large paintbrushes • pink and brown construction paper • scissors • markers • string • hole punch

What to do

1. This is a great activity for a fairy tale unit. After reading the story of the three little pigs, tell the children they will work in teams to create the pigs' houses for the Dramatic Play area.
2. Pair the children into teams.
3. Lay a sheet on each table and assign a team to each table to paint a house (one of straw, one of sticks, and one of bricks).
4. Pass out paints and brushes. Let the children decide which house they want to make. When they are done painting, let the sheets dry. Sheets take about one to two days to dry.
5. The next step is to make pig masks and wolf mask. Beforehand, cut out pig masks and wolf masks using the patterns (pages 522-523). Give each child a mask pattern to color with markers.
6. Help them cut out the eyes, punch holes in each side, and tie string through the holes.
7. When the sheets are dry, hang them from the ceiling, side by side, or in a grouping in your dramatic play area.
8. Show the children how they can put on their masks and act out the story of the three little pigs as they move from house to house. Explain that they can act out their own version of the story and have more than one pig living in each house.

Tip: Extend the activity by reading more than one version of the fairy tale. It is interesting to observe the children and see which version of the story they act out.

 Joy M. Tuttle, London, OH

A Variety of Three Little Pigs

Materials

Several versions of the *Three Little Pigs* • Post-it notes

What to do

1. This is a great activity to help children learn to compare and contrast stories, and also to help them learn to re-tell stories in proper sequence. It can be done in a similar way with any folk tale that has more than one re-telling available.

2. First, find several different versions of the *Three Little Pigs*, including those that are more non-traditional such as *The Three Little Javelinas* and *The Three Little Wolves and the Big Bad Pig*.

3. As you read the stories, compare how they are alike and how they are different. This is a chance to do some graphing, too. At the end of the week, after you have read several versions, put out all the versions.

4. Give each child a Post-it note with his name on it. Encourage the children to "vote" for their favorite version by placing their Post-it on that book.

5. Discuss what they liked best about their favorite, or make a language experience chart to show what each child said. This really gets the children using some higher-level critical thinking skills. They never get bored with a good story!

6. Extend the activity by putting out puppets to dramatize the story, put plastic figures and materials for house building in the Block Center, and costumes in Dramatic Play for acting out the story.

 Tracie O'Hara, Charlotte, NC

The Three Bears Go to Bed

Materials

Colored construction paper • crayons • scissors • paste • 12" x 18" manila paper • wallpaper or fabric scraps, optional

What to do

1. Read or tell the story of *Goldilocks and the Three Bears*. Then say, "The three bears were so tired after a long walk in the fresh air, then arriving home to find their house a mess and a stranger sleeping in one of their beds, they needed some rest. Will you help them get ready for bed?"
2. Give the children colored construction paper. Ask them to draw three beds— one large, one middle-sized, and one small—and cut them out.
3. Ask the children to glue the beds on a piece of manila paper. Encourage them to draw pillows on the beds or cut them out of construction paper and glue them to the bed.
4. When the beds are finished, they can draw the three bears sleeping on the beds.
5. Ask the children to cut out quilts for the beds from construction paper. If desired, provide wallpaper or fabric scraps and demonstrate how to cut or tear the pieces and paste them on the quilt to make a patchwork quilt.
6. The children can paste the quilts on top of the bears. Help them write the bears' names on their quilts.
7. Encourage the children to make up a bedtime story to tell Baby Bear before he falls to sleep.

Related books

Bedtime for Frances by Russell Hoban
If You Give a Mouse a Cookie by Laura J. Numeroff
Ira Sleeps Over by Bernard Waber
There's an Alligator Under My Bed by Mercer Mayer
The Three Bears illustrated by Paul Galdone

 Wendy Pfeffer, Pennington, NJ

Mixing Colors Like Mice

Materials

Mouse Paint by Ellen Stohl Walsh • primary colors of paint • liquid soap detergent • washing tub • towels

What to do

1. Talk about the three primary colors—red, blue, and yellow.
2. Read the book *Mouse Paint*. Pretend to turn the children into the little mice (from the book).
3. Ask the children to take off their shoes. Mix each primary color of paint with some liquid detergent (for easier cleanup). Label a large washing pan (for feet) "CAT." Tell the children that they will be stepping into the primary colors and mixing them to make new colors.
4. Take the children outside. Ask them to sit while you pour paint puddles about one foot apart on the sidewalk. Pour three puddles of each color.
5. Let the children walk through the paint, mixing it. When ready, let one child at a time wash off his feet in the "cat bowl."

 Vera M. Peters, Elizabethton, TN

Movin' in the Grass

Materials

In the Tall, Tall Grass by Denise Fleming • flash cards or chart paper • marker

What to do

1. Read the book to the children. Follow up with appropriate comprehension questions, discussing the movement words from the story.
2. Encourage the children to use motions to demonstrate movement words as you re-read the story.
3. Build a word bank with movement words on flash cards or chart paper to explore at other times.
4. Use *In the Small, Small Pond* by Fleming in a similar manner.

 Margery A. Kranyik Fermino, Hyde Park, MD

Nature and Creative Movement

Materials

Earthdance by Joanne Ryder

What to do

1. Read the book *Earthdance* and encourage the children to act it out.
2. As you read the book, describe what certain things mean and how they can be acted out.
3. Then, ask the children to stand up (give yourselves plenty of "wiggle room"), and as you read the book again, act it out with the children. The children will love it, and it makes a much more powerful impression on them.
4. End with a discussion on how we can take care of our Earth.

 Tracie O'Hara, Charlotte, NC

Owling

Materials

Owl Moon by Jane Yolen • park guide or naturalist

What to do

1. Read *Owl Moon* to the children. In the book, the author describes exactly what you do when you go owling.
2. If possible, obtain a recorded copy of the story from Scholastic and play it while you read the story to make it seem more real.
3. If desired, close the blinds in your classroom to give the effect of night.

Author Note: The children in my class loved this. When I was reading the story, if a child talked the children all said, "Shh! You have to be quiet when you go owling."

4. Talk about owls. Call you local metropolitan parks office and make arrangements to have a guide or naturalist take your class owling.

5. If possible, go to the Nature Center at the park and see if there is an owl there that the children can see before going owling. Owling can be done in the day, but nighttime is more effective. If an evening can be done, invite parents to come along.

6. Be sure to ask if the guide or naturalist has a copy of the story *Owl Moon*. If not, bring your copy and read it before starting your owling adventure.

More to do

Science and Nature: Contact a school supply store or catalog, or look up "owl pellets" on the Internet to order some owl pellets. Use them as a supplement to a classroom study of owls, food webs, and mammal anatomy. It's great fun to match the bones found in the pellet to various animals that the owls eat (on the sheet of paper you can get with the pellets).

Related books

All About Owls by Jim Aronsky
The Barn Owls by Tony Johnston
Good-Night, Owl! by Pat Hutchins
Owl Babies by Martin Waddell
Owly by Mike Thaler
Screech Owl at Midnight Hollow by Drew Lamm
The Sleepy Owl by Marcus Pfister

 Cookie Zingarelli, Columbus, OH

Making an Insect

Materials

Books on insects, such as *Bugs* by Joan Richards Wright • construction paper in various colors • scissors • glue • pipe cleaners

What to do

1. Read the book *Bugs* by Joan Richards Wright or any other basic insect book.

2. Identify the parts of an insect. As you identify each part, draw it on a board to create an insect. All insects have three body parts (head, thorax, and abdomen), antennae, six legs, and most have wings.

(continued on the next page)

3. Talk about the difference between insects and spiders (spiders have eight legs). To encourage critical thinking, give clues about various insects and let the children take turns trying to guess the name of the insect. (For example, "This insect has strong back legs for hopping and is green.")

4. Encourage the children to create their own insects using construction paper, scissors, glue, and pipe cleaners. The insects will all look different, but should include the necessary parts. Let them create a name for their insect.

5. If desired, ask the children to show their insect creation to the class and tell a story about it. They should include in what area of the world the insect is found, what it eats, and whether it does damage or is helpful to humans.

More to do

Games: Have a scavenger hunt. Split the class into teams. Hide construction paper insect parts around the room. Ask the teams to locate all the parts necessary to complete their insect. The first team to complete their insect wins.

 Sandra Suffoletto Ryan, Buffalo, NY

Tadpoles and Frogs

Materials

From Tadpole to Frog by Wendy Pfeffer • large paper • crayons • paint • paintbrushes • paste • green paper • aquarium with tadpoles, optional

What to do

1. Read *From Tadpole to Frog* to the children. Point out all the times the text says, "Where are the (tadpoles, frogs)?" Then ask, "Where are the frogs in winter? In spring? In summer? In the fall?" Talk about the word "hibernate."

2. Ask the children questions about the book. For example, "How are the frogs and tadpoles different?" "Are the frog's eggs like bird's eggs?" "What animals eat tadpoles?" "How do tadpoles/frogs swim?"

3. Talk about all the sounds that frogs make, such as "ribbet," "ba-ra-room," "croak," and so on. Then encourage the children to hop around like frogs, making frog sounds.

4. With the children, paint a big pond on large paper placed on the floor. When the pond is dry, let the children draw, paint, or paste frogs on the pond. Decide which season it will be and draw appropriate flowers, animals, fish, and so on.

5. If possible, set up an aquarium with a few tadpoles in it. Leopard or grass tadpoles are good to have because they are large enough for the children to see, but don't take too long to change into frogs. (Leopard tadpoles take a few weeks; bullfrog tadpoles take two years!) Watch the metamorphosis take place.

6. If you don't have frogs in your classroom, take the children to see frogs, perhaps at a local pond, lake, or aquarium.

 Wendy Pfeffer, Pennington, NJ

Polar Express Day

Materials

Polar Express by Chris Van Allsburg • hot chocolate mix, cups, and spoons • small silver bells (one for each child) • ribbon

What to do

1. Send a note home to parents asking them to let their child wear pajamas to school on the designated Polar Express Day. Teachers should wear pajamas, too!
2. When the children arrive at school, read the book *Polar Express*. Have a variety of activities in each center that relate to the story.
3. Set up a table for making and tasting hot cocoa. Supply this center with cocoa mix, cups, plastic spoons, and mini marshmallows. Have an adult help with the hot water.
4. Using the chairs in the room, set up a pretend train. Encourage the children to dramatize the story.
5. Let the children make snowy pictures in the Art Center. Put out black or blue paper and white chalk. Use a die-cut machine or scissors to cut out trains. Encourage the children to glue the trains on the paper and add "snow" using chalk.
6. Present each child with a silver bell on a piece of pretty ribbon as a keepsake of your Polar Express Day.

 Gail Morris, Kemah, TX

It Looked Like...

Materials

It Looked Like Spilt Milk by Charles G. Shaw • white paint • black paper • dropper or spoon • pen

What to do

1. Read *It Looked Like Spilt Milk* by Charles G. Shaw to the children.
2. Give each child a piece of black paper. Ask them to fold it in half.
3. Show them how to drop white paint on one side of the paper.

4. Ask the child to fold the paper and then smooth it.

5. When the child opens the paper, let him dictate what the picture reminds him of as you write his words underneath.

 Sandy L. Scott, Vancouver, WA

It Looked Like Spilt Milk Paint Blots

Materials

It Looked Like Spilt Milk by Charles G. Shaw • Option A: flannel board and white felt or heavy interfacing • Option B: Magnetic board and self-stick magnetic tape • copy machine • navy blue or black construction paper • white tempera or acrylic paint • white pencils • sentence strips • markers

What to do

Preparation: Copy the patterns from the book, enlarging as desired. For option A, pin the patterns to white felt and cut out the flannel board shapes. For option B, laminate or cover the patterns with self-adhesive paper, cut them out, and attach 1" magnetic strips to the pattern backs. Number the back of the patterns to follow the story sequence for both options.

1. Set up art tables with the following items: construction paper pre-folded (crosswise), bowls of paint with plastic spoons, white pencils, and sentence strips that read "Sometimes it looks like a…"

2. Gather the children in the circle area in view of the story board. First, read the story from the book. Then, invite the children to participate as you retell the story on the board. Say, "Sometimes it looked like a… (put the shape on the board and let them complete the sentence), but it wasn't a…" If the children are still enthralled, you can invite them to take turns picking shapes to put on the board and reciting the appropriate sentence.

3. Now, move the group to the Art Area to make blot prints. Show them how to place a spoonful of paint on the fold, close the paper, and press down with both hands. Then open the paper to reveal a "spilt milk" shape. Ask the children to suggest what it might be—a pumpkin, a ladybug, a football?

(continued on the next page)

4. Encourage the children to create and identify their own paint blots. Help the children print sentences across the top or bottom of their papers, such as "Sometimes it looked like a strawberry."

Related books

The Milk Makers by Gail Gibbons
Oliver's Milk Shake by Vivian French

 Susan A. Sharkey, La Mesa, CA

Sponge-Painted Swimmy

Materials

Swimmy by Leo Lionni • sponges • scissors • tagboard • 12 "x 18" blue paper • newspaper • paint smocks • black and red paint • shallow containers • crayons

What to do

1. Beforehand, cut sponges into small fish shapes. Make a copy of the fish pattern (see next page), cut it out, and trace around it onto tagboard. Cut one out for each child.
2. Over several days, read *Swimmy* frequently so that the children are very familiar with it. During circle time, demonstrate how to print with sponges—how to put paint on the sponge, scrape off the excess on the edge of the container, and print over and over again until the paint is used up.
3. Cover the work surface with newspaper and ask the children to put on paint smocks. Give each child a 12" tagboard fish pattern, crayons, and a 12" x 18" piece of blue paper. Ask the children to trace the tagboard pattern onto their papers, making the outline of the large fish.
4. Show them how to dip the sponge into the red paint to make fish on their papers, reminding them to print over and over again until the paint is gone. Ask the children to fill in the entire fish outline with smaller red fish.
5. When the children finish filling the large fish outline with small red fish prints, remind them to add a small black sponge print to be the eye. Let dry.

Related books

The Magic School Bus on the Ocean Floor by Joanna Cole
The Underwater Alphabet Book by Jerry Pallotta

 Susan Oldham Hill, Lakeland, FL

TAG BOARD FISH PATTERN

A Bunny and a Duck

Materials

The Golden Egg Book by Margaret Wise Brown • 9" x 12" brown and yellow construction paper, one piece each per child • stapler • cardboard paper • markers • scissors • orange, pink, and black construction paper • glue • cotton balls • yarn, optional

What to do

1. Read *The Golden Egg Book* to the children.
2. Give each child one piece of brown paper and one piece of yellow paper. Ask them to put the papers together and staple them at the corners.
3. Trace the bunny/duck pattern onto cardboard and cut it out. Let the children take turns tracing the pattern onto the yellow paper.
4. Encourage the children to cut out both papers together so the shapes match. Glue them together.
5. Cut orange construction paper into a beak shape (see illustration) and pink construction paper into an ear shape (see illustration). Cut out pink and black circles (for eyes). Give one of each to each child.
6. Encourage the children to glue the black eye and beak onto the yellow side of paper (as shown below) and draw feet.
7. Encourage them to glue the pink eye and pink ear as shown, and draw a nose and whiskers. Give them a cotton ball to glue on the back (for a tail).
8. The children can flip them back and forth to show the two characters in the story.
9. If desired, add yarn at the top and hang them so they will spin.

More to do

Circle Time: Give each child a plastic egg to take home. Ask them to find something that fits inside and bring it back to class for show and tell. Encourage the child to give clues so the children can guess the contents.

Music and Movement: Add gravel, crayon pieces, and other small objects to plastic eggs to make shakers.

 Sandra Gratias, Perkasie, PA

Where Do I Live?

Materials

Me on the Map by Joan Sweeney • paper • crayons and markers • world globe • maps (city, state, United States, and world) • *This Is My House* by Arthur Dorros

What to do

This project will take a week to finish. It can be part of a "Me" theme, where the children learn about themselves and the world around them.

Monday

1. Read *Me on the Map* during circle time. This book follows a girl as she learns about the world around her, and it will help the children understand what they will be doing during the week. The children will go on the same type of journey that the girl in the book goes on. (As the week progresses you may want to refer back to the book to reinforce what the children have already learned.)

2. After reading the book, ask the children questions such as: "Where do you live?" "What does your house look like?" "What does your bedroom look like?" "Do you have a favorite place in your house?"

3. After the discussion, encourage the children to draw a picture of their bedroom and their house. Help them label the different items in their bedroom. Hang the pictures so everyone can see each other's homes and bedrooms.

4. An alternate idea is to ask parents to take pictures of the child's bedroom and house and bring them in. Glue the pictures to construction paper and label them.

(continued on the next page)

Tuesday

1. Before class, make copies of a small house (to fit on a map) and cut them out.

2. During circle time, review what the children did the day before. Explain that today they are going to learn about their neighborhood and the town they live in.

3. Ask the children about their neighborhood. "What does your street look like?" "Are there stores where you live?" "Do you have a library nearby?" "Do you have a park in your neighborhood?"

4. After the discussion, place a map of your town on a table and ask the children to sit around it. Show them on the map where their school is and circle it. Now help each child find the street he lives on. When you find each street, place a house there and add the child's name on the house.

5. If there is a park, library, or other interesting place near the child's home, point it out and put a circle around it. Also point out interesting places in their town, such as airports, zoos, and museums. This will help the children become familiar with the different places in their town outside of their neighborhood.

6. When you are finished with the town map, hang it on the wall.

Wednesday

1. Before class, make copies of a state map.

2. During circle time, review what you have done so far. Talk about how they are going to learn about the state they live in and where their town is located in the state. Explain that there are many towns in the state, and children just like them in each town.

3. Lay the state map on a table and ask the children to sit around it. Talk about the interesting shape of the state. Explain that the star on the map represents the capital of the state. If desired, tell them a little about their state, its history, what crops are grown there, and so on.

4. After the discussion help the children find their town on the map and circle it. When you are finished hang the map on the wall next to the town map.

5. Hand out the state maps and help them put their town on it. Encourage them to color their maps if they want to. Hang the maps on the wall or put them aside to use in a book at the end of the lesson.

Thursday

1. Before class, make copies of a United States map.

2. During circle time, review what you have done so far. Explain that their state is part of the United States.

3. Show them a map of the United States. Explain that many states make up the United States. Ask them to count the states. "How many states did you count?" "Can we find our state?" When they find the state on the map, circle it. Hang it next to the state map.

4. Give each child a copy of the United States map. Ask them to find their state on the map and color it. Help them write the state's name. Hang them on the wall or put them aside to use in a book at the end of the lesson.

Friday

1. Before class, make copies of a world map. Find pictures of different children representing different cultures around the world and cut them out.

2. During circle time, read *This Is My House* by Arthur Dorros. This book has pictures of different homes that children live in around the world. After reading the story review what you have done so far. Explain that the United States is part of the world.

3. Show them a world globe and explain that it shows all the countries in the world. Point out the United States, and slowly turn the globe so the children can see the other countries that make up the world. Name a few of the countries and explain that there are children just like them who live all over the world. They go to school and play with toys. Referring back to the book *This Is My House*, talk about how the children live in houses like they do, but their houses are different from theirs.

4. Show them a world map and ask them to circle the United States.

5. Show them pictures of children from different countries. Encourage them to match the pictures to the countries where they live. When you are finished, hang the map next to the United States map.

6. The children can look at the maps to see that they live in a house, which is in a town, which is in a state, which is in the United States, which is a part of the world!

7. Give each child a world map to color. Set it aside to use in a book at the end of the lesson.

Summary: Putting the Book Together

1. Give each child a piece of construction paper to make a cover for the book.

2. Write or type the following paragraph on a piece of paper. Make copies and give one to each child to use as the introduction page.

> _____ (child's name) is a very special person. This book tells the story of the world he/she lives in. _____ lives in a house on _____ (child's address) in _____ , ____(city, state). This is just a small part of the world surrounding me. I have learned there are children who live around the world and go to school and play just like I do. As I grow up I will learn more about the world I live in, and one day when I am grown I will be able to go and see the world around me._

(continued on the next page)

3. Encourage the children to put their books together, with the cover, introduction page, drawings, and maps.

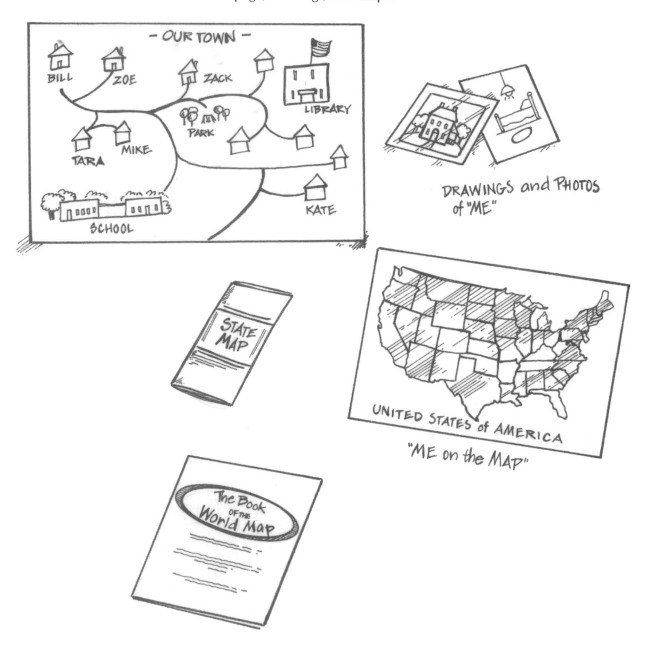

Related books

All Kinds of Children by Norma Simon
A First Atlas by Scholastic First Encyclopedia
My Map Book by Sara Fanelli
The Young People's Atlas of the United States by James Harrison

 Sherri Lawrence, Louisville, KY

Carpet Squares

Materials

Carpet squares (available at carpet retailers and outlets) • 2"-wide masking tape • black permanent marker

What to do

1. Write each child's first name on a carpet square.
2. The children will sit on their own carpet square during circle time.
3. This helps the children learn to recognize their names, as well as the names of their classmates.
4. If desired, replace the first names with last names mid-year.

 Sandy L. Scott, Vancouver, WA

Friendship Flag for Circle Time

Materials

Piece of muslin material • permanent markers or fabric paint in different colors • dowel rod • stapler

What to do

1. Make a friendship flag with the children the first week of school.
2. Each child writes her name or draws a small picture of herself on a piece of muslin. Make sure that each child is represented on the flag.
3. Staple the muslin to a dowel rod and put it with the American flag.
4. With the children, say the following "Friendship Pledge" along with the "Pledge of Allegiance" every morning. Assign a different pledge leader each day to hold the flag.

(continued on the next page)

I pledge to myself, on this day,
To try to be kind, in every way.
To every person, big and small,
I will help them, if they fall.
When I love myself and
others too,
That is the best that I can do.

5. This is a nice way to start the day with a friendly reminder to be kind to each other.

☆ Wanda Guidroz, Santa Fe, Texas

Circle Time by Month

Materials

Stickers or cutouts for different months of the year (see activity)

What to do

1. Purchase the following stickers for each month of the year:
   - ☆ September—apples
   - ☆ October—ghosts or pumpkins
   - ☆ November—turkeys
   - ☆ December—Christmas trees, menorahs, and Kwanzaa symbols
   - ☆ January—snowmen
   - ☆ February—hearts
   - ☆ March—shamrocks
   - ☆ April—umbrellas
   - ☆ May—flowers

2. For each month of the year, place the appropriate stickers in the circle area to mark the spots where children sit. This helps them learn to form a circle when they sit.

 Lisa Chichester, Parkersburg, WV

Holiday Circle Time Helpers

Materials

Props for each month of the year (see activity) • pointer

What to do

1. Collect props for each month of the year. For example:
   September—apples
   October—witch hats
   November—pilgrim hats or American Indian wear
   December—Santa beard and hat
   January—snowflake mask
   February—Cupid sash
   March—leprechaun hat
   April—umbrella and galoshes
   May—flower mask

2. During circle time, the helper for the day wears the appropriate props and uses the pointer to do the calendar and other preparations for the day.
3. This continues until all the children have had a turn to be helper.

 Lisa Chichester, Parkersburg, WV

Whose Is It?

Materials

Objects from home for the children

What to do

1. Before the first day of school, ask the parents if their child has a favorite pillow, blanket, stuffed animal, or other item the child feels connected to. Ask them to send in the item before school starts. (They can bring it in a bag the first day of school.)
2. Make sure the child's name is on the object.
3. At circle time, hold up one item at a time and ask, "Does this belong to someone?" The children's faces will light up!
4. After you have handed out all the special items, tell the children they can come back to it for a hug or comfort throughout the day.
5. You can send the items home that day or keep them for a week.

 Sandra Hutchins Lucas, Cox's Creek, KY

Star of the Day

Materials

Sturdy canvas or vinyl tote bag • yellow felt or fabric star shape • fabric glue or thread and needle

What to do

1. Prepare a tote bag by attaching a felt star to the front of the bag. Write a letter to parents explaining the purpose of the bag and examples of what the child can bring to school the next day to show.
2. As the school year begins, each day give a different child the "Star of the Day" bag to bring home and fill with special objects to show the class the next day. This activity will help children learn more about their new friends
3. Examples of items from home might be family pictures, pictures of family pets, favorite stories, favorite toys or games, a favorite doll or stuffed toy, pictures of the child as a baby, and enough of their favorite snack to share with the class.

 Christine Maiorano, Duxbury, MA

Hobbies and Collections

Materials

Items from home

What to do

1. Send a note home asking parents to let their children bring in a small sample of their favorite collection in a container on "Hobby and Collection Day."
2. On the designated day, ask each child to come to the circle and show her collection. Ask the child questions about it. For example, "Where did you get it?" "Why do you collect it?" "Which is your favorite in the collection?"
3. Encourage the children to ask questions, too.

 Lisa Chichester, Parkersburg, WV

Class Weather Forecaster

Materials

Laundry basket • weather-appropriate clothing, such as sunglasses, hats, gloves or mittens, umbrellas, and so on

What to do

1. Each day, choose a child to be the weather forecaster for the class.
2. The child looks out the window to check the weather, and then comes to the front of the room and picks out appropriate clothing for the weather from a laundry basket.

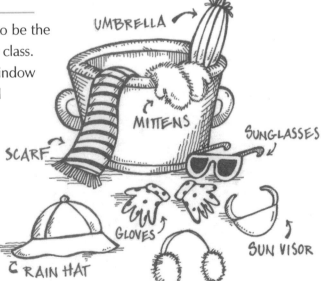

UMBRELLA

MITTENS

SCARF

SUNGLASSES

GLOVES

RAIN HAT

SUN VISOR

EAR MUFFS

(continued on the next page)

3. After the child puts on what she considers appropriate clothing for the day, prompt her to forecast the weather to the class.

 Lisa Chichester, Parkersburg, WV

Dress-Up Song

Materials

Dress-up clothes (such as bow tie, feathery hat, fringed vest, flowered shirt, ruffled skirt, Western belt, colorful apron, bib) • suitcase or bag

What to do

1. Gather dress-up clothes (both ordinary and unique) and place them into a suitcase or bag. The suitcase or bag will invite the children's curiosity and interest. Remove the dress-up items from the suitcase and lay them out for all the children to see.

2. Ask one child at a time to pick an item, describe it, and put it on while everyone sings the following song to the tune of "The Farmer in the Dell."

   I'm putting my (wooly scarf) on.
   I'm putting my (wooly scarf) on.
   I'm getting all dressed to look my best.
   I'm putting my (wooly scarf) on.

3. It is important to use the children's words in the song. (Don't change or rearrange their descriptive words.) This activity helps to develop observation skills, encourages language development, and validates their input.

 Judy Fujawa, The Villages, FL

Colors, Colors, Colors

Materials

None

What to do

1. During circle time, ask the children to close their eyes. Go around the circle and ask each child to name something that is a particular color. For example, ask a child to name something red in the classroom.
2. Play a guessing game by giving color clues. For example, a child might say, "I am thinking of something black- and white-striped. What is it?" Encourage the children to guess what it is.
3. The child continues to give clues until the children guess the answer. For example, "It is an animal," "It is large," and so on.

More to do

Math: Have different pieces of colored paper. Hold up a piece of blue paper. Ask the children who like the color blue to stand up. Count how many children stand up and write it on the paper. Hold up another color. Ask the children who like this color best to stand up. Count how many and write it on the paper. When you have shown all the papers, tally the results. Ask the children which color was most popular? The least? Any tie votes?

 Wendy Pfeffer, Pennington, NJ

Pet Store

Materials

Pictures of animals that make good pets (cats and dogs) and bad pets (tigers and elephants)

What to do

1. Ask the children to sit in a circle. Give each child an animal picture.

(continued on the next page)

2. Let the children take turns telling the group if their picture is a good pet or not. The children can discuss why the animal is a good pet or not.

Related books

Arthur's Pet Business by Marc Brown
A Name for Kitty by Marcia Trimble
The New Puppy by Anne Civardi
Pet Show by Ezra Jack Keats

☆ Liz Thomas, Hobart, IN

Safety School

Materials

Paper squares • markers • poster board

What to do

1. Write "Good for a Ride at Safety School" on small paper squares. Decorate the tickets with markers. Make traffic signs from poster board and hang them around the playground.
2. Give the children tickets to "Safety School." The children can use the tickets to take turns on the riding toys.
3. Explains what the traffic signs mean and rules for riding bikes and similar toys outside.
4. Practice the rules outside or in a hallway or gym.

☆ Andrea Clapper, Cobleskill, NY

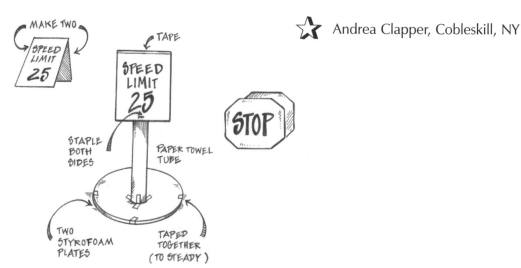

Chicka Chicka Boom Boom These Are the Letters I've Learned in My Room

Materials

Chicka Chicka Boom Boom by Bill Martin Jr. • poster board • scissors • bulletin board paper • Ticky Tac or tape • marker • pointer or yardstick

What to do

1. Read *Chicka Chicka Boom Boom* at the beginning of the year.
2. Cut out two large palm trees swaying into each other from poster board. Also cut out 26 coconuts for the alphabet plus a few others for decoration.
3. Label each of the 26 coconuts with a letter of the alphabet (upper- and lowercase.)
4. Glue or tape the trees to a large piece of bulletin board paper. Attach it to the bulletin board or a wall in the classroom. Write the title "Chicka Chicka Boom Boom These Are the Letters I've Learned in My Room" above the palm trees.
5. As the children learn the letters of the alphabet, let them attach the coconut to the tree or near the tree. At the end of the year, the tree will be full.
6. Every time you add a letter to the tree, review the letters already on the tree. Choose a child to stand by the tree with a pointer (to point to the letter). As you call out a letter, the whole group says the phonetic sounds for that letter.

COCONUT PATTERN

(continued on the next page)

Author Note: The children love standing in front of the class and using the pointer like the teacher. One year, this activity covered half of one of the walls in the room and the children loved it.

 Wanda Guidroz, Santa Fe, Texas

Are You Game?

Materials

Variety of board games • poster board • paper • markers • spools and small stones or jewels • dice • scissors • tape • glue

What to do

1. During circle time, have a discussion about board games. Ask questions such as, "What is your favorite game?" and "How did you learn to play it?"
2. Show the group several different board games with which they are familiar, such as checkers, Old Maid, Trouble, Chutes and Ladders, Go Fish, and Candy Land. Ask them to tell you what they know about each game. Make a list of their observations.
3. Ask the children what kind of game they would like to make. Show them the materials and encourage them to develop a game either individually or in small groups.
4. Support their creativity by helping to turn their ideas into concrete game pieces (cards, markers, boards) and documenting their rules.
5. Play and refine the games.

More to do

Have a family game night. Invite parents and siblings to come to school and play the games the children made. You might invite families to bring along commercial games as well.

 Ann Kelly, Johnstown, PA

Let's Pretend

Materials

Props from the Housekeeping Center

What to do

1. Put out props such as wigs, hats, shoes, mustaches, batons, stethoscopes, capes, and so on.
2. Ask the children to choose a prop and then pretend to be whomever they think the owner of the prop is.
3. Encourage them to dramatize stories of their choosing. Some examples are *The Little Engine That Could, Three Billy Goats Gruff,* and *Caps for Sale.* Nursery rhymes such as "Little Miss Muffett" and "Little Boy Blue" are also fun to dramatize.

 Wendy Pfeffer, Pennington, NJ

Jester Hat

Materials

Corrugated paper • scissors • pencil • cardboard • red, yellow, and purple construction or wrapping paper • gold or silver shiny paper or aluminum foil • 1" pompoms • bright colored yarn, ribbon, or rickrack • white glue • stapler

What to do

1. Cut corrugated paper into long strips, 24" long and 3" wide, for headbands.
2. Draw the outline of a jester hat (see illustration on the next page) on a piece of cardboard and cut it out to make a pattern.
3. Encourage the children to trace the jester hat pattern on the reverse side of a piece of corrugated paper and cut it out. Decorate the hat with construction paper or wrapping paper.
4. Help the children cut out several diamond shapes from shiny paper or foil and glue them on the hat.
5. Encourage the children to decorate their jester hats by gluing a pompom ball on each hat tip and their choice of trim to the bottom edge of the hat.

(continued on the next page)

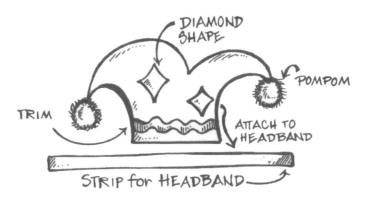

6. Glue or staple the headband to the hat.

7. Staple the headband to fit the size of the child's head.

Related book

The Jester Has Lost His Jingle by David Saltzman

 Mary Brehm, Aurora, OH

Blast Off Into Space

Materials

Foil • rubber bands • audiotape of space shuttle take-off sound • space music • space snacks such as Tang and squeezable yogurt

What to do

1. After doing a unit on space, schedule a "Blast Off in Space" day.

2. Gather the children in a circle and show them how to make "space shoes" by covering their shoes with foil and securing with rubber bands.

3. Tell the children they will now be taking a trip to space. Play the take-off sound and count down from ten. "10, 9, 8, 7, 6, …1, BLAST OFF!"

4. Explain that when the space music comes on, they are in space.

5. Encourage the children to get out of the "spaceship" and walk around. They can even look for pretend moon rocks.

6. Finally, settle down for a space snack. Talk to the children about the foods that astronauts eat.

 Lisa Chichester, Parkersburg, WV

Delivering the Mail

Materials

24 envelopes • cancelled stamps or stickers • pen • paper mailbox shapes or small boxes • small bag (mailbag)

What to do

1. Label each envelope with a name and address (real or fictional). Make about six different sets of four envelopes each.

2. Place a stamp or sticker on each envelope and place it in the mailbag.

3. Label each mailbox shape or box to match the mail you addressed.

4. Encourage the children to empty the mailbag, sort the mail, and deliver it to the correct address by matching the words and numbers on the envelopes.

 Vicki L. Schneider, Oshkosh, WI

Dinosaur Dig

Materials

T-shirts from home • dinosaur-shaped sponges • paint • dinosaur-related items • zipper-closure plastic bags • drawstring bag • numbered flags • paper and marker

(continued on the next page)

What to do

1. After a unit on dinosaurs that includes talking about the characteristics of dinosaurs, what happened to them, and what we know about dinosaurs roaming the earth, end the study by pretending you are paleontologists going on a dinosaur dig.

2. Several days before the dig, ask each child to bring in a t-shirt. Encourage the children to sponge paint a couple of dinosaur shapes on their shirts. The children will wear these on the day of the dig.

3. Ask parents to bring in dinosaur-related items, such as small dinosaurs, dinosaur erasers, dinosaur pencils, dinosaur eggs (candy), dinosaur eggs instant oatmeal, and so on (one for each child).

4. Put the items into zipper-closure bags. (This is to prevent the candy from getting dirty.) Fill enough bags so that each child will get one.

5. Put the zipper-closure bags inside a drawstring bag with a picture of a dinosaur on it (can be purchased from a librarian's catalog).

6. If possible, have your dinosaur dig on your playground. Draw a map of your playground and make copies. Ask a group of willing parents to bury the treasure bags.

7. After each bag is buried, the adult places a numbered dinosaur flag to indicate where the bag is.

8. Each map should have one number on it—where one of the bags is buried. Give each child a map and encourage him to look for the corresponding dinosaur flag. This may sound like an easy task, but some bags are buried deeper than others and the child may need an adult to help him find it.

9. After all the bags are found, enjoy a dinosaur picnic. This is fun for the children as well as the parents.

☆ Janet Nobles, Tulsa, OK

The Circus Comes to Town

Materials

16 brown grocery bags • gray and dark yellow paint • paintbrushes • scissors • glue • brown and yellow construction paper • broomstick • paper plates and cups • hula-hoop • red and yellow streamers • child's umbrella • marching music

What to do

1. Cut out two eyeholes in each of the paper bags.
2. Paint four bags gray and four yellow.
3. Trace and cut out huge ears (a large circle cut in half works well), then cut out four elephant trunks from the extra paper bags. Paint the ears and trunks gray and glue them to the gray bags to make elephants.
4. Cut out narrow strips from yellow and brown paper and glue them around the top portion of the yellow bags to make lions' manes.
5. Cut a hole in the middle of each paper plate (adult only). Paint the plates black and let them dry. Attach them to a broomstick to make "strong man's" weights.

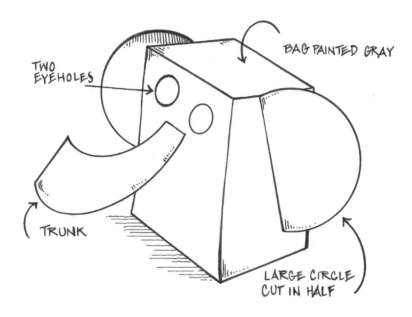

TWO EYEHOLES

BAG PAINTED GRAY

TRUNK

LARGE CIRCLE CUT IN HALF

6. Unevenly glue five paper plates or cups on the top of each cane for jugglers.
7. Tear a few streamers and attach them to a hula-hoop to represent fire for the lions to walk through.
8. Select clothes from the dress-up corner for clowns.
9. Set up a balance beam for tightrope walkers. Use an open umbrella for balance.
10. Ask the children which part they would like to perform. Rehearsing routines once is sufficient.

 Ingelore Mix, Gainesville, VA

Dramatic Play Circus

Materials

Popcorn • paper bags • paint and paintbrushes • paper plates • scissors • yarn • glue • big sheet • balloons • clown dolls or blow-ups • hat for ringmaster

What to do

1. Tell the children they will be creating a classroom circus.
2. Assign jobs to prepare the circus. Some might help you pop popcorn and paint paper bags. Help them write "popcorn" on the front.
3. Some can create tickets by cutting paper into ticket shapes and drawing on them.
4. Let the children decide what they will be in the circus (ringmaster, lions, clowns, and so on). Help them create masks using paper plates, yarn, and paint.
5. Decorate the room. Use a sheet to make a tent, and hang balloons and streamers from the ceiling.
6. Designate a ticket taker to take the audience's tickets and let the show begin!

 Lisa Chichester, Parkersburg, WV

Flying Carpet

Materials

Big colorful blanket

What to do

1. Ask the children to sit on the blanket. Tell them they are going to go on a magic carpet ride.
2. Let the children know where they are going. Your destination can go along with a theme you are going to be working on (such as space or the zoo). To get everybody's attention, ask them to buckle up.
3. Talk to them as you pretend to fly. Encourage them to add movements. For example, if you say, "We are turning right," lean right.

4. When you get there ask them what they see. Let everyone have a turn. Do the same thing while pretending to go back home.

 Darleen A. Schaible, Stroudsburg, PA

Funky Fashion Show

Materials

Period clothing

What to do

1. Send home a note asking parents to dress their children in their parents' or grandparents' time period clothing for a funky fashion show.
2. On the big day, ask each child to model his attire and tell a little about it.
3. If desired, have books about fashion history and how it has changed.

 Lisa Chichester, Parkersburg, WV

Grow an Indoor Garden

Materials

White or brown roll or mural paper or grocery bags • scissors • tape • crayons and markers • play garden tools • cardboard rolls

What to do

1. Place the brown or white roll paper on the floor. If using brown paper grocery bags, cut them open and tape them together. Explain to the children that they will be drawing an indoor garden.
2. Ask them to color plants on the paper and mark the areas with cardboard row markers (labeled "carrots," "peas," and so on).
3. Encourage them to use the play garden tools and the garden in dramatic play. This can be done any time, any season!

(continued on the next page)

Related books

The Carrot Seed by Ruth Krauss
Growing Colors by Bruce McMillan
Planting a Rainbow by Lois Ehlert
Sunflower House by Eve Bunting
The Tiny Seed by Eric Carle
Wild Wild Sunflower Child Anna by Nancy White Carlstrom

 Andrea Clapper, Cobleskill, NY

Learning to Count

Materials

Monopoly money • plain white tag tickets • pretend cash register • markers • tape

What to do

1. In the Housekeeping area, set up a play cash register, money, markers, and tags.
2. Tell the children to pretend it is a store. Encourage them to price items and mark prices on the tags.
3. Help them attach the tags to different items.
4. Encourage the children to play store. This is a good activity for practicing how to count change.

 Lisa Chichester, Parkersburg, WV

Let's Camp Out

Materials

Red and yellow paper • blue bulletin board paper • scissors • pop-up tent • sleeping bags • sticks • string • small magnets • construction paper • paper clips • cotton balls • flashlights • toy lanterns • play dishes and food

What to do

1. Make a fire "ring" using red and yellow paper, and a stream using a long sheet of blue bulletin board paper. Set up a tent with sleeping bags near the stream and fire ring.
2. Make fishing poles by attaching string to sticks and magnets to the end of the string. Cut out paper fish and attach paper clips to their mouths. Put the fish in the stream for the children to catch.
3. Provide flashlights, toy lanterns, play dishes and food, and sticks for roasting marshmallows (cotton balls). Encourage the children to pretend they are camping.

Related books

Meeting Trees by Scott Russell Sanders
Where the River Begins by Thomas Locker

 Andrea Clapper, Cobleskill, NY

Dramatic Play Library

Materials

Books • tape player and headsets • computer

What to do

1. Discuss the things a librarian does. Demonstrate by role playing:

   ☆ Putting books on and off the shelves
   ☆ Talking quietly
   ☆ "Reading" stories to dolls and stuffed toys
   ☆ "Checking out" books by stamping index cards

2. Encourage the children to play library. They can take turns being librarians or patrons reading and checking out books.
3. Record books on tape for the children to use with the tape players and headsets.

 Barb Lindsay, Mason City, IA

Ocean Life

Materials

Swimmy by Leo Lionni • construction paper • markers • scissors • old sheet • glue • green paint • sponges • 2 rolls of blue crepe paper • tape • poster board • paint and paintbrushes

What to do

1. Talk about how fish survive in the ocean. Read the story *Swimmy* by Leo Lionni. Then, work with the children to create an under-the-ocean environment in your Dramatic Play area.
2. Pre-draw or help the children draw fish and undersea life on construction paper with markers. Cut out the fish and glue them to an old sheet.
3. Encourage the children to dip sponges into green paint and stamp around the sea creatures on the sheet. This helps to give the illusion of underwater plants. When the sheet is dry, drape it over a play kitchen set to create a coral reef effect.
4. While the children are working on the coral reef, hang strips of blue crepe paper from the ceiling to the floor around the coral reef area and Dramatic Play area. Explain that this is the ocean.
5. The last step is for the children to create the giant ocean creatures from the story *Swimmy*. Draw giant ocean creatures on the poster board (one to a poster). Encourage the children to paint in teams.

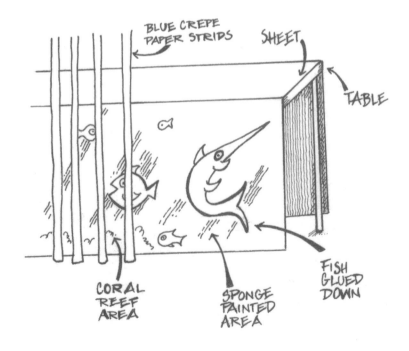

6. When they are dry, cut them out and put them in the Dramatic Play area.

7. It's a good idea to cut out several smaller fish, so the children can use these with the "giant" ocean creatures to act out the story of Swimmy. Show them how they can "swim" in and out of the blue crepe paper with their fish.

 Joy M. Tuttle, London, OH

Puppet House

Materials

Empty cardboard egg carton • X-acto knife (adult only) • wooden ice cream spoons or jumbo craft sticks • markers • paper and fabric scraps • craft supplies such as pompoms, yarn, and wiggly eyes • glue • scissors

What to do

1. Prior to doing this activity, remove and discard the lid of an egg carton. Cut the carton in half so you have six cups. Turn it bottom side up and slit each cup to hold a jumbo craft stick or ice cream spoon. It is a good idea to do this without the children because X-acto knives are not developmentally appropriate or safe for young children.
   Note: Spray the carton with sanitizing spray to assure no bacteria is spread to the children.

2. Encourage the children to create puppets using the wooden spoons or craft sticks. Provide markers, paper and fabric scraps, craft supplies, scissors, and glue. Help as needed.

3. Model how to stick the puppets in the slot of the egg carton to serve as a house for the puppets.

4. This activity can be done in conjunction with a family theme (they can make puppets to represent each member of their families) or the children can read a story, create puppets to represent key characters, then tell and retell the story using their own puppets.

 Bev Schumacher, Dayton, OH

Sledding and Winter Fun

Materials

Sleds • hats • scarves • boots • mittens

What to do

1. Add a touch of winter to your classroom by bringing sleds that don't have runners on them to school. You can do this any time of the year—even summer!
2. Encourage the children to pretend they are outside playing in the snow. Provide scarves, hats, boots, and mittens to add a real touch of winter to their dramatic play.
3. The children can take turns pulling one another on the sleds around the classroom, hallway, or gym. They can also place dolls or stuffed animals on the sleds.

More to do

Bring winter ice-skating into your classroom, too! Help the children cover their shoes with wax paper and secure it with masking tape. Pull the wax paper up high around the child's ankles for best results. (You can also try small plastic bags.) Encourage the children to wear hats and scarves as they skate. Play winter-type music or waltzes (such as the "Waltz of the Snowflakes" from the *Nutcracker*).

NEWSPAPER SNOWBALLS

MILK CRATE

STUFFED TOY WITH SCARF

TOBOGGAN SLED

 Cookie Zingarelli, Columbus, OH

A Snowman That Won't Melt

Materials

2 plastic white trash bags • old newspaper • wide, clear packing tape • hat • scarf • 2 small tree branches • construction paper for face or hair

What to do

1. Bring winter into your classroom by building a snowman that won't melt.
2. Stuff two white plastic trash bags with old newspaper. Twist the ends closed on both bags.
3. Stack them on top of each other with the twisted ends in the middle. Tape the two bags together using clear packing tape.
4. After they are taped, complete the snowman by adding stick arms, a hat, a scarf, facial features, and hair. Make the face and hair using construction paper or anything else you desire.
5. Add a magic touch by cutting out a red heart and writing "I love you" on it.
6. Let each child make his own snowman to create a snow family.

Related books

The Biggest, Best Snowman by Margery Cuyler
The Biggest Snowball of All by Jane Belk Moncure
One Snowy Day by Jeffrey Scherer
Snow by Roy McKie and P.D. Eastman
Snow Dance by Lezlie Evans
Snow Is Falling by Franklyn M. Branley
Snowballs by Lois Ehlert
The Snowman by Raymond Briggs
The Snowy Day by Ezra Jack Keats

 Cookie Zingarelli, Columbus, OH

Study the Arctic

Materials

White bed sheet or white fabric • box that children can crawl through • tape • books on the Arctic

What to do

1. Teach the children how the Eskimo people live in the Arctic by building your own igloo.
2. Cover a round table with a white bed sheet or white fabric.
3. Then cover a box with white paper, leaving both ends open so children can crawl through the box into the igloo. Let the children take dolls, play dishes, and so on into the igloo. This will help them understand that igloos are houses that the Eskimo people live in made out of snow.
4. Read books about how the Eskimo people really live. Talk about the different kinds of homes people live in.

Related books

Arctic Dreams by Carole Gerber
Building an Igloo by Ulli Steltzer
Caribou Girl by Claire Rudolf Murphy
Kitaq Goes Ice Fishing by Margaret Nicolai

 Cookie Zingarelli, Columbus, OH

Indoor Shanties

Materials

Books and magazines with photos of the inside and outside of different shanties (ice fishing houses) and people fishing • large appliance boxes • variety of art supplies • three 5-gallon buckets • plastic or cardboard fish • flat piece of Styrofoam (at least 2" thick and large enough to rest on the top of a bucket) • craft sticks • several sticks, dowel rods, or 1" x 1" pieces of wood approximately 2' long • yarn • magnets

DRAMATIC PLAY

What to do

1. Introduce ice fishing to the children using the books and magazines. Invite a parent or community member who has participated in the sport into the classroom to speak to the children and answer their questions.
2. Invite the children to decorate large appliance boxes to create shanties for their Dramatic Play area. These can also be used in the playground.
3. When the children are finished help them push their shanties onto the pretend ice and prepare the inside.
4. The children can use two of the 5-gallon buckets as seats or they can sit on classroom chairs or hollow blocks.
5. Use the third bucket to represent ice. Place the plastic or cardboard fish in the bucket. Then put a piece of Styrofoam on the bucket (ice) and encourage the children to "drill" or chop a hole in the ice using craft sticks.
6. Help the children make fishing poles from sticks and yarn. Add magnets to the fish and the end of the yarn on the poles so that the children are able to catch some fish.

More to do

Science: Add sheets of ice to a water table. Predict and chart the time it takes to melt. Compare sheets of ice that are inside with sheets that are outside. Observe different thicknesses and discuss the differences in melting times. Begin to hypothesize on the safety of the frozen lake or river.

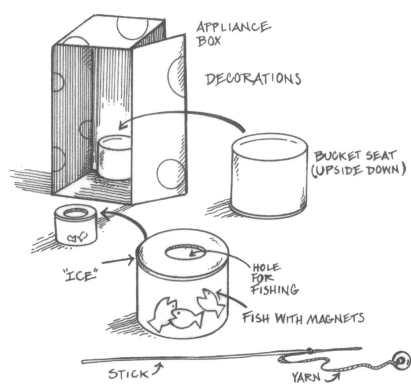

APPLIANCE BOX

DECORATIONS

BUCKET SEAT (UPSIDE DOWN)

"ICE"

HOLE FOR FISHING

FISH WITH MAGNETS

STICK

YARN

 Ann Kelly, Johnstown, PA

Play Restaurant

Materials

Construction paper • glue • old home and cooking magazines • markers • aprons • trays • pretend food, dishes, and so on • toy cash register • play money

What to do

1. Help the children make pretend menus by folding construction paper in half, gluing on pictures of food, and writing the names of items and prices.
2. Set up your Dramatic Play area with a table for customers, pretend food, dishes, aprons for waiters/waitresses, cooking toys on the stove, and so on.
3. Let the children take turns playing the different roles such as customers ordering food, cook preparing the meals, waiters/waitresses taking orders and serving food, cashier, and so on.

 Sandra Suffoletto Ryan, Buffalo, NY

Taking Restaurant Orders

Materials

Photo album pages • old magazines • ring clips • pencil or marker • restaurant check pad (available at office supply stores) with carbon paper to make copies

What to do

1. Make several pages of a menu using pages from a photo album and pictures of food cut from magazines. Make a cover such as "Welcome to the Washington School's Kindergarten Class Restaurant." Ring-clip the pages together. Be sure to include a variety of foods including fruits, vegetables, combination foods such as hamburgers and tacos, and desserts.
2. Invite a child to join you in demonstrating the new game for the class. One person plays the role of customer and the other is the waiter or waitress.
3. The waitperson presents the menu to the customer and invites him to place his order.
4. The customer chooses, one at a time, as many foods as desired. The waitperson writes his order on the order form using invented spelling by

sounding out the words and writing them phonetically. For example, "apple" could be written as "apl."

5. After the order is placed, the waitperson may act out serving it to the customer, who may act out eating it. The customer then gets to keep the copy of the order and the waitperson keeps the original.

6. The customer and waitperson reverse roles and play again.

 Susan Jones Jensen, Norman, OK

Wagons Ho!

Materials

Maps of the Oregon and/or Santa Fe Trails • brown wrapping paper or grocery bags • colored pencils, markers, or crayons • stickers and magazines, optional • queen- or king-size flat sheet • silver pie tins • small sticks of wood

What to do

1. This is a great activity for a unit on pioneer life. First, show the children a map of the trails that were popularly used in pioneer days. If one can't be found, make your own by drawing mountains, rivers, American Indian teepees, cacti, and small towns on brown wrapping paper or butcher paper.

(continued on the next page)

2. Talk about what life was like living out of a Conestoga wagon for months while being on these trails. Talk about the animals that were needed for these long journeys (horses, mules, oxen, cattle).

3. Discuss the tribes of American Indians along these trails. Talk about how people dressed, what they ate, the states they passed through, and the states where they were heading (Oregon, Washington, and California).

4. Help the children make their own maps. Tear brown wrapping paper into a square. It doesn't matter if the edges are jagged; this is the look you want.

5. Encourage them to draw mountains, lakes, teepees, and so on. If desired, let them use stickers or pictures from magazines (Western-themed magazines are great to use). Ask them to make red dots beside places that are important such as towns, American Indian camps, state capitals, and so on.

6. To play wagon train, drape a large sheet over a long table and put two or three chairs in the front of it for the seat (called a buckboard). Other children may sit under the table as though they are riding in the back of the "wagon."

7. Encourage children to use their imagination! For example, they can pretend to hold the horses' reins or oxen reins. They can also pretend to camp.

8. Sing pioneer songs such as "O Susanna," "Sweet Betsy from Pike," "Yankee Doodle," "Old Dan Tucker," "When Johnny Comes Marching Home," and so on. Learn some square dances and teach them to the children. Make up square dances and play lively music.

☆ Penni Smith, Riverside, CA

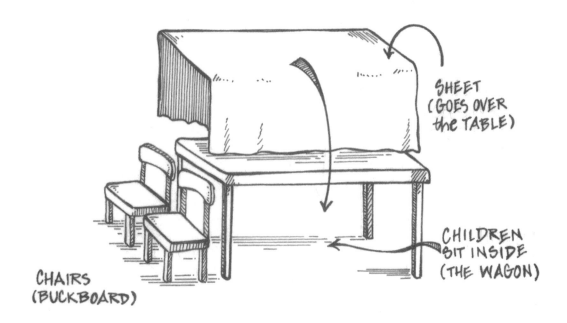

SHEET (GOES OVER the TABLE)

CHILDREN SIT INSIDE (THE WAGON)

CHAIRS (BUCKBOARD)

Button Buzzers

Materials

Buttons (2 holes, flat on both sides, at least 1" wide) • permanent color markers, optional • heavy-duty string (cotton or cotton-poly mix) • scissors

What to do:

1. If desired, let the children decorate the buttons with color markers before assembling buzzers.
2. Cut 2' of string per button (the string must be strong enough to withstand twists and rubbing but fine enough to slide easily through buttonholes). Thread the string through both buttonholes. If desired, pre-treat one tip of the string with glue and shape it to a point for easier threading.
3. Knot both ends of the string. Placing the button in the middle of the string, the child places the knotted end of string over one index finger, and the other end of the loop over the other index finger.

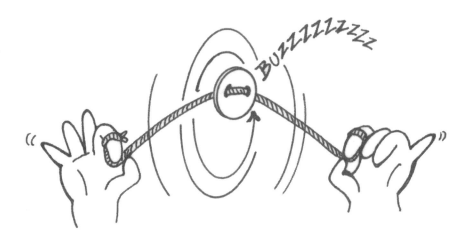

4. Touching index fingers to thumbs, the child swings the button in a circular motion until the string is tightly twisted.
5. The child, always holding onto the string, gently pulls and releases the twisted string in accordion fashion. The button will make a buzzing sound.

Note: Versions of this toy were used by colonial children, American Indian children, and pioneer children. This activity could enrich a unit on any of these three subjects.

 Christina Chilcote, New Freedom, PA

Candy Cane Ornaments

Materials

6″ long red pipe cleaner per candy cane • 6″ long white pipe cleaner per candy cane • 12 red beads per candy cane • 12 white beads per candy cane
Note: The hole in the beads should be large enough to thread the chenille stem through.

What to do

1. Encourage the children to twist the red and white pipe cleaners together at one end. Twist two times.
2. Encourage the children to slide three red beads on the red pipe cleaner and three white beads on the white pipe clearner.
3. Ask the children to twist the two pipe cleaners together once.
4. Repeat steps two and three, three more times.
5. Show the children how to bend the beaded "stick" so that it is in the shape of a candy cane.

 Melissa O. Markham, Huddleston, VA

Hopping Origami

Materials

3 ¼″ x 5 ¼″ stiff white paper • assorted markers • gummed reinforcements

What to do

1. Give each child a piece of stiff white paper. Demonstrate each step first, and then help the children follow along.
2. Fold side AB down to meet side BD and crease along BC. Open and fold back to the other side along the same crease. Open the paper flat again. (Figure 1)
3. Fold side AB down to meet side AC and crease along AD. Open and fold back to the other side along the same crease. Open the paper flat again. (Figure 1)

4. Fold down so that corner A meets C and corner B meets D. Crease along EF. Open the paper flat again. (Figure 1)

5. Push in the center crease of the paper so E and F are touching and fold edges GD and GC down. At the same time A should meet C and B should meet D. You will now have a triangle-pointed top on the paper. This is the head. (Figure 2)

6. Bend up the corners A and B to form front legs under the snout. (Figure 3)

7. Fold in the sides of the frog to form a more narrow body. (Figure 4)

8. Accordion fold the straight edge opposite the snout, one fold up and one down. (Figure 5)

9. Turn the frog over so it stands on its front legs and the accordion fold. The smooth back is on top. Decorate brightly with the markers. (Figure 6)

10. Add two gummed reinforcements to create big eyes.

11. Push down on the back fold and slide your finger off the end of the frog to make it jump and flip!

Related books

Fantastic Frogs by Fay Robinson
Flashy Fantastic Rainforest Frogs by Dorothy Hinshaw Patent
From Tadpole to Frog by Wendy Pfeffer
Red-Eyed Tree Frog by Joy Cowley

 Sandra Gratias, Perkasie, PA

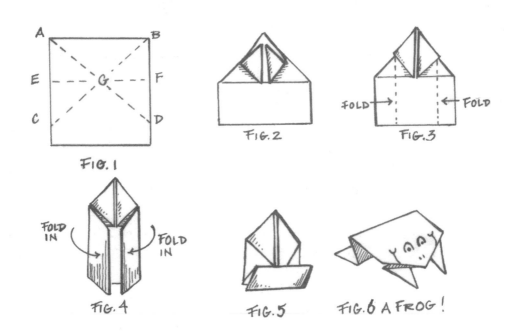

FIG. 1

FIG. 2

FIG. 3

FIG. 4

FIG. 5

FIG. 6 A FROG!

Make a Quilt

Materials

Real quilt or picture of a quilt • old wallpaper sample books • scissors • hole punch • yarn • masking tape

What to do

1. Show the children a real quilt. Talk about how it was made, and encourage them to look at it closely and touch it. If you don't have a real quilt available, show them a picture of a quilt.
2. Ask the children to sit at a table. Let them cut out a few pages of wallpaper to use for their own "quilt."
3. Demonstrate how to punch holes around the edges of each page of wallpaper. Help them as needed.
4. Give each child a long piece of yarn with masking tape around one end (this will make it easier for the children to thread it through the holes).
5. Demonstrate how to sew two of the pages together. Encourage them to try.
6. When everyone is done sewing, sew all of the children's pages together to make one big quilt.
7. Display it in the classroom.

 Darleen A. Schaible, Stroudsburg, PA

Cereal Box Puzzles

Materials

Empty cereal boxes • scissors • plastic storage bags

What to do

1. Ask the children to bring in empty cereal boxes from home.
2. Cut off the front of each box and cut it into various-shaped puzzle pieces. This step should be done by an adult. The number of pieces to cut varies depending on your group's skill level.
3. Store each puzzle in a separate plastic storage bag.

4. If you get duplicate boxes, use the extra box front as a puzzle board or as a reference for the children to look at as they work the puzzles.

 Vicki L. Schneider, Oshkosh, WI

Name Puzzles

Materials

Index cards or sentence strips • marker • scissors • plastic baggies or envelopes

What to do

1. Print each child's name on an index card or sentence strip.
2. Ask the children to cut their own name cards into three pieces.
3. Keep each name puzzle in a separate plastic baggie or envelope.
4. Encourage the children to match the pieces together to spell the name.
5. Once the children master the name puzzles, try doing the activity using vocabulary or other words.

 Sandra L. Nagel, White Lake, MI

Photo Puzzles

Materials

Photographs, preferably at least 4" x 6" • cardstock paper • scissors • glue • ruler • pencil • envelopes or baggies

What to do

1. Cut the cardstock so it is the same size as the photograph.
2. Glue the cardstock to the back of the photograph.
3. On the cardstock side, lightly draw horizontal and vertical lines, at least 1" apart (they do not have to be equally spaced). Use a ruler so they are straight.
4. Make enough so that each child will get one. Encourage them to cut along the lines to make a puzzle.
5. Store them in envelopes or baggies.

 Jean Daigneau, Kent, OH

Paper Pizzas

Materials

Large empty pizza boxes • poster board • manila paper • red construction paper • scissors • variety of construction paper: yellow (cheese), brown (sausage), pink (ham), white (onions), and green (peppers) • glue

What to do

1. Cut poster board into circles (to make the base). Cut manila paper the same size as the poster board circles, and red construction paper slightly smaller than that.
2. Cut the construction paper into thirds. Label each paper with the topping it represents.
3. Place each item on the counter as if ready to make pizzas.
4. Talk about the steps in making pizza: Place the dough (manila paper) on top of the cardboard, then add the sauce (red circle), cheese, and finally the toppings.
5. Give each child a poster board circle, a manila circle, and red circle. Encourage them to glue on the manila paper (dough) and red paper (sauce).
6. Let them choose whatever toppings they desire. Encourage them to tear the paper so that the pizza looks like a torn collage; this helps their small muscles.
7. This is a good activity when you have a "pizza parlor" in your Dramatic Play area.

 Vera Peters, Elizabethton, TN

The Scissors Store

Materials

Store props • scissors • variety of paper to cut (different sizes, colors, and textures) • variety of material to cut (sheets of aluminum foil, waxed paper, yarn, fabric, and so on) • pretend dollars and coins • paper lunch bags, optional

What to do

1. Set up an area in your room to be a pretend store.
2. Stock the shelves with scissors and cutting material.
3. Give each child two pretend coins to use for shopping.
4. One at a time, each child purchases scissors and something to cut with their two coins. Depending on the children's abilities, either an adult or a child can be the sales clerk.
5. Children return to their spots (on the floor or at the table) to cut.
6. Consider giving children more coins to shop for more materials to cut.
7. If desired, give the children paper lunch bags to bring home their cuttings.
8. Any undesired scraps either go in the trash or recycling—a great sorting activity!

 Barbara Reynolds, Smithville, NJ

See-Through Pockets

Materials

Laminating scraps • scissors • transparent tape • age-appropriate sorting activity • Sticky-Tac

What to do

1. For a hands-on sorting activity, use your classroom wall to display clear, plastic pockets to hold items to be sorted.
2. Make pockets out of laminating scraps left over from past projects. Cut them to the desired size to fold in half for a pocket.
3. Use transparent tape to tape the sides of the pockets.
4. Add sorting activities to each pocket.
5. Attach the pockets to the wall using Sticky-Tac.
6. This eye-catching idea draws children from across the room to the activity. Invite each child, in turn, to do the activity.
7. Children really enjoy this variation of a floor or table activity. Their classification skills and visual discrimination skills are sure to take root and grow with this clever idea.

 Jackie Wright, Enid, OK

Sew Fun

Materials

Any large, uncolored drawing suitable for five-year-olds (no larger than 7" x 10")
• cardstock paper • glue • hole punch • crayons or markers • shoelace or
length of yarn with each end knotted to prevent fraying

What to do

1. Glue cardstock to the back of the picture or photocopy the drawing onto cardstock paper.
2. Cut out the picture, leaving a 1" border around the edges.
3. Punch holes in the border area, approximately 1" apart, around the entire picture.
4. Write sequential numbers or letters of the alphabet, one next to each hole.
5. Give one to each child. Encourage them to color their pictures.
6. Encourage the children to use shoelaces or yarn to "sew" around their cards in numerical or alphabetical order.

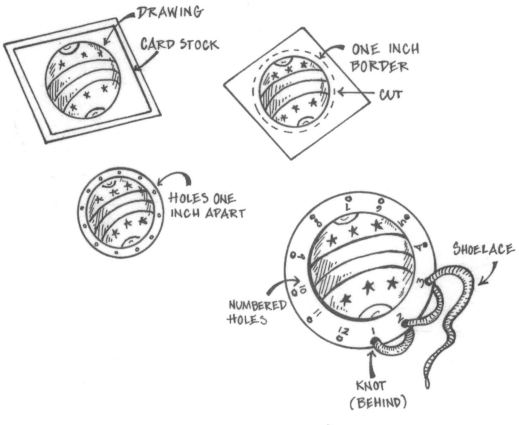

⭐ Jean Daigneau, Kent, OH

Scented Seaside Playdough

Materials

3 cups flour (may need 5 cups, see below) • 3 tablespoons cream of tartar • ¾ cups salt • 3 tablespoons oil • 3 cups hot water • 1 tablespoon coconut extract • large bowl • mixing spoon • yellow food coloring • gold glitter • chart paper

What to do

1. Combine flour, cream of tartar, salt, oil, and water in a large bowl. Mix until smooth.
2. Stir in coconut extract, yellow food coloring, and gold glitter.
3. Knead the mixture and add additional flour (you may need up to an additional 2 cups) until it is the desired smooth consistency.
4. Use various ocean-themed cookie cutters: fish, shells, boats, sea animals, and so on.
5. Prepare a large visual poster of the recipe and let the children assist by following the recipe, measuring the ingredients, mixing and kneading the playdough.

 Kaethe Lewandowski, Centreville, VA

Scented Playdough

Materials

2 ½ cups flour • ½ cup salt • 1 tablespoon alum • 1 package unsweetened Kool-Aid • 3 tablespoons vegetable oil • 1 ¾ cups boiling water • large bowl

What to do

1. Mix all of the ingredients together in a large bowl. Knead well.
2. Use as you would any playdough, enjoying the aroma.
3. Store in a covered container.

 Jackie Wright, Enid, OK

Squiggle Pen Mazes

Materials

Maze sheets • squiggle pens

What to do

1. Children this age love to do mazes. Keep a collection of maze books and incorporate them into all your themes.
2. To keep things fresh, add squiggle pens to your writing table for the children to use while doing mazes. They love the added challenge of keeping the pen inside the lines.
3. Encourage the children to color in different items on the maze in addition to completing the maze. This is a great problem-solving activity, and it develops fine motor skills and eye-hand coordination.

 Debbie Barbuch, Sheboygan, WI

Sad Little Rabbit Story

Materials

Shoelaces

What to do

1. As you tell the following story to the children, use shoelaces to demonstrate each step.

Once upon a time there was a little rabbit that was very sad. He cried and cried because his ears were so long that every time he tried to hop, he tripped on them. One day a fairy landed on the bunny's head. She carefully lifted the bunny's ears and crossed one over the other in the shape of an X. Then she put one ear through the bottom of the X and pulled. Next, she made each long ear into a loop and made another X like before. She put an ear under that X and pulled again to make a bow. The bunny looked in the mirror and saw his beautiful ears. This made the bunny laugh and he was never sad again.

2. Encourage the children to follow along and try to tie their own shoelaces.

⭐ Jean Potter, Charleston, WV

Teach Me to Tie

Materials

Styrofoam trays • hole punch • marker • long shoelaces or yarn

What to do

1. Draw a large shoe shape on a Styrofoam tray. Make one for each child.
2. Use a hole punch to make two rows of holes down the center of the "shoe."
3. Show the children how to lace the string through, and how to crisscross in and out.
4. Before long the children will do it over and over. Let the children take their shoe home to practice with their parents.

 Sandra Hutchins Lucas, Cox's Creek, KY

Calendar Snowmen

Materials

Large white paper • scissors • 25mm wiggly eyes • markers • white glue • all colors of construction paper • heart wrapping paper, optional • pencil • straight pins, tape, or Plasti-Tac • yarn for hanging, optional

What to do

1. Decide if you want snowmen on your bulletin board for just the winter months (November, December, January, February, and March) or if you want the display all year long.
2. Cut out a large basic snowman from white paper.
3. Cut out or draw arms to hold monthly decorations (see illustration).
4. Draw a mouth using a black marker and glue on wiggly eyes. Cut out and attach a hat, nose, and buttons.
5. Cut out a different seasonal object for the snowman to hold each month (see illustration for ideas).
6. You can make one snowman and attach monthly props using straight pins, tape, Velcro, or Plasti-Tac, or you can make separate snowmen and glue on the decorations.
7. Sing or chant the following song with the children.

Monthly Holidays by Mary Brehm

*January is a cold month
And the beginning of a new year.*

*February has President's Day
And Valentines do appear.*

*March brings the luck of the Irish
Sporting colors green and white.*

*April has the Easter holiday
And it rains day and night.*

*May honors our dear mothers
And flowers emerge from the ground.*

June is graduation time
And cards for fathers can be found.

July is the time for picnics
And our flag is everywhere.

August is the garden month
And going to the state fair.

September starts the school year
And riding the school bus too.

October brings Halloween
And apples and pumpkins come into view.

In November we think of Pilgrims
And that first Thanksgiving Day.

December brings Christmas time
A child's favorite holiday.

(continued on the next two pages)

VELCRO ON HEAD and MIDDLE (TO ATTACH ITEMS)

FOR HEAD

JANUARY

FEBRUARY

FOR MIDDLE

MARCH

APRIL

MAY

JUNE

JULY

AUGUST

SEPTEMBER

OCTOBER

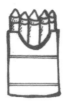

NOVEMBER

DECEMBER

And so twelve months have flown by
As we recall each one.

Then we look forward to a new year
And more holiday fun.

 Mary Brehm, Aurora, OH

Dame Cinco, Give Me Five

Materials

None

What to do

1. Say each of the following phrases—first in Spanish, then in English.
   - ☆ "Ojos. Miran a me." "Eyes on the teacher."
   - ☆ "Orejas. Escuchan a me." "Ears listening."
   - ☆ "Bocas. Silencios." "Mouths quiet."
   - ☆ "Brasos. Abajo." "Arms by your side."
   - ☆ "Pies. Immovil." "Feet still."

 Stacy Edwards, Jermyn, PA

Buenos Dias Greeting Song

Materials

None

What to do

1. Use the following song to teach the children how to say "good morning,"
   "good afternoon," "good evening," and "see you later" in Spanish.

(continued on the next page)

Buenos Dias (Tune: Frère Jacques)

Buenos dias, buenos dias, (pronounced bway-nose-dee-as)
Good morning, good morning.
Buenos tardes, buenos tardes, (pronounced bway-nose-tar-days)
Good afternoon, good afternoon.
Buenos noches, buenos noches, (pronounced bway-nose-no-chays)
Good evening, good evening,
Hasta luega, hasta luega, (pronounced ahs-tah-loo-egg-ah)
See you later, see you later.

 Lisa Chichester, Parkersburg, WV

Cinco Vaqueros

Materials

None

What to do

1. Do the following fingerplay with the children.

Cinco Vaqueros

Cinco vaqueros (hold up appropriate amount of fingers)
Riding in the desert (pretend to ride a horse)
On a hot, hot day. (wipe brow)
Un vaquero stops, (hold hands as in protest)
Stops to say, (cup hands around one side of mouth)
"Mucho calor!" (wipe brow, look tired)
"No mas, por favor!" (shake head from side to side)
"No, no, no, no, (shake your finger and shake head from side to side)
Not anymore!" (hold up hands in protest)
Ride, ride, ride, ride into town, (pretend to ride a horse)
As the sun goes down. (motion with hand like you are pushing something down)

2. Repeat the fingerplay, with descending numbers: quatro, tres, dos, and uno.

Translation guide:

cinco vaquero(s): five cowboy(s)

quatro: four

tres: three

dos: two

uno: one

mucho calor: it's very hot

no mas, por favor: no more, please

Related books

The Cat in the Hat/El Gato Ensombrerado by Dr. Seuss

Eight Animals on the Town (Ocho Animales) by Susan Middleton Elya

Just Like Home/Como En Mi Tierra by Elizabeth I. Miller

Say Hola to Spanish by Susan Middleton Elya

 Stacy Edwards, Jermyn, PA

Call a Friend

Materials

None

What to do

1. Sing the song below to the tune of "Row, Row, Row Your Boat."
2. If desired, sing it using different languages, including American Sign Language (ASL).
3. Encourage the children to learn a friend's phone number and practice dialing a pretend phone while learning the number.

Call, call, call a friend,
Friend, I'm calling you.
Hi, hello, how are you?
Very well, thank you!

 Kaethe Lewandowski and Nikoia Steward, Centreville, VA

Silly Songs

Materials

None

Songs or Poems

1. Sing the following song for Halloween to the tune of "If You're Happy and You Know It."

Halloween Song by Penni Smith

If you're a cat and you know it say, "Meow." (meow)
If you're a cat and you know it say, "Meow." (meow)
If you're a cat and you know it then your meow will surely show it.
If you're a cat and you know it say, "Meow." (meow)

If you're a witch and you know it cast a spell…. (Abracadabra!)
If you're a ghost and you know it then shout, "Boo!"…(boo!)
If you're a scarecrow and you know it wave your arms… (wave, wave)
If you're a spider and you know it spin your web… (spin, spin)
If you're a vampire and you know it flash your teeth… (ha, ha)
If you're a skeleton and you know it clink your bones… (clink, clink)
If Halloween makes you happy, clap your hands… (clap, clap)

2. Sing the following song to the tune of "Row, Row, Row Your Boat."

See Your Dentist by Penni Smith

Brush, brush, brush your teeth,
Do it every day.
If you don't, know what you'll have?
Dreadful tooth decay.
See, see, see your dentist
Do it, don't delay.
If you don't, know what you'll have?
Dreadful tooth decay.
Buzz, buzz goes the drill
To fill a rotting tooth.
Take good care of them today
Or they'll fall out—that's the truth.

 Penni L. Smith, Riverside, CA

Craft Stick Count

Materials

5-10 craft sticks per child

What to do

1. Sing the following song to the tune of "Frère Jacques." The teacher holds up three sticks at the beginning of the song.

   I have three sticks.
   I have three sticks.
   Yes I do.
   Yes I do.
   Anybody else?
   Anybody else?
   How about you?
   How about you?

2. Ask the children to hold up the same amount of sticks at the end of the song.
3. Continue singing the song, using a different amount of sticks each time.
4. This is a great way to help children learn to count with meaning.

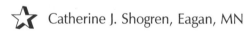 Catherine J. Shogren, Eagan, MN

Did You Ever Hear a...?

Materials

Pictures of animals • glue • Popsicle sticks • animal puppets

What to do

1. Pick out several animals (cut out pictures and glue them to Popsicle sticks or use hand puppets) that make sounds familiar to young children.
2. At the appropriate time, hold up the corresponding animal.
3. As you sing, hold up the picture or puppet of a tiger (or whatever animal you use) and let the children fill in the appropriate sound.

(continued on the next page)

4. Sing the following song to the tune of "Did You Ever See a Lassie?"

   Did you ever hear a tiger?
   A tiger, a tiger,
   Did you ever hear a tiger?
   One sounds like this. (roar like a tiger)

5. Ask the children to point to animal figures or pictures of animals in the room by changing the word "hear" to "see." End the song with "point to one now."

 Nancy A. Johnson, Cottage Grove, MN

Flag Salute Song

Materials

None

What to do

1. Help the children learn which hand is their right hand by singing the following song.

   This is my left hand, la la la la
   This is my right hand, la la la la
   That is the reason I'm so happy with delight
   I know my left hand from my right!

2. Now ask the children to raise their right hand and put it on their heart. Say the "Pledge of Allegiance" together.

 Sandy L. Scott, Vancouver, WA

"Green Frog"

Materials

None

What to do

1. Sing the following song with the children and do the actions.

   Glump, (clap) *glump,* (clap) *went the little green frog one day,*
   Glump, (clap) *glump,* (clap) *went the little green frog.*
   Glump, (clap) *glump,* (clap) *went the little green frog one day,*
   And they all went glump, (clap) *glump,* (clap) *glopp.* (hands clap knees)
   But we all know frogs go (clap)
   La-ti-da-di-da (wriggle fingers in air) (clap)
   La-ti-da-di-da (wriggle fingers in air) (clap)
   La-ti-da-di-da! (wriggle fingers in air)
   We all know frogs go (clap)
   La-ti-da-di-da (wriggle fingers in air)
   They don't go glump, (clap) *glump,* (clap) *glopp.* (hands clap knees)

 Sandy L. Scott, Vancouver, WA

"Little White Duck"

Materials

Colored felt in white, blue, light green, dark green, and black • scissors • black permanent marker • orange permanent marker • flannel board • recording of the song "Little White Duck"

What to do

1. Make this simple flannel board activity to use while listening to the song "Little White Duck."
2. Cut out a duck from white felt, a frog from dark green felt, a pond from blue felt, a lily pad from light green felt, and a bug from black felt.

(continued on the next page)

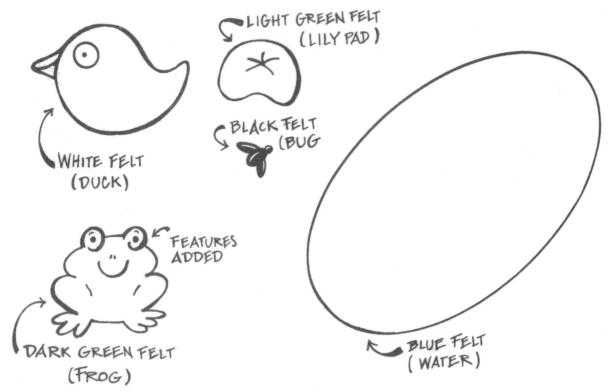

3. Add features using a black permanent marker.

4. Color the duck's bill orange with an orange marker, or cut it out from orange felt and attach it with glue.

5. Put a recording of the song along with the flannel board and characters in a center.

6. Encourage the children to listen to the song and place the characters on the flannel board: duck sitting in water, green frog swimming in the water, black bug floating on the water, red snake playing on the water, and so on.

☆ Jackie Wright, Enid, OK

My Ears

Materials

None

What to do

1. Sing the following song to the tune of "Frère Jacques."

They are listening!
They are listening!
My two ears, my two ears.
Sounds are all around me.
Their vibrations found me.
Through the air,
Through the air.

 Sandy L. Scott, Vancouver, WA

My Eyes

Materials

None

What to do

1. Sing the following song to the tune of "Mary Had a Little Lamb."

I have two eyes so I can see
Flowers, trees, birds and bees.
I have two eyes so I can see.
I can see you and me.
My two eyes see left and right,
Black and white and colors bright.
My two eyes see left and right.
I see day and night.

 Sandy L. Scott, Vancouver, WA

My Nose

Materials

None

What to do

1. Sing the following song to the tune of "My Little Red Wagon."

My nose it knows
How to smell a rose.
My nose it knows
Not to smell my toes.
My nose it knows
Which cookie I chose.
What a smart nose
Have I!

 Sandy L. Scott, Vancouver, WA

My Skin

Materials

None

What to do

1. Sing the following song to the tune of "On Top of Old Smokey."

On top of my elbow,
On top of my knee,
On top of my wiggly ears
Skin stretches on me.
Just like elastic,
And like rubber bands,
Skin shrinks and stretches
Right over my hands.

My skin's very special
And yours is too.
Our fingerprints are unique
To me and to you.

 Sandy L. Scott, Vancouver, WA

My Tongue

Materials

None

What to do

1. Sing the following song to the tune of "I'm a Little Teapot."

   I have a tongue with taste buds
   So when I eat
   I know if my food is bitter or sweet.
   My tongue can tell salty
   From sour too.
   It tells me what I like to chew!

    Sandy L. Scott, Vancouver, WA

Bubble Game

Materials

None

What to do

1. Ask the children to stand in a circle and join hands.
2. The children walk forward while holding hands and form as small a circle as possible.
3. Sing the following song to the tune of "Ring Around the Rosie" and do the motions.

(continued on the next page)

Blow air in our bubble, (move one step back while holding hands)
Blow air in our bubble, (move another step back while holding hands)
Bigger, bigger (move another step back while holding hands)
We stop and pop! (drop hands and fall to the ground)

⭐ Sandy L. Scott, Vancouver, WA

Rainbow Bubbles

Materials

None

What to do

1. Sing the following song to the tune of "Twinkle, Twinkle, Little Star."

Rainbow bubbles everywhere
Floating slowly through the air,
Sometimes big and sometimes small,
I wish I could catch them all!
Rainbow bubbles everywhere
Floating slowly through the air.

⭐ Sandy L. Scott, Vancouver, WA

"Five Brown Teddies"

Materials

Brown felt • scissors • flannel board • recording of "Five Brown Teddies" • tape player

What to do

1. Cut out five teddy bears from brown felt.
2. Put the teddy bears and flannel board in the Listening Center along with a recording of the song "Five Brown Teddies."

3. Encourage the children to manipulate the desired number of teddy bears on the flannel board as the song progresses.

Five Brown Teddies

Five brown teddies sitting on a wall.
Five brown teddies sitting on a wall.
And if one brown teddy should accidentally fall,
There'd be four brown teddies sitting on a wall.
Four brown teddies….
Three brown teddies...
Two brown teddies...
One brown teddy...
And if one brown teddy should accidentally fall,
There'd be no brown teddies sitting there at all!

 Jackie Wright, Enid, OK

Funtime Fair Time
(An Action Rhyme)

Materials

None

What to do

1. Read or recite each line of the following poem with the children and perform the motions.

Today's the day we go to the fair! (clap hands)
So many people everywhere! (look side to side)
Run over to the merry-go-round, (run in place)
Pick a horse, ride up and down. (rise up on tiptoes, squat down, repeat)
A fire engine ride? If you dare. (point and shake finger three times)
Hear its siren in the air. (put hands over ears)
A Ferris wheel! See it spin! (twirl around)
A wooden ring? Let's toss it in! (make a throwing motion)

(continued on the next page)

No more games, I tried my best. (shake head "no," shrug, hands up at sides with palms up)
Whew! I need to go home and rest! (stretch and yawn)

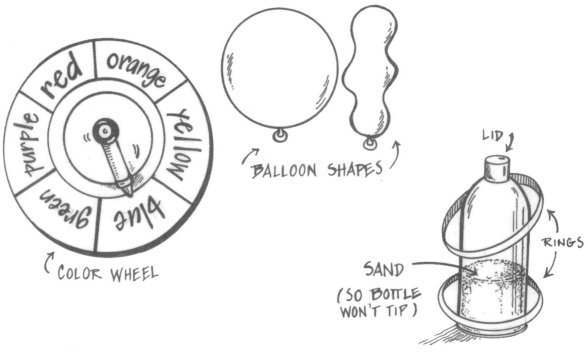

More to do

Games: Help the children create their own fair. Draw or cut out balloon shapes, have a ring toss over soda bottles, make a wheel spin for colors or numbers, put plastic ducks marked with numbers on the bottom in a small swimming pool, apply face paint, dig in a sandbox for small surprises, and so on. Prizes can include small containers of popcorn, pretzels, or raisins, or bright pencils.

 Theresa A. Usilton, Easton, MD

"Little Bunny"

Materials

Paper • markers • copy machine

What to do

1. Make a little book using the text from the fingerplay "Little Bunny." Make enough copies so that child gets one to illustrate and keep.

Page one text:

Here is a bunny
With ears so funny.

Page two text:

And here is his
Hole in the ground.

Page three text:

When a noise he hears,
He pricks up his ears.

Page four text:

And he jumps into his
Hole in the ground.

 Jackie Wright, Enid, OK

Effie Lee Newsome

Materials

None

What to do

1. Tell the children about Effie Lee Newsome. She was an African American poet in the 1920s who primarily wrote poems for children. She is considered a pioneer in children's literature.
2. Tell the children the following poem.

Effie Lee Newsome by Patricia Murchison

Effie Lee Newsome was a bright young girl,
The poems she wrote influenced the world.
Effie began writing at age five,
When she wrote, her words came alive.
When Effie wrote, her words did sing,
They came alive with zest and zing.
Effie Lee knew what it took,
Her poems where published in a book.
When Effie wrote, her words did sing,

(continued on the next page)

She wanted children to see the nature and beauty of things.
When Effie wrote, her words did sing,
They came alive with zest and zing.

 Patricia Murchison, Chesapeake, VA

"Mice Are Nice"

Materials

Construction paper (gray or black) • scissors • hole punch • adhesive paper reinforcementss • rubber bands • string • tape • construction paper

What to do

1. Make mouse masks with the children to use while reciting the poem.
2. Cut out the outline of a mouse face for each child.
3. Show the children how to punch a hole into each side of the mouse's face and then put a paper reinforcement on each hole.
4. Tie a rubber band through the holes.
5. Encourage the children to tape string on the masks for tails.
6. Cut out the numbers one through 10 from construction paper to use with the poem.

Mice Are Nice

1 mouse peeking out of a hole,
2 mice nibbling on a roll,
3 mice eating stinky cheese,
4 mice are about to sneeze.
5 mice running on the rail,
6 mice playing chase the tail,
7 mice climb in a shoe,
8 mice dancing two by two.
9 mice quickly build a nest,
10 mice tired—time to rest.

 Joan Stevenson, North Fort Myers, FL

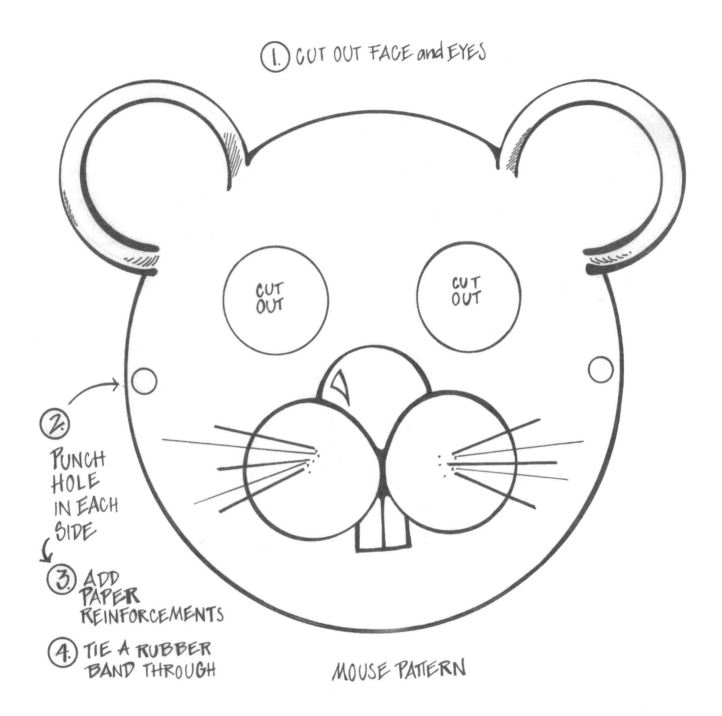

1. CUT OUT FACE and EYES

CUT OUT

CUT OUT

2. PUNCH HOLE IN EACH SIDE

3. ADD PAPER REINFORCEMENTS

4. TIE A RUBBER BAND THROUGH

MOUSE PATTERN

Phyllis Wheatley

Materials

Chart paper • crayons or markers • assorted nursery rhymes charts

What to do

1. Tell the children about Phyllis Wheatley, who was the first African American to write poetry. She even wrote a poem for our country's first president, George Washington.
2. Explain what a poem is to the children, and tell them that they will be writing their own poems about the seasons.
3. Title the poem "Spring Is…," "Fall Is…," "Summer Is…," or "Fall Is…" To help the children get started, the teacher should begin the poem. For example, "Summer is hot sun, summer is so much fun." The children can complete the poem.
4. Show the children assorted nursery rhymes on charts.
5. Say the following poems with the children.

Phyllis Wheatley by Patricia Murchison

Phyllis Wheatley loved to write,
She wrote poems into the night.
A poem is a rhyme you see,
A verse for you.
A verse for me.

Stephen Square by Patricia Murchison

Stephen Square is my name,
My four sides are the same.
You can turn me around—I'm not ashamed,
And I don't change.
Stephen Square is my name.

 Patricia Murchison, Chesapeake, VA

Scarecrow Fun

Materials

Chart paper • marker

What to do

1. Write the poem on a piece of chart paper so the children can follow along.

2. As you read the poem, encourage the children to act out the motions of the scarecrow.

The Scarecrow (author unknown)

> The old scarecrow is such a funny man,
> He flops in the wind as hard as he can.
> He flops to the right,
> He flops to the left,
> He flops back and forth
> 'Til he's almost out of breath.
> His arms swing out; his legs swing too.
> He nods his head, "How do you do?"
> See him flippity flop when the wind blows hard,
> The funny scarecrow in our back yard.

 Jackie Wright, Enid,

OK

Sister Sky

Materials

Felt in various colors • large and small star stickers • planet sticker • shiny silver paper or cardboard • felt board

What to do

1. Cut out clouds, the moon, and a rainbow from felt.
2. Stick small stars on the moon to make a face and use large stars for hands.
3. Cut out lightning bolts from shiny silver paper.
4. Create Sister Sky on the felt board as you sing the song to the children.
5. Once the children know the song, they can take turns adding body parts as the song is sung.

Sister Sky (Tune: "Aiken Drum")

There was a girl lived in the sky, lived in the sky, lived in the sky,
There was a girl lived in the sky, and her name was Sister Sky.
And her hair was made of rainbows, of rainbows, of rainbows.
And her hair was made of rainbows, and her name was Sister Sky.

And her head was a giant moon, a giant moon, a giant moon.
And her head was a giant moon, and her name was Sister Sky.

A constellation made her face, it made her face, it made her face,
A constellation made her face, and her name was Sister Sky.

And her tummy was a cumulus cloud, a cumulus cloud, a cumulus cloud...
And her arms were made of thunderclouds...
And her hands were made of shooting stars...
And her legs were made of lightning bolts...
A planet was her belly button... and her name was Sister Sky.

 Barbara Anthony, Boston, MA

Flower Poems

Materials

None

What to do

1. Say the following poems with the children.

Little Flowers (author unknown)
The sun comes out and shines so bright
And then we have a shower.
The little bud pushes with all its might
And soon we have a flower.
Flowers in the garden on their tall stems sway
I think I hear them whisper, "What a lovely day."

 the sun comes out and shines so bright

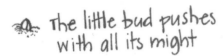 And then we have a shower.

 The little bud pushes with all its might

And soon we have a flower.

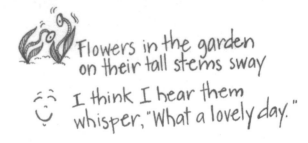 Flowers in the garden on their tall stems sway

I think I hear them whisper, "What a lovely day."

Little Crocus by Mary Brehm
Little crocus, little crocus,
I watch for you each spring
To pop your head out of the soil
As if you're going to sing.

(continued on the next page)

At first I see a tip of green
And then the rest of you.
What color will you be
When your blossom is in view?
You might be striped or yellow,
Lavender or white.
In the daytime you are lovely,
At night you close up tight.
Little crocus you are beautiful
For everyone to see.
But I think you are special
Because you're short like me.

 Mary Brehm, Aurora, OH

"Sounds at Night" Poem

Materials

Large chart paper or poster paper • marker • paper • crayons

What to do

1. Print the poem "Sounds at Night" on a large piece of chart paper.
2. Read the poem to the children. Discuss other sounds we hear at night. Then discuss sounds we hear during the day (for example, children's laughter during play). Could these sounds still be heard at night? Why or why not? (The children are asleep at night.)
3. Read the poem again and ask the children to illustrate something mentioned in the poem, such as a train or rain falling on a roof.

Sounds at Night

I like to go to bed at night
Lying still with no one around.
For if I'm very quiet,
I can hear many a sound.
Maybe the raindrops are falling
On our roof and maple tree.
I think it's typing a letter

Especially for me.
Sometimes I hear a dog bark
Or a train whistle blow.
I listen for cars and trucks
Still going to and fro.
I like the sound of crickets
Chirping on a summer's night.
Then I begin to get sleepy
Feeling the world's just right.

☆ Mary Brehm, Aurora, OH

Summer Sun

Materials

None

What to do

1. Talk about weather conditions with the children. How does weather affect people and plants?
2. Demonstrate the rhyme play below. Encourage the children to do the motions with you.

Summer sky means summer sun (reach up)
And it rises very high. (reach up on tiptoes)
When people want to look around (look from side to side)
They have to shade their eyes. (hand shades eyes)
But when a seed far in the ground (squat down)
Hears its warm invite (cup hand to ear to "listen")
It tries and tries to climb right out (hand over hand "climb" to stand)
So its leaves can greet the light. (wave hello)

☆ Theresa A. Usilton, Easton, MD

"Visiting the Farm" Poem

Materials

Poster board • black marker • file card

What to do

1. Write the poem on a poster board in large print. Also copy the poem on a file card for quick reference.

Visiting the Farm by Mary Brehm

I like to go to a farm
And see the animals there,
I think that is more fun
Than visiting a fair.
The cows say, "Moo,"
The kittens mew, and the horses neigh.
The frisky lambs and calves
Kick up their heels in play.
The farmer gives me corn
To scatter in the yard.
Feeding the noisy chickens
Isn't very hard.
I watch him milk the cows
And fill the water pail.
He feeds the cows and horses
And I see them swish their tails.
The pigs are very funny
As they roll in mud and dirt.
They squeal and push each other
But they really don't get hurt.
The farmer tries to keep
The animals from harm.
I wish I could come often
To help him on the farm.

 Mary Brehm, Aurora, OH

Weather Moves
(An Action Rhyme)

Materials

Optional props: leaves or trees • gray clouds • yellow and gray construction paper • raindrops • grass • sun • blue construction paper

What to do

1. Assign one or several children sections of the following poem to recite and act out (actions are in parentheses).
2. The items in the brackets could be worn by the children to illustrate their parts, if desired.
3. The last two lines should be said and acted by everyone.

First there comes a sleepy breeze (puff a breath of air)
It gently moves the dangling leaves. (sway back and forth) [leaves or trees]
Dark clouds bounce along their way (bounce in place) [gray clouds]
They turn the sky from bright to gray. (hand above eyebrows to "peer" into
  the dark) [a piece of paper, half yellow and half gray]
The warm, soft rain falls down so (reach hands up, bring down slowly in
front, wiggling fingers) [raindrops]
It helps the new green grass to grow. (bring hands back overhead) [grass]
At last the hot sun rises high (hands over head, reach up on tiptoes) [sun]
It brightens up the clear blue sky. (bring arms out to sides, then down) [blue
  sky/sun]
Since it's such a sunny day (big smile)
I think I'll run around and play! (run in place)

☆ Theresa A. Usilton, Easton, MD

Changing Old to New

Materials

Objects about to be discarded • pencil • black construction paper • scissors • glue stick • letter-size folder • laminate • self-adhesive Velcro with a sticky back • zipper-closure plastic bag

What to do

1. Salvage any items that are about to be discarded or buy inexpensive items at garage sales that can be used to make new teaching materials. Choose small items that have simple shapes and flat backs.
2. To prepare, trace the actual objects onto black construction paper.
3. Cut out the outlines.
4. Glue the black images to the inside of a letter-size file folder.
5. Laminate the file folder (opened).
6. Attach Velcro to the backs of the actual objects and to the black images on the file folder.
7. Store the actual objects in a zipper-closure plastic bag attached to the back of the folder.
8. Encourage the child to match the actual object to its "shadow." Something old has become a new activity for your classroom!

 Jackie Wright, Enid, OK

Learning Mats

Materials

30" x 24" learning mat • cylinder-shaped container • contact paper • label, optional • learning mat activity in a container

What to do

1. Purchase a 30" x 24" learning mat from a discount store (made by Learning Playground), or make your own.
2. In advance, collect an empty container to hold the rolled-up mat. A cylinder that is 9" tall and 5" in diameter works great.

3. Cover the container with contact paper. If desired, add a decorative label and write "Learning Mat" on it.
4. Place the container with the learning mat, rolled crosswise, in a designated area of the classroom.
5. Next to it, place any teacher-made, learning-mat activity you wish to feature. The activity should be in its own container. For example, it could be in its own file jacket labeled with the contents.
6. Invite a child to unroll the mat, place it on the floor where she wants to work, and use it as the work surface for the matching activity.
7. Each week or so, replace the learning mat activity with a new one.
8. The visual enticement will keep the children busy all year long!

☆ Jackie Wright, Enid, OK

Alphabet Hopscotch

Materials

Large construction paper squares • marker • clear contact paper or laminate, optional

What to do

1. Write the letters of the alphabet on large construction paper squares (one letter per square). If possible, laminate the squares or cover them with clear contact paper.
2. Make a hopscotch board on the floor with the squares. Use whichever letters the children are working on or need to review. Do not set them up in alphabetical order. You may wish to tape the squares down.
3. Call children in turn to begin the hopscotch game.
4. As you call out a letter of the alphabet, the child hops to that letter. Give each child three to five letters to jump to, and then call another child.
5. If the class has moved on to identifying beginning consonant sounds, expand the activity and call out a word beginning with one of the letters. Ask the child to jump to the letter that starts the word.

(continued on the next page)

6. If the class is working on lowercase letters, adapt the activity accordingly.

Related books

Alpha Bugs by David A. Carter

Alphabatics by Suse MacDonald

 Sandra Suffoletto Ryan, Buffalo, NY

Dart Balls

Materials

Cardboard • scissors • colored felt • glue gun (adult only) • 4 to 6 Ping-Pong balls • small strips of Velcro

What to do

1. Cut a piece of cardboard into a large circle and cover it with felt.
2. Cut two progressively smaller circles, cover them with different colors of felt, and glue them to the circle to be used as a target.
3. Glue a small strip of Velcro to each Ping-Pong ball.
4. Two or more children take turns throwing Ping-Pong balls, one at a time, at the target. The object is to hit the center circle. If desired, keep score and after two or three turns, the winners get a badge.

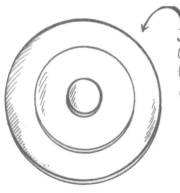

3 DIFFERENT COLORED CIRCLES COVERED in FELT and GLUED DOWN

PING-PONG BALL with VELCRO STRIP GLUED ALL the WAY AROUND

LOOK at my BADGE!

BADGE

ROUND CIRCLE

BLUE RIBBON

 Elaine Commins, Athens, GA

Doggie, Doggie, Where's Your Bone?

Materials

Brown paper lunch bags • white construction paper • black marker • brown and black tempera paint • paint trays • paw print stamps • treats for children • stapler • glue • crayons

What to do

1. In advance, trace dog bone and puppy head patterns (see illustration) on white construction paper and cut them out, one for each child.
2. Pour black and brown liquid tempera paint into separate trays. Place paw print stamps in each paint tray.
3. Give each child a paper bag. Encourage them to stamp paw prints all over their bags.
4. Allow the bags to dry.
5. After the bags have dried, let each child fill her bag half full with treats.
6. Demonstrate how to fold over the top half of the bag and staple closed.
7. Give each child a dog bone and puppy head. Help the children write their name on the bone with a black marker.

(continued on the next page)

FOLD DOWN

STAPLE

PAW PRINTS

GOES HERE LAST

ALI

CHILD'S NAME

PATTERN

8. Encourage the children to glue the doggie and bone on the half of the bag that is folded.

9. Later, while the children are outside playing, hide all the bags around the room. When the children re-enter the room, ask them to find their treat.

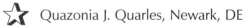 Quazonia J. Quarles, Newark, DE

Wrapping Paper Dominoes

Materials

Pattern of a giant domino (3 ½" x 7 ½" rectangle divided in the middle) • tagboard or oak tag • copy machine • wrapping paper with several different objects on it • scissors • glue stick • laminate

What to do

1. Make a giant set of dominoes by copying a domino pattern onto oak tag using a copy machine.

2. Using wrapping paper with several different kinds of objects on it, such as birds or dinosaurs, cut out each picture and glue it onto a separate end of a domino.

3. Laminate the dominoes for durability.

4. To play, mix up the dominoes and stack them face down in the center of the playing area on the floor.

5. Give five dominoes to each player.

6. Begin by placing one domino face up.

7. Invite each player, in turn, to put the end of one of her dominoes next to the matching end of a domino on the floor.

8. If the child does not have a matching domino, invite her to draw a domino from the stack. Players may draw a maximum of three dominoes per turn.

9. The first player to get rid of all of her dominoes is the winner.

 Jackie Wright, Enid, OK

Button Math Game

Materials

Buttons, acorns, or any other small object • craft sticks • glue • bowl • dice (purchased or homemade)

What to do

1. Glue five buttons onto each stick. Make about 20 sticks.
2. Glue five buttons onto five more sticks, and glue the five sticks to two empty sticks to make a rack. Let dry overnight.
3. Put a bunch of buttons in a bowl.
4. Two to four children can play together. The child rolls the dice and counts out the same amount of buttons. Each child takes a turn.
5. When the child has five buttons, she can trade it in for a five-button stick. When the child has five sticks, she can trade it in for a rack.
6. Play until a pre-determined number of buttons are collected. A good number is 50 buttons (two racks) or 25 buttons (one rack).
7. To make dice, cut a sponge into square cubes and draw or glue dots on each side.

 Audrey F. Kanoff, Allentown, PA

Insect Match Card Game

Materials

Pictures of insects (two copies of each insect) • cardboard or oak tag • glue • laminate

What to do

1. Mount each insect picture on cardboard to make insect cards, making sure there are two copies of each insect to make pairs. Laminate for durability.
2. To play the game, mix up the cards and place them face down in a pile.
3. One player takes the first card and says the name of the insect on the card. Then she puts the card face up in front of her.

(continued on the next page)

4. The second player takes a card and says the name of the insect on it. If it matches the card the first player picked, she can take the first player's card to make a pair. If she cannot make a pair, she also puts her card face up in front of her.

5. The players take turns drawing cards, saying the insects' names, and trying to make pairs. A player can make a pair with her own cards or by taking a matching card from another player.

6. When all the cards are gone from the pile, the player who has the most pairs is the winner.

 Jackie Wright, Enid, OK

Listening Game

Materials

Set of ten seasonal stick puppets numbered one to ten • basket or container

What to do

1. Ask the children to sit in a circle on the floor.
2. Walk around the outside of the circle carrying a basket of seasonal stick puppets.
3. Stop behind one child. That child must now close her eyes, and the rest of the children must remain quiet.
4. Hold up one stick puppet for the other children to see.
5. Make a clicking sound with your tongue (or tap your foot) the number of times indicated on the stick puppet.
6. The designated child counts to herself and guesses the number without opening her eyes.
7. If she guesses incorrectly, she may open her eyes and turn around to see the correct answer. You may repeat the activity with another stick puppet for two more tries.
8. If the child guesses correctly, the game continues until each child has had a turn.

 Jackie Wright, Enid, OK

Action Words for Sight Words

Materials

Colored pictures of action words (approximately 30 pictures) • file folder • scissors • glue stick • colored card stock • laminate

What to do

1. Collect cute, brightly-colored action pictures depicting action words, such as run, clap, sit, dance, skate, stand, and so on.
2. Print the action word, in small print, under each action picture.
3. Glue the pictures to the inside of a file folder.
4. Now make word cards for each action word depicted by a picture. Print the words in large print.
5. Glue the words to colored card stock sized to cover the pictures on the file folder (approximately 2" x 2 ½").
6. Laminate the file folder and the word cards for durability.
7. To play, each player selects one side of the folder as her game board.
8. Place the action word cards face down on the playing surface.
9. Then each player, in turn, selects a card with one of the action words. She reads the word aloud and places it on her game board covering the action picture.
10. If she does not have the picture on her side, she discards the word card.
11. Continue until one player has covered her side completely.

 Jackie Wright, Enid, OK

Matching Body Parts to Actions

Materials

None

What to do

1. Gather a group of about 5-6 children around you. Ask the children to stand for this activity.
2. Tell them they will match the body part that goes with the activity or action you name. For example, if you say, "Feed yourself," what body parts are involved in this action (hands and mouth)?
3. Tell them that you will name an action and then point to a child, who will either name the body part or show it.
4. Make sure everyone is attentive, then begin stating actions one at a time. Below is a list to get you started:

talking	brushing teeth
tying shoes	running
jumping	swimming
drawing	walking
playing drums	reading books
listening to music	kicking a ball
ice skating	setting the table

5. Each time you state an action, point to a new child to label or show the appropriate body part.
6. Be sure all the children are given an opportunity to participate. Either go around the group again or have the children take turns naming actions that the others need to match for body parts.

 Kate Ross, Middlesex, VT

Monkey, Monkey Game

Materials

Caps for Sale by Esphyr Slobodkina • hat

What to do

1. This game is a variation of the game, "Doggie, Doggie, Where's Your Bone?" Ask the children to sit in a circle.
2. Pick one child to be the monkey. Ask her to sit in the center of the circle and close her eyes.
3. Take a hat and put it behind one of the children in the circle. Then everyone chants, "Monkey, Monkey, where's your cap? Somebody took it. Give him a tap."
4. Then the child who is the monkey tries to guess who has the cap. The child gets three guesses.
5. The child who has the cap then becomes the monkey in the center, and the play continues.

 Catherine J. Shogren, Eagan, MN

Mystery Box

Materials

Small sturdy cardboard box • marker • interesting objects • thick piece of cardboard

What to do

1. On each side of the box, draw a large question mark.
2. Put an object inside that is of interest to the children, perhaps a lead-in to a topic you'd like to introduce. For example, to begin a project on butterflies, you might put a chrysalis inside the box.
3. Each child gets to ask one question and provide one guess about what's inside the box. The child whose turn it is holds a large cardboard cutout of a "?" (question mark). Record their comments and periodically read them aloud to the group as the activity progresses.
4. Let the children have a chance to place something in the box for others to guess.

 Sharon Dempsey, Mays Landing, NJ

Mystery Clothes Box

Materials

Grocery bag, box, or other item with an opening big enough for an adult hand to reach inside • clothing items, such as a mitten, watch, bracelet, glove, hat, belt, swimsuit, shoe, bib, tie, and so on

What to do

1. In preparation, you may wish to decorate the bag or box to make it more enticing.
2. Ask a group of no more than eight children to sit in a circle around you.
3. Show the children the Mystery Box or Bag and tell them that there are pieces of clothing inside. You may wish to display the articles before starting, especially the first time.
4. The children will take turns reaching in, and without looking, trying to guess the one item that they grab. (You may wish to have an adult demonstrate this activity first.)
5. After the child has chosen an item and revealed it, an adult might ask, "On what part of the body do you wear this item?" "What time of the year do you wear this item?"
6. Give each child a turn finding an item.
7. A variation of this activity might be for the child to describe with three clues what she feels inside the bag or box so the rest of the children can guess what the item is.

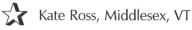 Kate Ross, Middlesex, VT

Secret Items Bag

Materials

10 items from a particular category, such as vehicles, foods, clothing, animals, and so on • paper bag, shoebox, or other small enclosed object that can conceal the objects

What to do

1. With a group of about 4–5 children in a circle, display all the items you have chosen.
2. Transfer the items to another place in the room and let the children know where they are.
3. Let the children take turns leaving the circle and choosing one of the items. The child places the item into the box or bag, and then returns to the group, keeping the item in the bag a secret.
4. The rest of the children guess what is hidden. After each wrong guess, the "secret holder" provides a clue. For example, the child might say, "No, it's not a car. It has a propeller."
5. The children continue guessing until they figure it out. The child then returns the item and another child has a turn.

 Kate Ross, Middlesex, VT

Name and Toss

Materials

Ball or beanbag

What to do

1. Ask the children to sit in a circle. Explain the directions.
2. The children carefully toss or roll the ball or beanbag around the circle to whoever they wish.
3. Before the child holding the ball or beanbag passes it, she must name the person to whom she will pass the ball.
4. The game continues until all the children are given an opportunity to participate. An adult should remain in the circle in order to facilitate participation.
5. If desired, add an additional step. The children can add a distinguishing characteristic or name an item of clothing on the child to whom they will pass the ball after they have said their name. This could be performed as a second time around the circle. For example, "I'm throwing to Sam who's wearing striped socks."

 Kate Ross, Middlesex, VT

Tablecloth Fun

Materials

Small vinyl tablecloth • permanent markers • assorted props

What to do

1. To prepare, draw a 16- to 20-square grid on the tablecloth using permanent markers. The number of grids will depend on the size of the cloth. You will need different props to put into each square, such as an empty two-liter bottle, plastic or stuffed animals, beanbags, poker chips, and so on.
2. Spread the tablecloth on the floor and put objects ("pins") into some of the squares and leave some empty.
3. Give each child a beanbag and take turns knocking down the "pins." Tell the children that they may play with their beanbags in their own space while waiting to play.
4. If a child knocks over a pin, she can put it back up in any square she desires. If she lands on an empty square, she may move a pin to that square. This way the pins are always moving around.

 Susan E. May, Madison Heights, VA

Nursery Rhyme Game

Materials

Tagboard • scissors • stickers or pictures of Mother Goose rhyme characters • container, such as a margarine container

What to do

1. Cut tagboard into 2" squares.
2. Affix one sticke to each square to depict different nursery rhymes.
3. Put the cards inside a container and label the lid with the game title.
4. To play, a child draws one card from the container, then announces what rhyme is represented on that card.
5. The class recites or sings the rhyme together.

6. The child places the card face down near the container.
7. Continue asking another child to play in the same manner until every child who wishes to play has had an opportunity.

 Jackie Wright, Enid, OK

Old Maid Sequence

Materials

Two decks of Old Maid playing cards • poster board • glue stick • clear contact paper or laminating film • poker chips, at least ten each of four colors

What to do

1. To make the game board, take one set of Old Maid cards and remove the old maid card. Place the rest of the cards in random order on the piece of poster board. Make sure the cards are not touching and are in the shape of a square or large rectangle when all are on the board.
2. Glue the cards in place.
3. Cover the finished board with clear contact paper or laminating film.
4. To play the game, gather two to four players. Shuffle the second deck of cards and add the extra old maid card to the deck.
5. Each player gets four cards to start and ten poker chips. Each player should have a different color of chips. The object of the game is to be the first player to get four of her colored chips in a row. Rows may be horizontal, diagonal, or vertical.
6. Players take turns removing a card from their hand and covering the corresponding card on the board with a poker chip. The player then discards the card into the discard pile.
7. After each turn, the player draws a new card, keeping four cards in her hand at all times. Players also may choose to block an opponent. If a player is dealt or draws the Old Maid, she may use it as a Wild Card. The Old Maid card may be used to remove another player's chip or to cover any card on the board with a chip.

 Tammy Byington, Columbia, MO

On the Road Again

Materials

Yellow and black tagboard or poster board • scissors • glue stick • matching or classifying, transportation-themed game board and game pieces • laminate • self-adhesive Velcro (sticky backed) • sticky-backed storage pocket

What to do

1. Draw the outline of a bus (approximately 12" x 17") on a sheet of yellow tagboard or poster board. Cut it out.
2. Cut out three wheels approximately 3 ½" in diameter from black tagboard or poster board.
3. Glue the wheels to the bus.
4. Select any age-appropriate transportation game board intended for use as a file-folder game. (For example, you might use one with a grid of 1 ½" squares that requires the child to classify vehicles by color and shape.)
5. Color the game pieces (vehicles) and the game board, if needed.
6. Mount the game pieces on tagboard squares (1 ½" x 1 ½") and laminate them for durability.
7. Attach Velcro to the back of the game pieces and the squares on the grid of the game board.
8. Attach a sticky-backed pocket on the bus to hold the game pieces.
9. Mount the bus on the wall and encourage children to try this fun, hands-on activity.

 Jackie Wright, Enid, OK

Part of the Whole

Materials

Pictures of objects • large hat or item to hold the pictures

What to do

1. Gather the children in a circle around you.
2. Explain that they will be playing a guessing game. They will receive clues about some parts of a mystery item and then try and guess what the item is.
3. Choose one child to start the game. Ask the child to choose a picture and hide it from the other children.
4. The child then names three parts to the item. For example, pepperoni, sauce, and cheese (pizza).
5. The other children take turns guessing what the item is.
6. Continue until all the children have been given an opportunity to participate.

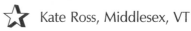 Kate Ross, Middlesex, VT

Photo Memory Game

Materials

Photographs of each child in the class • copy machine • laminate

What to do

1. Make two copies of each child's photo and laminate them.
2. To play the game, lay the pictures face down on the table in no particular order.
3. Each child (four can play at a time) takes a turn turning over two pictures.
4. If the pictures match, the child puts the photos in a pile in front of him.
5. Play continues to the left until all the pictures have been matched and taken.
6. Count the number of pictures each child has. The highest number wins.

Hint: Laminate the names of the children and have children match the printed name to the face in the photo.

 Nancy DeSteno, Andover, MN

Photo Name Match

Materials

Digital or 35mm camera • two 3″ x 5″ cards for each child • laminate or clear adhesive paper

What to do

1. Take a photo of each child in the room. Print them or have them developed in a 3″ x 5″ format.
2. Glue each photo to a 3″ x 5″ card. Laminate or cover with clear adhesive paper for durability.
3. Print each child's name on a 3″ x 5″ card. Laminate or cover with clear adhesive paper for durability.
4. Turn the cards (both photo and name) over on a table in a typical Memory game format.
5. Let the children take turns turning over the photos and names. Help them to read the names on the card and decide if the name matches the child in the photo. If they match, the child keeps the cards; if not, they go back on the table in their original positions.
6. Continue to play until all cards have been matched.

 Virginia Jean Herrod, Columbia, SC

Play the Game

Materials

Construction paper • circle stickers • markers • dice or cards with numbers or colors • caps of old markers

What to do

1. Give each child a piece of construction paper to make a game board. Ask each child to place a circle sticker near the upper left corner of the paper and one at the lower right-hand corner.
2. Then ask each child to use a marker to draw a wiggly line from one sticker dot to the other and mark one dot as the start and one as the finish.

3. Encourage the children to place circle sticker dots along the wiggly line. Any extra stickers can be used to decorate the game boards.

4. The children use cards or dice to play the game.

5. Children play the game by rolling the dice and moving the playing pieces (marker caps) or using the cards to go to a particular color.

6. This game helps children work on taking turns, counting, and numeral or color identification.

 Sandra Nagel, White Lake, MI

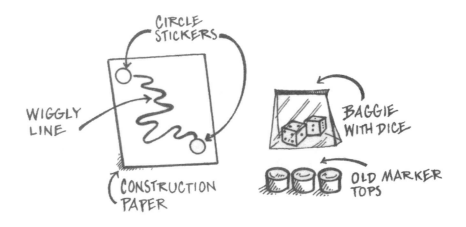

Roll a Collage

Materials

2 Styrofoam cubes • patterned adhesive paper • 6 pieces of collage material such as glitter, yarn, paper scraps, buttons, felt scraps, and sequins • permanent marker • glue • sturdy construction paper

What to do

1. Use the two Styrofoam cubes to create a pair of dice. Cover both cubes with the patterned adhesive paper. Decide what collage materials the children will be using for their collages. Mount a sample of each collage material on the six sides of one cube. On the other cube, label the six sides with the numbers one through six.

2. Give each child a piece of sturdy construction paper. Let the children take turns throwing the dice. The child who rolls names the collage material and number that land on top.

(continued on the next page)

3. The children add materials to their collages according to the dice. For example, if the dice land with the number two and the yarn sample up, then the children should each take two pieces of yarn and add them to their collages.

4. Continue play until the children have created a collage with which they are satisfied.

5. Change the materials on the collage cubes by carefully peeling the clear layer of adhesive paper off the cube. Remove the old samples and add some new ones. Cover with adhesive paper again.

 Virginia Jean Herrod, Columbia, SC

Spin Art

Materials

Sorting tray • collage materials (one for each section of the sorting tray) • lazy Susan (spinning serving tray) • heavyweight paper • glue • digital kitchen timer

What to do

1. Fill the sorting tray sections with collage materials.

2. Place the sorting tray on the lazy Susan and put it in the middle of the table.

3. Invite as many children as the table will hold to join in a rousing game of Spin Art.

4. Give each child a piece of paper and a bottle of glue.

5. Explain the game to the children. One child will spin the sorting tray. The children will all have one minute to place as many collage items as they want on their paper. They must use the materials from the sorting tray compartment nearest them. Then another child will spin the tray and the game continues until all the collages are completed.

6. Ask the first child to spin the sorting tray, set the timer for one minute, and cheer the children on as they spend one minute collecting collage items from the compartment nearest them to add to their collages.

7. When the timer rings, have another child spin the sorting tray.

8. Continue play until each child has had a turn. From there the children can decide if they want to keep working on the same collage for the second round or if they want to start a new collage.

9. Continue play for at least two rounds or until interest wanes.

 Virginia Jean Herrod, Columbia, SC

Spinner Board Games

Materials

Pattern intended for a mobile • copy machine • oak tag • scissors • black felt-tip pen • glue stick • laminate • markers • spinner that snaps into place

What to do

1. Use reproducible patterns intended for making mobiles as your inspiration for making spinner board games for your classroom.
2. Search your teacher resource books for patterns with six main parts such as one with a rabbit's head, body, arms, legs, basket of eggs, and paintbrush with paint.
3. Duplicate the pattern the number of times you want players (two times for two players) and once for the spinner board.
4. To make the spinner board, cut an 8 ½" x 8 ½" piece of oak tag into a circle and use a black, felt-tip pen to divide it into six sections.
5. Glue a picture of a different body part or item in each section. Reduce the size of the pictures, if necessary.
6. Color the pictures on the spinner board.
7. Mount the players' pictures on oak tag using a glue stick. Then, cut out and color the players' oak tag-backed pictures. These will be the game pieces.
8. Laminate the game board and spinner pieces.
9. Attach a spinner to the center of the board.
10. To play, have the children spin one at a time. As the spinner lands on a specific part or item, the child picks the corresponding piece from the game pieces.
11. If she does not need the item, she skips a turn.
12. Play continues until one child collects all six of the body parts and items.

 Jackie Wright, Enid, OK

The Busy Month of February

Materials

Large, wall-size February calendar or white poster board and markers • beanbag • candy hearts • maraschino cherries • pennies • groundhog or other animal stickers • M&Ms or other small reward of your choosing

What to do

1. If you don't have a large calendar with the month of February, make your own from poster board.
2. Label the following days on the calendar in large print or with colorful stickers: Groundhog Day, Valentine's Day, Washington's birthday, and Lincoln's birthday.
3. Lay the calendar on the floor at a predetermined distance from the children.
4. The children take turns tossing the beanbag at the calendar and are rewarded as follows:
   - ☆ hitting the calendar anyplace wins one M&M
   - ☆ landing on Groundhog Day wins a sticker
   - ☆ landing on Valentine's Day wins a candy heart
   - ☆ landing on Lincoln's birthday wins a penny
   - ☆ landing on Washington's birthday wins a cherry

5. This activity can be played with any calendar month; February lends itself well because of all its special days.

Note: This game can only be played if the children in your group no longer put things such as pennies in their mouths. Other rewards can be substituted as you see fit.

 Vicki L. Schneider, Oshkosh, WI

Valentine's Heart Game

Materials

Pastel paper • marker or pencil • laminate • stickers or candy treats • basket

What to do

1. Prepare hearts in advance by tracing a heart shape onto pastel paper. Prepare enough hearts for the amount of children in your class. Make sure that at least three of the hearts are yellow.
2. Laminate the hearts for longevity.
3. Ask the children to sit in a circle. Put a basket of stickers or candy hearts in the middle of the circle.
4. Give each child a heart to hold.
5. As the children pass the hearts around the circle clockwise, sing the following song to the tune of "Pop Goes the Weasel."

   All around the circle now
   The hearts are passing by,
   Whoever gets the yellow heart
   STOP!
   Will you be mine?

6. When you sing "Stop!" everyone stops passing the hearts and the children who have a yellow heart pick a treat.
7. Keep playing until everyone has picked a treat.

 Quazonia J. Quarles, Newark, DE

"Who Goes First?" Box

Materials

Sturdy small box labeled "Who goes first?" • markers • small cards • laminate

What to do

1. To prepare, label a small box "Who goes first?" Write the numbers 1 through 10 on small cards (one number per card) and laminate them. Put the cards inside the box.

2. Invite two children to help introduce the game to the class. Let them choose a two-person game and ask who wants to go first. (If, in the unlikely event that they don't both want to go first, ask them to pretend that they do.) Discuss the need for a fair and impartial way to decide who goes first.

3. Show the "Who goes first?" box and all the numbers in it, turning the cards so the numbers show.

4. Turn the cards over and mix them up in the box.

5. Explain that both children will draw one number each, and whoever gets the largest number will get to go first.

6. Ask the children to draw and compare their numbers to see which is larger.

7. Make the box available in the classroom to be used as needed and encourage the children to use it on their own.

8. If children are having difficulty deciding which is the larger number, post a number line from 1 to 10 near the box.

Tip: Extend the use of the box to decide other minor disputes, such as who gets to use a school material that both choose simultaneously, who gets to sit in a favorite spot, and so on.

 Susan Jones Jensen, Norman, OK

Social Development of Five-Year-Olds

Materials

None

What to do

1. Five is a fun and enjoyable age. Five-year-olds are cheerful, cooperative, and uninhibited in displaying emotions. They have hearts full of hugs!

2. Learning language is an important stage of development for five-year-olds. Before they can read and write, children must have a large vocabulary, which they add to every day. They practice by chatting during activities and are experts at listening to adults and acting out what they see and hear. Phonemic awareness (listening to sounds that are the same and different) is normally developed at this time.

3. Children become moe independent at age five. An exciting environment that they can explore usually supersedes separation from their family. They do worry about when they will be picked up and mention it from time to time, but as long as they are given an answer, they move forward in play.

4. Schedules are essential to a five-year-old. They will be the first ones to tell you what happened yesterday at this time and remind you to keep to the same plan. A combination of teacher-chosen and independent selections makes for a good balance in activities. Mentally engrossing activities should be followed by free play in about twenty minute periods.

5. Five-year-olds can be clumsy and often run into things. Large motor activities such as running, climbing, hopping, riding, and reaching help them develop more coordination.

6. Singing, painting, listening, and movement are the multi-sensory ways in which five-year-olds learn. They love to imitate the doctor's office, riding on a school bus, and activities with which they are familiar. By mimicking these experiences, they are able to make them their own.

7. Writing comes at many different developmental levels at the age of five. Wavy lines, writing imitation, letter practice, and legible words are some examples. Keep pencils and paper at learning centers as well as books, so the

(continued on the next page)

children can write recipes, notes, building plans, and letters. Usually the children's names are the first words they can write. They delight in learning to write the names of their family members and the children that are around them.

8. This is an age where children develop social interaction. Anger may be followed shortly by laughter and friendliness. Children's emotions are fleeting and they get over things in a short time.

9. Above all, five is fun! Talking, climbing, writing, singing, and listening are ways that they make friends and discover their environment in their venture to independence.

☆ Barbara Saul, Eureka, CA

"Kinder" Garden

Materials

Container for each child • Popsicle stick • picture cut out of each child • small plant

What to do

1. Explain that *kindergarten* is a German word meaning "children's garden."
2. Take a photo of each child.
3. After the photos have been developed, give the children their photos.
4. Ask each child to cut out his face and glue it to a Popsicle stick.
5. Give each child a small plant in a container. Ask them to stick their Popsicle in the container with the plant.
6. Group the plants in an old wagon or on a windowsill. Place a sign on or near the garden that says "Our Kinder Garden."

☆ Lisa Chichester, Parkersburg, WV

Teachable Moments

Materials

None

What to do

1. There are many moments in the day when the children express interest in something that is not on the daily lesson plan. Take advantage of these "teachable moments" every time you can. Use the phrase, "What do you think?" when asking children open-ended questions. This way children are not pressured to get the "right answer" because there is no wrong answer to this question. Do not correct the children's answers by providing facts. Remember, you asked what they thought and they told you! Accept what they tell you. Keep a notepad and pencil handy for recording the children's answers, or use a hand-held recorder and transcribe their answers later. Following are some examples of teachable moments:

2. When the children are outside and see some construction trucks and they express interest in the equipment, stop to talk about it. Ask the children to describe the equipment to you. "What color is it? How long do you think it is?" Then ask the children to brainstorm. "What do you think that piece of equipment is called? What do you think it is used for?"

3. If the children hear a train whistle and express interest in it, it can lead to great discussion. "Where do you think the train is? Which direction do you think the sound came from? What do you think the train is carrying?"

4. If a plane goes overhead and someone notices, you can talk about a lot of things. "Where do you think the plane is going? How high do you think the plane is? How fast do you think it is going? Where would you go if you could fly a plane anywhere in the world?"

5. If maintenance personnel visit the classroom one day to fix something, do not ignore them. Introduce them to the class. Ask the children questions. "Why do you think they are here? What are they fixing? How do you think that broke?"

6. If a bird or other small animal appears outside the window, take advantage of the situation. "What type of bird do you think that is? Where do you think that bird came from? What do you think the bird is doing? Where do you think the bird lives?"

(continued on the next page)

7. Feel free to draw the children's attention to something interesting that they might not have noticed. Children are greatly interested in the world around them and love it when you challenge them to notice what is going on around them.

 Virginia Jean Herrod, Columbia, SC

Tips and Techniques for Working With Five-Year-Olds

Materials

None

What to do

1. Remember that five-year-olds are just that. They are five years old—not young adults or big babies. They are five, unique and special.

2. Five things you should never say to a five-year-old:
   ☆ "Act your age!" They are already acting their age!
   ☆ "Grow up!" or "It's time to grow up now." Why? Being young is fun!
   ☆ "Why did you do that?" Children don't always know why they do things, and to force them to explain is to teach them to lie to adults to get out of trouble.

☆ "What did I just tell you?" They might not know.

☆ "Good job!" This is a pat, overused phrase. Instead, say something specific about the situation. For example, when Ralphie finally makes up his naptime mat by himself, you could say, "Wow, Ralphie, I know you must feel great about yourself. You finally conquered that mat!"

3. Five things you should say to five-year-olds at least once a day:

☆ "I love you!" Say it and mean it!

☆ "I care about you." You convey this message by noticing what the child is doing throughout the day. Comment on the children's play daily and take time to stop and really listen when they talk. Look at children when you are talking together.

☆ "You are special to me." You can say this in many ways: a smile, a gentle look, a kind word, a morning greeting, or noticing when the child does something special or conquers a task.

☆ "You are strong!" Say this by entrusting your fives with daily chores and classroom tasks. This goes beyond "Calendar Helper" or "Door Monitor." There are many little things that need to be done in a typical early childhood classroom each day and you have a classroom full of willing volunteers at your disposal!

☆ "You are independent." Zippers need zippering, buttons need buttoning, and laces need tying every day. Most fives are able to achieve these tasks if given adequate time. Give them that time and remember to not hover over them.

4. If you are going to be gone for a few days, leave some "Happy Notes" hidden around the room for the children to find in your absence. Print some happy and encouraging messages on memo pad paper or 3" x 5" note cards. Hide these around the room. Think of places where the children will be sure to find them, but not too fast. Following are some examples of Happy Notes:

☆ "Try mixing red and blue paint for a happy surprise. Let me know what you discover when I get back." Tape this one to the art easel.

☆ "The animals here in the Block Center need a home. Can you build one for them? If you do, ask (substitute teacher's name) to take a photograph so I can see it when I get back." Hide this behind the blocks.

☆ "I miss you all so much. Will you draw some pictures for me? I would love to have them waiting for me when I get back." Hide this on the art shelf.

☆ "Take one cup of love. Add one big hug. Mix well together and save it for me until I get back." Hide this in the play refrigerator.

(continued on the next page)

☆ "Go find (child's name) and whisper, '(teacher's name) loves you very much' in his or her ear." Make one of these for each child and hide them throughout the room.

5. Is it hot enough to fry an egg on the sidewalk outside? Try it! Or try this fun activity. Fill buckets with water and give the children large paintbrushes. Let them paint the building, the playground equipment, the fence, or anything at all. They may try to paint each other!

6. Remember that there is no wrong answer to the question, "What do you think?" Ask this question to each child at least once a day. Ask them what they think about their lunch, the truck that just went by, the color of the sky, and so on. You will be amazed by the amount of knowledge children have!

7. Remember that the children in your care are experiencing something they will never get a chance to experience again: their childhoods. You undoubtedly have schedules to follow and requirements to meet, but remember to meet the most important requirement of all—the needs of the children in your care. Give them time to be children. Let them run and play. Give them time to be noisy and time to be quiet. Provide quiet areas for resting and relaxing. Do not require them to participate in something every minute of the day. Give them a few moments for just doing nothing at all. Talk with them, listen to them, and most of all, love them.

 Virginia Jean Herrod, Columbia, SC

Bear Hugs

Materials

Black permanent marker • small thin pieces of craft hobby wood • paint • small paintbrushes • clothespins • wood glue • basket or bucket

What to do

1. This is a wonderful way to be sure you talk individually with each child at the start of each day—and to give each one a "bear hug." The children will have their own bear hug clothespins to clip on when they arrive in the morning. During morning free play, go to each child and say hello, give them a "bear hug," and ask about his day and his family. Then take the child's clothespin and clip it on your clothes. Children love to see their bear hugs on their teacher.

2. To make the bear hug pins, pre-draw a small bear on each piece of hobby wood with a black permanent marker. Make one for each child in the class. **Note:** Some craft stores have hobby wood pre-cut in the shape of a bear or other animals.

3. Give one bear to each child. Encourage them to paint their bears using small brushes.

4. Next, give each child a clothespin to paint.

5. Allow 24 hours for the pieces to dry.

6. Use wood glue to glue the bears on the clothespins. You can write their names on their clothespins with the permanent black marker.

7. Store the "bear hugs" in a basket or bucket. Or, clip the bear hugs to a large stuffed bear.

Note: If the children keep their bear hugs in their cubbies, they often take them home and forget to return them.

☆ Joy M. Tuttle, London, OH

Community Adventure

Materials

Field trip pre-planning • simple birdhouse kits • wood glue • hammers and nails • toy binoculars

What to do

1. This theme was designed to help children develop, in a "five-year-old way," an appreciation for the exciting opportunities a community offers. Select experiences that are very recognizable to the children and add a twist.

(continued on the next page)

2. Here are some popular five-year-old field trips:

☆ McDonald's: This fast food restaurant is very popular with five-year-olds, but before lunch and playground time, take a behind-the-scenes tour. Let the children experience, for example, the cold of the freezer, how ketchup squirts, and making biscuits.

☆ A Nature Center: Before the trip, let each child construct a very basic birdhouse. The children can hammer in the nails, and an adult can add wood glue to help hold loose nails. (With the help of the glue, an adult does not need to re-hammer nails, helping children feel more independent.) When at the center, experience only the outdoors. Stay on the grounds armed with sack lunches and binoculars. Ordinary birds become very exciting when viewed through binoculars or seen eating a crumb dropped from a sandwich.

☆ Transportation: Children see city buses daily, but riding them is a field trip in itself. So, board the bus and ride downtown. Scenes look very different seen from a bus by five-year-olds. Downtowns offer a wide variety of opportunities. Board the bus and ride back to school. Experiencing different modes of transportation is a first for most of the children.

Related books

Big Blue Engine by Ken Wilson-Max
Long Train by Sam Williams
Maisy Drives the Bus by Lucy Cousins

 Diane L. Shatto, Kansas City, MO

Lining Up

Materials

Paint (appropriate for use on cement) • paintbrush

What to do

1. At the beginning of the year, paint a 12"-long line on the cement outside your classroom door. Allow enough room for the door to open and you to stand.

2. When it's time to line up, ask the children to form a line behind the painted line.

3. Tell them that as they pass through the door, they "throw away" their outside voices and come inside quietly.

 Jackie Wright, Enid, OK

"Off to Kindergarten" Button

Materials

Stickers or markers • button-making kit or 3″ round cardboard circles • self-adhesive pins

What to do

1. Attach a sticker with a positive comment on it ("Super Star," "Way to Go") on a cardboard circle or button.

2. Write the child's name on the front and let the child decorate around his name with star stickers or markers.

3. Attach a pin on back and a message from you, such as "You are special to me." The child can wear this the first day of kindergarten, bringing love from preschool to a new school experience.

 Andrea Clapper, Cobleskill, NY

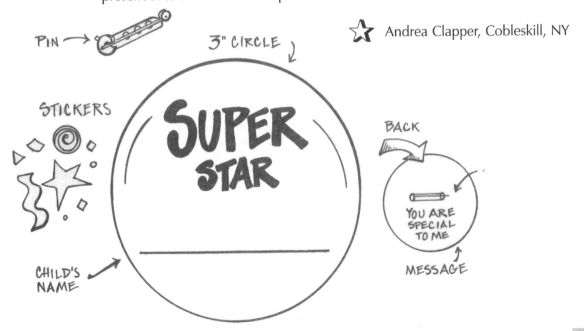

Welcome Board

Materials

White board • dry-erase markers

What to do

1. Hang a white board outside of your classroom.
2. Each morning write a greeting to the parents and mention some of the things the children will be doing that day. This way, they can talk with their child about what to expect for the day.
3. Following is an example:

   "Fabulous Friday"
   Make feathery friends
   Share bird nests
   Paint with feathers
   Make a birdseed picture

4. Also include reminders, such as "Don't forget to sign up for the field trip to the zoo."

 Sandy L. Scott, Vancouver, WA

Swap Day

Materials

Unwanted items from home • large table • hat

What to do

1. Send home a note to parents announcing "Swap Day" at school.
2. On the big day, the children bring in old toys or things they no longer want
3. Place all of the items on a large table, like a garage sale.
4. Draw names from a hat so that a few children at a time can go to the table and pick a certain number of items they would like to have.
5. In this way, the class can get rid on things they no longer want and swap for things they do.

 Lisa Chichester, Parkersburg, WV

Cinco Vaqueros to Centers: "Colores"

Materials

Construction paper in a variety of colors • paper bag

What to do

1. Assign a color to each center.
2. Fill a paper bag with construction paper squares matching the colors of each center.
3. Pass around the bag and let each child choose a color randomly.
4. Call out a color in English and Spanish.
5. When a child hears his color called, he looks around at the centers to find the matching color. For example, if Housekeeping is yellow/amarillo and a child has that color square, he will play in that center.

 Stacy Edwards, Jermyn, PA

Class Photo Album

Materials

Digital camera or camera and film • photo album

What to do

1. Preserve special memories throughout the year by taking pictures of the children.
2. In a photo album, place a collection of pictures showing children participating in classroom activities. Label the pictures with children's names and an explanation of the activity captured on film.
3. By using a digital camera, you can import the digital photos into a word-processing program, add captions, and print them onto paper. Bind the pages together to make a book.

(continued on the next page)

4. Leafing through the pages during Circle Time and remembering special events together will become a favorite pastime.

 Jackie Wright, Enid, OK

A Tip for Saving Work Samples

Materials

Paper • rubber date stamp

What to do

1. Keeping work samples to show the parents can be hard.
2. An easy way to do this is to staple several pieces of paper together to make a journal for each child.
3. Each day the child has a chance to draw or write in his journal. Use a rubber date stamp to put the day's date on each page. This makes the samples easier to save so you can show progress to the parents.

Tracie O'Hara, Charlotte, NC

Weekly Parent Note

Materials

Pen • paper (or computer and paper)

What to do

1. Parents enjoy being a part of their children's education. Send home a weekly letter telling them what is going on in class. Parents really appreciate this.
2. In your note include any of the following:

☆ The current theme

☆ Phonetics lessons and how they can help their children hear sounds

☆ What the children are learning in math

☆ Field trips being planned

☆ General school instructions

☆ Menus

☆ Any part of the curriculum that the parents can help with

☆ Any special occurrences, such as parties, visitors, and so on

3. If your school has a website, put the weekly letter on the site for families to read. Or, make a class letterhead to write the messages on.

 Barbara Saul, Eureka, CA

Take-Home Games

Materials

Canvas bags • fabric marker • activities and books to take home • paper • laminate

What to do

1. Label the outside of canvas bags "Take-Home Bag."

2. Place a book and activity in each bag with the directions written on a laminated piece of paper.

3. Send home a permission slip for parents that notifies them of the take-home activity packs and get their signed permission that they will be responsible for the items in the bag.

4. Make a chart to keep track of who has which bag. For example, label the bag with a number and a letter (1A, 1B, 1C).

5. Following are some examples for activity packs:

☆ The book *26 Letters and 99 Cents* by Tana Hoban, magnetic or plastic letters, and play money. Children can label the money and place the letters in order.

☆ Any alphabet book and magnetic letters to place in order.

☆ Any number book and ten plastic cups with the numbers written on the outside and small counters to match the amount to the number.

☆ A story with a matching puppet that the children can use to retell the story after they have read the book.

(continued on the next page)

☆ A simple story such as "The Three Little Pigs" and picture cards for the children to sequence after reading the story.

☆ A shape book and pattern blocks that the child can use to create designs or learn to make patterns.

 Melissa Browning, Milwaukee, WI

Observation Sticky Notes

Materials

Pads of sticky notes • pens or pencils

What to do

1. Have pads of sticky notes and pens or pencils available throughout your classroom. When you see a child engaging in positive behavior (such as performing a new skill or engaging in a social interaction) or negative behavior (such as striking out at another child), you can take a moment to jot a brief note to yourself. Stick these notes anywhere and gather them at the end of each day. Then, add them to the child's file at a later date.

2. Once you start using this strategy, your observation skills will improve. You will also discover that you don't necessarily observe every child in your classroom on equal terms. You may need to "catch" active children doing quiet activities, aggressive children engaged in sharing activities, or quiet children initiating an activity with another child. You will also find yourself making more of an attempt to identify positive behaviors instead of focusing on the negative ones.

3. You can add the child's initials for confidentiality and the date, if necessary. These notes are great reminders when preparing report cards or progress notes for parents.

4. Use different colors of sticky notes to depict certain days of the week so that when you collect the notes at the end of the week, you can remember the day the behavior occurred.

5. Encourage extra classroom staff such as assistants, therapists, and volunteers to utilize the note pads, too.

 Mary Volkman, Ottawa, IL

Assigned Seats for Snack

Materials

Large labels • marker • clear mailing tape

What to do

1. Be ready for snack time by having assigned seats.
2. Write each child's name on a label and tape it to his assigned place with mailing tape.
3. By having children sit in the same place each day, much unnecessary confusion and noise are eliminated. It is also another opportunity for children to practice name recognition skills.

 Jackie Wright, Enid, OK

Days-of-the-Week Seating

Materials

None

What to do

1. At the beginning of the year, divide the total number of children in your class into five different groups—one for each day of the school week.
2. On Monday, the children in group one get to wash their hands first for snack.
3. On Tuesday, the children in group two get the honor.
4. Continue in this manner for the remaining days of the week and begin again on Monday. In no time at all the children will be able to tell you which day of the week it is.

Author Note: This works well for my class because we sit in groups of three and have assigned places for snack.

 Jackie Wright, Enid, OK

Where Will I Sit?

Materials

None

What to do

Purpose: To provide a variety of ways to break up cliques, mix boys and girls, move children closer to the teacher, and stop inappropriate behavior and talking at circle time without singling out individual children.

Methods:

1. Ask children to sit on mats or chairs at circle time. Call out two names and have those children switch places. Call out two more names and continue until all the children are mixed up!

2. Place name cards on the tables and ask children to find their names to find their seats. When first names become easy, use last names or initials.

3. Place numerals on the tables. Give out cars with dots or stickers for the children to count and then find the corresponding number to find their seat.

4. Give out numerals or letters to match the ones put out on the tables. Give uppercase letters to match with lowercase letters.

5. Place objects on the table at each seat and give each child a letter. The child must find the object that starts with the letter.

6. Whisper a color in each child's ear as he enters and have him go to the table with that color on it. As an alternative, give out colored tickets.

7. Label the tables with categories and give out pictures that fit into those categories. Children find the category and sit there. For example, two-legged, four-legged, and swimming dinosaurs, or things that start with the letters of the month.

8. To mix up children during playtime in order to help them make new friends and learn cooperation, start by getting large paint sample chips, three of each color. Punch holes at the tops of each one. Hang hooks on the back of each section of the toy shelf and hang one different color chip in each section. As children arrive, give out color chips so that two children get matching colors. They go to the shelf, hang up their chip with the matching one, and get the toy from that section of the shelf. They play with the toy with their matching color partner. When they are done, they put it back and may have free choice time.

 Virginia Jean Herrod, Columbia, SC

Magic Scrap

Materials

None

What to do

1. To facilitate cleaning the room, tell the children there is a "magic scrap" somewhere on the floor.
2. Play a song while the children pick up everything they find on the floor. Before throwing anything away, the children show it to you to see if it's the "magic scrap."
3. Glance around the floor and designate to yourself what will be the magic scrap and then announce the child who finds it. Other times decide who will be the winner and then point to something that the child cleaned up and say, "Suzy found the magic scrap."
4. You can give the winner a little surprise, or simply say, "Surprise! Clean room!"

 Lynn Cagney, Lutz, FL

Cleaning Tip

Materials

Hand-held vacuum cleaner • duster and snap-on dustpan • hokey (mechanical carpet sweeper) • feather duster

What to do

1. Give children the opportunity to clean up after themselves. Have available a hand-held, cordless vacuum cleaner, a duster and dustpan, a Hokey, and a feather duster.
2. These four tools are sized perfectly for preschoolers and kindergarteners. They are easy for the youngsters to use and perfect for promoting independence. Cleaning up is a snap when the needed tools are made available.

 Jackie Wright, Enid, OK

Iron Unstuck Lamination

Materials

Laminated teaching materials • iron

What to do

1. This is a good tip for fixing laminated materials.
2. If you don't have a good seal after laminating your teaching materials, iron over the page once or twice with a dry iron on a low setting. Use just the tip of the iron.
3. Many times the lamination will reseal.

 Jackie Wright, Enid, OK

Remove Crayon Markings

Materials

De-Solve-It citrus solution (in a 12 oz. spray bottle) • paper towels

What to do

1. A great product for removing tough crayon markings is De-Solve-It citrus solution.
2. Spray it on walls or floors. Then rub with a paper towel to remove crayon markings.
3. You can also use it to remove any writing from permanent markers from laminated materials.

 Jackie Wright, Enid, OK

Substitute or Volunteer Roll Sheet

Materials

Computer • sheets of computer labels • small photocopied pictures of each child • piece of card stock

What to do

1. Set up your computer to print the correct size of labels.
2. Type half-sheets of labels for each of the children's names in large print.
3. Remove the labels and attach them to card stock.
4. Glue each of the children's photos next to the correct name.
5. Substitutes, volunteers, and visitors can use this picture roll sheet to learn the children's names.
6. Make copies of this sheet to be used at other times.
7. Put a photocopy of the roll list at each learning center. Ask the children to cross out their name when they play at the center. This helps them to take turns.

 Barbara Saul, Eureka, CA

For the Substitute

Materials

Blank cassette tape • children's records • CDs, and cassettes • tape recorder • basket

What to do

1. Collect many favorite songs, musical games, fingerplays, and so on and make your own cassette recording of them. Make the recording about 15 to 20 minutes long.
2. Be sure to include songs that the children will love to hear when they are engaged in high-energy activities.

(continued on the next page)

3. If the weather is bad and children must stay inside during recess, your substitute will have the inside recess period covered with this great sing-along cassette tape.
4. Store it in a "substitute basket" along with other activities.

☆ Jackie Wright, Enid, OK

Substitute Plans Box

Materials

Gallon-size zipper-closure plastic bags • box or container • sets of materials to complete an activity for each day you'll be gone • copy of the daily schedule • copy of your roll sheet

What to do

1. When you must be away unexpectedly, have a substitute plans box already prepared. In advance, prepare a set of lesson plans for five to six days, incorporating a theme or topic that could be used at any time during the year.
2. Store the plans along with any needed worksheets, books, or special material in a zipper-closure plastic bag for each day.
3. Store in a decorated box labeled "Substitute Box" and place it in an easy-to-find location.
4. Include a schedule for the day, roll sheet, and any specific instructions on the front of the box.
5. Now your substitute will quickly be able to find the materials and schedule he or she needs for a successful day.

☆ Jackie Wright, Enid, OK

A Place for Everything

Materials

Classroom materials • variety of storage containers

What to do

1. Make the most of valuable storage space. Keep everything in the room organized and easy to reach.
2. With all the many storage containers on the market today, it is easy to select ones that best suit your needs. Use clear, see-through containers when possible so the contents are visible.
3. Label every box, drawer, book, container, and so on with its contents. This system really cuts down on lost materials and helps keep you organized.

 Jackie Wright, Enid, OK

Covered Boxes

Materials

Wrapping paper • scissors • laminate • cardboard box • rubber cement • mailing tape

What to do

1. This is a great way to make attractive boxes for your classroom without covering them with contact paper.
2. Cut wrapping paper to the desired length and laminate it.
3. Cut the paper to fit the box.
4. Glue the paper on the box using rubber cement.
5. Secure the seams with clear mailing tape, if needed.
6. Decorate the box with a cute teddy bear or other age-appropriate character, if desired.

 Jackie Wright, Enid, OK

Big Book Box

Materials

Corrugated box (preferably with two sections) • contact paper or laminated wrapping paper • scissors • rubber cement • label

What to do

1. Convert a corrugated box into a storage container for your big books. If possible, find a two-section box with a 15"-high divider down the middle lengthwise. The box should be at least 21" long and 6" deep (each section should be 3" deep).
2. Cover the box with contact or decorative paper to improve its appearance and life span. If using laminated wrapping paper, cut it to the desired size and glue it to the box with rubber cement.
3. Label the outside of the box with an attractive label.
4. Slide your big books into the top of the box for quick and easy storage. A two-sectioned box should hold up to sixteen big books securely in place (eight big books in each section).
5. This portable and durable box can be moved easily to any location in the classroom. During class time, put it in the reading area where children have easy access to the books.
6. After reading a big book to the children, place it in the box. Leave the book accessible to the children for a month or so. Rotate the books monthly so that each big book can be displayed for at least a month.

☆ Jackie Wright, Enid, OK

Recycle Book Boxes

Materials

Corrugated boxes (14"W x 11"D x 1 ½"H) with lids

What to do

1. Save the boxes from book orders (or whatever is available) to make a supply of uniform-size containers.

2. These sturdy boxes stack neatly in closets or on shelves.

3. Label each box along the side to identify the contents.

4. Use a separate box to sort and store things such as lesson plan masters, Internet resources, bulletin board ideas, teaching guides, arts and crafts ideas, music and movement, game ideas, new fingerplays and poems, teaching back-ups, tissue paper patterns, projects to start, pictures and color copies, patterns, teaching expenses, databases, cooking activities, science activities, book extensions, craft recipes, and so on.

5. These boxes provide a place to store copies of new ideas you come upon or patterns you use in making teacher-created material for your classroom. Use the boxes as holding places for loose pages and ideas either before or after you put them in your permanently-bound or filed organizers.

6. Using this organizational tip helps keep your desk and room uncluttered and frees up room in your filing cabinets.

 Jackie Wright, Enid, OK

Monthly Sacks

Materials

Paper shopping bags with handles • labels

What to do

1. Here is a tip for storing all kinds of classroom supplies.

2. Collect a container, such as a shopping bag with handles, for each month of the school year. These bags are perfect for storing supplies.

3. Label each sack with the months of the year.

4. Now, gather together many of the supplies needed in your classroom and store them in the paper sacks according to the month you plan to use them.

5. As each month arrives, pull out the sack for that month and quickly locate items such as holiday-themed cookie cutters, bows made of seasonal ribbon to decorate baskets, seasonal-shaped containers, special holiday or seasonal dice, Jell-O molds, sponge painters, themed classroom decorations, and so on.

6. Store the sacks on a shelf in an out-of-the way location until the following year.

 Jackie Wright, Enid, OK

Paper Collection Tray

Materials

Tray or paper box lid • decorative contact paper

What to do

1. Place a tray in a central location in your classroom for the children to place their completed projects.
2. If a tray is not available, cover a paper box lid with decorative contact paper.
3. Turn the box lid upside down to make an easy organizer tray.

☆ Jackie Wright, Enid, OK

Quick Solution for Storage Containers

Materials

Empty one-quart water bottles • scissors • small game pieces • file-folder activities • tray or easy-slide drawer

What to do

1. Save empty water bottles.
2. Cut off the tops of the water bottles, leaving only the bottom portions. Cut them to your desired height.
3. Fill them with small game pieces and classroom items you want to keep off the floor.
4. Store them along with the game boards or file-folder activities they accompany on a tray or slide-out drawer. This technique gives children easy access to materials.

☆ Jackie Wright, Enid, OK

Table Set Up

Materials

Small baskets • crayons • glue sticks • pencils • scissors

What to do

1. On each table, set up a basket with crayons and another divided basket with pencils, scissors, and glue sticks.
2. This keeps them readily available to the children for projects, journaling, or free choice time.

 Melissa Browning, Milwaukee, WI

Art Sorting Box

Materials

White hanging file folder box • hanging file folders of any color, one for each child • glue • tape • scrap paper and fabric scraps, glitter, and sequins • markers or crayons • construction paper • oak tag or card paper

What to do

1. Put an end to the clutter in your room by creating this classy Art Box to store children's artwork.
2. Explain to the children that they will have a special place to store completed artwork. Show them the file folder box and hanging files. Tell them that you are going to work together to create an Art Box.
3. Encourage the children to use scrap paper, fabric scraps, glitter, and sequins to decorate the hanging file folder box. Avoid using large items such as beads or macaroni because they tend to fall off.
4. Create a label for the box and apply it to the front end.
5. Give each child a hanging file folder. Let them use colored markers, pencils, and crayons to decorate it as they please. (Since these folders will be used daily, avoid using glitter, sequins, and other glued items—they will not withstand the constant handling.)

(continued on the next page)

6. Print each child's name on a 2" x 4" piece of oak tag. Tape these to the top of the children's file folders. Do not use the folder tags included with the pack of file folders. They are too small to be seen once the artwork is stored in the box. The child's name should stick up at least 1" above the folder.

7. Place the Art Box near the supply shelf. Encourage the children to put their completed artwork in their own file folder. Remind the children that collage and other glued artwork need to dry thoroughly before being put in the box.

8. Send the collected artwork home at least twice a month, but do not send the file folder itself home. You will need it for more artwork.

OAK TAG BOARD
(2"×4"/ 1" ABOVE FOLDER)

DECORATED
FILE FOLDER
BOX

Artists' Works

ART WORK
INSIDE

SEQUINS

DECORATIONS

LABEL

☆ Virginia Jean Herrod, Columbia, SC

Art Area Set Up

Materials

Variety of art materials • shoeboxes or plastic baskets • photos • tape

What to do

1. Place items that can be used in the Art Area into baskets or boxes. Items could include scissors, hole punch, sticky tape, ribbon, stick and liquid glue, paper of various sizes, fronts of greeting cards, and various buttons.

2. On the outside front of each box, tape a picture of the item that is stored inside. This will help the children clean up the area.
3. Place the boxes on a shelf in the Art Area. Make sure the shelf is within easy reach of the children.
4. This same method can be used in the Science Area. Store items such as magnifying glasses, binoculars, kaleidoscope, various rocks, feathers, bones, and shells in baskets.

 Melissa Browning, Milwaukee, WI

Classroom Display Index

Materials

Copy of all your poems and songs on chart paper, posters, and bulletin boards • index tabs • copy machine • camera, optional • binding machine, optional

What to do

1. Set up a book for the school year with index tabs to divide each month.
2. Keep an 8 ½" x 11" copy of each song and poem you have on chart paper. Also write down the items you display on the wall with the song or poem, or take a photo of the items arranged on the wall.
3. Also keep a copy of each poster, bulletin board, worksheet from the bulletin board kit, and so on.
4. Arrange the copies in the order you plan to display them.
5. Store them by months behind the index tab dividers.
6. Assemble the pages into a book.
7. This book will serve as a reminder of all your wall and bulletin board displays.

 Jackie Wright, Enid, OK

Lesson Plans Made Simple

Materials

Copy machine • binding machine

What to do

1. Design a lesson plan form that indicates your daily routines such as lunch, snack, naptime, center times, recess, and time for various planned activities or subjects. Leave room for special activities that change each week.
2. Reproduce multiple copies of the form, one for each week of the school year.
3. Bind the pages together using a binding machine.
4. Each week, simply fill in the areas that change.

 Jackie Wright, Enid, OK

Materials List

Materials

Teaching materials • paper • pencil

What to do

1. Organize your teaching units with this handy tip. Complete a one-page record listing all the materials you have available for a particular unit such as: big books, puppets, flannel board stories, songs and games, rhymes and chants, as well as chart and posters, and so on.
2. Once your list is complete for each unit, use it to speed you along as you write your lesson plans.
3. Add to the list as new materials are acquired.
4. Reuse the lists from year to year. It's a great way to jog your memory about the many resources you have collected.

 Jackie Wright, Enid, OK

Make Your Own Page Protectors

Materials

Laminating scraps • scissors • mailing tape or clear tape • binding machine, optional

What to do

1. Take extra film from past laminating projects and fold it in half.
2. Create a pocket of the desired size by taping the sides with clear mailing tape or Scotch Crystal Clear tape.
3. Leave the top open to slip in papers.
4. Make as many as needed. If desired, bind these together into a book using a binding machine.
5. This is a terrific way to organize and protect important papers, children's work, photos, and so on. Now children can handle and view the contents without damaging the material.

 Jackie Wright, Enid, OK

Windowed File Jackets

Materials

5 file folders • scissors • laminating scraps • transparent tape • Mini Sorter, purchased from an office supply store or discount store

What to do

1. Taking a peek at what work is available is much easier when you put it inside windowed file jackets.
2. Cut out a 5" x 8" opening from the front of a file folder.
3. Cut out a slightly larger rectangle from laminating scraps.

(continued on the next page)

4. Center this on the opening in the file folder and tape it to the inside of the folder.

5. Now you have created a window for viewing the contents inside.

6. To create a pocket, simply tape the sides closed, leaving the top open to insert the materials.

7. Make one file jacket for each day of the week. Inside, display little books, activity sheets, craft projects, alphabet puppet pages, cut-and-paste projects, and so on.

8. Display these upright in a Mini Sorter, designed to hold envelopes on a desk top. Keep all five file jackets in one of the three sections of this handy holder. Place it in a central location where children can access it during free choice time.

9. Rotate the materials that go inside on a regular basis, putting out a new activity each day and removing ones that everyone has had a chance to complete.

10. This system allows for more than one day to complete a project. Children who are absent can easily see what they missed as soon as they return and can catch up on their own without feeling left out. Those who are not interested in doing an activity one day might be eager to do it another day.

☆ Jackie Wright, Enid, OK

Color Words Songbook

Materials

Words to color songs • computer • construction paper in colors matching the songs • glue stick • scissors • laminate • binding machine or hole punch and yarn

What to do

1. Have you ever wondered what to do with those cute color songs that reinforce the spelling of color words? Make a booklet of all the songs.

2. Using your computer, print the words to each color song on separate pages.

3. Glue each song copy to a sheet of construction paper of the same color, leaving a border showing around all four sides.

4. Cut the colored pages of the book to different lengths, each ½" longer than the preceding page, to create a rainbow effect with bands of each color showing at the bottom.

5. Make a front cover ½" shorter than the first page and a back cover ½" longer than the last page.

6. Laminate the pages and the covers.

7. Align the booklet pages and covers at the top, ensuring that the bands of color of each page are unobstructed when the booklet is closed.

8. Bind the booklet at the top, using a binding machine or hole punch and yarn, with the shortest page first and each progressively longer page following so that each color is showing.

9. The children love having this book available. They can quickly turn to the color they want to sing and their spelling skills are enhanced as well.

 Jackie Wright, Enid, OK

Game Booklet

Materials

Spiral-bound pack of 4" x 6" index cards • copy machine • rubber cement • scissors • copy of favorite classroom games

What to do

1. Keep classroom games at your fingertips with this handy booklet.

2. Make a copy of your favorite games so that each one will fit on a 4" x 6" index card.

3. Organize the games in alphabetical order.

4. Glue one game on each index card and keep them in alphabetical order. Number the pages.

5. Make an index with the game titles and page numbers.

6. Keep the game booklet in a basket of substitute teacher supplies so he or she will have a choice of games while you are away.

 Jackie Wright, Enid, OK

Hang It Up!

Materials

String • scissors • pinch-type clothespins • hot glue gun (adult only) • wrapping paper and laminate, optional • paper clips or Christmas ornament hooks

What to do

1. Here's a space-saving idea: use ceiling space to display children's artwork!
2. Cut a 16" length of string for each child. Knot the ends together to form a loop.
3. Glue a pinch-style clothespin to the end of the looped string.
4. Decorate the front of the clothespins with something attractive such as bows cut from wrapping paper and laminated. Glue in place using a hot glue gun (adult only).
5. Suspend the clothespins from the ceiling of your classroom with paper clips or Christmas ornament hooks attached to the top loop of the strings.
6. The clothespins are ready to hold the children's artwork for a lovely display.

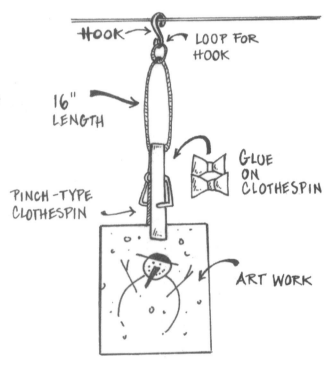

⭐ Jackie Wright, Enid, OK

Long Reach Stapler

Materials

Long-reach stapler

What to do

1. Purchase a long-reach stapler to staple in the middle of folded papers.

☆ Jackie Wright, Enid, OK

Time-Saving Tip for a Book Cover

Materials

Book jacket with appropriate picture • color copier • oak tag • laminate

What to do

1. Whenever you need to decorate a cover for a book you or the children are making, make a color copy of a cute book jacket that has a great picture to depict the contents of your book.
2. Label the cover, if necessary.
3. If you use oak tag through your printer, you save the step of having to glue the color copy to the oak tag. Laminate.
4. Use as a cover when you bind your books.

☆ Jackie Wright, Enid, OK

Our Book of Poems and Songs

Materials

Copy of favorite poems, songs, fingerplays, and rhymes • pictures for illustrations • glue stick • sheet protectors • three-ring binder (or use a binding machine) • stick puppets, optional

What to do

1. Throughout the year, make copies of age-appropriate poems from a variety of sources, such as children's poetry books, magazines, the Internet, and so on.
2. If desired, add a corresponding illustration or photograph to each poetry page for easy identification.
3. Place each page into a separate sheet protector.
4. If desired, glue poems to the backs of stick puppets for the children to handle. Put these in a sheet protector, also.
5. Put the pages in a three-ring binder or bind them with a binding machine.
6. Label the front of the book with an appropriate title.
7. Keep in the reading area for children to enjoy all year long.

 Jackie Wright, Enid, OK

Poem and Song Cards

Materials

5" x 8" tagboard or index cards

What to do

1. Collect songs and fingerplays that are often used in the classroom.
2. On the front of each card, draw a picture that represents the song or fingerplay.
3. On the back, write the poem or song so that anyone can use the flash cards with ease.
4. For thematic songs and fingerplays, mount all of them on a larger card to display for a period of time.

 Melissa Browning, Milwaukee, WI

Stories on Tape

Materials

Picture books • cassette tapes • tape player

What to do

1. Build a library of audio recordings with page-turning signals to accompany the picture books.
2. On days when you need to consult with a parent or complete a task, simply grab one of your book/tape sets and start the tape.
3. Select a child to hold the book and show the illustrations to the other children. The child can follow along and turn the pages at the signal.
4. This allows children to enjoy listening to a story while you take care of business.

 Jackie Wright, Enid, OK

Children's Favorite Poems on Tape

Materials

Blank cassette tape • tape recorder • book of poems

What to do

1. Create a rich environment where children can learn, listen, relax, and grow by making your own classroom tape of your children's favorite poems.
2. Listening to poetry helps the children improve their listening skills. It also helps them develop an awareness of rhyme and rhythm and helps build their early reading skills.
3. A wonderful source is *Read-Aloud Rhymes for the Very Young* with poems selected by Jack Prelutsky. This book is an essential resource for any early childhood classroom or childcare center.

 Jackie Wright, Enid, OK

Laundry Bag for Flannel Board Storage

Materials

Large, drawstring laundry bag • flannel board

What to do

1. Purchase a drawstring laundry bag (or make your own) large enough to hold all your flannel boards, stands, and so on.
2. By using this organizational method, your flannel boards are kept in a clean, safe place and are easy for you to remove as needed.
3. This method also makes your flannel boards easily identifiable as yours. This is particularly useful if there are several teachers in your facility who share materials or who use your classroom during different parts of the day.
4. Store the laundry bag containing the flannel boards in an out-of-the-way location, such as behind a piece of furniture, until they are needed.

☆ Jackie Wright, Enid, OK

Build a Large Library of Flannel Board Stories

Materials

Flannel board story sets (stories, characters, tapes) • gallon-size zipper-closure plastic bags (10" x 12") • labels

What to do

1. Organize your flannel board stories with this easy-to-use system. Place each flannel board story (script) in a zipper-closure plastic bag along with the characters and cassette tape telling the story.

2. Label each bag with the name of the story. If desired, also include the running time of the cassette tape.

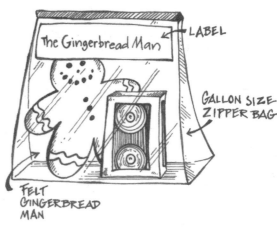

3. You may also place other related materials such as a picture book of the story, reproducible images, book notes, and so on.

4. Store the bagged stories in a large box or file drawer in the order you plan to use them. After using one, place it in the back.

5. Continue adding to your flannel board story collection throughout the year.

☆ Jackie Wright, Enid, OK

Reading on a Bench

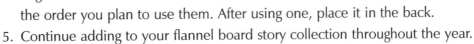

Materials

Child-size bench • children's books

What to do

1. Find a quiet corner in your classroom to create an area for children to browse through books and read.
2. If a child-sized bench is available, put it in your reading area.
3. Put your books near the bench. Provide theme-related literature, and include big books, picture books, and class-made books.
4. Change the books weekly to correlate with your current classroom themes.
5. Add new class-made books as soon as they are constructed. Keep them out throughout the year for the children to enjoy.

☆ Jackie Wright, Enid, OK

Build a Reading List for Character Education

Materials

Children's books • computer with a database program, optional

What to do

1. Compile a list of easy-to-find children's books that teach values.
2. Jot down the title and author when you find a book that supports any of the following themes: acceptance, compassion, cooperation, courage, cultural diversity, fairness, friendship, generosity, hard work, helpfulness, honesty, kindness, love, patience, peace-making, perseverance, respect for the environment, respect for others, responsibility, self-discipline, self-esteem, sharing, unconditional love, and so on.
3. The books on this list can be used to support your character education program. By using your computer to store the list, you can refer to it as needed and update it throughout the year.
4. Following are a list of books that teach values:

Reading List for Character Education

Title	Author	Thematic Units
Alexander the Wind-Up Mouse	Leo Lionni	Mice, Value of friendship
A Bargain for Frances	Russell Hoban	Friendship/Value of fairness/Honesty
Brave Irene	William Stieg	Snow/Value of courage and responsibility
The Bremen-town Musicians	Ruth Belov Gross	Farm/Value of friendship
The Carrot Seed	Ruth Krauss	Plants/Food/Value of perseverance
A Chair for My Mother	Vera B. Williams	Mother's Day/Value of cooperation
The Chicken Book	Garth Williams	Spring/Value of work
Courtney	John Burningham	Pets/Value of respect
Crow Boy	Taro Yashima	Value of respect for diversity and kindness
Eggbert—The Slightly Cracked Egg	Tom Ross	Individuality/Eggs/Value of self-esteem
Finders Keepers	William Lipkind	Value of sharing

Frederick	Leo Lionni	Seasons/Fall/Mice/Value of respect
Frog and Toad Are Friends	Arnold Lobel	Frogs/ Value of friendship/ Kindness
George and Martha	James Marshall	Value of friendship
I Know a Lady	Charlotte Zolotow	Friends/Value of kindess/Empathy
If You Give a Mouse a Cookie	Laura Numeroff	Mice/Value of kindness/Patience
Inch by Inch	Leo Lionni	Value of respect
Ira Sleeps Over	Bernard Waber	School begins/Value of friendship/Cooperation
Just for You	Mercer Mayer	School begins/Value of helpfulness
Knots on a Counting Rope	Bill Martin, Jr.	American Indians/Value of compassion
The Legend of the Indian Paintbrush	Tomie de Paola	Plants/Value of respect
The Little Black Truck	Libba Moore Gray	Transportation/Value of perseverance
Little Blue and Little Yellow	Leo Lionni	Value of perseverance
The Little Engine That Could	Watty Piper	Transportation/Value of perseverance
The Little House	Virginia Lee Burton	Seasons/Community/Value of perseverance
The Little Mouse, The Red Ripe Strawberry, and the Big Hungry Bear	Don and Audrey Wood	Mice/Food/Value of sharing
The Little Old Lady Who Was Not Afraid of Anything	Linda Williams	Halloween/Value of courage
Little Toot	Hardie Gramatsky	Transportation/Value of responsibility
Loudmouth George and The Big Race	Nancy Carlson	Value of self-discipline
Mike Mulligan and His Steam Shovel	Virginia Lee Burton	Value of perseverance
Miss Nelson Is Missing	Harry Allard	School begins/Value of cooperation
Miss Rumphuis	Barbara Cooney	Flowers/Value of respect
The Mother's Day Mice	Eve Bunting	Mother's Day/Value of kindness
My Friends	Taro Gomi	Family and friends/Value of friendship
My Red Umbrella	Robert Bright	Rainy days/Value of friendship
Over in the Meadow	John Langstaff	Value of responsibility

Petunia	Roger Duvoisin	Safety/Value of humility/Honesty
The Pied Piper	Alan Benjamin	Value of honesty
Pigsty	Mark Teague	Value of honesty
A Pocket for Corduroy	Don Freeman	Teddy bears/Value of helpfulness
The Quarreling Book	Charlotte Zolotow	Feelings/Value of peacemaking/Kindness
The Runaway Bunny	Margaret Wise Brown	Easter/Rabbits/Value of love
Song and Dance Man	Karen Ackerman	Grandparents/Value of kindness
Stellaluna	Janell Cannon	Bats/Value of respect
The Story of Ferdinand	Munro Leaf	Flowers/Value of respect/Diversity
Swimmy	Leo Lionni	Water animals/Value of cooperation
Three Little Kittens	Paul Galdone	Mittens/Value of responsibility
A Tree Is Nice	Janice May Udry	Arbor Day/Value of respect for the environment
The Velveteen Rabbit	Margery Williams	Rabbits/Value of love/Friendship
Where the Wild Things Are	Maurice Sendak	Feelings/Value of unconditional love
The Wild Christmas Reindeer	Jan Brett	Christmas/Value of kindness
William's Doll	Charlotte Zolotow	Feelings/Value of respect
The Worst Person's Christmas	James Stevenson	Christmas/Value of generosity

 Jackie Wright, Enid, OK

Literature List

Materials

Collection of children's books • computer with a database program • binding machine, optional

What to do

1. Do you find it difficult to keep track of the many books, stories, and poems you use every year? Try creating a database to keep an inventory of your resources.
2. List the books by thematic unit as well as title and author. (I also like to list the week I plan to use each thematic unit.)
3. Print out these pages and assemble them into a book.
4. Now you will have a record that's easy to update from year to year.
5. Following is a list of books to get you started.

   Author Note: I have included themes for many of the books. Change or add to the themes as you see fit.

Book Title	Author(s)	Theme(s)	Time of Year
1 Is One	Tasha Tudor	Numbers, Time, Calendar	
1, 2, 3 to the Zoo	Eric Carle	Zoo/Safari	
12 Ways to Get to 11	Eve Merriam	Counting/Math	
26 Letters and 99 Cents	Tana Hoban	Counting/Math	
A Apple Pie and Traditional Nursery Rhymes	Kate Greenaway	Apples/ABCs	
A Bad, Bad Day	Kirsten Hall	Sense of Humor	
A Chair for My Mother	Vera B. Williams	Mother's Day/Values of Cooperation, Sharing, & Perseverance	
A Dog Named Sam	Janice Boland	Pets	
A Holiday for Mister Muster	Arnold Lobel	Zoo/Safari	
A House for Hermit Crab	Eric Carle	Houses/Animals	
A House Is a House for Me	Mary Ann Hoberman	Spring/Earth Day	
A January Fog Will Freeze a Hog	Hubert Davis	Folklore	
A Letter to Amy	Ezra Jack Keats	Friendship	
A My Name Is Alice	Jane Bayer	ABCs	
A Pair of Red Clogs	Masako Matsuno	Friends Around World	
A Pair of Socks	Stuart J. Murphy, illus. Lois Ehlert	Pairs/Clothing	
A Picture Book of Abraham Lincoln	David Adler	Presidents/American History	

Book Title	Author(s)	Theme(s)	Time of Year
A Piece of Cake	Jill Murphy	Mother's Day	
A Pocketful of Seasons	Doris Van Liew Foster	Seasons	
A Spoon for Every Bite	Joe Hayes	Moral choices	
A Story, a Story	Gail E. Haley	Friends Around the World	
A Tiger Called Thomas	Charlotte Zolotow	Halloween	
A Tree Is Nice	Janice May Udry	Arbor Day/Respect for the Environment	
A Turkey for Thanksgiving	Eve Bunting	Thanksgiving	
A Very Special House	Ruth Krauss	Houses	
A Visit to Grandma's	Nancy L. Carlson	Family	
Abe Lincoln's Hat	Martha Brenner	Presidents	
Abiyoyo	Pete Seeger	Folk Tales and Myths	
Across the Stream	Mirra Ginsburg	All About the Farm	
The Adventures of Spider: West African Folktales	Joyce Arkhurst		
The Adventures of Taxi Dog	Debra and Sal Barracca		
Ahoy There, Little Polar Bear	Hans de Beer	Adventure/North Pole	
Alejandro's Gift	Richard Albert	Desert/Wildlife	
Alexander and the Terrible, Horrible, No Good, Very Bad Day	Judith Viorst	Feelings	
Alexander and the Wind-Up Mouse	Leo Lionni	Mice/Value of Friendship	
Alexander, Who Used to Be Rich Last Sunday	Judith Viorst	Value of Money/Feelings	
All By Myself	Mercer Mayer	Totally Terrific Me	
All Fall Down	Brian Wildsmith	Zoo Safari	
Alphabears	Kathleen Hague	Bears/ABCs	
The Alphabet Book	P. D. Eastman	ABCs	
The Alphabet Tree	Leo Lionni	ABCs/President's Day	
Amazing Grace	Mary Hoffman	Value of Self-Esteem	
Amelia Bedelia Goes Camping	Peggy Parish	Camping/Adventure	
Amelia's Nine Lives	Lorna Balian	Pets	
American Tall Tales	Mary Pope Osborne	History/Folktales	
Amos and Boris	William Steig	Sea Animals/Boats	
An Extraordinary Egg	Leo Lionni		
Anansi and the Talking Melon	Eric Kimmel	Folk Tale/Tricksters	
Anansi the Spider: A Tale From the Ashanti	Gerald McDermott	Folk Tale/Tricksters	
Angel Child, Dragon Child	Michele Maria Surat	Vietnamese culture	
Angry Arthur	Haiwyn Oram	Anger/Self-control	
Angus and the Ducks	Marjorie Flack	Pets/Curiosity	
The Animal	Lorna Balian		

Book Title	Author(s)	Theme(s)	Time of Year
The Animal Atlas	Barbara Taylor		
Animal Homes	Brian Wildsmith	Animal Homes	
Animalia	Graeme Base	Alphabet	
Animals in Danger	Marcus Schenck	Environment	
Annie and the Wild Animals	Jan Brett Winter	Days/Snow Pets	
Annie Bananie	Leah Komaiko	Family & Friends	
Anno's Alphabet	Mitsumasa Anno	ABCs	
Anno's U. S. A.	Mitsumasa Anno	United States	
Antarctica	Helen Cowcher	Environment/Penguins	
Appelemando's Dreams	Patricia Polacco	Dreams/Acceptance	
Apples and Pumpkins	Anne Rockwell	Halloween/Fall	
April Fools	Fernando Krahn	April Fools Day	
Are You My Mother?	P.D. Eastman		
The Armadillo From Amarillo	Lynne Cherry		
Armadillo Rodeo	Jan Brett		
The Art Lesson	Tomie dePaola	Occupations/Art	
Arthur's Eyes	Marc Brown	Five Senses	
As the Crow Flies	Gail Hartman		
At Daddy's on Saturdays	Linda Walvoord Girard		
Aunt Chip and the Great Triple Creek Dam Affair	Patricia Polacco		
Baby Animals	Karen Rissing	Baby Animals	
Baby Farm Animals	Garth Williams	Baby Animals	
Back Home	Gloria Jean Pinkney		
The Balancing Act—A Counting Song	Merle Peek	Elephants	
Barn Dance!	Bill Martin, Jr.	Scarecrows	
Barnyard Banter	Denise Fleming		
Bartholomew the Bossy	Marjorie Weinman Sharmat		
Batholomew and the Oobleck	Dr. Seuss		
Batter Up!	Andrew Gutelle	Springtime	
Be Nice to Spiders	Margaret Bloy Graham	Spiders	
Beady Bear	Don Freeman		
The Bear's Cave	Regine Schindler		
Bears on Wheels: A Bright and Early Counting Book	Stan and Jan Berenstain	Counting	
Bee My Valentine!	Miriam Cohen	Valentine's Day	
The Bee-Man of Orn	Frank Stockton		
Benny's Pennies	Pat Brisson		
Bentley & Egg	William Joyce		
The Berenstain Bears Go to School	Stan & Jan Berenstain	School Begins	
Berlioz the Bear	Jan Brett	Music	
Best Friends	Steven Kellogg	Friends	
The Best Nest	P. D. Eastman		

Book Title	Author(s)	Theme(s)	Time of Year
The Big Bunny and the Magic Show	Steven Kroll	Easter/Rabbits	
The Big Fat Enormous Lie	Marjorie Weinman Sharmat		
Big Fat Hen	Keith Baker	Counting/Eggs	
Big Old Bones—A Dinosaur Tale	Carol Carrick	Dinosaurs	
The Big Sneeze	Ruth Brown	All About the Farm/Spiders	
The Big Snow	Berta Hader & Elmer Hader	Groundhogs/Winter	
The Biggest House in the World	Leo Lionni	Animal Homes	
Biggest Machines	Dennis Kiley	Construction	
The Biggest Nose	Kathy Caple		
The Biggest Pumpkin Ever	Steven Kroll		
The Black Snowman	Phil Mendez		
Blue Sea	Robert Kalan; illus. Don Crews	Water Animals/ Sizes & Shapes	
Boat Book	Gail Gibbons	Boats	
Borreguita and the Coyote	Verna Aardema	Lions & Lambs	
The Boy Who Would Be a Helicopter	Vivian Gussin Paley		
Brave as a Mountain Lion	Ann Herbert Scott	Lions & Lambs	
The Brave Cowboy	Jane Walsh Anglund	L'il Cowpokes	
Brave Irene	William Steig	Snow/Values of Courage & Responsibility	
Bread and Jam for Frances	Russell Hoban	Foods/Nutrition	
Bread Bread Bread	Ann Morris	Foods/Nutrition	
Bremen Town Musicians	Jacob Grimm		
Brian Wildsmith's ABC	Brian Wildsmith	ABCs	
Brian Wildsmith's Birds	Brian Wildsmith	Birds	
Bringing the Rain to Kapita Plain	Verna Aardema		
Brother Eagle, Sister Sky	Susan Jeffers	Birds/Environment	
Bubble Bubble	Mercer Mayer	Bubbles	
The Bug Book	William Dugan	Insects	
Building a House	Byron Barton	Homes/Construction	
Bumper to Bumper, A Traffic Jam	Jakki Wood	Transportation	
The Button Box	Margaret S. Reid		
Caps for Sale	Esphyr Slobodkina	Clothing	
Caps, Hats, Socks, and Mittens	Louise Borden	Weather/Seasons/Fall	
Carl Goes Shopping	Alexandra Day	Pets	
The Carousel	Liz Rosenberg		
The Carrot Seed	Ruth Krauss	Plants/Food/Value of Perseverance	
Cat Goes Fiddle-I-Fee	Paul Galdone	All About the Farm	
The Cat in the Hat	Dr. Seuss		

Book Title	Author(s)	Theme(s)	Time of Year
Changes, Changes	Pat Hutchins	Shapes	
Charlie Needs a Cloak	Tomie dePaola	Sheep/Clothing	
Check It Out! The Book About Libraries	Gail Gibbons	Library Week	
Cherries and Cherry Pits	Vera B. Williams	Plants	
Chicka Chicka Sticka Sticka	Bill Martin, Jr. & John Archambault	ABCs	
Chickens Aren't the Only Ones	Ruth Heller	All About the Farm	
Child's Book of Art	Lucy Micklethwait	Art Appreciation	
Choo Choo: The Story of a Little Engine Who Ran Away	Virginia Lee Burton		
Christopher Columbus	Stephen Krensky	Columbus Day	
Circus	Lois Ehlert		
City Green	Dyanne DiSalvo-Ryan		
City in the Winter	Eleanor Schick	Winter Days/Snow	
The Cloud Book	Tomie dePaola	Clouds/Picnic	
Cloudy With a Chance of Meatballs	Judi Barrett	Food	
Cock-a-Doodle Dudley	Bill Peet	All About the Farm	
Color Dance	Ann Jonas	Colors	
Colors Are Nice	Adelaide Holl	Springtime/Colors	
Colors Everywhere	Tana Hoban	Colors	
Come a Tide	George Ella Lyon		
The Complete Story of Three Blind Mice	Paul Galdone		
Cornelius	Leo Lionni	Alligators	
Count and See	Tana Hoban	Counting	
Counting Rhymes	Sharon Kane, illus.	Counting	
Cowboy Dreams	Dayal Kaur Khalsa	Cowpokes	
Coyote Steals the Blanket	Janet Stevens		
Creak, Thump, Bonk! A Very Spooky Mystery	Susan L. Roth		
Creepy, Crawly Caterpillars	Margery Facklam	Insects	
Crictor	Tomi Ungerer		
Crinkleroot's Guide to Knowing the Trees	Jim Aronsky	Trees	
Crow Boy	Taro Yashima	Values of Respect for Diversity & Kindness	
Curious George	H. A. Rey	Occupations/Monkeys	
Cyrus the Unsinkable Sea Serpent	Bill Peet		
Dad and Me in the Morning	Patricia Lakin		
Daddy Makes the Best Spaghetti	Anna Grossnickle Hines		
Daisy-Head Mayzie	Dr. Seuss		

Book Title	Author(s)	Theme(s)	Time of Year
Dandelion	Don Freeman	Lions & Lambs	
Dandelions	Eve Bunting		
Danny and the Dinosaur	Syd Hoff	Dinosaurs	
The Day Jimmy's Boa Ate the Wash	Trinka Hakes Noble	All About the Farm	
The Day the Goose Got Loose	Reeve Lindbergh	Geese/Farm Animals	
The Day the Teacher Went Bananas	James Howe		
De Colores and Other Latin-American Folk Songs	Jose-Luis Orozco		
Dear Benjamin Banneker	Andrea Davis Pinkney		
Digging Up Dinosaurs	Aliki	Dinosaurs	
The Dinosaur Alphabet Book	Jerry Pallotta	Dinosaurs/ABCs	
Dinosaur Bones	Aliki	Dinosaurs	
Dinosaurs Are Different	Aliki	Dinosaurs	
Dinosaurs to the Rescue!	Laurene Krasny Brown	Dinosaurs	
Dinosaurs, Dinosaurs	Byron Barton	Dinosaurs	
Discovering Seashells	Douglas Florian		
Do You Want to Be My Friend?	Eric Carle	Mice	
Doctor De Soto	William Steig		
The Dog Who Had Kittens	Polly M. Robertus		
Dogs	Gail Gibbons	Dogs	
The Doorbell Rang	Pat Hutchins		
Dragon ABC Hunt	Loreen Leedy	ABCs	
Draw Me a Star	Eric Carle	Shapes/Artist	
Dreams	Ezra Jack Keats	Shadows/Nighttime	
Drylongso	Virginia Hamilton		
Ducks Don't Get Wet	Augusta Goldin Water	Animals	
Each Peach Pear Plum	Janet & Allan Ahlberg	Mother Goose	
The Earth and I	Frank Asch		
Eating the Alphabet	Lois Ehlert	ABCs/Vegetables	
Edward the Emu	Sheena Knowles	Zoo Safari	
Eggbert, the Slightly Cracked Egg	Tom Ross	Individuality/Eggs/Value of Self-Esteem	
The Eggs: A Greek Folk Tale	Aliki		
Elbert's Bad Word	Audrey Wood		
The Elephant's Child	Rudyard Kipling		
Elephants Aloft	Kathi Appelt		
Emergency!	Gail Gibbons		
The Empty Pot	Demi	Plants & Seeds/Value of Honesty	
Eric Carle's Animals	Eric Carle		
Everybody Needs a Rock	Byrd Baylor		
Everyday Mysteries	Jerome Wexler		
Exploring the Night Sky	Terence Dickinson		

Book Title	Author(s)	Theme(s)	Time of Year
Fables	Arnold Lobel		
The Fall of Freddie the Leaf	Leo Buscaglia		
Fanny's Dream	Caralyn Buehner		
The Farm Alphabet Book	Jane Miller	Farm/ABCs	
Farmer Duck	Martin Waddell		
Farming	Gail Gibbons	All About the Farm	
Fathers, Mothers, Sisters, Brothers: A Collection of Family Poems	Mary Ann Hoberman		
Feathers for Lunch	Lois Ehlert	Birds	
Feelings	Aliki		
Fiddle-I-Fee	Melissa Sweet	All About the Farm	
Finger Rhymes	Marc Brown		
The Fire Engine Book	Jesse Younger	Safety/Fire Prevention	
Fire Engines	Anne Rockwell	Fire Prevention	
Fire on the Mountain	Jane Kurtz		
Fire! Fire!	Gail Gibbons		
Fireflies in the Night	Judy Hawes	Insects/Night & Day	
The First Snowfall	Anne & Harlow Rockwell	Winter Days/Snow	
Fish Is Fish	Leo Lionni	Frogs	
Flap Your Wings	P. D. Eastman	Eggs/Alligators	
Flossie and the Fox	Patricia McKissack		
The Flower Alphabet Book	Jerry Pallotta	Plants/ABCs	
Flower Garden	Eve Bunting		
Flying in a Hot Air Balloon	Cheryl Walsh Bellville		
Fortunately	Remy Charlip	Opposites	
Fossils Tell of Long Ago	Aliki	Dinosaurs	
Four Valentines in a Rainstorm	Felicia Bond	Valentine's Day	
Fraction Action	Loreen Leedy		
Franklin in the Dark	Paulette Bourgeois	Feelings/Turtles	
Frederick	Leo Lionni	Seasons/Fall/Mice/ Value of Respect	
Freight Train	Donald Crews	Transportation	
Friday Night Is Papa Night	Ruth A. Sonneborn		
Friends	Helme Heine	Friendship	
The Frog Alphabet Book	Jerry Pallotta	Frogs/ABCs	
The Frog Prince	Edith H. Tarcov	Frogs	
Frog Went A-Courtin'	John Langstaff	Frogs	
Froggy Gets Dressed	Jonathan London		
From Pictures to Words: A Book About Making a Book	Janet Stevens		
The Furry Alphabet Book	Jerry Pallotta	Animals/ABCs	

Book Title	Author(s)	Theme(s)	Time of Year
The Gadget War	Betsy Duffey		
The Garden of Happiness	Erika Tamar		
George and Martha	James Marshall	Value of Friendship	
George Washington's Breakfast	Jean Fritz	Presidents	
Geraldine's Blanket	Holly Keller	Feelings/Pigs	
The Giant Jam Sandwich	John Vernon Lord	Food	
Gila Monsters Meet You at the Airport	Marjorie Weinman Sharmat		
Gilberto and the Wind	Marie Hall Ets		
The Gingerbread Boy	Paul Galdone		
The Gingerbread Man	John A. Rowe	Gingerbread	
The Girl Who Loved Wild Horses	Paul Goble		
Give Me Half!	Stuart J. Murphy		
The Giving Tree	Shel Silverstein		
Glad Monster Sad Monster: A Book About Feelings	Ed Emberley	Feelings	
Go Away, Big Green Monster!	Ed Emberley	Body Parts/Monsters	
The Goat in the Rug	Charles L. Blood		
Goggles!	Ezra Jack Keats		
The Golden Christmas Tree	Jan Wahl	Christmas	
Goldilocks and the Three Bears	Jan Brett		
Good Dog, Carl	Alexandra Day		
Good Morning, Chick	Mirra Ginsburg	All About the Farm	
Good Night, Gorilla	Peggy Rathmann		
The Good, the Bad, and the Goofy	Jon Scieszka		
Goodbye Geese	Nancy White Carlstrom	Fall	
Good-Night Owl!	Pat Hutchins	Night & Day/Owls	
Gooseberry Park	Cynthia Rylant		
Grandfather Twilight	Barbara Berger		
Grandmother's Pigeon	Louise Erdrich		
The Grasshopper and the Ant	Aesop	Insects	
The Great Kapok Tree: A Tale of the Amazon Rainforest	Lynne Cherry		
The Great Pumpkin Switch	Megan McDonald		
The Greedy Python	Richard Buckley		
The Greedy Zebra	Mwenye Hadithi	Sound of Z/Animals	
Green Eggs and Ham	Dr. Seuss	Five Senses	
Gregory, the Terrible Eater	Mitchell Sharmat	Goats/Food	
The Grey Lady and the Strawberry Snatcher	Molly Bang	Strawberries	
The Grouchy Ladybug	Eric Carle	Insects	
Growing Vegetable Soup	Lois Ehlert	Foods/Nutrition	
Guess Who?	Margaret Miller	Careers	

Book Title	Author(s)	Theme(s)	Time of Year
Guess Who?	Anne W. Ball	Community Helpers	
Hailstones and Halibut Bones	Mary O'Neill	Colors	
Hand Rhymes	Marc Brown	Five Senses	
Hands Off!	Mario Mariotti		
Hansel and Gretel	Brothers Grimm		
Happy Birthday, Dear Duck	Eve Bunting	Farm/Birthdays	
Happy Birthday, Sam	Pat Hutchins	Totally Terrific Me	
The Happy Day	Ruth Krauss	Zoo/Safari/Winter/ Snow/Groundhogs	
Happy Easter, Little Critter	Mercer Mayer	Easter	
Harbor	Donald Crews	Boats/Transportation	
Harriet and the Promised Land	Jacob Lawrence		
Harry and the Terrible Whatzit	Dick Gackenbach		
Hattie and the Fox	Mem Fox	All About the Farm	
Have You Seen Birds?	Joanne Oppenheim	Birds	
Have You Seen My Cat?	Eric Carle	Pets	
Have You Seen My Duckling?	Nancy Tafuri	Water Animals	
Hear Your Heart	Paul Showers	Valentine's Day	
Her Seven Brothers	Paul Goble		
Here Are My Hands	Bill Martin, Jr.	My Body	
Hi Mom, I'm Home!	Kees Moerbeek	Rabbits/Animal Homes	
Hi, Cat!	Ezra Jack Keats	Pets	
Hide and Seek Fog	Alvin Tresselt	Clouds/Picnic	
Home for a Bunny	Margaret Wise Brown	Easter/Rabbits/Homes	
Hooray for Me	Remy Charlip	Totally Terrific Me	
Hooray for Mother's Day!	Marjorie Weinman Sharmat	Mother's Day	
Hopper	Marcus Pfister		
Horton Hatches the Egg	Dr. Seuss		
Hosie's Alphabet	Leonard Baskin	ABCs	
The House That Jack Built	Tony Brice, illus.	Houses	
Houses and Homes	Ann Morris	Houses & Homes	
How a Book Is Made	Aliki		
How a House Is Built	Gail Gibbons		
How a Seed Grows	Helen J. Jordan		
How Droofus the Dragon Lost His Head	Bill Peet	Dragons	
How Many Days to America? A Thanksgiving Story	Eve Bunting		
How Much Is a Million?	David M. Schwartz	Math	
How Teddy Bears Are Made	Ann Morris		
How the Grinch Stole Christmas	Dr. Seuss		

Book Title	Author(s)	Theme(s)	Time of Year
How the Guinea Fowl Got Her Spots	Barbara Knutson	Friendship/African Tale	
How the Ostrich Got Its Long Neck	Verna Aardema		
How the Sun Was Brought Back to the Sky	Mirra Ginsburg	Sun	
Huge Harold	Bill Peet	Easter/Rabbits	
The Hungry Thing	Jan Slepian & Ann Seidler	Food	
Hurry Up, Franklin	Paulette Bourgeois	Birthdays/Turtles	
I Have a Pet!	Shari Halpern		
I Know a Lady	Charlotte Zolotow	Friends/Values of Kindness & Empathy	
I Like Me	Nancy Carlson		
I Like the Library	Anne Rockwell	Library	
I Love Animals	Flora McDonnell		
I See Animals Hiding	Jim Aronsky		
I Spy Two Eyes: Numbers in Art	Lucy Micklethwait		
I Want to Be	Thylias Moss		
I Want to Be an Astronaut	Byron Barton		
I Was So Mad!	Norma Simon		
I Wish I Were a Butterfly	James Howe		
I'll Always Love You	Hans Wilhelm		
I'm in Charge of Celebrations	Byrd Baylor		
I'm Not Sleepy	Denys Cazet		
The Icky Bug Alphabet Book	Jerry Pallotta	Insects/ABCs	
If Anything Ever Goes Wrong at the Zoo	Mary Jean Hendrick		
If I Ran the Circus	Dr. Seuss	Circus	
If I Were a Penguin	Heidi Goennel	Totally Terrific Me	
If I Were in Charge of the World and Other Worries	Judith Viorst		
If the Dinosaurs Came Back	Bernard Most	Dinosaurs	
If You Give a Moose a Muffin	Laura Joffe Numeroff		
If You Give a Mouse a Cookie	Laura Numeroff; illus. Felicia Bond	Mice/Values of Kindness & Patience	
If You Give a Pig a Pancake	Laura Numeroff	Pigs/Pancakes	
Iktomi and the Boulder	Paul Goble		
I'm a Little Teapot	Iza Trapani	Around the World/ Incredible Journey	
The Important Book	Margaret Wise Brown	Totally Terrific Me	
In a Scary Old House	Harriet Ziefert	Halloween	
In the Night Kitchen	Maurice Sendak	Bakers	
In the Rain With Baby Duck	Amy Hest	Rainy Days	

Book Title	Author(s)	Theme(s)	Time of Year
In the Tall, Tall Grass	Denise Fleming		
Inch by Inch	Leo Lionni	Insects/Value of Respect	
Insects in the Garden	Dorothy M. Souza		
Inside a Barn in the Country	Alyssa Satin Capucilli	All About the Farm	
Ira Sleeps Over	Bernard Waber	Teddy Bears/Values of Friendship, Courage, Honesty, & Self-Respect	
Is It Larger? Is It Smaller?	Tana Hoban		
Is It Red? Is It Yellow? Is It Blue?	Tana Hoban		
The Island of the Skog	Steven Kellogg	Mice/Imaginary Creatures/Value of Communication	
It Could Always Be Worse	Margot Zemach	Feelings	
It Goes Eeeeeee!	Jamie Gilson		
It's Halloween	Jack Prelutsky		
It's Thanksgiving	Jack Prelutsky		
It's Pumpkin Time!	Zoe Hall	Halloween	
It's Raining, It's Pouring	Kin Eagle	Rainy Days	
Itsy Bitsy Spider	Iza Trapani	Spiders	
The Jack Tales	Richard Chase		
The Jacket I Wear in the Snow	Shirley Neitzel		
Jamaica's Find	Juanita Havill		
Jamie O'Rourke and the Big Potato	Tomie dePaola		
Jasmine	Roger Duvoisin	Farm Animals/Hats	
Jelly Beans for Sale	Bruce McMillan		
Jemima Puddle-Duck	Beatrix Potter	Water Animals	
Jennie's Hat	Ezra Jack Keats		
Jesse Bear, What Will You Wear?	Nancy White Carlstrom	Clothing	
Jimmy, the Pickpocket of the Palace	Donna Jo Napoli		
John Henry: An American Legend	Ezra Jack Keats		
Johnny Appleseed	Steven Kellogg	Apples	
The Jolly Postman or Other People's Letters	Janet and Allan Ahlberg		
Joseph's Other Red Sock	Niki Daly		
Jump!: The New Jump Rope Book	Susan Kalbfleisch		
Jump, Frog, Jump!	Robert Kalan	Water Animals/Frogs	
June 29, 1999	David Wiesner		
The Jungle	Carroll Norden		
Just a Dream	Chris Van Allsburg		
Just for You	Mercer Mayer	School Begins/Value of Helpfulness/Caring	

Book Title	Author(s)	Theme(s)	Time of Year
Just Go to Bed	Mercer Mayer	Feelings	
Just Me and My Little Sister	Mercer Mayer	Family & Friends	
Katy No-Pocket	Emmy Payne	Mother's Day	
Keep Looking	Millicent Selsam and Joyce Hunt		
The Keepers of the Earth	Michael J. Caduto and Joseph Bruchac		
Kitten Can…	Bruce McMillan	Pets	
Kittens Are Like That	Jan Pfloog	Pets	
Knights of the Kitchen Table	Jon Scieszka		
Knots on a Counting Rope	Bill Martin, Jr.	American Indians/ Values of Compassion & Courage	
Koala Lou	Mem Fox		
The Lady and the Spider	Faith McNulty		
The Lady With the Alligator Purse	Nadine Bernard Westcott	Water Animals	
Ladybug, Ladybug	Ruth Brown	Insects	
The Last Pupp	Frank Asch	Pets	
The Last Tales of Uncle Remus	Julius Lester		
Latkes and Applesauce: A Hanukkah Story	Fran Manushkin		
The Legend of Earth, Air, Fire, and Water	Eric and Tessa Hadley		
The Legend of the Blue Bonnet	Tomie dePaola		
The Legend of the Poinsettia	Tomie dePaola		
Lentil	Robert McCloskey	Music	
Let's Go to the Library	Lisl Weil		
Let's Make Rabbits	Leo Lionni	Easter/Rabbits	
Liar, Liar, Pants on Fire!	Miriam Cohen		
The Library	Sarah Stewart		
The Life and Times of the Honeybee	Charles Micucci		
Linnea in Monet's Garden	Christina Bjork and Lena Anderson		
The Lion and the Mouse	Gail Herman	Lions and Lambs/Mice	
Lion Dancer: Ernie Wan's Chinese New Year	Kate Waters		
The Listening Walk	Paul Showers	Five Senses	
Little Bear's Christmas	Janice Christmas		
Little Beaver and the Echo	Amy MacDonald		
Little Cloud	Eric Carle		
The Little Drummer Boy	Ezra Jack Keats		
Little Grunt and the Big Egg	Tomie dePaola	Dinosaurs	

Book Title	Author(s)	Theme(s)	Time of Year
The Little Match Girl	Hans Christian Andersen		
The Little Mouse, The Red Ripe Strawberry, and the Big Hungry Bear	Don and Audrey Wood	Mice/Food/Values of Sharing & Generosity	
Little Mouse's Big Valentine	Thacher Hurd	Valentine's Day	
Little One Inch and Other Japanese Children's Favorite Stories	Florence Sadake		
Little Penguin's Tale	Audrey Wood	Arctic Animals	
Little Polar Bear	Hans de Beer		
Little Rabbit's Loose Tooth	Lucy Bates	Rabbits	
The Little Red Hen	Paul Galdone	All About the Farm	
Lon Po Po	Ed Young		
London Bridge Is Falling Down	Peter Spier		
The Lorax	Dr. Seuss		
Lost	Paul Brett Johnson		
Lost at the White House: A 1909 Easter Story	Lisa Griest		
The Lotus Seed	Sherry Garland		
Loudmouth George and the Big Race	Nancy Carlson	Value of Self-Discipline	
Louise's Search	Ezra Jack Keats		
Lovable Lyle	Bernard Waber	Water Animals	
Love You Forever	Robert Munsch		
Loving	Ann Morris	Friends Around the World	
Lunch	Denise Fleming	Mice/Food	
Madeline	Ludwig Bemelmans	Friends Around the World	
The Maestro Plays	Bill Martin, Jr.	Musical Sounds	
The Magic Dreidels	Eric A. Kimmel		
The Magic Fish	Freya Littledale		
The Magic School Bus series	Joanna Cole		
The Magic String	Francene Sabin	Totally Terrific Me	
Mama Went Walking	Christine Berry		
Mama Zooms	Jane Cowen-Fltecher		
Mama, Do You Love Me?	Barbara M. Joosse		
Maps: Getting From Here to There	Harvey Weiss		
Market Day	Eve Bunting		
Martin Luther King Day	Linda Lowery		
Marvin the Mouse—Opposites Book	Jane Harvey	Opposites/Mice	
Mary Had a Little Lamb	Colin & Moira Maclean	Lions & Lambs	
Mary Wore Her Red Dress & Henry Wore His Green Sneakers	Merle Peek	Clothing/Colors/Birthdays	

Book Title	Author(s)	Theme(s)	Time of Year
Math Curse	Jon Scieszka		
Max	Rachel Isadora		
Max Found Two Sticks	Brian Pinkney		
Mean Soup	Betsy Everitt		
Merry Christmas, Strega Nona	Tomie dePaola		
Mice Twice	Joseph Low		
Mighty Tree	Dick Gackenbach		
Mike Fink: A Tall Tale	Steven Kellogg		
Mike Mulligan and His Steam Shovel	Virginia Burton	Value of Perseverance	
The Milk Makers	Gail Gibbons		
Milton the Early Riser	Robert Kraus	Friends Around the World	
Ming Lo Moves the Mountain	Arnold Lobel		
Mirandy and Brother Wind	Patricia M. McKissack		
Mirette on the Highwire	Emily Arnold McCully		
Miss Bindergarten Gets Ready for Kindergarten	Joseph Slate	School Begins	
Miss Mary Mack	Mary Ann Hoberman	Elephants	
Miss Nelson Is Back	Harry Allard	School Begins	
Miss Rumphius	Barbara Cooney	Flowers/Value of Respect	
Miss Spider's Tea Party	David Kirk		
Mister Momboo's Hat	Ralph Leemis		
The Mitten	Jan Brett	Mittens	
The Mixed-Up Chameleon	Eric Carle		
Mojave	Diane Siebert		
Molly's Pilgrim	Barbara Cohen		
Monarch Butterfly	Gail Gibbons	Butterflies	
The Monkey and the Crocodile	Paul Galdone		
Moon Lake	Ivan Gantschev		
Moon Rope	Lois Ehlert		
Moongame	Frank Asch		
More Than Anything Else	Marie Bradby		
The Most Wonderful Egg in the World	Helme Heine	Eggs	
The Mother's Day Mice	Eve Bunting	Mother's Day/Values of Kindness & Courage	
Mouse Paint	Ellen Stoll Walsh		
Mouse Soup	Arnold Lobel		
Mr. Gumpy's Outing	John Burningham	Safety/Transportation	
Mr. Rabbit and the Lovely Present	Charlotte Zolotow	Mother's Day/Birthday	
Mrs. Merriwether's Musical Cat	Carol Purdy		
Mud Puddle	Robert N. Munsch		

Book Title	Author(s)	Theme(s)	Time of Year
Mufaro's Beautiful Daughters An African Tale	John Steptoe		
Mushroom in the Rain	Mirra Ginsburg	Rainy Days/Plants/ Safety	
My Barber	Anne & Harlow Rockwell	Occupations	
My Brother, Ant	Betsy Cromer Byars		
My Father's Hand	Joanne Ryder		
My First Book of Time	Claire Llewellyn		
My First Kwanzaa Book	Deborah M. Newton	Chocolate	
My Five Senses	Aliki	Five Senses	
My Friend John	Charlotte Zolotow	Friendship	
My Friends	Taro Gomi	Family & Friends/Value of Friends	
My Hands Can	Jean Holzenthaler	My Body	
My House/Mi Casa	Rebecca Emberley		
My Mama Had a Dancing Heart	Libba Moore Gray		
My Mama Says There Aren't Any Zombies, Ghosts, Vampires, Creatures, Demons, Monsters, Fiends, Goblins, or Things	Judith Viorst	Feelings/Family	
My Spring Robin	Anne Rockwell	Spring	
My Teacher Sleeps in School	Leatie Weiss	Elephants/School	
My Very First Mother Goose	Iona Opie	Mother Goose	
The Mysterious Rays of Dr. Rontgen	Beverly Gherman		
The Mysterious Tadpole	Steven Kellogg	Pets	
Nana Upstairs & Nana Downstairs	Tomie dePaola		
The Napping House Wakes Up	Audrey Wood	Night & Day	
Nate the Great and the Boring Beach Bag	Marjorie Weinman Sharmat		
Nature's Green Umbrella: Tropical Rain Forest	Gail Gibbons		
Never Spit on Your Shoes	Deny Cazet	School Begins	
Night Creatures	Susan Santoro Whayne		
Night in the Country	Cynthia Rylant	Night & Day	
Night of the Gargoyles	Eve Bunting		
Night, Circus	Mark Corcoran	Night & Day	
Nine Days to Christmas: A Story of Mexico	Marie Hall Ets & Aurora Labastida		
No Jumping on the Bed	Tedd Arnold		
No Moon, No Milk	Chris Babcock		
No Nap	Eve Bunting	Families	
Noah's Ark	Peter Spier	Animals	
Nora's Surprise	Satomi Ichikawa		

Book Title	Author(s)	Theme(s)	Time of Year
Norma Jean, Jumping Bean	Joanna Cole	Zoo/Safari	
Norman the Doorman	Don Freeman	Mice/Snowy Days	
The Not-So-Jolly Roger	Jon Scieszka		
Now I Know Birds	Susan Kuchalla	Birds	
Now One Foot, Now the Other	Tomie dePaola		
The Ocean Alphabet Book	Jerry Pallotta	Water Animals/ABCs	
Of Colors and Things	Tana Hoban	Colors	
Officer Buckle and Gloria	Peggy Rathmann	Safety	
Old Bear	Jane Hissey	Friendship/Teddy Bears	
Old Black Fly	Jim Aylesworth	Insects/ABCs	
Old MacDonald Had a Farm	Carol Jones	All About the Farm	
The Old Woman and Her Pig	Paul Galdone	All About the Farm	
Oliver Pig at School	Jean Van Leeuwen		
On Market Street	Arnold Lobel	Occupations/Friends/ World/ABCs	
On Monday When It Rained	Cherr Kachenmeister		
On Mother's Lap	Ann Herbert Scott		
On the Day You Were Born	Debra Frasier	Totally Terrific Me	
On the Go	Ann Morris		
Once a Mouse	Marcia Brown		
One Bear in the Hospital	Caroline Bucknall		
One Fish, Two Fish, Red Fish, Blue Fish	Dr. Seuss	Water/Animals	
One Hundred Hungry Ants	Elinor J. Pinczes	Insects	
One Hungry Monster	Susan Heyboer O'Keefe		
One Is Good, But Two Are Better	Louis Slobodkin	Family & Friends	
One Small Candle	Thomas J. Fleming		
One Sun: A Book of Terse Verse	Bruce McMillan		
One Tough Turkey: A Thanksgiving Story	Steven Kroll		
Ooops!	Suzy Kline		
Opposites	John Burningham	Opposites	
Opposites	Rosalinda Kightley	Opposites	
The Orchard Book of Nursery Rhymes	Zena Sutherland		
Out and About	Shirley Hughes		
Outside and Inside Birds	Sandra Markle		
Over and Over	Charlotte Zolotow	Birthdays/Holidays	
Over in the Meadow	Olive A. Wadsworth	All About the Farm	
Over the River and Through the Woods	Brinton Turkle, illus.	Thanksgiving/ American Indians	
Owl Moon	Jane Yolen		
The Ox-Cart Man	Donald Hall	Fall Harvest	

Book Title	Author(s)	Theme(s)	Time of Year
Pancakes, Crackers, and Pizza: A Book of Shapes	Marjorie Eberts & Margaret Gisler		
Pancakes, Pancakes	Eric Carle		
Panda	Caroline Arnold		
Papa, Please Get the Moon for Me	Eric Carle		
Parade	Donald Crews	Music	
The Patchwork Quilt	Valerie Flournoy		
Paul Bunyan	Steven Kellogg		
Peace at Last	Jill Murphy		
Peanut Butter and Jelly	Nadine Bernard Westcott	Foods	
Pelle's New Suit	Elsa Beskow	Lions & Lambs	
Perfect Father's Day	Eve Bunting	Father's Day	
Perfect Pigs: An Introduction to Manners	Marc Brown		
Perfect the Pig	Susan Jesch		
The Perky Little Pumpkin	Margaret Friskey	Halloween	
Pet Show	Ezra Jack Keats	Pets	
Peter's Chair	Ezra Jack Keats		
Petunia	Roger Duvoisin	Safety/Values of Humility & Honesty	
Picnic	Emily Arnold McCully	Family/Picnics/Mice	
Pig Pig Gets a Job	David McPhail	Pigs/Occupations	
Piggies	Audrey Wood		
Pigs	Peter Brady		
Pigs Ahoy!	David McPhail		
Pigs Aplenty, Pigs Galore!	David McPhail		
Pigsty	Mark Teague		
Pink and Say	Patricia Polacco		
Pinkerton, Behave!	Steven Kellogg	Pets	
Pirates	Brenda Thompson & Rosemary Giesen	Pirates	
Planes	Anne Rockwell	Transportation	
The Planets	Gail Gibbons		
Planting a Rainbow	Lois Ehlert	Plants	
Play Ball, Amelia Bedelia	Peggy Parish		
Play Rhymes	Marc Brown		
Play With Me	Marie Hall Ets	Insects	
The Pledge of Allegiance	Francis Bellamy	Back to School	
The Poky Little Puppy	Janette Lowrey	Pets	
Polar Bear, Polar Bear, What Do You Hear?	Bill Martin, Jr.		
The Polar Express	Chris Van Allsburg	Christmas	

Book Title	Author(s)	Theme(s)	Time of Year
The Post Office Book: Mail and How it Moves	Gail Gibbons		
Pretend You're a Cat	Jean Marzollo	Animal Movements	
The Puffins Are Back!	Gail Gibbons		
Puffins Climb, Penguins Rhyme	Bruce McMillan		
Pumpkin Pumpkin	Jeanne Titherington	Pumpkins	
The Puppy Who Wanted a Boy	Jane Thayer	Christmas/Pets	
The Purse	Kathy Caple		
Puss in Boots	Charles Perrault		
Quacky Duck	Paul and Emma Rogers		
The Quarreling Book	Charlotte Zolotow	Feelings/Values of Peacemaking, Kindness, Empathy, & Respect	
Quick as a Cricket	Audrey Wood	Feelings	
The Quilt	Ann Jonas		
The Quilt Story	Tony Johnston	Family & Friends	
Raccoons and Ripe Corn	Jim Aronsky		
Rachel Carson	William Accorsi		
Rachel Fister's Blister	Amy MacDonald		
The Rag Coat	Lauren A. Mills		
Rain Forest	Helen Cowcher		
Rain Makes Applesauce	Julian Scheer	Apples/Rainy Days	
The Rainbow Bridge	Audrey Wood		
The Rainbow Fish	Marcus Pfister	Sea Animals	
Rainbow Fish and the Big Blue Whale	Marcus Pfister	The Ocean/Value of Communication	
Rainbow Fish to the Rescue!	Marcus Pfister	Friendship/Values of Kindness & Acceptance of Others	
Rapunzel	Brothers Grimm		
The Rattlebang Picnic	Margaret Mahy		
Raven: A Trickster Tale From the Pacific North	Gerald McDermott		
Red Is Best	Kathy Stinson	Colors	
Red Light, Green Light	Golden MacDonald	Safety	
Regards to the Man in the Moon	Ezra Jack Keats	Imagination/Space	
Regina's Big Mistake	Marissa Moss		
The Relatives Came	Cynthia Rylant		
Richard Scarry's Chipmunk's ABC	Roberta Miller	Springtime/ABCs	
The Right Number of Elephants illus. Felicia Bond	Jeff Sheppard;	Elephants	
River Day	Jane B. Mason		
Roll-Over: A Counting Song	Merle Peek		

Book Title	Author(s)	Theme(s)	Time of Year
Rosie's Walk	Pat Hutchins	All About the Farm	
Roxaboxen	Alice McLerran	Rocks	
The Runaway Bunny	Margaret Wise Brown	Easter/Rabbits/Value of Love	
The Runaway Chick	Robin Ravilious		
Sadako	Eleanor Coerr		
The Salamander Room	Anne Mazer		
Sam and the Tigers	Julius Lester		
Sam Who Never Forgets	Eve Rice	Zoo/Safari	
Sam's Sandwich	David Pelham	Insects/Food	
Say It!	Charlotte Zolotow		
Scary, Scary Halloween	Eve Bunting	Halloween	
School	Emily Arnold McCully	School Begins	
School Bus	Donald Crews		
Seashore Story	Taro Yashima	Friends Around the World	
The Seasons of Arnold's Apple Tree	Gail Gibbons	Weather/Seasons/Fall	
Secret Valentine	Laura Damon	Valentine's Day	
Seven Blind Mice	Ed Young	Mice/Colors	
Shapes	Guy Smalley	Sizes & Shapes	
Shapes, Shapes, Shapes	Tana Hoban		
Sheep in a Shop	Nancy Shaw	Lions & Lambs	
Sheep on a Ship	Nancy Shaw	Lions & Lambs	
The Sheepish Book of Opposites	George Mendoza	Opposites	
The Shoemaker and the Elves	Adrienne Adams, illus.	Clothing	
Shoes	Elizabeth Winthrop	Clothing	
Shy Charles	Rosemary Wells		
The Sign Book	William Dugan	Safety	
Silly Tilly's Thanksgiving Dinner	Lillian Hoban	Thanksgiving/Food	
Sing a Song of Popcorn: Every Child's Book of Poems	Beatrice Shenk de Regniers		
Six Foolish Fishermen	Benjamin Elkin	Friends Around World/Occupations	
The Skeleton Inside You	Philip Balestrino	My Body	
Sleepy Bear	Lydia Dabcovich	Hibernation/Seasons	
Sleepy Book	Charlotte Zolotow	Night & Day	
Sleepy Heads	Aileen Fisher	Night & Day	
Small Green Snake	Libba Moore Gray		
Small Pig	Arnold Lobel	Pigs/Mud & Dirt	
The Smallest Cow in the World	Katherine Paterson		
Smokey	Bill Peet	Transportation	
Snakes	Seymour Simon		
Snap!	Marcia Vaughan		
Snowballs	Lois Ehlert		

Book Title	Author(s)	Theme(s)	Time of Year
The Snowman	Raymond Briggs	Snow	
The Snowy Day	Ezra Jack Keats	Winter Days/Snow	
Some Things Go Together	Charlotte Zolotow	Valentine's Day	
Something Big Has Been Here	Jack Prelutsky		
Something Special for Me	Vera B. Williams	Music/Birthday/ Money	
Somewhere in the World Right Now	Stacy Schuett		
Song and Dance Man	Karen Ackerman	Grandparents/Values of Kindness, Loyalty, Diversity, & Empathy	
Soup Should Be Seen, Not Heard	Beth Brainard and Sheila Behr		
Space Case	Edward Marshall	Space/Halloween	
Spider on the Floor	Raffi		
Splish, Splash!	Joan Bransfield Graham	Water	
Spots, Feathers, and Curly Tails	Nancy Tafuri	All About the Farm	
Squirrel Nutkin	Beatrix Potter	Fall	
St. Patrick's Day in the Morning	Eve Bunting	St. Patrick's Day	
Stand Back, Said the Elephant, I'm Going to Sneeze!	Patricia Thomas	Zoo Safari	
Stanely	Syd Hoff		
The Star Spangled Banner	Peter Spier		
Stellaluna	Jannell Cannon		
Stevie	John Steptoe		
The Stinky Cheese Man and Other Fairly Stupid Tales	Jon Scieszka		
Stone Soup	Marcia Brown		
The Storm Book	Charlotte Zolotow	Rainy Days	
Storm in the Night	Mary Stoltz		
Storms	Seymour Simon		
The Story of Ruby Bridges	Robert Coles		
The Story of the Pilgrims	Katharine Ross		
The Stranger	Chris Van Allsburg		
Stringbean's Trip to the Shining Sea	Vera B. & Jennifer Williams		
Suddenly!	Colin McNaughton	Pigs/Creepy Crawlers	
The Supermarket	Anne & Harlow Rockwell	Food/Community Helpers	
Sukey and the Mermaid	Robert D. San Souci		
The Summer Snowman	Gene Zion	Winter Days/Snow	
The Sun's Asleep Behind the Hill	Mirra Ginsburg		
Sunshine	Jan Ormerod		
Sunshine Makes the Seasons	Franklyn Mansfield Branley		

Book Title	Author(s)	Theme(s)	Time of Year
Swamp Angel	Anne Isaacs		
The Swapping Boy	John Langstaff	Friends Around the World	
Swimmy	Leo Lionni	Water Animals/ Value of Cooperation	
Sylvester the Mouse With the Musical Ear	Adelaide Holl	Music	
Tacky the Penguin	Helen Lester	Friendship/ Penguins	
Tail Twisters	Aileen Fisher	Rabbits	
The Tale of Benjamin Bunny With Peter Rabbit	Beatrix Potter	Springtime/Rabbits	
The Tale of Peter Rabbit	Beatrix Potter	Springtime/Rabbits	
The Tale of Two Bad Mice	Beatrix Potter	Mice	
Tales of Oliver Pig	Jean Van Leeuwen	Pigs	
The Talking Eggs	Robert D. San Souci		
The Teddy Bears' Picnic	Jimmy Kennedy		
The Teeny Tiny Woman	Jane O'Connor	Halloween	
Ten Apples Up on Top!	Theo LeSieg		
Ten Black Dots	Donald Crews		
Ten Little Ladybugs	Melanie Gerth	Insects	
Ten, Nine, Eight	Molly Bang		
Thanksgiving Day	Gail Gibbons		
That's What a Friend Is	P. K. Hallinan	Family & Friends	
There's No Such Thing as a Dragon	Jack Kent		
There's a Nightmare in My Closet	Mercer Mayer	Night & Day	
Thidwich, the Big-Hearted Moose	Dr. Seuss		
The Third Planet: Exploring the Earth From Space	Sally Ride		
This Is the Bear and the Scary Night	Sarah Hayes		
This Is the Farmer	Nancy Tafuri		
This Is the Way We Go to School	Edith Baer		
This Old Man	Robin Michal Koontz		
This Year's Garden	Cynthia Rylant	Seasons/Gardens	
Three Ducks Went Wandering	Ron Roy	Easter/Mother's Day	
The Three Bears	Paul Galdone	Bears	
Three by the Sea	Edward Marshall		
Three Cheers for Tacky	Helen Lester	Penguins	
Three Little Indians	Gene S. Stuart	Thanksgiving/ American Indians	
The Three Little Pigs	James Marshall	Fairy Tales	
The Three Little Wolves and the Big Bad Pig	Eugene Trivizas	Contemporary Fairy Tale	
Through Grandpa's Eyes	Patricia MacLachian		

Book Title	Author(s)	Theme(s)	Time of Year
Through Moon and Stars and Night Skies	Ann Warren Turner		
Thumbelina	Hans Christian Andersen		
Tico and the Golden Wings	Leo Lionni	Birds	
Tidy Titch	Pat Hutchins	Clean Rooms	
Tigress	Helen Cowcher		
Tilabel	Patricia Coombs		
Tim O'Toole and the Wee Folk	Gerald McDermott		
Time Flies	Eric Rohmann	Dinosaurs	
Time for Bed	Mem Fox		
Timothy Goes to School	Rosemary Wells		
The Tiny Seed	Eric Carle		
Titch	Pat Hutchins	Totally Terrific Me	
To Space and Back	Sally Ride and Susan Okie		
To Think I Saw it on Mulberry Street	Dr. Seuss		
Toad for Tuesday	Russell E. Erickson	Animals/Fantasy	
Today Is Monday	Eric Carle		
Tomie dePaola's Mother Goose	Tomie dePaola		
The Tomten	Astrid Lindgren	Winter Days/Snow	
Tops and Bottoms	Janet Stevens		
The Tortilla Factory	Gary Paulsen		
The Tortoise and the Hare	Janet Stevens		
The Town Mouse and the Country Mouse	Lorinda Bryan Cauley		
Train Song	Diane Siebert	Transportation	
Trains	Anne F. Rockwell		
The Trek	Ann Jonas	Zoo/Safari	
The Trip	Ezra Jack Keats		
The True Story of the Three Little Pigs	Jon Scieszka		
The Tub People	Pam Conrad		
Tyrannosaurus Was a Beast	Jack Prelutsky		
Umbrella	Taro Yashima	Clothing	
Under the Moon	Dyan Sheldon		
Uno, Dos, Tres: One, Two, Three	Pat Mora		
Valentine's Day	Gail Gibbons		
The Vanishing Pumpkin	Tony Johnston	Halloween	
The Very Busy Spider	Eric Carle	Five Senses	
The Very Hungry Caterpillar	Eric Carle	Insects/Food	
The Very Lonely Firefly	Eric Carle		
The Very Quiet Cricket	Eric Carle	Five Senses/Insects	
Village of Round and Square Houses	Ann Grifalconi		
The Village Tree	Taro Yashima	Japan	

Book Title	Author(s)	Theme(s)	Time of Year
Wake Up, Little Children: A Rise-and-Shine Rhyme	Jim Aylesworth		
Walter the Baker	Eric Carle		
We Are Best Friends	Aliki		
The Wednesday Surprise	Eve Bunting		
Weird Parents	Audrey Wood	Family	
The Whales' Song	Dyan Sheldon	Water Animals/Whales	
What About Ladybugs	Celia Godkin		
What Does Word Bird See?	Jane Belk Moncure	Animal Homes	
What Happened to Patrick's Dinosaurs?	Carol Carrick	Dinosaurs	
What Makes a Bird a Bird?	Mary Garelick		
What Sank the Boat?	Pamela Allen		
What Would You Do if You Lived at the Zoo?	Nancy White Carlstrom		
The Wheels on the Bus	Paul Zelinsky	Transportation	
When Autumn Comes	Robert Maass	Fall Harvest	
When I Am Old With You	Angela Johnson		
When I Was Five	Arthur Howard	Identity/Friendship	
When the Wind Stops	Charlotte Zolotow		
Where Do They Go? Insects in Winter	Millicent E. Selsam	Insects	
Where Does the Sun Go at Night?	Mirra Ginsburg	Sun	
Where Is Spot	Eric Hill		
Where the Bald Eagles Gather	Dorothy Hinshaw Patent		
Where the Sidewalk Ends	Shel Silverstein		
Where the Wild Things Are	Maurice Sendak	Feelings/Unconditional Love	
Where's My Teddy?	Jez Alborough	Sizes & Shapes	
Whistle for Willie	Ezra Jack Keats	Pets/Air	
White Snow, Bright Snow	Alvin Tresselt	Winter Days/Snow	
Who Said Red?	Mary Serfozo	Colors	
Who Says That?	Arnold L. Shapiro		
Who Uses This?	Margaret Miller	Occupations/ Construction/Tools	
Who Will Be My Friends?	Syd Hoff		
Who's in Rabbit's House? A Masai Tale	Verna Aardema		
Whose Mouse Are You?	Robert Kraus	Family & Friends/Mice	
Whose Shoe?	Margaret Miller	Shoe Week	
Why the Chicken Crossed the Road	David Macaulay	Birds	
Why the Sun and the Moon Live in the Sky	Elphinstone Dayrell	Friends Around the World/Space	

Book Title	Author(s)	Theme(s)	Time of Year
Will I Have a Friend?	Miriam Cohen	School Begins/ Family & Friends	
William the Backwards Skunk	Chuck Jones		
The Wild Christmas Reindeer	Jan Brett		
The Wind Blew	Pat Hutchins	Wind	
Window	Jeannie Baker		
The Wump World	Bill Peet		
Wynken, Blynken, and Nod	Eugene Field		
Yankee Doodle	Edward Bangs		
The Year at Maple Hill Farm	Alice & Martin Provensen	All About the Farm	
Young Martin Luther King, Jr.	Joanne Mattern		
Your Mother Was a Neanderthal	Jon Scieszka		
Your Skin and Mine	Paul Showers	My Body	
The Yucky Reptile Alphabet Book	Jerry Pallotta	Animals/ABCs	
Yummers!	James Marshall	Pigs/Food	
Zin! Zin! Zin! A Violin	Lloyd Moss	Music	
Zinnia and Dot	Lisa Ernst Campbell		
Zomo the Rabbit: A Trickster Tale From the West	Gerald McDermott		
The Zoo Book	Jan Pfloog	Zoo/Safari	
Zoo Dreams	Cor Hazelaar	Night	

 Jackie Wright, Enid, OK

Blindfold

Materials

Black cotton fabric • ¾"-wide black elastic • black thread • sewing machine or needle

What to do

1. Make your own blindfold out of black fabric. Sew black elastic on the back to make it easy for the children to put on by themselves.
2. Encourage the children to wear the blindfold when playing favorite games that require a child to keep his eyes closed.
3. The blindfold may be used for other tactile activities.

 Jackie Wright, Enid, OK

Make Your Own Bubbles

Materials

Distilled water • liquid soap (Ivory, Joy, or Sunlight) • glycerin, optional • sugar

What to do

1. Make your own bubbles using one of the following methods:
   - ☆ Mix ½ cup water and ½ cup liquid soap (make as much as needed using equal amounts of both).
   - ☆ Mix together ⅓ cup liquid soap, ⅓ cup glycerin (a small amount of glycerin makes stronger bubbles, but is not necessary), ⅓ cup distilled water, and 1 cup sugar per quart of solution.

   Tip: Use distilled water because hard water does not work well.
2. Keep the bubble mixture at room temperature.
3. Bubbles can be used for pure enjoyment indoors and out. They can be used for a science, art, or math project.

   Tip: If using bubbles indoors, cover the floor because it can become very slippery from the bubble mixture.

 Sandy L. Scott, Vancouver, WA

Stress Jars

Materials

Labels • marker • clean, empty, plastic peanut butter jars, one for each child • clay

What to do

1. Write each child's name on a label and attach it to his peanut butter jar.
2. Place a chunk of clay into each child's jar and replace the lid.
3. Give each child a jar to keep in his cubby or desk.
4. Explain that whenever you feel they might need a little stress relief or escape from routine, they can take out their "stress jars" and pound on their clay.

 Lisa Chichester, Parkersburg, WV

Science Jars

Materials

Plastic soda or juice bottles • small objects such as beads, glitter, letters, small animals, and marbles • food coloring • hot glue gun (adult only) • tape

What to do

1. Fill bottles with water, and add small objects according to the theme. Seal with hot glue (adult only) and tape.
2. You can make a variety of theme bottles. For example, make a sea theme by adding blue food coloring, small plastic fish, and seashells; a color theme by adding the same color objects; or an alphabet theme by adding a plastic letter and other items that begin with the letter.
3. Another idea is to fill the bottles with thick liquids such as shampoo, add marbles, and watch them slowly sink.

 Audrey F. Kanoff, Allentown, PA

Treasure Box

Materials

Empty baby wipe boxes, one for each child • permanent marker • stickers

What to do

1. At the end of the school year (or when a child moves up), give each child an empty baby wipe box to decorate. Using a permanent marker, write on the box "My (or child's name) Treasure Box."
2. At group time, tell the children they are going on a treasure hunt. Explain that anywhere in the room they see their own name tag (name-writing cards, birthday signs, cubby tags, photos, and so on), they should pick it up and put it in their box.
3. Ask them to collect other small belongings, such as toothbrushes. Tell them these are their treasures, and they are now theirs to take home.

Author Note: The first time I did this with my class, they had a ball. It took them about 20 minutes to look all around. They helped each other, and as an unanticipated bonus, they took out their names and counted them, lined them up, sorted them by type, and compared them with others. One little girl even stopped teachers in the hall to show them her treasure as she left for the day.

⭐ Tracie O'Hara, Charlotte, NC

Balloon Fun

Materials

Balloons, one for each child plus extra • hula hoop

What to do

1. Beforehand, blow up all the balloons and place in a container until game time. Place the hula hoop in the center of the room.
2. Ask the children to sit in a circle around the hula hoop.
3. Give each child a balloon. Ask them to hold their balloons still until they start playing the game.
4. On your signal, the children will try to roll the balloons into the hula hoop using their hands. When all the balloons are in the hoop, take them out and play again.
5. Encourage the children to try and roll the balloons into the hoop using other body parts.

 Susan E. May, Madison Heights, VA

Crawl Under Smoke

Materials

Plastic or wooden hula hoops with stands, cardboard blocks set up with a top to crawl under, or commercial play equipment with circle opening

What to do

1. As part of a unit on fire safety, tell the children that if their house is on fire, they should crawl close to the ground to get away from the smoke above.
2. Encourage the children to crawl one by one under the "smoke" (hula hoop, block "tunnel" or play equipment). This could be part of an obstacle course.
3. Use in connection with "Stop, drop, and roll" practice. This could be a life-saving activity.
4. This is great to set up as a demonstration if the fire department visits the class.

 Andrea Clapper, Cobleskill, NY

Butterfly Hunt

Materials

Metal clothes hangers • net fruit bags (usually used for citrus fruit) • glue • tissue paper

What to do

1. Bend a hanger into a circular shape. Make one for each child.
2. Show the children how to glue a net fruit bag to the hanger to make a net.
3. Encourage the children to make butterflies from rectangles of tissue paper by twisting them in the center.
4. The children can throw the butterflies into the air and catch them with the net.

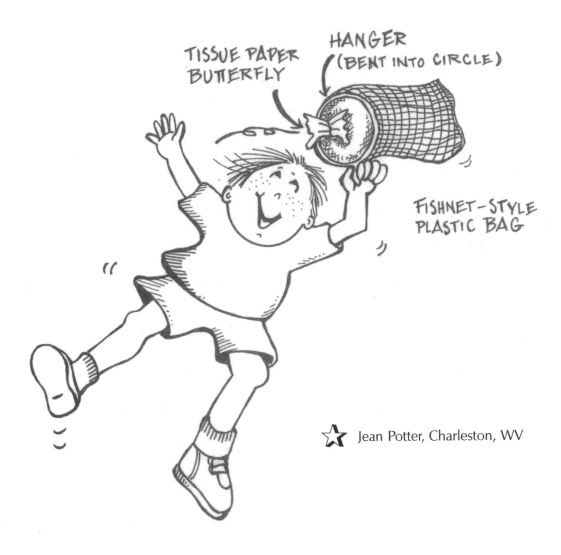

TISSUE PAPER BUTTERFLY

HANGER (BENT INTO CIRCLE)

FISHNET-STYLE PLASTIC BAG

☆ Jean Potter, Charleston, WV

Clothespin Drop

Materials

3 large plastic containers (ice cream containers work well) • masking tape • clothespins • stickers or small pictures related to your theme • ribbon • chair

What to do

1. Tape three containers together using masking tape.
2. Attach stickers and ribbons to clothespins to give them a party look. You may also decorate the containers with ribbons and stickers.
3. Place the containers next to a chair. Ask the children to sit in a circle around the chair.
4. Give each child a clothespin. Explain that they are going to take turns trying to drop their clothespins into the bucket.
5. Sing the following song as each child tries to drop her clothespin in the bucket.

   Drop the clothespin, dear _____(child's name), dear _____, dear _____.
   Drop the clothespin, dear _____.
   Drop the clothespin right now!

 Susan E. May, Madison Heights, VA

Gross Motor Fun With Colors and Shapes

Materials

4 different colors of paper • scissors

What to do

1. Cut out four different shapes (about 4–6") from four different colors of paper (for example, red circle, yellow triangle, blue square, and green rectangle). Cut out enough so that every child playing will have each of the four different colored shapes.

2. Give each child four colored shapes.

3. Ask them to lay the shapes in any order around their body: one in front, one in back, and one on each side. There should be enough room for the child to stand in the middle of all four without touching any shape.

4. Call out a body part, color, and shape. The children then try and put that body part on the colored shape. Sometimes it is a balancing act, and sometimes it is silly but no matter what, the children enjoy the challenge.

5. After they have all tried it, ask them to stand in the middle of their shapes again, not touching any of the shapes.

6. Repeat, using a different body part, shape, and color for the children to try.

7. After doing a couple more, you can go around the circle and ask each child to take a turn to pick some combination of body part, color, and shape for everyone to try.

 Tracey Neumarke, Chicago, IL

Paper Bubble Catch

Materials

Bubble solution (or bubble machine) • construction paper

What to do

1. Go outside with the children and blow bubbles together.

2. Give each child a sheet of construction paper (rough paper pops bubbles better).

3. Encourage the children to catch bubbles on the paper.

 Jean Potter, Charleston, WV

Party Bowl

Materials

Six 2-liter bottles • sand or small pebbles • stickers • paper or metallic party grass • ball or beanbag for each child • masking tape

What to do

1. Fill each bottle with 1 cup of sand or pebbles for stability. Add party grass and decorate the outside with theme-appropriate stickers or picture. Secure lids so the sand and grass do not spill out.
2. Arrange the six bottles in a triangle shape and use masking tape to mark a place on the floor for bowlers to stand.
3. Give each child a ball or beanbag to play with while waiting for her turn.
4. The children take turns bowling by tossing their beanbags at the bottles.
5. Encourage the children to cheer on their classmates and applaud all their efforts.

 Susan E. May, Madison Heights, VA

Pumpkin Patch

Materials

Large box • white paper • tape or glue • markers • cardboard • scissors • orange yarn • tissue paper balls, optional

What to do

1. Cover a large box with white paper, leaving the top open. Draw vines and leaves on the outside of the box. This will be the "pumpkin patch."
2. Make yarn balls using orange rug yarn. Wrap yarn around a 6" piece of cardboard. When it is the desired size, tie in the middle and cut the loops. It will look like a big pompom. Make one "pumpkin" for each child.
3. You could also make "pumpkins" by covering balled-up newspaper with orange tissue paper and tipping the top to look like a stem.
4. Give each child a "pumpkin." Explain that they will take turns trying to throw their pumpkin into the "pumpkin patch."

5. Sing the following song as each child throws her pumpkin.

Throw the pumpkin in, ___(child's name), dear _____, dear _____.
Throw the pumpkin in, _____.
Throw it right in!

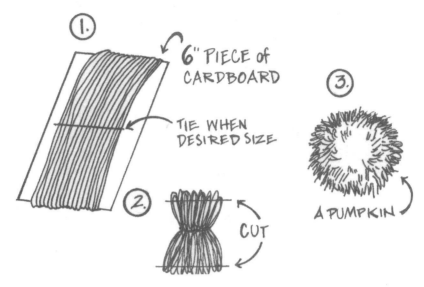

☆ Susan E. May, Madison Heights, VA

Beanbag Toss

Materials

Large poster board • large pictures relating to your theme • glue • laminate, optional • beanbags for every child • masking tape • chart paper

What to do

1. Arrange and attach pictures on the poster board. If you plan on using the game often, you may wish to laminate it or cover with clear adhesive paper. **Tip:** A good source for pictures is a paper products store. These stores frequently have inexpensive paper placemats with assorted pictures.

2. If you don't already have beanbags, make your own. Fill an old sock with beans and cut off the top, leaving enough so that you can close it with a rubber band. Or use 6" x 6" fabric squares. Sew all the way around except for a 2" opening. Fill with beans and sew the opening closed.

(continued on the next page)

3. Place the poster on the floor or attach it to a wall. Mark a spot for throwers to stand.

4. Give each child a beanbag. Explain that they will take turns tossing their beanbags at the different pictures.

5. Each child gets three tries to throw the beanbag. Encourage the children to play with and manipulate their beanbags as they wait for their turn.

6. If desired, use large chart paper to record the number of times each picture was hit or which picture the children tried to hit most. Asking follow-up questions gives closure to the game.

☆ Susan E. May, Madison Heights, VA

Airplane Toss

Materials

Paper airplanes • stickers and markers • hula hoops • masking tape

What to do

1. Make a paper airplane for each child plus a few extra. If desired, let the children decorate them with stickers and markers as a lead-in activity.

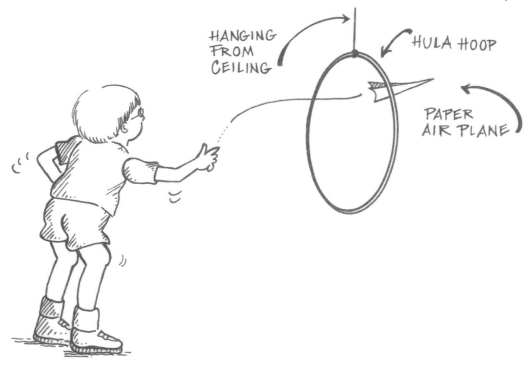

2. Hang a hula hoop from the ceiling or tape the bottom edge to the back of a chair. Mark a spot on the floor for throwers to stand.

3. Let the children take turns tossing their airplanes through the hula hoop. Give each child three tries. Encourage them to count how many times their airplane goes through the hoop.

4. Let the children fly their airplanes outside during free time.

 Susan E. May, Madison Heights, VA

Snowman Toss

Materials

Styrofoam packing peanuts • large, white plastic trash bag • white pillowcase • string • black buttons • needle and thread • marker • brimmed hat • beanbags

What to do

1. Fill a large trash bag with packing peanuts and seal the bag with a twist tie.

2. Place the plastic bag inside a white pillowcase and tie or pin shut.

3. Using twine or string, tie around the pillowcase one third from the top to create a head and lower body.

4. Sew on buttons for eyes and a nose, and draw a mouth.

5. Cover the tied-off top of the pillowcase with a brimmed hat.

6. Give each child a beanbag. Standing 5' away from the snowman, the children take turns tossing their beanbags to try to knock the snowman's hat off.

 Christine Maiorano, Duxbury, MA

Texture Balance Beam

Materials

Two 2" x 4" boards • glue • feathers • variety of soft fabrics (corduroy, fur, burlap)

What to do

1. Cover the 4" sides of the 2" x 4" boards with the feathers and fabric. Use glue to secure the materials.
2. You can also use glue to create a texture by using dime-sized drops of glue and allowing them to dry.
3. Each material should cover at least a 3' section to ensure the children step on each kind.
4. Use the boards as balance beams that the children walk on in their stocking feet.

☆ Ann Kelly, Johnstown, PA

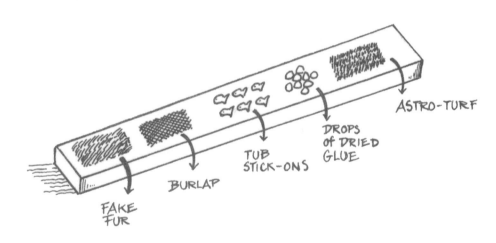

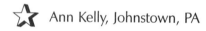

ASTRO-TURF

DROPS of DRIED GLUE

TUB STICK-ONS

BURLAP

FAKE FUR

OTHERS: FLAT MARBLES   DOWELS (GLUE SIDE BY SIDE)

Styrofoam and Saw

Materials

Large blocks or pieces of Styrofoam • toy saw from workbench or tool kit

What to do

1. Let the children use a toy saw to "cut" the Styrofoam. It should go right through very easily.
2. Replace the Styrofoam when the pieces get too small.
3. The Styrofoam may break into very small pieces on the floor. Use this opportunity to teach the children about static electricity. Rub a balloon or a piece of wool very quickly on your head and it should lift those pieces off the floor!

 Nancy A. Johnson, Cottage Grove, MN

Any-Holiday Lacing Cards

Materials

Assorted greeting cards for the targeted holiday, one per child • scissors • hole punch • yarn • white glue • wax paper • masking tape, optional

What to do

1. Cut off the fronts of greeting cards. Punch holes around each card.
2. Cut pieces of yarn about 18" in length.
3. Make "sewing needles" by pouring white glue on wax paper and rolling about 2" of one end of the yarn into the glue. Another way to make needles is to wrap a 2" strip of masking tape around one end of the yarn.
4. Dry by laying flat on another sheet of wax paper. Make sure that the glued end is straight and not kinked or curved.
5. When dry, tie a piece of yarn with a "needle" to each card.
6. Encourage the children to sew the yarn through the holes in the card.

CARD FRONT

PAPER PUNCH

NEEDLE END

July 4th!

 Linda Hodge, Minnetonka, MN

All-Occasion Hats

Materials

Paper bowls and plates • scissors • glue • hole punch • colorful yarn and ribbons • variety of art materials, such as tissue paper in many colors, feathers, sequins, cotton balls, paint, and so on

What to do

1. To make a basic hat, remove and discard the middle from the center of a paper plate. Put the outer rim of the paper plate over the paper bowl. This makes a hat brim. Glue it on, if necessary.
2. Punch holes on each side of the paper plate and attach yarn or ribbon.
3. Let the children decorate their hats according to the holiday or occasion. Any number of things can be used to create these hats.

   For example:

   ☆ Winter Hats: Glue cotton balls and paper snowflakes all around the hat.

   ☆ Valentine's Day: Glue red, pink, silver, and gold hearts all over the hat. Trim doilies and glue around the edges. This looks like lace.

   ☆ St. Patrick's Day: Paint the entire hat with tempera paint or watercolors. Glue shamrocks, leprechauns, and spray-painted gold play coins all over it.

   ☆ Cinco de Mayo Hats: Twist red, green, and white ribbons or yarn together to make a hatband. Glue this around the middle of the hat. Add tiny flags of Mexico (found at party supply stores). Find pictures from magazines of Mexican foods and glue them on the hat. On the rim of the hat, glue red, green, and white pompoms.

   ☆ 4th of July Hats: Paint hats with red and blue paint. Use white ribbon or yarn for the hatband. Stick tiny American flags in the hatband or attach flag stickers.

   ☆ August No-Holiday Month Galaxy Hats: Paint the hats black or dark blue. Glue suns, moons, stars, comets, space ships, and so on to the hat.

   ☆ Autumn Hats: Paint hats yellow, brown, or light green. Glue a variety of leaves (real or made from paper) to the hats. Add nuts, acorns, or small shafts of wheat.

 Penni Smith, Riverside, CA

Albuquerque Turkey and Song

Materials

Brown lunch bags, one for each child • newspaper • string • red and orange construction paper • scissors • stapler • glue • construction paper feathers

What to do

1. Encourage children to stuff their paper lunch bags with newspaper. Then help them tie off the bag 3" from the top and twist the bag into a small "stem."
2. Give each child a piece of red construction paper. Ask them to fold the paper in half, trace a turkey face, and cut out two faces.
3. Ask them to staple a face onto each side of the bag top.
4. Encourage the children to trace and cut out orange feet and glue them on the bottom of the bag.
5. Children then glue on colored tail feathers.

STUFFED WITH NEWSPAPERS

BROWN LUNCH BAG

TIED OFF and TWISTED INTO STEM

FACE ADDED

COLORED TAIL FEATHERS

FEET

Related song

Albuquerque Turkey Song
(Tune: "Oh My Darling Clementine")

Albuquerque is my turkey, he's got feathers like a fan,
And he wobbles and he gobbles and he struts when he can.
He's the best pet that you can get, better than a dog or cat
We won't eat him for Thanksgiving and I'm mighty glad of that!

 Christine Maiorano, Duxbury, MA

Edible Hanukah Menorahs

Materials

Homemade or purchased cupcakes • candles • bread • peanut butter • raisins • celery • marshmallows • chocolate kisses

What to do

1. Make, enjoy, and eat any of the following Hanukah menorahs.

   ☆ Make or purchase cupcakes. Line up eight cupcakes in a row, leaving a space in the middle. Put two cupcakes on top of one another and put them in the middle of the row. This will be the shamash holder. Add candles to each cupcake and light them for Hanukah.

   ☆ Spread peanut butter on bread. Make a menorah by laying pretzel sticks on the peanut butter and adding raisins for flames.

   ☆ Spread peanut butter on a celery stick and put pretzels in it for candles.

   ☆ Make edible dreidels (a spinning top game played during Hanukah). Put a pretzel stick into a marshmallow, and then use peanut butter to stick a chocolate kiss onto the end of the marshmallow.

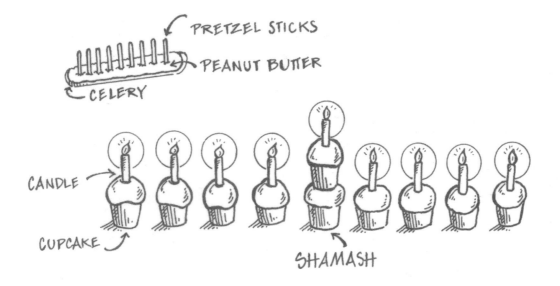

 Audrey F. Kanoff, Allentown, PA

Horn O' Plenty

Materials

Paper • scissors • markers and crayons • gardening and food magazines and seed catalogs • fruit and vegetable stickers, optional • glue • old manila file folders

What to do

1. Draw a cornucopia and make a copy for each child (see illustration).
2. Ask the children to cut out the cornucopia and color it.
3. Cut out pictures of fruits and vegetables from magazines.
4. Encourage the children to glue the pictures (or attach stickers) onto the mouth of the cornucopia.
5. Cut old manila file folders into the shape of a "T" (2" for the vertical line and 3" inches for the horizontal line). Make one for each child.
6. Show the children how to fold the T in half along the vertical line. This will make two L's when opened up part way.
7. Glue one side of the upside down T to the back of cornucopia. This will act as a stand so the cornucopia can be displayed on the table.

☆ Melissa O. Markham, Huddleston, VA

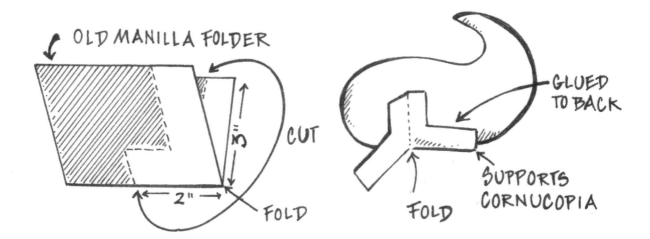

OLD MANILLA FOLDER

CUT

FOLD

2"

GLUED TO BACK

SUPPORTS CORNUCOPIA

FOLD

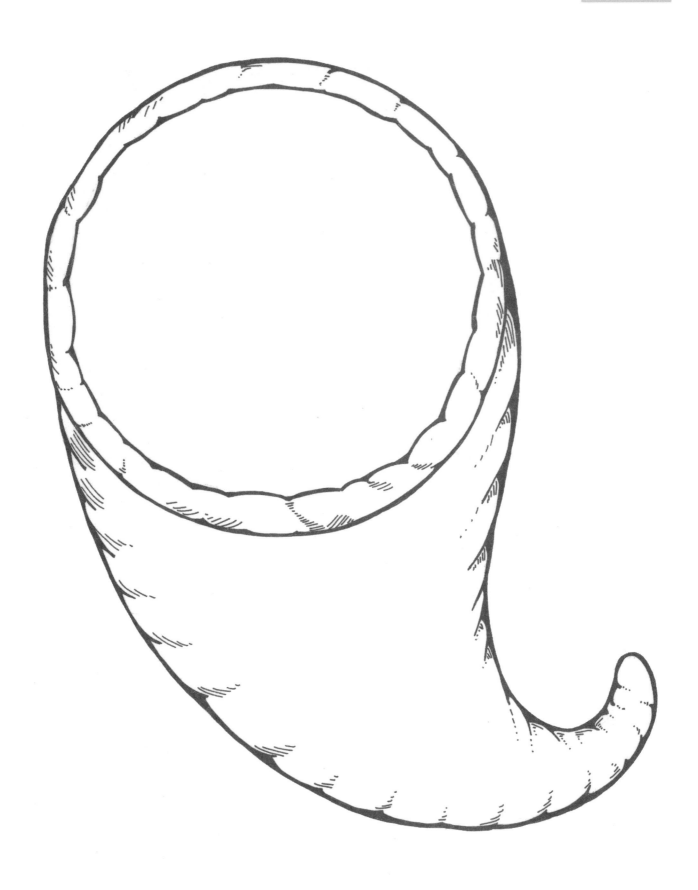

Thankfulness Cornucopia

Materials

Construction paper • scissors • markers or crayons

What to do

1. Cut out fruits and vegetables from construction paper.
2. Encourage the children to choose a paper fruit or vegetable and write what they are thankful for on it.
3. Let the children color their fruit or vegetable.
4. Hang them on the bulletin board near a large cornucopia.

 Sandy L. Scott, Vancouver, WA

Hanukah Handprint Menorahs

Materials

Fingerpaint • paper • glitter • real menorah or pictures of one

What to do

1. Give each child a piece of paper. Ask them to make two handprints next to each other, with thumbs touching.
2. When the paint is dry, they can draw a candle on each finger. Tell them to draw one big candle, larger than the others, where the thumbs meet. This is called the "shamash" or the helper candle.
3. Let the children add glitter for the flames on the candles.
4. Show the children a real menorah with candles in it. If you don't have one available, show them pictures of a variety of different types of menorahs. Explain why there are eight candles and what the shamash is.

 Audrey F. Kanoff, Allentown, PA

Tree of Hands

Materials

Large green paper triangles • tempera paint or fingerpaint • paintbrushes • scissors • markers

What to do

1. Give each child a large green triangle.
2. Help each child paint one hand and then make a handprint on his triangle.
3. When the handprints are dry, ask the children to snip the base edge of the triangle using scissors.
4. Using one finger or the side of a marker, the child rolls the snipped area to give the tree a three-dimensional look.
5. Mount the triangles in a large triangle formation to make a tree.

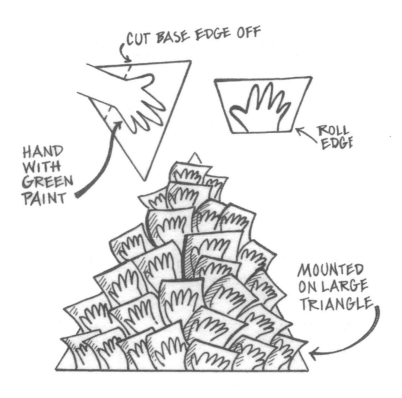

CUT BASE EDGE OFF

HAND WITH GREEN PAINT

ROLL EDGE

MOUNTED ON LARGE TRIANGLE

 Sandie Nagel, White Lake, MI

Tissue Christmas Tree

Materials

Newspaper • liquid starch • containers • 9″ x 12″ wax paper • paintbrushes • 1″ squares of tissue paper in shades of green and blue • pens • tagboard tree patterns • scissors • gold metallic paint • pencils with erasers (or very small sponges)

What to do

1. Cover the work surface with newspaper. Pour liquid starch into containers and give each child a 9″ x 12″ piece of waxed paper positioned vertically.

2. Ask the children to paint half the paper with starch. Show them how to place tissue squares on the starch, overlapping the squares.

3. Repeat with the second half, encouraging them to fill in enough squares of blue and green to create a large vertical triangle like a Christmas tree. Let dry.

4. When the starch has dried, ask the children to use pens to draw a large tree shape on the waxed paper. Make sure the tree outline is large enough to take in most of their tissue triangle. Another option is to provide 9″ tagboard tree patterns to trace.

5. Ask the children to cut out their tree along the lines they draw.

6. Pour small amounts of gold paint into shallow containers. Show the children how to dip the eraser of the pencils into the gold paint and make randomly-spaced dots of gold on the trees to resemble ornaments.

7. When the trees have dried, flatten them with heavy books overnight, if necessary.

 Susan Oldham Hill, Lakeland, FL

Toilet Roll Santa

Materials

Red, pink, and black construction paper • red tissue paper • scissors • empty toilet tissue rolls • stapler • hot glue gun (adult only), assorted wrapped candies • red curling ribbon • glue • cotton balls

What to do

1. Cut red construction paper into 3" x 6" strips, pink or peach construction paper into 2" x 6" strips, and red tissue paper into 4" x 6" strips. Cut black construction paper "M" shapes for feet.
2. Give each child an empty toilet tissue roll. Show them how to cover the bottom with a red strip and the top with a pink strip. Help them staple in place.
3. Hot glue (adult only) black paper feet to the bottom of the tube (adult only).
4. Let the children count out the desired candies and drop them inside the roll.
5. Glue the tissue paper strip around the top of the roll and tie it shut with a curling ribbon.
6. Encourage the children to draw a face on the pink strip and glue a cotton ball beard under it.

   Tip: These Santas make great gifts for parents; they are also nice to bring to residents of a nursing home or to needy families.

 Christine Maiorano, Duxbury, MA

Holiday Treat Container

Materials

Clean, empty 4-oz. fruit cup cans • construction paper • scissors • bits of lace, ribbon, sequins, yarn, pompom balls of various sizes, and cotton balls • 10mm wiggly eyes • white glue • cinnamon, optional

What to do

1. Cut construction paper strips the width of the can.
2. Give each child a clean can and a strip to glue on it.
3. Cut out gingerbread man shapes from construction paper and give one to each child.
4. The children can decorate the gingerbread man as desired. Provide wiggly eyes, yarn, sequins, and so on. Ideas include a gingerbread boy, snowman, or Santa.
5. Ask the children to glue their holiday gingerbread design to their can.
6. If desired, encourage the children to spread glue on the design and sprinkle cinnamon on it.

 Mary Brehm, Aurora, OH

Home for the Holidays

Materials

Un-colored playdough, Christmas cookie cutters, rolling pins, spatula, bowl, plastic knives, cookie sheets • play oven, optional • tape • wrapping paper • small empty boxes • scissors • small Christmas tree • art supplies for making ornaments

What to do

1. Set up three holiday dramatic play centers: one for cookie baking, one for wrapping gifts, and one for trimming a tree. Keep them up during the holiday season.

2. In the Cookie Baking Center, put out "cookie dough" (un-colored playdough) in a bowl with the cooking supplies, baking sheets, and cookie cutters. The children love baking pretend cookies. Set up this center in the Housekeeping area, if possible, so they can use the play oven to bake the cookies.

3. In the Wrapping Center, put out wrapping paper, tape, and boxes. Children love to wrap, so have lots of supplies! Let the children wrap the empty boxes over and over again. If desired, let them put their wrapped gifts under a tree. **Tip:** Ask parents to buy and donate inexpensive wrapping paper.

4. Set up a small tree in the Tree Trimming Center. Encourage the children to make decorations and then decorate the tree as desired. Provide plenty of supplies, such as Christmas cards, pipe cleaners, small bells, string or yarn, and so on.

5. These centers give the children the chance to do these holiday activities any way they want. How often do they get the opportunity to do these things during the busy holiday season? These centers give them a chance to get ready for the season, and all offer great fine motor practice.

 Gail Morris, Kemah, TX

New Year's Hat

Materials

Large sheet of newsprint paper • colored masking tape • paint • paintbrushes • glue • scrap material, sequins, and feathers

What to do

1. Shape the newsprint over the child's head.
2. Put masking tape around the newsprint to begin the hat's rim (and hold newsprint together if using more than one piece).
3. Roll up the ends of the paper to form the rim of the hat.
4. After shaping the paper to the child's head, remove and let the child use colored tape to keep the hat's shape.
5. Encourage the children to decorate their hats as desired.
6. Wear the hats during a parade or for other celebrations.

 Sandy L. Scott, Vancouver, WA

National Soup Month (January)

Materials

Snow or crushed ice • fresh or frozen vegetables • large pot • beef or chicken broth • large spoon • several white sheets • Styrofoam cups and plastic spoons

What to do

1. Celebrate National Soup Month (January) in your class by making "snow soup." The story "Snow Soup" can be found in "Kidactivities" in *Kidstuff, a Treasury of Early Childhood Enrichment Materials,* vol. 6, no. 2, 1992, or *Is Your Storytale Dragging?* by Jean Stagl. If available, read the story to the children using real and felt board props.
2. To begin, go outside and gather some clean snow (to add to the soup). If clean snow is not available, use crushed ice.
3. Cut up vegetables or use a couple of packages of frozen vegetables. (The amount of vegetables will depend on the size of your class.)
4. Pour ready-to-use canned chicken or beef broth into a pot along with some snow and let it simmer (adult only). Add vegetables.
5. When the soup is ready, lay several white sheets on the floor to represent snow.

(continued on the next page)

6. Ask the children to put on hats, scarves, and mittens, and then sit on the sheets.

7. Pour soup into Styrofoam cups and eat.

 Cookie Zingarelli, Columbus, OH

George Washington Carver

Materials

Peanuts in shells • paint and paintbrushes • containers • graph paper

What to do

1. Celebrate George Washington Carver's birthday, January 10th. Explain to the children that George Washington Carver was an African American botanist, scientist, artist, and singer. He was a great scientist who experimented with peanuts and invented over 300 items from the peanut. He also studied soybeans and sweet potatoes.

2. Encourage the children to paint peanuts (in their shells). When the peanuts have dried, the children can sort them by size, color, and shape.

3. Count a bag of peanuts with the children.

4. Play a Peanut Number Game. Number five containers from 1 to 5 or higher. Place them on a table along with a basket containing 15 or more peanuts. Let the children take turns placing the appropriate number of peanuts in each container

5. Help the children sort and graph peanuts, different nuts, and seeds.
   Safety Note: Check for peanut allergies before doing this activity. Many children who are allergic to peanuts cannot even touch peanuts or be around them.

Related poem

George Washington Carver by Patricia Murchison
> *George Washington Carver*
> *An outdoors man.*
>
> *He grew plants in dirt and sand,*
> *Soybeans, peanuts, sweet potatoes, too.*
> *George grew these plants just for you.*

He had his own garden,
Took care of his own plans,
George worked hard in his blue jean pants.

George could paint,
George could sing,
He made the peanut do many things.

 Patricia Murchison, Chesapeake, VA

Groundhog and Its Cave

Materials

Stuffed animals • brown paper grocery bags • brown paint • paintbrushes • scissors • stapler

What to do

1. Ask the children to bring in small stuffed animals from home. Have a few extra for children who forget to bring one in.
2. Give each child a grocery bag to paint. Placing the grocery bag on an upside-down garbage can makes it easier for the child to paint.
3. When the bags are dry, cut open the bottom of the bag on three sides to make a flap for the "cave."

(continued on the next page)

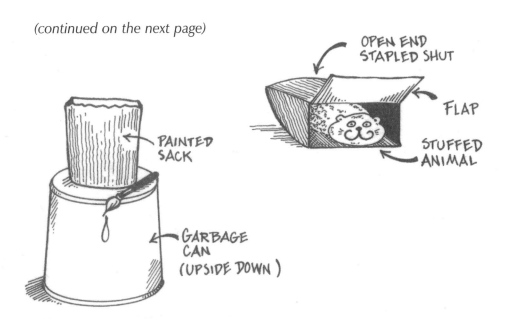

OPEN END STAPLED SHUT

FLAP

STUFFED ANIMAL

PAINTED SACK

GARBAGE CAN (UPSIDE DOWN)

4. Help the children staple the open end of the bags closed.
5. The children put their small stuffed animals in the cave opening.

 Sandy L. Scott, Vancouver, WA

Groundhog Looks for His Shadow

Materials

Foam cups • scissors • brown paint • paintbrushes • 2" brown pompoms • glue • tongue depressors or craft sticks • ½" wiggly eyes

What to do

1. Ahead of time, make a small slit in the bottom of each cup. Give one to each child.
2. Encourage the children to paint their cups with brown paint. Let dry.
3. Give each child a tongue depressor or craft stick. They can glue a brown pompom on the end of it, and then glue two wiggly eyes on the pompom.
4. Show the children how to put the depressor into the slit in the cup.
5. The puppet goes inside the burrow and then peeks out to look for his shadow.
6. Talk about shadows with the children. Go outside with them during the day to measure their shadows. Record and discuss why the shadows are longer or shorter at certain times.

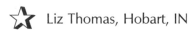 Liz Thomas, Hobart, IN

Chinese Dragon for the New Year

Materials

Cardboard box • scissors or knife (adult only) • string • paint • paintbrushes • egg carton or Styrofoam balls • glue • yarn • jewels • diaper pin • colorful blanket or material • small bed

What to do

1. Make a Chinese dragon with the children for the Chinese New Year (see illustration on the following page).
2. First find a box that will fit over a child's head and shoulders to create a dragon head.
3. Cut a square opening to be the mouth on three sides, leaving one side uncut. Attach a string so that you can open or close the mouth wearing the head.
4. Encourage the children to paint the box whatever color they choose.
5. When the box is dry, glue two egg carton cups or two halves of a Styrofoam ball on the box for eyes.
6. Cut long strings of thick yarn. Encourage the children to attach to the yarn to the top sides of the box for a mane. Mixing colors of yarn adds a beautiful effect to your dragon's mane.
7. Glue a jewel to the center an egg carton cup and glue it to the center of the dragon's head. This is the dragon's jeweled eye.
8. Add triangle-shaped ears to the head. Attach a small bell to the mane or ears.
9. When the dragon head is completed, choose one child to be the head. Use a diaper safety pin to attach the blanket or material on the child. Or, cut a hole in the material and put it over the child's head.
10. Select a few other children to stand in a line and hold onto each other's shoulders. Place the material over their bodies to represent the dragon's body. The custom is to keep the dragon moving at all times so the dragon never stands still.
11. Encourage the other children in the class to make loud noises using drums, bells, and other musical instruments. They should accompany the dragon wherever he goes to bring him good luck. Bring the dragon around the school to other classrooms or around the neighborhood to bring good luck for the New Year.

(continued on the next page)

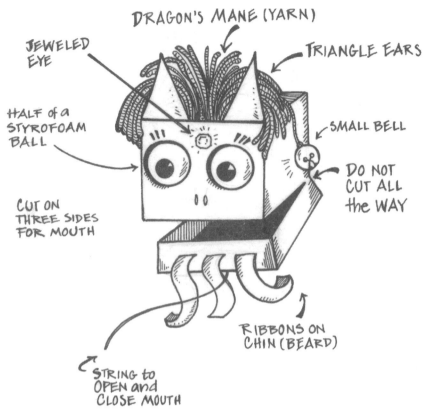

DRAGON'S MANE (YARN)

JEWELED EYE

TRIANGLE EARS

HALF of a STYROFOAM BALL

SMALL BELL

DO NOT CUT ALL the WAY

CUT ON THREE SIDES FOR MOUTH

RIBBONS ON CHIN (BEARD)

STRING to OPEN and CLOSE MOUTH

12. Read books to learn about more customs, such as how it is customary to feed the dragon a red envelope, or salad from shopkeepers.

Related books

The Last Dragon by Susan Miho Nunes
This Next New Year by Janet S. Wong

 Cookie Zingarelli, Columbus, OH

Chinese Dragon and Feast

Materials

Old full-size sheet • construction paper scraps • glue • medium-size box • marker • small knife (adult only) • paint and paintbrush • stapler • CD or cassette tape of Chinese music • books on the Chinese New Year celebrations

What to do

1. This is a great activity if you are learning about other cultures and their holidays.
2. Spread the sheet on a large table and ask the children to gather around it.
3. Give each child a bottle of glue and a pile of construction paper scraps. Explain that the scraps of paper will be the dragon scales and the sheet is the dragon's body.
4. The children can glue the construction paper scraps all over the sheet.
5. As the children are working on the body, draw a dragon face on the long side of the box.
6. Next, cut out the dragon's eyes with a small knife. Then paint the face. If desired, ask the children to help paint the rest of the box red.
7. When the face and "scales" are dry, attach the box to the end of the sheet with a stapler.
8. When the dragon is finished, show the children how to line up behind each other and put their hands on the waist of the child in front of them. Practice moving to the Chinese music before you place the "dragon" over them. Select a line leader to wear the head of the dragon and lead the dragon around the room. It is also great fun to visit other classes.

   Tip: If you have Chinese-American children in your class, you could invite their parents to speak to the class about their culture, traditions, and foods.

☆ Joy M. Tuttle, London, OH

Five Little Valentines

Materials

5 paper plates with large hearts (preferably with lace on them) • scissors • black, felt-tip pen • contact cement or hot glue gun (adult only) • 5 craft sticks

What to do

1. Look for paper plates with a heart in the center the next time Valentine's Day rolls around. If you can't find any, make your own.
2. Cut out the hearts from the center of five plates. Discard the remainder of the plates.
3. Write the five spoken parts of the verse on each of the five hearts. For example, write "Will you be mine?" on one heart, and so on.

(continued on the next page)

Five Little Valentines

Five little valentines pretty with lace
Standing in a row, each in his own place.
The first one says, "Will you be mine?"
The second one says, "Be my Valentine."
The third one says, "I love you."
The fourth one says, "I will be true."
The fifth one says, "Let's all run away and find a little friend today."

4. Attach a craft stick behind each Valentine using contact cement or a hot glue gun.
5. Encourage a group of five children to hold the Valentines and recite the first two lines of the fingerplay together and then one of each of the remaining five lines.

 Jackie Wright, Enid, OK

Valentine Fun Candy Making

Materials

Chocolate playdough (flour, cocoa powder, salt, cream of tartar, oil, water) • plastic candy molds • assorted Valentine candy boxes • mixing bowls • rolling pins and other playdough cutters

What to do

1. Make chocolate playdough with the children.
2. Mix together 1 ¼ cups flour, ½ cup cocoa powder, ½ cup salt, and ½ teaspoons cream of tartar. Add 1 ½ tablespoons oil and 1 cup boiling water and stir quickly.
3. Encourage the children to make playdough candy using the molds.
4. The chocolate playdough smells like real chocolate, and the children love filling the boxes with the pretend candy to give to someone special.

 Diane Hennington, League City, TX

Edible Peppermint Valentine Hearts

Materials

Oven • two candy canes for each heart • cookie sheet • aerosol cooking spray • 2 metal spoons

What to do

Author Note: You could try this at school using a toaster oven, but it's a little too difficult for the children to do much except watch. The children love receiving the hearts as a treat from their teacher, so you might want to make them at home and bring them in.

1. Preheat the oven to 300° F.
2. Remove the wrappers from candy canes.
3. Lightly spray the cookie sheet with oil.
4. Place the candy canes on the cookie sheet, forming heart shapes. Be sure the ends touch, but leave some space between the hearts.
5. Place in the oven for a few minutes until the candy softens. (About three minutes, but check so the candy doesn't melt completely.)
6. Remove the tray and use the spoons to join the ends where the candy canes meet.
7. Allow them to cool completely.
8. Wrap hearts individually in clear plastic wrap.
9. If desired, do a simpler version of this activity with the children. Show them how to tape together the ends of two wrapped candy candles to form hearts.
   Tip: When candy canes go on sale after Christmas, buy a lot!

 Mary Jo Shannon, Roanoke, VA

Paul Revere Williams

Materials

Architecture books • rulers • markers and crayons • pencils • drawing paper • construction paper • tagboard • scissors • glue

What to do

1. Celebrate the birthday of Paul Revere Williams, who was born on February 18, 1894. Explain that Paul Revere Williams was a famous African American architect. Discuss the meaning of the word "architect" (one skilled in the art of building or designing), and show them a book of different types of architectural buildings and designs.

2. Show the children a ruler. Ask them if they know what it is and how it is used. When you finish the discussion, give the children rulers, pencils or markers, and drawing paper.

3. Ask them to place the rulers on the paper and draw lines going in many different directions.

4. Before doing this part of the activity, cut out a variety of shapes from multi-colored paper. Explain to the children that they will be using the different shapes to design their own building.

5. Give each child a piece of tagboard. Encourage them to choose a few paper shapes and glue them to the tagboard to make a building.

6. Encourage the children to write a story about their buildings. Attach the story to their picture and display.

Related poem

Paul Revere Williams by Patricia Murchison

Paul R. Williams was an architect
No finer one have we met.
Building and construction was his thing,
Boy, could he make his pencil sing.
With a ruler and pencil in his hand,
Paul's buildings became famous throughout the land.

 Patricia Murchison, Chesapeake, VA

President's Day Hats

Materials

2 pieces of white construction paper (12" x 18") per child • stapler • red and blue crayons, markers, or paint

What to do

1. Put two pieces of paper together and fold as if making a newspaper hat. Staple at both ends to hold the hat together.
2. Encourage the children to decorate their hats using red and blue crayons, markers, or paint. This is a nice time to show the American flag and talk about the colors in the flag. See if anyone knows the name of our president.
3. After the hats are finished, have a parade using rhythm band instruments or homemade instruments.

 Phyllis Esch, Export, PA

Harriet Tubman

Materials

Trail mix ingredients (see activity) • large bowl and mixing spoon • napkins • flashlight • outlines of the states of Maryland and Pennsylvania

What to do

1. Celebrate Harriet Tubman's birthday, which is March 10. Explain to the children that she was born a slave in 1820 and worked hard all her young life. She could not play or go to school, and she was very sad. One day she decided that she wanted to be free, so she planned her escape. Her family was too scared to go with her, but her father taught her things to help her find her way north. He told her about the sky and the North Star (the brightest star in the Little Dipper). He also taught her many things about the wilderness, such as how moss grows on the north side of trees. Harriet escaped to Philadelphia from Maryland, where she became free and very happy. Harriet went back to the South 13 times and rescued more than 300 people from slavery.

(continued on the next page)

2. Make trail mix for the freedom trail. Mix an assortment of dry cereal, raisins, nuts, M&Ms, sunflower seeds, pretzel sticks, and dried fruit in a large bowl. Put half-cup servings on large napkins or paper towels and wrap them up.

3. Pin the two outlines (one of Maryland and one of Pennsylvania) in two different areas. The children will begin in Maryland and end up in Pennsylvania.

4. Choose one child to role play Harriet Tubman, and the other children will be the escapees or Freedom Seekers.

5. Turn off the lights and give Harriet Tubman the flashlight. Ask her to point the flashlight up toward the ceiling (the sky). The flashlight will be the North Star. Have Harriet and the Freedom Seekers go quietly and swiftly toward the outline state of Pennsylvania.

6. Harriet should go back at least two to three times to get more Freedom Seekers.

Related poem

Harriet Tubman by Patricia Murchison

Harriet Tubman was a real go-getter,
She rescued her people so life would be better.
Life without Harriet wouldn't be the same,
Harriet Tubman was her name.
She traveled by night and not by day,
The stars in the sky lead the way.

 Patricia Murchison, Chesapeake, VA

Shamrock Ladder

Materials

Yarn • green and yellow construction paper • straws • scissors • masking tape

What to do

1. Cut out shamrock shapes from green and yellow construction paper. Cut straws into ½" pieces.

2. Give each child a 2' long piece of yarn.

3. Demonstrate how to attach a small piece of tape to the end of the yarn, and then string alternating straw pieces and shamrocks.

4. Hang the ladders from the ceiling for "leprechauns" to climb.

 Sandy L. Scott, Vancouver, WA

St. Patrick's Day Tic Tac Toe

Materials

Seasonal picture • color printer or markers • green tagboard • scissors • glue stick • felt-tip pen • laminator

What to do

1. Make your own Tic Tac Toe game for St. Patrick's Day.
2. First locate a seasonal picture to serve as game pieces instead of the traditional X's and O's (for example, two bears facing each other and holding a shamrock between them). You can download the graphic from the Internet and print it using a color printer, or make copies and color them yourself.
3. Reduce the size of the picture to approximately 1 ½".
4. Make five game pieces in one color (for the first player) and four in another color (for the second player).
5. Mount the colored pictures on green tagboard circles approximately 1 ½" to 2".
6. Cut out the circle-shaped game pieces.
7. Cut a 7 ½" square of green tagboard for the game board.
8. Using a felt-tip pen, mark a grid on the board to form 9 squares (2 ½" x 2 ½" each) with three across and three down.
9. Laminate the game board and game pieces.

REDUCE and GLUE ON TO 1½" – 2" CIRCLE of GREEN TAGBOARD

2" CIRCLE PATTERN

 Jackie Wright, Enid, OK

Clue Finder

Materials

Tagboard • scissors • green-colored cellophane • glue • Popsicle sticks

What to do

1. Cut out shamrock shapes from tagboard and then cut out the centers. Give two to each child.
2. Show the children how to cover the centers of the shamrocks with cellophane and glue in place.
3. Ask the children to glue a Popsicle stick to the bottom of one of the shamrocks, and then place the other shamrock on top (lined up) and glue it in place.
4. When the glue dries, the children have their own green clue finders.

⭐ Sandy L. Scott, Vancouver, WA

Bunny Easter Egg Basket

Materials

Half-gallon milk containers • sandpaper • construction paper • glue • hole punch • pipe cleaners • scissors • wiggly eyes • pompoms • Easter grass

What to do

1. Cut off the tops of milk containers and keep the bottom half. It is helpful to lightly sand the container so that glue sticks to it.
2. Give one to each child. Encourage the children to glue pink or white paper (depending on what color bunny they want) on the outside of the carton.

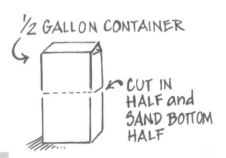

½ GALLON CONTAINER

CUT IN HALF and SAND BOTTOM HALF

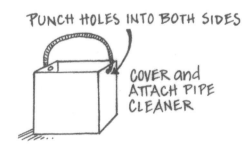

PUNCH HOLES INTO BOTH SIDES

COVER and ATTACH PIPE CLEANER

3. Punch two holes on each side of the carton and attach a pipe cleaner handle.

4. Cut out circles (for the face) and ears from construction paper.

5. Encourage the children to glue on the circle (face), ears, wiggly eyes, and pompom for the nose.

6. They can attach a pompom to the back for the tail.

7. Fill them with Easter grass or torn paper.

☆ Sandy L. Scott, Vancouver, WA

Duck Easter Bag

Materials

Tagboard or heavy paper (for patterns) • pencils • orange construction paper • scissors • yellow or white lunch bags • 23mm wiggle eyes • white glue • white or yellow paper • spring stickers, optional

What to do

1. Make patterns for a duck head (circle), feet, and bill.

2. Help each child trace two feet and a bill on orange paper and cut them out.

3. Also help each child trace the head on a lunch bag and cut it out (save the cut-out piece to make a tail).

4. Demonstrate how to fold out both sides of the bag (where the head was cut out). This forms the duck's two wings when the bag is open.

5. Encourage the children to glue on wiggle eyes, the bill (folded in half), and feet.

(continued on the next page)

6. Cut out 1 ½″ x 9″ strips from white or yellow paper and glue them to the bags to make handles.

7. If desired, let the children attach spring stickers to their bags.

8. Show the children how to make a tail by folding down the flap of the saved paper scrap and gluing it on the back of the bag.

9. Help the children write their names on the handle of their bags. If desired, let them fill their bag with goodies.

 Mary Brehm, Aurora, OH

Basket of Mother Goose Books

Materials

Mother Goose nursery rhyme books • basket

What to do

1. To celebrate Mother Goose Day on May 1st, fill a basket with nursery rhyme books, such as *My Very First Mother Goose* edited by Iona Opie or *Mother Hubbard's Cupboard* by Laura Rader.

2. Use these books to introduce the rhymes, a few each day, over the entire week of the celebration.

 Jackie Wright, Enid, OK

May Baskets

Materials

Paper plates • scissors • rolls of 1"-wide ribbon • colored tissue paper cut into 3" squares • white glue • small cups

What to do

1. Beforehand, cut two slits in each paper plate as shown below. The slits should be opposite of each other and 1" from the edge of the plates.
2. Give each child a plate and a long piece of ribbon.
3. Show the children how to weave the ribbon through one of the slits, push it through the back, and come up through the other slit to make a basket handle.
4. Demonstrate how to find the middle of a square of tissue paper, twist it, and dip it in the cup of glue.
5. Encourage the children to fill the middle of their plates this way, using a variety of colors.
6. When the tissue flowers are done, help the children tie the ribbon into a bow at the top of their basket.
7. Tell the children to surprise someone with the basket on May first, "May Day."

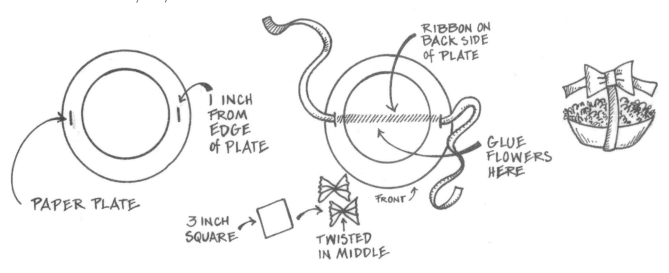

PAPER PLATE · 1 INCH FROM EDGE OF PLATE · 3 INCH SQUARE · TWISTED IN MIDDLE · RIBBON ON BACK SIDE OF PLATE · FRONT · GLUE FLOWERS HERE

 Barbara Saul, Eureka, CA

Mother's Day Tea

Materials

Paper • markers • tea • juice • finger foods, fruit, and cookies • napkins • cups • plates • spoons • decorations

What to do:

1. Mother's Day is a wonderful time to celebrate with mothers and grandmothers. Have a Mother's Day Tea for moms, grandmothers, or other special caregivers.
2. Help the children make invitations to send home.
3. Encourage the children to dress up for this event.
4. Before the event, the children can prepare the food and decorate the room.
5. The day of the tea, the children can sing songs or have background music playing. Encourage the children to bring drinks and food to their moms.
6. Everyone enjoys the food and tea together!

 Sandy L. Scott, Vancouver, WA

Father's Day Footprints

Materials

2 large shallow baking pans • bag of flour • 2-cup measuring cup • plaster of Paris • water • several small, soft vegetable brushes • shellac (adult only)

What to do

1. Make sure you start this great Father's Day gift well in advance. Completing it takes some time.
2. Fill the baking pans with finely sifted flour. Make sure the flour is level and does not come completely to the top of the pan.
3. Help each child carefully press one bare foot into the flour, leaving a foot impression. Make sure the child lifts his foot straight up when done so the sides of the flour footprint are not disturbed.
4. Mix the plaster of Paris according to the package directions. Quickly pour some into the measuring cup and help the child fill his footprint to the top. Be careful not to let the plaster overflow the footprint impression.

5. Set the footprints aside to harden. The plaster of Paris will warm as it hardens and will slightly cook the layer of flour closest to it.

6. When the footprints have hardened and cooled, remove them from the flour impression. Let the children help peel the cooked layer of flour away. This might be difficult for some children, so offer help as needed.

7. Give the children a vegetable brush and encourage them to gently remove any leftover flour from the footprint.

8. Spray the footprints with shellac for durability. Do this away from the children.

9. Print each child's name on the bottom of his footprint.

10. The children can give their footprints to the fathers (or other special man in their lives) for Father's Day.

 Virginia Jean Herrod, Columbia, SC

Silvery Star Banner

Materials

Pictures of flags • star stickers • large blue paper • 8 ½" x 11" paper • markers

What to do

1. These are great to do on Flag Day (June 14).
2. Show the children flags from other countries to compare colors and designs.
3. Provide 50 stars and a large blue rectangle. Encourage the children to arrange and count the stars.
4. Invite the children to create their own flags or a family flag.

 Susan Oldham Hill, Lakeland, FL

Making a Flag

Materials

Blue paper • glue • red and white crepe paper • star stickers

What to do

1. Talk to the children about the colors in the flag. Ask if anyone knows how many stripes there are, or how many stars. Does anyone know why there are 50 stars?
2. Give each child a piece of blue paper and strips or red and white crepe paper.
3. After the children glue on their stripes, they attach their stars.

 Sandra Hutchins Lucas, Cox's Creek, KY

Yankee Doodle Hat

Materials

Cardboard for pattern • red, white, and blue construction paper • pencils • scissors • stapler • glue • gold or silver glitter • red, white, or blue feathers • patriotic or star stickers, optional

What to do

1. Trace the hat pattern (see next page) on a piece of cardboard.
2. Ask each child to trace the hat on a piece of red paper, blue paper, and white paper.
3. Help the children cut out all three hats.
4. The children put a line of glue near the top of all three hat shapes and then sprinkle the glue with glitter.
5. Help the children staple the three shapes together near the ends to make a three-cornered colonial hat.
6. Staple a feather in the middle of the back blue piece.
7. If desired, give the children stickers to add to their hats.
8. March in a rhythm band parade wearing the hats.

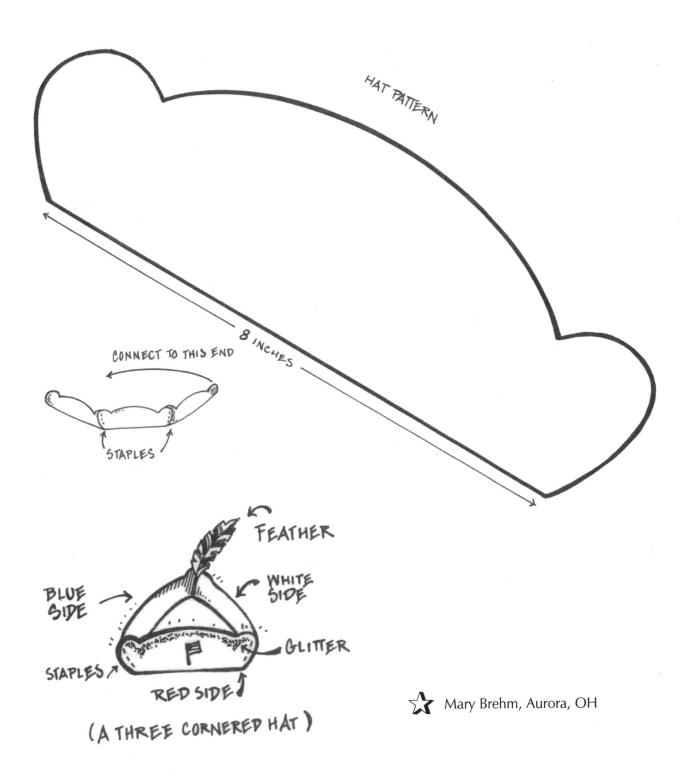

HAT PATTERN

8 INCHES

CONNECT TO THIS END

STAPLES

FEATHER

BLUE SIDE

WHITE SIDE

GLITTER

STAPLES

RED SIDE

(A THREE CORNERED HAT)

⭐ Mary Brehm, Aurora, OH

Mary McLeod Bethune

Materials
Pre-baked, small pie shells, one for each child • small bowls • assorted pie fillings in cans, assorted toppings for pies • spoons

What to do

1. Celebrate the birthday of Mary McLeod Bethune (July 10, 1875). She devoted her life to ensuring the right to education and freedom from discrimination for African Americans. In 1904, she opened the Daytona Normal and Industrial Institute for Negro Girls. Tell the children that Mary McLeod Bethune sold pies in order to save money to start her school.

2. Ahead of time, place assorted pie fillings into small bowls and keep in the refrigerator until ready to use. After the discussion is over, the children will make their own pies to eat.

3. Tell them they must "purchase" their small pie shells from you by telling you one reason why they like school. When all the children have their pie shells, they can fill them with any pie filling. (Make sure that each bowl of filling has at least two spoons next it.)

4. Then the children can top them as desired. Eat and enjoy!

Related poem

Mary McLeod Bethune by Patricia Murchison

Mary McLeod Bethune, the black rose of education,
She was determined to reach a nation.

Known by people everywhere,
She knew how to love and how to care.

She sold pies and sweets,
Just to make education a real treat.

With three nickels and a dime,
Education for me came right on time.

 Patricia Murchison, Chesapeake, VA

Felt Theme Boxes

Materials

Plastic videocassette boxes • felt with adhesive back (available in large sheets at hardware stores, with products designed to protect wooden floors) • felt • scissors

What to do

1. Over a period of time, you can create a variety of theme boxes. These provide great activities for the children to do during quiet times.
2. Cut adhesive-backed felt to fit flat outside the tape box. Adhere felt to the plastic case.
3. Cut or purchase felt pieces to match the classroom themes (for example, letters, numbers, shapes, farm animals, clothing shapes, story characters, and so on).
4. Put the felt cutouts into the box. Label the outside with words or pictures for easy identification and selection.
5. Let the play begin. Supervise and talk with the children about their use of the material provided. Encourage language.

 Bev Schumacher, Dayton, OH

The Art Critic

Materials

Pictures of all forms of art (for example, Norman Rockwell paintings, Frank Lloyd Wright's "Fallingwater" or other structures, Da Vinci's "Mona Lisa," Andy Warhol's "Campbell's Cans," a recognizable statue from your local area)

What to do

1. Display a single piece of art in the center of a bulletin board or other prominent area in the classroom. Make sure it is the only item displayed in that area.
2. If possible, draw attention to the picture by illuminating it as if it were hanging in a museum.

(continued on the next page)

3. Display the picture for a few days without pointing it out. Let the children discover it for themselves and talk to each other about it.

4. During snack, tell the children the artist's name and the name of the work. Begin to find out what the children think of the work of art. Ask questions such as:

   ☆ How do you feel about the picture?

   ☆ Does it make you think of anything?

   ☆ What is your favorite part?

   ☆ What, if anything, do you dislike about it?

   ☆ Does the picture tell a story?

   ☆ Do you like this work of art? Why or why not?

   ☆ Is there anything interesting about it?

   ☆ How did the artist make it?

5. Have the children write or dictate their thoughts about the picture and hang them around the picture.

6. When interest in the picture has died down, hang up a new picture and follow the same routine.

Related books

All I See by Cynthia Rylant
The Art Lesson by Tomie dePaola
Draw Me a Star by Eric Carle
No Good in Art by Miriam Cohen

☆ Ann Kelly, Johnstown, PA

Bare Bear

Materials

Bag • story props: ball, carpentry nails, toy rabbit, pear, sunglasses, leaves, toy meat, pen, toy bat (animal), and bowl • bear and overalls patterns • cardboard • scissors • 9" x 6" brown construction paper • markers • construction paper in various colors • small pear stickers or pre-cut pears

What to do

1. Beforehand, fill a bag with the story props. Tell the children the following story and pull out the appropriate props from the bag. Allow the children to giggle and correct your "mistakes."

My friend invited me to a ball and told me to dress up. Why do I have to dress for a ball? She said we should also paint our nails, but I don't know why. She said to brush our hare, too. My friend is going to get a new pair of shoes. Do they make shoes with pears? When we are at the ball we might get to dance with the king's son, so I'm bringing my sunglasses. To get to the ball we will take a bus. The bus leaves at seven so we will meat a little early. On the way we'll pass a farm with a pen full of pigs. How do the pigs fit in there? We will also pass a baseball game. My friend said we will hear the bats hit the balls. How do bats do that? After the ball we are going bowling. I don't know how to play, but I brought a bowl. Do you think that we will have fun?

2. Explain that some words sound the same but have different meanings, which is sometimes confusing. Other words the children might recognize are night/knight, pale/pail, I/eye, and not/knot.

3. Tell the children they will be making bare bears. Because the bears are bare, they will also make a pair (pear) of pants.

(continued on the next page)

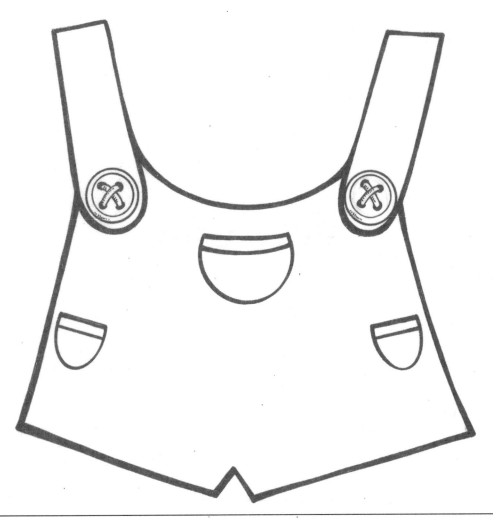

4. Beforehand, make a bear pattern and overalls pattern by tracing the illustrations onto cardboard and cutting them out.

5. Give the children brown paper and encourage them to trace the bear pattern and cut it out. Then ask them to draw a face and toes on the bear.

6. Let the children choose a piece of paper, trace the overalls pattern on it, and cut out.

7. Encourage them to decorate the overalls with patterns, stripes, plaid, dots, and so on. Let them attach the pears to the pants.
8. Show the children how to bend back the shoulder straps of the overalls over the bear's shoulders to give the bear a pair (pear) of pants.

 Sandra Gratias, Perkasie, PA

Little Red Riding Hood
(Left and Right)

Materials

None

What to do

1. This is a left and right story. Instruct the children to raise their left hands when they hear the word "left" and to raise their right hands when they hear the word "right."
2. Read the following story to the children.

   Little Red Riding Hood LEFT her house with a basket of goodies for Granny. "Now stay on the RIGHT path," her mother warned as Red started towards the woods. Red knew her granny was sick, and she was the only one LEFT to help out.

   But as she turned RIGHT on the forest trail, she noticed some lovely flowers to her LEFT, blooming with bright rainbow colors. What Red didn't notice was that there was a wolf standing RIGHT behind her, leaning against a tree.

   "Good afternoon," the wolf said, shifting his beady eyes LEFT and RIGHT. "It certainly is a beautiful day to pick flowers."

   Red LEFT her flowers by the basket and looked up at the wolf. "I really shouldn't be picking flowers RIGHT now," she said. "I'm supposed to take this basket of food to my granny. Now I'm late."

   "Don't worry," said the wolf in a deceiving voice. "I know a shortcut. If you go LEFT on the trail, you'll get to Granny's a lot sooner."

   "But my mother told me to stay on the RIGHT path," Red argued.

(continued on the next page)

"Believe me," the wolf lied, "I know these woods LEFT and RIGHT. This way is much faster."

So, Little Red Riding Hood LEFT the wolf and headed the long way to Granny's.

But that slick old wolf took the short cut and soon he was RIGHT at Granny's front door. He didn't bother knocking. He burst in, tied granny up, and LEFT her in the coat closet. Eventually, Red made it to Granny's house and tapped on the door.

"Who is it?" the wolf asked in a high voice.

"It's me. Little Red Riding Hood."

"Come RIGHT in, dear."

She slipped in, LEFT the basket and flowers on the table, and walked up to Granny, who was lying in bed. Red thought that Granny must be really sick. She looked downright awful!

"Granny, what big ears you have," Little Red Riding Hood said, a bit suspicious.

"The better to hear you with, my dear," the wolf said, perking up his LEFT ear a little.

"Granny, what a big nose you have," Little Red Riding Hood said.

"Wouldn't anyone in their RIGHT mind want a big nose to smell those lovely flowers you picked for me?" the wolf asked.

"Granny," Red blurted out nervously, "What big teeth you have!"

"The better to eat you with!" the wolf yelled as he sprang from the bed.

Red screamed and ran. The wolf chased her around and around the table, panting with what little breath he had LEFT.

A woodsman nearby heard the racket and knew RIGHT away that it was the pesky old wolf. He came charging in, looked the wolf straight in the eyes, and LEFT him no choice. "You leave RIGHT now and never let me catch you around these woods again!" the woodsman demanded.

So, the wolf LEFT.

Red and the woodsman helped Granny out of the closet, making sure she was all RIGHT. Red set the table and took the food from the basket.

"LEFTovers again!" Granny said with a wink.

They all had a big laugh, and lived happily ever after.

 Dotti Enderle, Richmond, TX

Word Card Flash

Materials

3″ x 5″ cards • black marker • crayons or picture and glue

What to do

1. Choose a book that has a word in it repeated several times throughout the story. Write the word on a 3″ x 5″ card using a black marker, and if possible, glue or draw a picture for even more reinforcement.
2. Review the flash card with the children before you start the story.
3. Explain to the children that you are going to read the story straight through the first time. Then you will read it again with their help. Tell them to say the word on the flash card every time you hold it up during the story.
4. As you read the book to the children, hold up the flash card each time you come to the word in the story, and the children say the word. The children catch on fast and will begin to say the word without your prompting.
5. When you are finished, leave the book and the flash card in the reading corner. The children can look for the word in the story themselves.
6. As the children become more comfortable with this technique, you can do more than one word at a time.

   Tip: Put the flash cards in a recipe box. Keep it in the reading corner for the children to use as they look through other books. At the end of the week, give the parents a word list of all the new words the children are working on.

 Joy M. Tuttle, London, OH

Categories Toll Booth

Materials

Appliance box or puppet theater • craft knife (adult only) • art supplies (crayons, paints, markers, material or paper scraps) • actual or created theater tickets

What to do

1. Make a tollbooth by cutting out a large hole from the side of an appliance box (adult only). This will become a window. (If desired, use a puppet theater instead.)

(continued on the next page)

APPLIANCE BOX

TOLL

BOOTH

WINDOW CUT OUT

ADMIT ONE

2. Encourage the children to decorate the box using the art supplies. This will become the tollbooth.

3. The children will pretend to drive up to the tollbooth and answer a question presented by the tollbooth operator. An adult may wish to be the first toll booth "operator" to demonstrate.

4. The tollbooth operator asks each child to name a member of a category, which is chosen ahead of time (such as animals, foods, clothing, or vehicles).

5. If the child answers correctly, she may give the tollbooth operator a ticket and proceed over the "bridge." If the answer is incorrect, the child may ask for help from another child, or "drive" around some more to think.

6. The children continue to take turns going to the tollbooth. Encourage the children to think of new answers each time.

7. When the game is understood, a child may become the tollbooth operator.

Related books

Go, Dog, Go! by P.D. Eastman

Gray Rabbit's Odd One Out by Alan Baker

 Kate Ross, Middlesex, VT

Character Cubes

Materials

4 clean, cardboard ½-gallon milk cartons • scissors • paper • tape • markers • contact paper

What to do

1. Make two dice by cutting the milk cartons in half and sliding the bottom of one carton inside another (two cartons make one cube).
2. Cut paper into 12 pieces. Cover each side of the cubes with a piece of paper and tape in place.
3. On one die, draw six items in which the children are currently interested (for example, a dinosaur, truck, horse, princess, and so on).
4. On the other die, write six action words and draw a picture that represents the action (for example, swim, fly, fall, brush, shop, and so on).
5. Cover the cubes with contact paper.
6. Gather a small group of children. Model using the dice to create a crazy story. Roll the item die and make up something about the picture that is facing up. For example, "Once upon a time, there was a very small *dinosaur* that lived all alone in a very small apartment." Then have a child roll the action die and add to the story that you began. For example, "His apartment was surrounded by soup so when he wanted to go anywhere, he had to *swim.*"
7. Keep adding to the silly story until every child has had a turn to roll a die.
8. If desired, write down or tape-record the silly story so that it can be shared with others and enjoyed again and again.

☆ Ann Kelly, Johnstown, PA

Fairy Tale Dice

Materials

4 Styrofoam cubes • patterned adhesive paper • clear adhesive paper • white typing paper • scissors • tape • construction paper • markers • hole punch • yarn

What to do

Phase One: Prepare the dice

1. Help the children cover the cubes with the patterned adhesive paper.
2. Print the following words or phrases on small pieces of typing paper that are cut to fit the sides of the cubes: bear, boy, girl, cat, queen, king, small, large, old, new, messy, clean, hut, house, castle, cave, city, farm, the store, a friend's house, Grandma's house, into the woods, into town, and to the park.
3. Tape the words on the cubes in the following order:
   - ☆ Cube One: bear, boy, girl, cat, queen, king
   - ☆ Cube Two: large, old, new, messy, clean
   - ☆ Cube Three: hut, house, castle, cave, city, farm
   - ☆ Cube Four: the store, a friend's house, Grandma's house, into the woods, into town, to the park
4. Cover the completed cubes with clear adhesive paper for durability. You have now completed your set of Fairy Tale Dice.

Phase Two: Write the story

1. Begin the story like this: "Once upon a time there was a..."
2. Roll the first die. Whatever character lands on top is now your main character for the story.
3. Insert the character into the story. For example, if the die lands with the cat on top: "Once upon a time there was a cat..."
4. Continue the story like this: "...who lived in a very ..."
5. Roll the second die and insert whatever descriptive word lands on top. For example, "Once upon a time there was a cat who lived in a very messy ..."
6. Roll the third die and insert whatever type of residence lands on top. For example, "Once upon a time there was a cat who lived in a very messy hut."
7. Continue the story like this: "One day the cat decided to go ..."
8. Roll the fourth die and insert whatever lands on top. For example, "Once upon a time there was a cat that lived in a very messy hut. One day the cat decided to go into town."

9. Now, put the dice to the side and ask the children to continue the story from there. Ask leading questions such as, "What do you think might happen next?" Keep a record of their responses. Continue to ask them what might happen next in the story. Shape their responses into a short story. For example:

Once upon a time, a cat lived in a very messy hut. One day the cat decided to go into town. While the cat was in town, he went to the store. In the store, he bought a vacuum cleaner and a mop. The cat decided to go back home and clean up his hut. The cat lived happily ever after. The end!

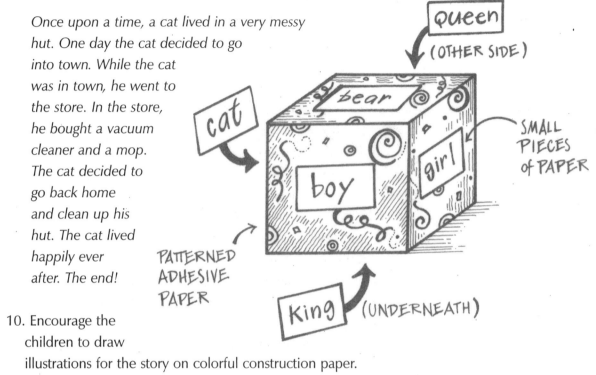

10. Encourage the children to draw illustrations for the story on colorful construction paper.
11. Add the text to the story, create a front and back cover, and bind the pages together into a book.
12. Put the new fairy tale book in the reading center for all to enjoy.

    Tip: Before binding the book, make multiple photocopies of the story. This way each child will have one to take home. If making multiple copies, have the children draw illustrations on plain white paper instead of construction paper.

 Virginia Jean Herrod, Columbia, SC

Cows Out to Pasture

Materials

Tagboard • paper • scissors • white and blue construction paper • pencils • black crayons • glue • grass

What to do

1. Ahead of time, cut out cow patterns from tagboard (see illustration).
2. Read a story about cows to the children. Explain that cows like to eat grass.
3. As a group, write two-line poems about cows. Encourage the children to think of words that rhyme with cow.
4. Ask the children to trace the cow patterns on white construction paper.
5. Invite the children to draw black shapes on their cows.
6. Go outside with the children and pick some blades of grass.
7. Ask the children to spread glue on the bottom half of the blue construction paper. Then they can spread the blades of grass on the glue.
8. While the glue is drying, the children cut out their cow shapes.

 Liz Thomas, Hobart, IN

Do You See What I See?

Materials

Large poster of an active image

What to do

1. Gather a few children (no more than four at a time) around the poster.
2. Encourage the children to look at the poster for a few minutes.
3. Ask them to find something in the picture and describ its color, shape, size, texture, and so on. For example, "I found something blue. Can you find it?" The other children guess what that child sees. Encourage them to use descriptors other than color and size.
4. Choose one child to begin the game.
5. Once the chosen child has asked the question, "Can you find it?" the other children take turns guessing what it is.
6. The child who guesses the correct item becomes the next child to pick an item and ask the others to find it.
7. Continue until all of the children have had a chance to choose an item for the others to guess.
8. At this point, you may wish to either change the group of children or change the pictures.

 Kate Ross, Middlesex, VT

Growth Flowers

Materials

Butcher paper in green and a variety of bright colors • scissors • small paper plates • glue • marker

What to do

1. Cut out stems from green butcher paper that are as tall as the tallest child in the class.
2. Cut out leaves so that every stem has two leaves.

(continued on the next page)

3. Cut out flower petals from bright colored butcher paper.

4. On one leaf, write: "When I was little I could…" Write: "Now that I am bigger I can…" on the other leaf.

5. Ask each child to complete the above statements. Write their responses on their leaves.

6. Encourage the children to attach the flower petals to their paper plate and draw a face on it.

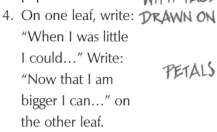

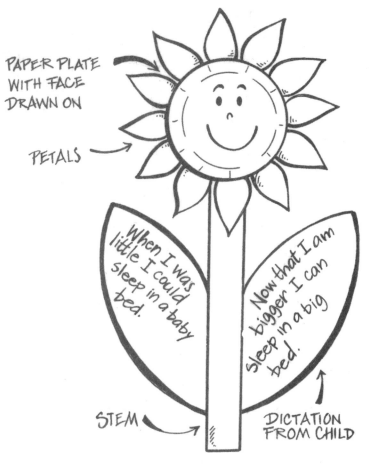

PAPER PLATE WITH FACE DRAWN ON

PETALS

When I was little I could sleep in a baby bed.

Now that I am bigger I can sleep in a big bed.

STEM

DICTATION FROM CHILD

7. The child attaches the flower head to the stem and adds the leaves.

 Sandy L. Scott, Vancouver, WA

Kinder Chatter

Materials

Red and green construction paper • scissors • craft stick • glue • red and green watercolor pens

What to do

1. Five-year-olds love to talk. This is a great way to involve your whole group in discussions.

2. Beforehand, cut the red and green paper into two circles of the same size, about 4" in diameter. Glue them back-to-back, inserting the craft stick in the middle with the stick extended to form a handle.

3. Ask each child to choose a partner.

4. Make a green dot on the back of one partner's hand, and a red dot on the other partner's hand.

5. When asking the group to answer a question or have a discussion, tell them to "kinder chatter." Hold up the color signal and say, "Red dots, kinder chatter the answer with your partner." Turn over the sign and say, "Green dots, kinder chatter with your partner." This enables all the children to have a turn.

6. While they are chatting, the adult working with them can hear their answers and say, "I hear someone saying…"

7. To promote listening skills, ask the children to tell what their partner said.

8. Let the children take turns holding the "kinder chatter" sign.

 Barbara Saul, Eureka, CA

Monster Moods

Materials

Paper • pencils • crayons or markers

What to do

1. Read the following poem out loud. Ask the children to repeat the refrain after every stanza.

Monster, Monster by Barbara Saul
Refrain:
Monster, Monster, I see you there
With purple eyes and long, green hair.

Late at night when I'm in bed,
A monster pops out his big head.

He's big and tall and very hairy,
You might even think he's scary.

He runs and jumps
And makes loud THUMPS.

(continued on the next page)

When Monster stands up on my rug,
He gives me a great, big hug.

2. Pre-print the following phrases at the bottom of each piece of paper. Give one to each child. Ask them to draw a monster.

   Monster feels sad when…
   Monster feels happy when…

3. Work with the children individually and have them fill in the phrases orally while you write down what they say. Children can write their own answers, if they are able.

 Barbara Saul, Eureka, CA

People in Motion Collage

Materials

Variety of magazines • construction paper • glue sticks or containers of white glue • scissors

What to do

1. Discuss the meaning of people in motion in conjunction with movement concepts. Show pictures of active people. Ask questions such as, "What is this person doing? What parts of this person's body would be moving? What game do you think they are playing? How do you know?"
2. Ask the children to select and cut out pictures of people who look like they are moving or playing a game. For children who are unable to use scissors, provide assistance as they tear pictures from the magazines.
3. Let the children glue the pictures to construction paper.
4. Encourage discussion about the collages by asking questions. For example, "What is this person doing?" "What parts of her body are moving?" "Name the body parts that are bent, …touching the ground, …up in the air." "Have you ever played that game or done that activity?"

 Margery A. Kranyik Fermino, Hyde Park, MD

Riddle Me This

Materials

Sturdy pet pictures • tagboard cards • markers • bag

What to do

1. Ahead of time, collect pet pictures and make a rhyming riddle card for each.

   I'm small and furry.
   I love to run.
   I live in a cage
   And sleep for fun.
   (hamster)

   I'm not in a cage
   Or up in the sky.
   I swim and I dart
   But I cannot fly.
   (fish)

   My fur is soft
   And my ears are long.
   My two back feet
   Are extra strong!
   (rabbit)

   My two feet hop.
   My two wings fly.
   You can see me
   Up in the sky.
   (bird)

2. Discuss the pet pictures, describing the characteristics of each animal.
3. Teach the children the following rhyme:

   Can you, can you, tell my name?
   Come and play my guessing game!

(continued on the next page)

4. Put the riddle cards into the bag. Chant the "Can you, can you" rhyme together. Ask a child to draw a card. When the riddle is read, let the child name the animal and choose the correct picture. If help is needed, prompt the child to choose a friend to help.

 Susan Oldham Hill, Lakeland, FL

Riddle Rhymes

Materials

20 sheets of construction paper • black marker

What to do

1. Write each of these words on a sheet of construction paper: fat, cat, funny, bunny, bug, jug, bony, pony, snake, cake, cool, tool, wee, bee, mad, dad, mouse, house, toad, road.

2. Spread the papers on the floor, mixing and separating the rhyming words. Ask the following riddles, and have the children match the rhyming words.
   - ☆ An overweight kitty (fat cat)
   - ☆ A silly rabbit (funny bunny)
   - ☆ A jar of insects (bug jug)
   - ☆ A skinny horse (bony pony)
   - ☆ A python dessert (snake cake)
   - ☆ A cold hammer (cool tool)
   - ☆ A tiny bug (wee bee)
   - ☆ An angry father (mad dad)
   - ☆ A rodent's home (mouse house)
   - ☆ A frog's street (toad road)

3. Think up more simple nouns and ask the children to come up with their own rhymes.

 Dotti Enderle, Richmond, TX

Spanish Days of the Week

What to do

1. Sing the days of the week in Spanish to the tune of "Row, Row, Row Your Boat."

   Lunes, martez,
   Miercoles, jueves,
   Viernes, sabado,
   Domingo.

 Lisa Chichester, Parkersburg, WV

Prop Storytelling

Materials

Small toy people (at least as many as the number of children plus teacher) • twice as many pieces of toy furniture, animals, or any other small toys

What to do

1. Gather the children in a circle.
2. Lay out all the people, furniture, animals, and so on in the center of the circle.
3. Ask each child to pick one toy person and two of any of the other objects. The children keep their items in front of them.
4. Say, "I will start our story, and I need everyone to take a turn and help out." Start by taking your toy person and making up one or two sentences about it. Then place it in the middle of the circle.
5. Ask the child next to you to tell something about her toy person, and then add it to the middle of the circle.
6. Go around the circle letting each child take a turn.
7. After everyone has a turn, choose one of your other objects and start a story about it as you add it to the middle of the circle. For example, "Once upon a time, there was a group of people sitting together when suddenly, a small dog (add this to the circle) ran up and sat down right in the middle of everyone."

(continued on the next page)

8. Then ask the child sitting next to you what happened next. Ask her to add one of her pieces and tell a couple more sentences.

9. Continue going around the circle until all the objects are in the middle. Then say, "The end!"

 Tracey Neumarke, Chicago, IL

Rhyming Objects

Materials

Rhyming objects • low table or flat surface

What to do

1. Collect pairs of rhyming objects ahead of time. Some suggestions are: car/star, mouse/house, book/hook, hat/cat, fish/dish, rose/bows, bug/rug, pin/tin, bee/tree, clown/brown, vase/lace, goat/boat, pot/knot, soap/rope, bear/pear, seed/weed, ring/king, moon/spoon, pan/fan, block/clock, ant/plant, wig/pig, dog/frog, and box/fox.

2. Collect as many pairs of rhyming objects as you have children, plus one or two extra, on a flat surface.

3. Let each child select a pair of rhyming objects. Encourage them to say what the objects are and use them in a sentence.

4. Sing songs that have many rhyming words such as "Down by the Bay," "This Old Man," and "Over in the Meadow."

5. Read a poetry book or rhyme book out loud. Read only the first rhyming word and let the children think of the second rhyming word.

 Mary Brehm, Aurora, OH

Story Box

Materials

Box • miscellaneous items (such as a car, cup, book, or clothing), one for each child • paper • markers

What to do

1. Put all of the items in a box. Make sure there are enough objects for each child to pick one.
2. Begin by helping the group pick a main character (any character will work).
3. Tell the first line of a story about that character.
4. Then, ask a child to select an item from the box. The child uses the object to tell the next line of the story.
5. Pass the box around the circle, so each child has a turn to add to the story.
6. Write each child's part on a separate sheet of paper and let her illustrate her page.
7. Assemble the pages and put the new book in the reading corner.

 Catherine Shogren, Eagan, MN

All Through the Week

Materials

Calendar • seven strips of colored construction paper • construction paper • pencils • crayons

What to do

1. Start on a Monday. Tell the children that today is Monday and write the word on a strip of paper.
2. Talk about what is special about Mondays. For example, it's the first day of the school week, there may be some special activities or snacks that happen on Monday, and so on.
3. Establish certain things that you or the school always does on Monday, such as music, art, or special food at lunch.
4. Encourage the children to copy the word Monday and decorate it with little pictures showing what happens on Mondays.
5. The next day, do the same activity with Tuesday, and so on.
6. After a number of weeks, the children will be able to identify each day of the week.
7. On Fridays, talk about Saturday; on Mondays, talk about Sunday.
8. Encourage the children to make up sentences about each day of the week. Challenge them to come up with ideas that begin with the same letter as the day of the week. For example: On Mondays we meet our friends in school (Monday, meet), on Tuesdays we take the bus to school (Tuesday, take), and so on.
9. Another idea is to ask them to name foods with the same letter of the day of the week. For example, Monday: macaroni, Tuesday: turkey, and so on.

 Lucy Fuchs, Brandon, FL

Adjectives

Materials

Objects around the room • pictures from magazines • strips of construction paper • markers

What to do

1. Hold up an object in the room, such as your sweater. Talk about the object. What does it look like? Is it big or little? What color is it? Is it soft or hard? Is it warm or cool? As each word is said, write it on a strip of construction paper with a marker.
2. Explain that these description words are all adjectives. Write "adjective" on the chalkboard.
3. Ask individual children to describe other objects, perhaps their own sweaters. As each new word is used, write it on a strip.
4. Place the strips of construction paper around the room. As children talk about things, ask them to select words and describe them. Keep adding new ones.
5. Later, perhaps the next day or week, introduce the children to new adjectives.

 Lucy Fuchs, Brandon, FL

A Is for Apple and Ads

Materials

Grocery ads from the local newspaper • construction paper • markers • glue • scissors

What to do

1. Explain to the children that they are going to do an activity that focuses on vowels.
2. Discuss the different vowels and the sounds that each one makes.
3. Divide the children into groups of five. Distribute the grocery ads to the children's work stations.

(continued on the next page)

4. Next, distribute five (six if you are teaching Y as a vowel) sheets of construction paper to each group of children. Ask them to print a different vowel on each sheet of paper.

5. Then, distribute the glue and scissors and demonstrate for the children how to cut out a picture from the grocery ads.

6. The group decides what vowel sound each item makes and then glues it to the appropriate vowel sheet. For example, an apple would make the short "a" sound, so the children would glue it on the vowel sheet titled "A."

7. The children continue until they have found several pictures for each vowel sheet.

8. When the children are done with this part of the activity, gather them together and ask each group to share their findings. The children who are not sharing can check to make sure that the pictures were assigned to the correct vowel sheets.

9. Display the sheets throughout the classroom.

10. Do the same activity another day, but use initial consonants instead of vowels.

 Mike Krestar, White Oak, PA

ABC Names

Materials

Photos of each child, teacher, classroom pet, or anyone important to the class • index cards or sentence strips • glue stick • computer, typewriter, or marker • alphabet chart • stapler

What to do

1. Glue each person's picture onto an index card, sentence strip, or piece of paper. (Sizes will depend upon the size of the photo and the size of your alphabet chart.)

2. Using a computer, typewriter, or marker, clearly write each person's name next to the picture.

3. As you study a letter of the alphabet, add the corresponding name and photo (if any) to your alphabet chart. Staple it below the chart so the children can see whose name(s) starts with that letter.

4. Add other important words such as "mom," "dad," and "love" to the alphabet chart.

 Linda N. Ford, Sacramento, CA

Alphabet Art Book

Materials

Construction paper in many colors • alphabet stencils (large enough to cover half a sheet of construction paper) • hole punch • reinforcements, optional • an art medium for each letter of the alphabet (for example apple stickers for A, macaroni for M, insect stamps for I, and so on) • ring for each child

What to do

1. Cut construction paper in half and divide the paper into 26 stacks. Cut enough sheets so that each child can take one sheet from each stack. (Have a few extra sheets in each stack for mistakes.)

2. Use stencils to trace the outline of each letter (upper- and lowercase) on each sheet of paper, again making sure you have enough for each child to have each letter.

3. Punch a hole in the top left corner of each page. If desired, add a reinforcement to the hole.

4. When you are ready to do your first letter, give each child an alphabet page and a corresponding art medium (one that starts with that letter). Encourage them to fill in the letter using the medium—gluing, drawing, stamping, etc.

5. On the first letter page, attach a ring to the top left corner and a letter to the parents that reads, "Dear parents: This is the beginning of your child's alphabet book. As we learn each letter of the alphabet, your child will bring home a new page for their book. Please help them to open the ring and add each new page to the book. At the end of the year, they will have a complete alphabet book to enjoy."

6. As you study each letter, try to come up with different items for the child to put on the letter. For example, feather F's, jewel J's, polka dot (bingo daubers) P's, Lego print L's, and kitten stickers for K. The possibilities are endless.

7. Be careful not to choose items that are too heavy because they weigh the book down.

   Author Note: When I start to prepare the pages for this book, I do the first 13 letters at the beginning of the year and the rest in the middle of the year. I cut and count the pages and then put about three to four letters together in kits with the stencils and reinforcements. Then I give these to parent volunteers to trace the letters, punch the holes, and stick on the reinforcements. This is a HUGE time saver!

 Gail Morris, Kemah, TX

Alphabet Fun

Materials

Fabric scraps (about 13 different fabric pieces) • scissors • red felt • sewing machine capable of making zigzag stitch • 26 pictures (one for each letter of the alphabet) • oak tag • rubber cement • laminator • felt • flannel board

What to do

1. Cut out 3" uppercase letters from fabric scraps. Each fabric scrap may be used to make two different letters.
2. Cut red felt into 26 pieces approximately 3 ½" x 4" each.
3. Appliqué each letter to a piece of red felt using a zigzag stitch on a sewing machine.
4. Locate 26 cute, colored pictures of objects beginning with each letter of the alphabet.
5. Glue the pictures to oak tag using rubber cement. Cut around each oak tag-backed picture so that each picture is approximately 3 ¼" x 3 ¾".
6. Laminate the pictures for durability.
7. Prepare for flannel board use by backing the pictures with felt using rubber cement.
8. To do the activity, the child matches each letter with a picture that has the same beginning sound on the flannel board.
9. This fun activity is great for reinforcing initial sound recognition.

Tip: If your flannel board is not large enough, put out only half of the activity at a time.

UPPER CASE

RED FELT 3½" x 4"

OAK TAG-BACKED PICTURE (LAMINATED ON FRONT and FELT ON BACK)

 Jackie Wright, Enid, OK

Alphabet Sorting Case

Materials

One machine screw case with 30 drawers • 26 white adhesive labels • black marker • four small items to represent each letter of the alphabet (104 items total) • one upper- and one lowercase small plastic magnetic letter for each letter of the alphabet

What to do

1. Obtain one machine screw case with 30 drawers (available at hardware stores).

2. Use the white adhesive labels and black marker to create A-Z labels for each drawer. Use one letter per drawer. Start at the upper left corner and work your way down the machine case going left to right. There will be four drawers left over in the bottom of the case.

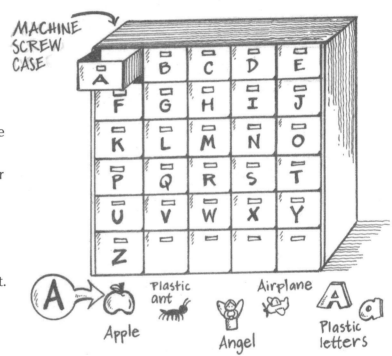

3. Place the objects that represent each letter in the appropriate drawers.

4. Put out the alphabet sorting case for free use.

5. Encourage the children to explore the sorting case. Encourage them to notice the lettered labels. Sound out the names of the objects in each drawer with them. Help them make the connection between the objects and the letter of the alphabet each one represents.

6. Keep the sorting case out for daily use. The children will enjoy playing with the small objects and trying to match them to the appropriate letter.

 Virginia Jean Herrod, Columbia, SC

Egyptian Cartouche

Materials

Egyptian alphabet sheets • cardboard • markers • scissors • rectangular shapes with rounded corners • pictures of hieroglyphics and Egypt from the library • heavy paper or construction paper • string • hole punch

What to do

1. Write/draw the Egyptian alphabet on a piece of paper (see illustration). Make a copy for each child in the class.

2. Make patterns of the Egyptian alphabet by drawing each letter (hieroglyphic) on a piece of cardboard and cutting it out. Then make a pattern of an Egyptian cartouche by tracing a rectangular shape with rounded corners on a piece of cardboard and cutting it out.

3. Explore and discuss the Egyptian alphabet or hieroglyphics. Show the children books and pictures of hieroglyphics and Egypt.

4. Tell the children that a cartouche is an oval figure enclosing a sovereign's (leader) name. Explain that they will make their own cartouche by writing their names using hieroglyphics.

MIRANDA

5. Ask the children to trace an oval shape on a piece of paper and cut it out.

6. Give each child an Egyptian alphabet sheet. Demonstrate how to find the symbol for each letter of their names. Encourage them to use the patterns to trace the symbols on their oval papers.

7. The children can decorate the outer edge of the cartouche, punch a hole in the top, and place a string through the hole.

8. Encourage them to try to read each other's names. If desired, let them make name and label cards for classroom pets and materials.

☆ Sandra L. Nagel, White Lake, MI

Bunnie's Bunches of B's

Materials

Brown paper lunch bags, one for each child • blue or black marker • assorted objects that start with B, one for each child • one large basket • bunny ears (one set to pass around or one set for each child)

What to do

1. Write "Bb" in blue or black marker on each paper lunch bag. Place one "B" object into each bag and fold the top down several times.

2. Ask the children to sit in a circle with a basket in the center.

3. Give each child a bag. Instruct them not to open the bags until it is their turn.

4. Point out that the words brown, bag, blue, and black all start with "B."

5. Teach this chant:

   Bunnies are bringing bunches of Bs.
   What did you bring in your bag, Bunny?

6. Place the ears on the first child, or if they have their own ears point to a child. The class repeats the chant and the child opens his bag, removes the object, names it, and places it in the basket.

7. If you have one set of ears, pass them around to another child, or point to another child already wearing ears. Repeat the chant and see what is in the next bag. Keep repeating until everyone gets a turn.

 Sandra Gratias, Perkasie, PA

Animal Alphabet Parade: Walrus

Materials

Construction paper • scissors • brown lunch bags • white glue • 23mm wiggly eyes • stickers • markers for detail

What to do

1. Make patterns for animal puppets. The example shown is for a walrus (see illustration). Make your own puppet first, and when you are done with each letter, let the children make their own puppets.
2. Help the children trace the patterns onto construction paper and cut them out. The children glue the pieces to a paper bag as shown.
3. Encourage the children to decorate their walrus puppet as desired, using wiggly eyes, stickers, and markers.
4. Post the animal puppet with the uppercase and lowercase letter as you study the phonics for that letter.
5. When the last letter animal is made, have an animal puppet parade and visit other classrooms.
6. If desired, vary the types of puppets you make (for example, stick puppets, paper tube puppets, and spoon puppets).

WALRUS

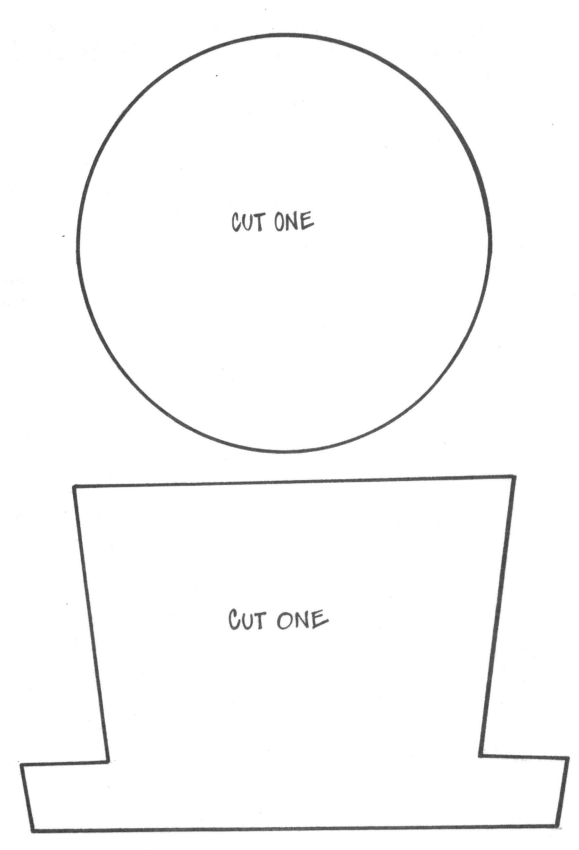

CUT ONE

CUT ONE

(continued on the next page)

7. Suggestions for the animal puppet to make for each letter:

Aa: Alligator
Bb: Bear
Cc: Cat
Dd: Dog
Ee: Elephant
Ff: Frog
Gg: Goat
Hh: Horse
Ii: Iguana
Jj: Jaguar
Kk: Koala
Ll: Lion
Mm: Monkey
Nn: Narwhal
Oo: Otter
Pp: Pig
Qq: Quail

Rr: Raccoon
Ss: Seal
Tt: Turtle
Uu: Umbrella bird
Vv: Vulture
Ww: Walrus
Xx: X-ray fish
Yy: Yak
Zz: Zebra
Long Vowels:
A: Ape
E: Eagle
I: Ibis bird
O: Orangutan
U: Unicorn fish

 Mary Brehm, Aurora, OH

Animal Name Game

Materials

Index cards • magazine pictures of animals • scissors • glue

What to do

1. Make pairs of animal cards by gluing pictures of animals to index cards. Pairs of cards must have the same animal but not necessarily the same picture. Write the names of the animals on the other side of the cards (without the pictures).
2. Spread the cards on the table with the names of the animals facing up.
3. Children take turns trying to match the names. If they find a match, they keep the cards.

Tip: Make cards depicting other themes, such as types of toys, clothing, colors, or objects beginning with the same letter.

 Deborah Litfin, Forest Hills, NY

Class ABC's Book

Materials

Large sheets of paper, one page for each letter • marker • old magazines • scissors • glue stick

What to do

1. On each page write a letter of the alphabet and a few words that begin with that letter.
2. It is helpful to work on only one letter each week. Introduce the letter of the week and talk about the sound the letter makes as well as some items that begin with that letter.
3. Ask the children to cut out pictures that begin with that letter from magazines and glue them to the letter page.
4. By the end of the year, all letters will be covered in the book.

 Sandy L. Scott, Vancouver, WA

Grocery Bag Books

Materials

Empty grocery containers • large brown paper bags • scissors • 9" x 12" manila paper • stapler • glue • markers

What to do

1. Set up a grocery store center. Ask parents to donate empty boxes and cans from food items. Place them on the shelves of the grocery store.
2. Open the bags and cut out the sides and bottom. Use the front and back of the bag as the front and back cover of a book.
3. Count out ten pages of manila paper and place them between the two covers. Staple the pages in place.
4. Encourage the children to "shop" for their favorite foods or choose foods from each food group in the grocery store center.
5. Give each child a blank book. Ask them to cut out and glue labels on each page of their books.

(continued on the next page)

6. Encourage the children to copy the labels on their pages. They can number the pages, copy letters from the labels, or find prices and write them down.

 Vera M. Peters, Elizabethton, TN

Leaf Baggie Books

Materials

Index cards • 5 zipper-closure plastic bags • stapler • white, green, red, and yellow (fall leaf colors) poster board cut into 8" x 20" pieces • scissors • string • masking tape or clear packaging tape

What to do

1. For children to do assembly-line book publishing, place step-by-step directions on cards in front of the supplies. Beforehand, read the steps to the children. If desired, include pictures.

2. Each child counts out five baggies.

3. Demonstrate how to staple the baggies together at the top (not the open end).

4. Let each child pick one piece of poster board and fold it in half.

5. Cut pieces of string approximately 24" (you may need to measure to child's height, as they will wear this book as a "pocketbook").

6. Tie the ends of the string together, forming a loop, and place the tied string loop around the folded poster board (see illustration). Tape it to the fold.

7. Add baggies; staple in place (make sure that the string and baggies are stapled).

8. Take the children on a nature walk and collect leaves in the baggies.

 Vera M. Peters, Elizabethton, TN

Bookmaking Center

Materials

Paper of all kinds, shapes, and sizes (notebook, typing, construction, wallpaper wrapping paper, graph paper, rolled paper) • tape • hole punch • stapler • string • glue • brads • rings • scissors • magazines • greeting cards • stickers • clip art • stamps and stamp pads • crayons • pencils • variety of markers • examples of different kinds of books, commercial and homemade

What to do

1. Bookmaking encourages creativity, literacy, language development, and fine motor skills. Discuss making books at circle time, and show examples of commercial and homemade books. Explain that a person who writes a book is called an author and that they will be authors of their own books.

2. Set up your bookmaking center on a regular basis. Put out a variety of materials, including interesting paper and writing instruments (for example, metallic colored pencils, glitter crayons, and cool gel pens). These give new encouragement to the uninterested writer.

3. Help children with the words and stories for their books. Let them dictate their stories or use inventive writing. Make word cards (picture and word together on a card) and put them in the bookmaking center to help facilitate their writing.

4. Encourage the children to cut out pictures or draw their own to make their stories come to life.

5. Encourage them to make a cover for their books and to come up with a title. Show them how to attach the pages together using staples, yarn or string, or brads and rings.

6. Read their stories to them or to the class if they wish.

7. Keep it fresh and new each time you put out the center by including plenty of supplies. Encourage them to be creative and try new things.

Tip: Some interesting ideas to try are accordion books, miniature books, gigantic books, books that roll up, and pop-up books.

 Gail Morris, Kemah, TX

How to Fetch a Rainbow

Materials

Several sheets of ruled paper • pen • hole punch • paper fasteners

What to do

1. Tell the children that you would like to have a rainbow. Ask them if they can think of ways you could get one. (For any five-year-old, this is not impossible!)
2. Write down each child's idea.
3. Punch a hole in each page and attach them together with paper fasteners.
4. If possible, make copies for each child and present them at the end of the school year. If not, display the book on parent/teacher conference day.

    Author Note: Following are some samples from my own classes:

    "A pilot can bring it back next time he lands."

    "My dad has a very long ladder and he can unhook it from the sky. My dad can do anything."

    "You have to wait until it comes to your garden."

    "When you see the rainbow, sneak outside and grab a small piece and put it in your pocket."

    "You can't have a rainbow because it's nailed to the clouds."

 Ingelore Mix, Gainesville, VA

I Can Read This Book!

Materials

Pictures of signs • magazines and newspapers • scissors • 9" x 12" white construction paper • stapler • glue • markers

What to do

1. Introduce this activity at circle time. Show the children pictures of various road, store, and fast food restaurant signs. Encourage the children to "read" them.

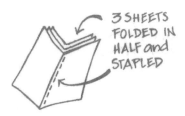

2. Give the children magazines and newspapers in which to find familiar signs. Allow the children to cut them out.

3. Fold three sheets of white construction paper in half and staple at the crease to form a book. Make one for each child.

4. Print the title and author (child's name) on the front cover. Ask the children to paste their pictures in their books.

5. Encourage them to take their books home and read them to their parents.
   Tip: Send a note home with the children informing parents of the environmental reading unit. Ask the parents to send in additional food or soap labels for children to add to their books.

 Susan R. Forbes, Daytona Beach, FL

If I Were a Dinosaur or Me as a Dinosaur

Materials

Close-up "head" shot of each child • scissors • paper • glue • markers

What to do

1. Take a close-up picture of each child in the room. Cut out the head only.

2. Give each child a piece of paper. Encourage them to glue the head onto the paper and then draw any kind of dinosaur body they wish.

3. Encourage each child to name his dinosaur creation (for example, Katie-O-Saurus and Ty-Matt-O-don).

4. Ask each child to dictate a few things about his dinosaur. For example, is it a meat eater (carnivore) or a plant eater (herbivore)? What does it like to do for fun? Where does it live?

5. At lunch or at the end of the day, read each child's page to the class. The children love it!

 Wanda Guidroz, Santa Fe, TX

My Me Book

Materials

Paper • crayons or markers • *The One and Only Me* by Marilyn Singer • *Me and My Family* by Paul Showers • magazines • scissors • glue • construction paper

What to do

1. This project will take a week to finish. It can be a part of a beginning-of-the-year theme, such as a "Me" theme.
2. Prior to doing this activity, send a note home asking parents to send in a small picture of their child.
3. Write the following titles on separate pieces of paper and make a copy for each child: "Me," "My Family," "My Birthday" (also draw a birthday cake for the children to decorate and add candles to), "What I Want to Be When I Grow Up," "My Favorite Color," "My Favorite Food," and "My Favorite Things" (write the following list of questions: What is your favorite book? What is your favorite game to play? What is your favorite toy to play with? Who are your best friends? What is your favorite color? Do you have a pet? What is your pet's name?).

Monday

1. During circle time, read the book *The One and Only Me* by Marilyn Singer.
2. Have a discussion about how each child is different from the other children in the room. For example, some children have blue eyes, and some have brown eyes. Ask each child, in turn, to describe the person sitting next to him.
3. After the discussion, explain that they will be making a "Me Book" all week. This book will be a story about them. After explaining the project, ask them to move to work tables and give them the page titled, "Me."
4. Ask them to draw a picture of themselves. When they are finished, put the pictures aside to use later in their book.
5. Hand out the page titled "My Birthday" and let the children decorate the cake. When they are finished, they can add the number of candles that they will be on their next birthday. At the bottom, write: "(Child's name) will be ___ years old on his/her birthday." Add the child's birth date and put the pictures aside to use later in the book.

Tueday

1. During circle time, read the book *Me and My Family* by Paul Showers.
2. Have a discussion about families. It is important to remember the many different family types we have in our society today. Ask questions such as,

"How many brothers or sisters do you have?" "Are they older or younger than you?" Do you know what your parent(s) do at work?" "When you have a family outing, what do you do?"

3. Give the children the page titled, "My Family." Ask them to draw a picture of their families and when they are finished, you can help them write the names of each family member under their picture.

4. When they are finished, give them the page titled, "My Favorite Things." Ask them to dictate their answers as you write down the information.

5. Set both pages aside to use later in their book.

Wednesday

1. Before class find pictures of different community workers, or use magazines for the children to find pictures of what they want to be when they grow up.

2. During circle time, read a book about community workers (see related books below).

3. Start a discussion by asking the children what they want to be when they grow up. Ask them why they would like to have that occupation.

4. Give each child a page titled, "What Do I Want To Be When I Grow Up?" Encourage them to choose a picture of what they would like to be and glue it to their page.

5. Help the children label the picture, for example, "I want to be a teacher."

6. When they are done, put the page aside for later.

Thursday

1. Before class, find pictures of different kinds of food or use magazines for the children to look through for their favorite foods.

2. During circle time, ask the children, "What is your favorite food?" "Why?" After your discussion, explain that they will be finding a picture of their favorite foods and adding it to their books.

3. Hand out the page titled "My Favorite Food." Encourage the children to glue pictures of their favorite foods on their pages.

4. Help them label their pages with the names of the foods.

5. When they are finished, set the pages aside for later.

Friday

1. Before class, prepare the covers for the books by printing, "(Child's name)'s Me Book" on a piece of construction paper. Make one for each child. Have their photos and pages ready to hand out.

2. Explain to the children that today's project will be to finish their books.

3. Move to a table where they can work. Hand out the covers, pages, and a photo to each child. Explain that they will glue the picture to their covers.

(continued on the next page)

4. When they are finished, help them staple together the pages inside the front and back covers.

5. Encourage the children to take their books home to share with their families.

Related books

(For "What I Want to Be When I Grow Up")
Books by Gail Gibbons
Career Day by Anne Rockwell
Construction Workers by Tami Deedrick
Fire Fighters by Norma Simon
I Want to be a Vet by Dan Liebman
I Want to be an Astronaut by Byron Barton

 Sherri Lawrence, Louisville, KY

My Opposite Book

Materials

9" x 12" white construction paper • hole punch • colored yarn • pencils • crayons • black, yellow, purple, green, and blue construction paper • paper cutter • glue • scissors • star stickers • cotton balls or strips • tongue depressors • small star stickers

What to do

1. Put two pieces of white construction paper together and fold them in half.

2. Punch two holes on the left-hand side and thread bright yarn through the holes to make a book. Make one for each child.

3. Show the children how to write "My Opposite Book" on the cover, one letter at a time.

4. Cut purple, black, green, and blue paper 6" x 4 ½" on a paper cutter prior to the project.

5. Ask the children to glue the black paper to the first inside page of the booklet. Encourage them to cut out moon shapes from yellow paper and glue them to the black paper. They can add star stickers, too. Help them write "Night" on the page.

6. On the opposite page (second page), help them write "Day." Encourage them to draw the sun and flowers on this page.

7. Help them write "Big" on the next page, and "Little" on the opposite page. Encourage them to draw something big (big snowman, ball, building) and something little.

8. Let each child choose a piece of purple, green, or blue paper and glue it on the second to last page of the book. Help them write "Soft" on the page and "Hard" on the opposite page.

9. Encourage them to glue cotton balls on the colored paper and a tongue depressor on the opposite page.

10. Add more pages, if desired, using any pairs of opposites you and the children can think of.

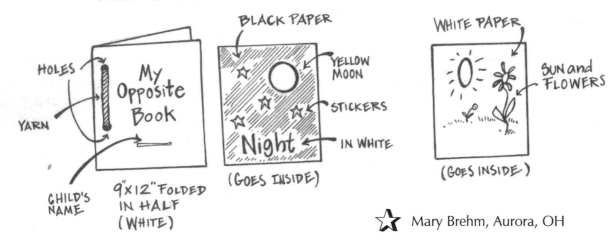

☆ Mary Brehm, Aurora, OH

Our Stories

Materials

Magazines • scissors • writing paper (lined at the bottom and unlined at the top) • glue • markers or crayons

What to do

1. Go through magazines (have a volunteer adult help you with this) and cut out pictures that go with a theme. Some ideas for themes are zoo, ocean, or space. Make sure that you have plenty of pictures for the children to choose from. The children could help with this, too.

2. Talk to the children about authors. Tell them they are going to be authors and write their own stories. Explain that a story has a beginning, middle, and an end.

3. Put out all the pictures, glue, and writing supplies. Explain that the bottom of the paper is for words and the top is for pictures.

(continued on the next page)

4. Have the children start with the pictures, as this helps them begin to visualize what their story may be about. Let them to choose the cut-out pictures that interest them.

5. Encourage them to glue a few pictures on the page and use crayons or markers to add to the scene. Tell them to start to think of the story that will go along with the picture as they are creating it.

6. When they are done, ask them to tell you their story. Write their words exactly as they dictate them to you. Allow the children to watch you as you put their words on the paper. If they want to write the stories themselves, be there to support their efforts.

7. Read the children's stories during lunch or circle time. Make sure to acknowledge the author. The children will beam with pride.

Tip: At the beginning of the year, ask parents to cut out pictures that relate to your themes. You could also collect a lot of interesting pictures without a theme and let the children create whatever kind of story they want.

☆ Gail Morris, Kemah, TX

Dictated Story Day

Materials

Story paper, top half blank, bottom lined, hole-punched • 3-prong folders, one for each child • markers

What to do

1. Introduce the story paper and folders to the children. Explain that they will make up their own books of stories.

2. Demonstrate how to make a story by doing the first one yourself. Draw a simple picture, then give your story a title, and write it (in print, not cursive) on the lines below. Date and sign your story at the end.

3. Read your story aloud and add it to a folder labeled "A Book of Stories" by (your name).

4. Explain to the children that after they have drawn their story picture, they can dictate their story to you or another adult in the room. Emphasize that their stories can be about anything they choose, true or make-believe, happy or sad, scary, silly, or whatever they want to write about.

5. Choose a day of the week to be story day at group time.

6. After the children finish their stories each week, give each child the option of choosing one of his stories to be read aloud to the class.

7. After the stories are chosen, go through the stack and read each one. Do not read stories that might be hurtful to other childern in the class.

8. After each child's story is read, let him show the picture to the class by carrying it around the circle.

9. The child may then call on three children who have raised their hands to speak. Those called on may make comments or ask questions about the story.

10. Each week, after the children finish their stories, they can add them to their folders.

 Susan Jones Jensen, Norman, OK

Snowman Big Book

Materials

12″ x 18″ white construction paper • scissors • markers • 12″ x 18″ white paper • hole punch and yarn, stapler, or binding machine

What to do

1. Draw a snowman shape (about 12″ x 16″) on two pieces of white construction paper. Cut out the shapes. These will be the front and back cover of a class big book.

2. Decorate the snowman using markers.

3. Make pages for the book by cutting white paper in the same shape, slightly smaller than the cover.

4. Use the pages for a favorite snowman poem, or ask each child to dictate what his snowman would like to eat. Let the children illustrate the book.

5. Attach the pages together using a stapler, yarn and hole punch, or binding machine. Keep it in your reading area for all to enjoy.

 Jackie Wright, Enid, OK

Rainy Day Big Book

Materials

11" x 17" paper • 12" x 18" tagboard or poster board • computer and printer • laminator, optional • binding machine, optional

What to do

1. Make a class big book (approximately 11" x 17") using one of your favorite songs about rain.
2. Print the text using a large font on your computer (if a computer is not available, use a felt-tip pen).
3. At the back of the book include these "Think Rain" phrases for the children to complete verbally.

Phrase	Suggested Answer
The color of the sky	Gray
Coat used for rain	Raincoat
Thunder and…	Lightning
Where you can't play when it rains	Outside
Put one up to stay dry	Umbrella
Pools of water	Puddles
What the earth is after rain	Wet
They keep your feet dry	Boots
Helps us to see while driving in rain	Windshield wipers
Colored arch in the sky	Rainbow

4. Decorate the cover of the big book with an appropriate picture. For example, use a duck wearing a raincoat, rain hat, and boots in the rain.
5. Laminate the covers and the pages, if desired.
6. Bind the pages together between the covers using a binding machine, if available.
7. Share the big book with the class and then put it in your reading area.

 Jackie Wright, Enid, OK

Christmas Cards for Book Illustrations

Materials

Old Christmas cards • scissors • glue stick • red and green construction paper • computer (or black water-based marker) • laminator • binder, optional

What to do

1. Old Christmas cards are great to use to illustrate a classroom book quickly. Get the whole class involved in looking through the cards to locate the needed pictures.
2. Cut out various Christmas items from the cards, such as a snowman, candle, Christmas tree, poinsettia, wreath, bells, sleigh, manger, pinecones, candy canes, stocking, reindeer, and so on.
3. Cut the desired number of construction paper pages approximately 8" x 9".
4. Glue one Christmas shape to the front and back of each construction paper page, alternating the pages between red and green.
5. Label the pictures using a large font on your computer or a black, water-based pen.
6. Cut the front and back covers 8 ½" x 10".
7. Label the front cover with an appropriate title such as "The Magic of Christmas."
8. Laminate the pages and covers for a longer shelf life.
9. Assemble the pages into a book and bind the book on the left using a binding machine, if available.
10. Put the book in your reading area.

 Jackie Wright, Enid, OK

Silly Salad

Materials

Chart paper • markers • 6" x 9" construction paper in various colors • scissors • large salad bowl

(continued on the next page)

What to do

1. Gather the children together and ask them to name some items that might go into a salad. List each item on a piece of chart paper. (You can have children draw icons next to each word during small group time.)
2. Next make a list of things that definitely would NOT go into a salad.
3. Ask the children to draw a picture of something that would not go into a salad on a piece of construction paper.
4. Pre-trace vegetable shapes on construction paper. Help the children cut out all the shapes.
5. Label the pictures and "toss" the word cards in the salad bowl.
6. The children may practice tossing different combinations of their own personal salad by selecting a vegetable card, "reading" it, and keeping the card if read correctly.

 Susan R. Forbes, Daytona Beach, FL

Unscramble

Materials

Note cards • marker

What to do

1. Write a variety of easy reading words on note cards (one per card), such as sight words or consonant-vowel-consonant words. Prior to the activity, think of a few sentences using the words on the note cards and keep them together.
2. Gather the children (8-12 is ideal) around you on a rug on the floor.
3. Explain that they are going to become editors. You may wish to explain that editors correct sentences to make them easier to understand.
4. Pass out three to five of the cards (that make a potential sentence) to some children (one card per child).
5. Read aloud a possible sentence (scrambled) using the words on the cards.
6. Ask the children to arrange themselves in a line in the order that the words were read.
7. Now say, "Unscramble," and the children must figure out by themselves how to create a grammatically correct sentence. There may be several possibilities. Help them to understand this concept. (Perhaps they can be guided to make a question out of their sentence when done?)

8. Read aloud the correct sentence or let the children read their own words aloud.

9. Choose another small group of children to create the next sentence.

10. Be sure all the children have been given the opportunity to participate before repeating the exercise or moving on to another activity.

 Kate Ross, Middlessex, VT

The Magic Letter Game

Materials

Large note cards • markers

What to do

1. Make a set of cards by writing the uppercase letters of the alphabet on each card (one letter per card), large enough for the children to read in a group setting.

2. Invite the children to sit in a circle with you. Explain that they will be playing the Magic Letter Game. Emphasize that it is important for them to pay attention and listen so they will know what to say when it is their turn.

3. Show the children the set of cards, one at a time in alphabetical order, and encourage them to name each letter.

4. Shuffle the cards and draw one at random for the "magic letter."

5. Show the card and invite the class to name the letter. Lay the card face up in front of you.

6. Beginning with the letter "A," go around the circle and have each child say a letter of the alphabet, in order, until someone gets to the "magic letter." For example, if the letter "R" was drawn, the game will go from "A" to "R," and the child who gets to say the letter "R" will be "Mr. R" or "Miss R." You might want to serve as the initial starting person and say "A," and then have the sequence move around the circle to your left (the child next to you says "B," and so on).

7. The person who gets to say the magic letter (in this case, "Miss R") stands up as everyone claps.

8. Choose a new "magic letter" by drawing another card and begin the alphabet sequence again, with the winner of the previous round starting the game by saying the letter "A."

9. Repeat the game as many times as you like, each time drawing a new letter.

(continued on the next page)

10. Sometimes a child may be unsure of what letter to say when it is his turn. Emphasize beforehand that it is always okay to ask for help if they don't know the answer—this is a learning game! Encourage the children to help their friends by raising their hands if they know the correct letter. The child can then call on a friend who may say the letter.

11. The game can continue until all the letters have been used, or can conclude after a pre-determined number of "magic letters" are chosen.

 Susan Jones Jensen, Norman, OK

Letter Carrier Game

Materials

Business-size envelopes • markers • scissors • oak tag • "mail" bag • paper for hats

What to do

1. Make labels for various things throughout the room, such as a desk, door, shelf, blocks, and sink, by writing the word on business-size envelopes and attaching the envelope on the item.

2. Cut oak tag the size of the envelopes and write the words of the labeled places on each one (desk, door, sink, and so on). This is the "mail." Place the "letters" in the mailbag.

3. Make paper mail carrier hats for each child by fitting a band around the child's head and attaching a visor made out of paper.

4. The child who is delivering the mail tries to match the "letters" in his bag with the signs throughout the room. When he finds a match, he places the mail in the proper envelopes.

5. If you would like to make this a self-checking activity, you can place a sticker or icon on the back of each piece of "mail" and a matching one somewhere on the envelope.

 Iris Rothstein, New Hyde Park, NY

Letter Hunts

Materials

Large pieces of construction paper or oak tag • glue sticks • magazines and catalogs

What to do

1. Prepare large pieces of construction paper or oak tag by pasting a selected letter (upper- and lowercase) in the center of each (for example, Pp, Mm, Ff).
2. Cut out a number of pictures from magazines that begin with the appropriate initial sound on the pages (for example, milk, meat, monkey, pie, puppet, fish, fan, and so on). Put the pictures in the middle of the work table.
3. Place a prepared letter paper in front of each of three or four children seated around the table.
4. Each child finds a picture that starts with the letter on his paper and glues it to the page.
5. When everyone has found a picture and glued it on, rotate the papers so that each child is now looking for a new picture with a different letter. Continue the rotation until all the pictures have been glued.
6. The children who participated can now display their work to the class and identify the pictures chosen for each letter. The class can offer suggestions for other pictures that might belong on a given paper.

Related books

26 Letters and 99 Cents by Tana Hoban
Alligators All Around by Maurice Sendak
Chicka Chicka Boom Boom by Bill Martin

 Iris Rothstein, New Hyde Park, NY

Magnetic Names

Materials

Magnetic letters • copy machine • scissors • construction paper • glue • photo of each child • clear contact paper or laminating machine, optional • magnet board or metal sheet

(continued on the next page)

What to do

1. Place magnetic letters on the copy machine and make multiple copies. Cut out each letter.
2. Glue the letters on a piece of construction paper to form a child's name in the class. Make one for each child. Add a photo (or photocopy) of the child. Laminate them, if desired.
3. Invite the children to place matching magnetic letters on top of their name cards. This can be done with or without a magnet board. (Use bar magnets to hold the name card down.) The children can try to find their friends' names as well.
4. Make word cards of other words with the magnets.

 Laura Durbrow, Lake Oswego, OR

Texture Book

Materials

5" x 6" paper • stapler • fabric with different textures (fur, burlap, corduroy, felt, silk, satin, bouclé, wool, cotton, and so on) • variety of other textured materials (corrugated material, bubble wrap, sandpaper, foil, feathers, cellophane, and thin wood pieces or sandpaper) • glue • marker

What to do

1. Make blank books for each child by stapling together five or six pieces of 5" x 6" paper. Give one to each child.
2. Put out a variety of textured materials for the children to choose from. Encourage the children to choose the textures they like and glue one on each page of their books.

3. Sit with each child and go through his book. Ask the child to touch each texture and use a word to describe how it feels. Help the child write the word next to the texture.
4. Now they have an interactive book that they can touch and read!
5. As a group, discuss some of the words that were used to describe the different textures in the books.

BUBBLEWRAP
THIN WOOD PIECES
SAND PAPER
CORRUGRATED MATERIAL
FEATHER

 Gail Morris, Kemah, TX

Sandpaper Letters

Materials

Sandpaper squares • scissors or X-acto knife (adult only) • alphabet stencils • pencil • poster board

What to do

1. Trace both the lower- and uppercase letters of the alphabet onto squares of sandpaper and cut them out.
2. Mount the letters onto a piece of poster board.
3. Place the letters in the book or writing area of the classroom.
4. You may want to discuss letter sounds during circle time or with the children one by one.

   Author Note: To aid in future reading abilities it is best NOT to state the letter name because some do not sound how the letter is pronounced. (For example, "G" makes "guh" and "juh" sounds but the letter is pronounced "gee."). Rather, discuss only the sound(s) it makes. Vowels and double-sounding consonants should probably be covered last to avoid confusion when first introducing this technique to the children.
5. When applicable, and as time permits, use one- or two-word books in the reading center and sound out words as you read along with the children.
6. Children can use the letters to trace their names or other words as interest peaks.

 Tina R. Woehler, Lebanon, TN

Reading With Your Hands

Materials

Tagboard • scissors • textured material, such as sandpaper or felt • glue • blindfold

What to do

1. Cut out 52 squares from tagboard. Then cut out a set of upper- and lowercase letters from a textured material, such as sandpaper or felt.
2. Glue a letter on each square.

(continued on the next page)

3. Show the children how they can "read" the letters by feeling them with their hands.

4. Let the children take turns putting on the blindfold and guessing what they're holding.

5. Later they can match uppercase letters with lowercase letters. You can also do this with numbers.

Related books

It Begins With A by Stephanie Calmenson
Tomorrow's Alphabet by George Shannon

 Sandra Hutchins Lucas, Cox's Creek, KY

Solomon Grundy

Materials

Sentence strips • marker • laminator • pocket chart

What to do

1. Write each line of the Mother Goose verse, "Solomon Grundy" on separate sentence strips.

Solomon Grundy

Solomon Grundy
Born on a Monday,
Christened on Tuesday,
Married on Wednesday,
Took ill on Thursday,
Worse on Friday,
Died on Saturday,
Buried on Sunday,
This is the end
Of Solomon Grundy.

2. Laminate the strips for durability.

3. This can be done first as a whole group activity and then individually as reading skills improve. Pass out the sentence strips to different children in the group.

4. Enlist the children's help in finding which sentence strip comes next.

5. As you read aloud, track the text with your finger to help youngsters focus on the individual words.

6. Put the sentence strips in your literacy center or near a pocket chart. Encourage the children to revisit the poem during free choice time.

 Jackie Wright, Enid, OK

Rebus Rhymes

Materials

Computer and printer • three pictures for each rebus rhyme • oak tag • scissors • glue stick • colored, string-tie envelope for each rhyme • laminator • X-acto knife (adult only) • self-adhesive Velcro with a sticky back • container for the activity

What to do

1. Using a large font on your computer, type four-line rebus rhymes (making sure the last words of the second and fourth line rhyme). Make as many rhymes as desired.

2. Collect three pictures to replace the words in each rhyme. Label the words on the pictures.

3. Mount labeled pictures on 2" x 2 ½" rectangles of oak tag using a glue stick.

4. Glue the printed text to the front of a colored, string-tie envelope.

5. Laminate the string-tie envelopes and the labeled pictures.

6. Use an X-acto knife to cut around the top openings of each envelope.

7. Attach Velcro to the back of the rebus pictures and to the location in the text where a word was omitted.

8. Decorate a container to hold the envelopes, each with three pictures inside. Label the front with instructions for the activity.

9. The child opens the envelope, reads the rhyme, and attaches the picture to the correct location to complete the rhyme.

10. When finished, he returns the pictures to the inside of the envelope and returns the envelope to the container.

 Jackie Wright, Enid, OK

Rhyming Words

Materials

Novel Notes or shaped notepads • pictures from old workbooks • scissors • glue stick • rubber cement • poster board • laminator

What to do

1. Purchase Novel Notes or find different-shaped notepads that correspond to your theme, such as butterflies and flowers.
2. Save pictures appropriate for rhyming words from old workbooks and worksheets.
3. Cut out pictures of pairs of rhyming words (for example, cat and hat).
4. Glue the picture of one rhyming word to the center of a butterfly-shaped notepad page and the corresponding rhyming picture to the center of a flower-shaped notepad page. Make as many rhyming pairs as desired.
5. Using rubber cement, attach the pages to poster board for durability.
6. Cut around the shapes, laminate, and trim off the excess laminating film.
7. Encourage the child to match rhyming pairs.

 Jackie Wright, Enid, OK

Signing Letters/Signing Words

Materials

Alphabet signing chart

What to do

1. Practice signing the letters of the alphabet using the chart. Children enjoy signing the letters of their names.
2. Sing the alphabet song with the children. Encourage them to sign the letters as they sing the song.
3. Practice signing the letters of other familiar words. It is a great way to practice words, spelling, and sequencing of letters.

Related books

My First Book of Sign Language by Joan Holub
Signing at School by S. Harold Collins
Simple Signs by Cindy Wheeler

 Sandra L. Nagel, White Lake, MI

Visit the Local Library Frequently

Materials

List of suggested books • computer with a database program

What to do

1. To help you find good book selections, take a list of books each month to the library. Use books suggested in your favorite teaching magazines and resource books. (Also see the list of recommended books on page 239.)
2. Look up the titles on the computer in your local library and jot down the call numbers next to the titles.
3. Check out the available titles to preview.
4. Keep a record on your computer at home of all the books your children will enjoy at the public library, as well as those in your school library. List by title, author, and call number.
5. Print out the pages and assemble into a book.
6. By keeping track of the themes in which these books are appropriate, you have a wonderful supply of thematic book titles right at your fingertips.

 Jackie Wright, Enid, OK

Counting Cards

Materials

Deck of playing cards

What to do

1. Add a deck of playing cards to the manipulatives area of your classroom or provide them in a math center.
2. Encourage the children to sort the cards by color, suit, face value, and so on.
3. Challenge them to count the number of shapes depicted on each card, the number of red or black cards, or all the cards.
4. If desired, let the children make their own set of cards using shapes of their choice. Instead of hearts, spades, diamonds, and clubs, they may choose to make crescents, rectangles, triangles, hexagons, or other shapes.

☆ Ann Kelly, Johnstown, PA

Creating Games Using Old CDs

Materials

Demo CDs from various companies

What to do

1. Recycle demo CDs that come in the mail. By asking everyone you know to donate these to you (a simple memo in a school flier should produce all that you need), you have a fantastic resource for making games in the early childhood classroom! They are durable and easy for children to manipulate, and are much easier to work with than cutting out cardboard backings. You can use them to:
   ☆ Teach the alphabet, numbers, and shapes. Children could create their own flashcards by painting on the CDs with tempera paints.

☆ Create sequencing games. Cut out comic strips and glue each frame onto a separate CD. (Rubber cement works well for gluing paper onto the CDs.)

☆ Create self-correcting sight word games. Glue pictures on one side of the CD and write the name of the object on the other side.

☆ Make any number of matching games. Let the children make these using their imaginations!

 Anne M. Slanina, Slippery Rock, PA

Picket Puzzles

Materials

8 jumbo craft sticks or tongue depressors for each child • colored markers • masking tape • rubber bands • scratch or drawing paper • pencils

What to do

1. Preparation: Align eight sticks in a row (like a picket fence) for each puzzle. Secure the sticks with two 6" long pieces of tape placed crosswise about 1" from the top and bottom of the "fence." This taped side will form the back of the puzzle. Test your markers on an extra stick; most washable brands will work on wood. Cut out 6" squares of scratch paper.

① STICKS TOUCHING

NUMBERED → |1|2|3|4|5|6|7|8|

(BACK)

TAPE (REMOVE AFTER ART IS APPLIED)

CHILD'S DESIGN

②

COLOR

FLIP OVER and DRAW ON THIS SIDE (FRONT)

(continued on the next page)

2. Invite the children to create designs that fill an entire 6″ square of paper (otherwise the completed puzzle may have blank pieces).

3. Ask the children to copy their design onto the wooden squares (the side without tape) using a pencil. They can then use markers to trace and color the artwork.

4. Ask the children to flip over their puzzles to backside. Help them number the top of each stick one to eight (from right to left).

5. Now ask the children to remove the tape strips from the puzzle backs and gather their sticks in a bundle. Provide space for each child to shuffle her sticks and solve her own puzzle by lining the sticks back into their original order. The numbers on the back can be used as reference if needed.

6. Conclude the activity by securing each child's puzzle with a rubber band. **Tip:** The numbered sticks can be used in the teaching of math sequencing concepts.

 Susan A. Sharkey, La Mesa, CA

Pipe Cleaner Bead Rings

Materials

Pipe cleaners in various colors • plastic beads with holes big enough to slide onto cleaners

What to do

1. Give each child pipe cleaners and beads.
2. Encourage the children to string the beads as desired.
3. Show them how to adjust the pipe cleaner so they can wear it as a toe ring or bracelet!

 Lisa Chichester, Parkersburg, WV

Math Every Day

Materials

None

What to do

1. Tell the children that they can use math all day, every day!
2. At circle time, count each child as he sits down.
3. Before snack, ask them to pair up to wash their hands. Ask them to count out a certain number of crackers to eat. Count out loud when passing out napkins and cups. Encourage the children to join in.
4. As the children line up for outdoor time, count and touch each child's head. Encourage them to count how many steps it takes to walk to the back door, how many hops around the sidewalk, and how many tricycles are outdoors.
5. Encourage them to count their fingers while waiting.
6. Count, count, count, all the time, out loud, for children to hear and join in!

 Susan M. Myhre, Bremerton, WA

Adding Box

Materials

Markers • index cards or note cards • small shoebox with lid • scissors • small objects (buttons, pompom balls, acorns)

What to do

1. Write simple equations on separate index cards.
2. Cut two holes in the lid of the box approximately 2" apart. Print a plus sign between the holes.
3. Put small objects and a stack of cards by the box. A child holds up an equation card, and then counts and drops the amount shown into each hole. For example, if the equation is 2 + 2 = __, the child puts two objects in one hole and two in the other.
4. The child then removes the lid and counts how many objects are in the box to get the total amount.

 Sandra L. Nagel, White Lake, MI

Sticker Counting

Materials

Small smiley face stickers

What to do

1. Use small smiley face stickers to teach the meaning of numbers. They are fun for the children to use and provide a visual cue.
2. For example, give each child five smiley stickers. Ask them to put one on each finger. Then ask, "If you take off two stickers, how many do you have left?"
3. Continue asking them to add and remove a different number of stickers.

 Lisa Chichester, Parkersburg, WV

Bear Counting

Materials

Teddy bear counters or poker chips • sandwich-size plastic bags • masking tape • marker

What to do

1. Prepare several bags with various numbers of counters or chips. You might choose to fill a bag with four, one with five, one with six, and another with seven. The number of items in the bag depends on the children's comfort level with counting.
2. Seal each bag securely with masking tape. Write how many counters are in the bag on the masking tape.
3. Review the number of objects in each bag with the children.
4. Demonstrate how the items can be manipulated through the plastic to create a number of different combinations.
5. Encourage the child to manipulate the objects in as many ways as he can think of. He can record his efforts on a work sheet that you provide.

Related books

12 Ways to Get to 11 by Eve Merriam
What Comes in 2's, 3's, and 4's by Suzanne Aker

 Iris Rothstein, New Hyde Park, NY

Let's Learn About Money (Coins)

Materials

Coins (pennies, dimes, nickels, quarters) • sturdy paper and tape • magnifying glass • crayons with paper torn off

What to do

1. Here are a few ways for children to become familiar with the names and values of different coins.

   ☆ Provide a container of coins and a container for sorting (egg cartons, muffin tins, divided dish).

   ☆ Encourage the children to sort the coins by color, size, or denomination.

   ☆ Tape each kind of coin to a sturdy piece of paper and write the name of the coin and how much it is worth next to each coin.

   ☆ Demonstrate how to make rubbings of the coins using the flat side of unwrapped crayons.

   ☆ Hide a certain number of one kind of coin in your sandbox. Ask the children to find them (tell them how many to look for). When they are done, ask them if they can count the coins.

   ☆ Talk about each coin at group time.

   ☆ Put a few of each type of coin at the science table along with a magnifying glass or two. Encourage the children to examine the coins.

 Gail Morris, Kemah, TX

Money Activity

Materials

Old books or workbooks • scissors • blue and orange tagboard or card stock • glue stick • laminator, optional • felt • rubber cement • flannel board

What to do

1. Look through old books or workbooks for brightly colored pictures of merchandise labeled with price tags (such as a comb for 10 cents, a ball for 25 cents, a sailboat for 7 cents, and so on) and the correct number of coins needed to purchase each item. You can also draw pictures of different items with price tags and pictures of coins.
2. Cut the blue tagboard or card stock to make the desired number of cards, approximately 3 ½" x 2 ¼". Cut enough for each picture of merchandise you have.
3. Cut the orange tagboard or card stock to make coin cards for each item of merchandise.
4. Glue the pictures of the merchandise a blue tagboard rectangle.
5. Glue the pictures of the coins needed to purchase each item to an orange rectangle.
6. Laminate both sets for durability, if desired.
7. Prepare the cards for flannel board use by gluing felt to the back of the cards using rubber cement.
8. To do the activity, the child places merchandise cards on the flannel board. Then he matches the coin set card to the corresponding merchandise card.

PICTURE GLUED to BLUE TAG BOARD

COINS GLUED to ORANGE TAG BOARD

(ALL LAMINATED for DURABILITY)

 Jackie Wright, Enid, OK

$100

Materials

11" x 6" construction paper • 10 photocopied $10.00 bills per child (copy on green paper, if available) • glue or paste • markers or crayons

What to do

1. On the 100th day of school, make wallets filled with ten $10.00 bills.
2. Show the children how to fold their piece of construction paper in half lengthwise. The folded paper will measure 11" x 3".
3. Glue the two short sides closed, leaving the top open.
4. Encourage the children to decorate their wallets with markers or crayons.
5. Count the money together with each child, counting by tens to 100.
6. The children can put their money into their wallet and fold it in half like a real wallet.

 Lynn Cagney, Lutz, FL

Zero the Hero

Materials

Roll of paper from calculator • marker • small prizes

What to do:

1. Each day add a number to the roll of paper to indicate how many days the children have been in school.
2. Whenever you reach a number that ends in zero, the children get a visit from "Zero the Hero" (this can be a puppet). Use the puppet to give each child a small prize.
3. The prizes can be simple things such as stickers, coins, and small trinkets. It is nice if the prizes can correspond to the season, a particular activity, or classroom theme.
4. Children enjoy counting and looking forward to special days.
   Tip: On the 100th day of school, have a special party. Ask the children to bring in 100 of an item to share with classmates (for example, pennies, paperclips, marbles, cards, and so on).

 Sandy L. Scott, Vancouver, WA

Book of 100

Materials

8 ½" x 11" newsprint or construction paper • stapler • marker • stamp pads • a variety of stamps (happy faces, animals, stars, and so on)

What to do

1. Fold four pieces of 8 ½" x 11" paper in half and staple them together to make a 10-page book. Make one for each child. Help the children number the pages, or do it ahead of time depending on their level.
2. Tell the children that they will be making a book of 100 stamps. This is a nice activity to do on the 100th day of school.
3. Encourage the children to choose one type of stamp and stamp it 10 times on the first page of their books. They can choose a different stamp and stamp 10 on the second page, and so on.
4. The child is done when he has stamped 10 "pictures" on 10 pages. Encourage them to come up with a title for their books.
5. Help the children count by tens to 100.

 Lynn Cagney, Lutz, FL

The Count to 100 Game

Materials

None

What to do

1. Invite the children to sit in a circle with you. Explain that they will be playing a counting game called Count to 100. Emphasize that it will be important to pay attention and listen so that they will know what to say when it is their turn.
2. Explain that they will count around the circle until someone gets to 100. Whoever gets to say "100" will become "Mr. 100" or "Miss 100." If you feel that the children need it, have a practice count first. Lead the class in counting in unison from 1 to 100.

3. Choose a starting point. (You may wish to be the person to start the count.) The starter says, "One," the person to the starter's left says, "Two," and so on. When a child gets to 100, he stands up and everyone claps.
Note: If there are exactly 20 or 25 people in the circle, the same child will always get to say "100." Taking yourself out or putting yourself into the circle can solve this problem.

4. The next round begins with Mr. 100 or Miss 100 saying, "One." Continue as before until someone gets to 100. The game may be repeated as many times as desired.

5. For an added challenge, after about four counts to 100 by ones, make the rounds shorter by counting by twos, fives, or tens depending on the ability of the class. Precede each of these new ways of counting with a practice count.

6. Sometimes a child may not know what number to say when it is his turn. Emphasize beforehand that it is always okay to ask for help if they don't know the answer; this is a learning game! Encourage the children to help by raising their hands if they know the correct number. The child can call on a friend who may say the correct number and the count can continue. If this happens too often, do another practice count or go to a lower number such as 50 or 25.
Tip: You may wish to hang a chart with the numbers 1 to 100 to help the children who need it.

 Susan Jones Jensen, Norman, OK

Build Your Own Pizza

Materials

Construction paper in a variety of colors • scissors • glue • markers • laminator or clear contact paper • dice

What to do

1. Cut out 9" circles from brown construction paper to make the crust of the pizza. Make six circles so that six children can play at one time.

2. Cut out five different types of pizza toppings, 2" to 3" in size, enough for the number of pizza crusts you made. For example, cheese, tomato, pepperoni, mushrooms, green peppers, onions, and so on.

(continued on the next page)

3. Draw six squares on a 9" x 12" sheet of white construction paper. Turn the squares into a die by drawing the dots one through six in the squares.

4. In the squares 1 through 5, add a construction paper ingredient. Next to the number 6 write, "Take off one item."

5. Laminate the pieces or cover them with contact paper to keep the pieces durable.

6. Give each child a pizza crust and one piece of each different topping.

7. Encourage the children to take turns rolling the dice and putting the topping on according to the number on the die. For example, if a child rolls a five, he would add the ingredient listed on the chart for number 5. If the child rolls a 6, he would take one item off. Continue to play until everyone makes a complete pizza. How long you play depends on if you want one or all of the children to finish.

Author Note: I have used this game with children from the ages of three to five. Everyone loves it. At first you will need a teacher to introduce the game and help the children learn, but after that the children will play the game with very little teacher help.

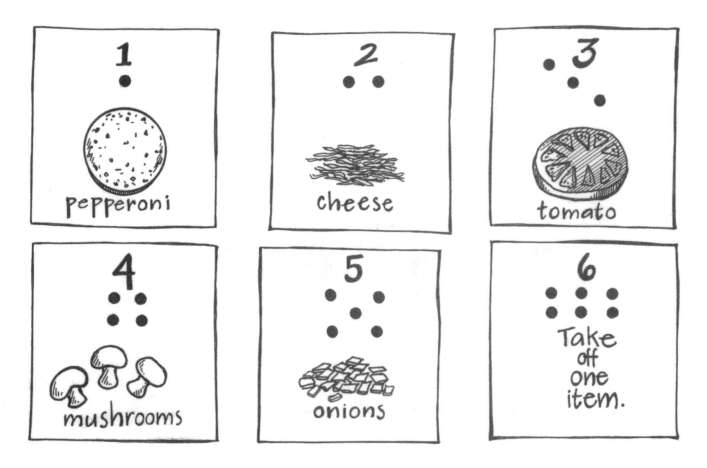

 Maggie Dugan, Oshkosh, WI

Finding Numbers in the Environment

Materials

File cards • marker

What to do

1. Write the numbers 0 through 9 on file cards (one number per card). You may wish to make several sets of these cards.
2. Gather a group of about four children around you at a small table.
3. Display a set of the number cards on the table in front of the children. Ask them if they know what the symbols are. Can they name the numbers?
4. Ask the children, either one at a time or as a group, to find number matches within the room (for example, on boxes, chalkboards, pieces of paper, blocks, and so on).
5. Once they have found a match, encourage them to share what they found with the rest of the group. Ask if they know what the number is used for (price tag, the object's weight, and so on).
6. Let the children exchange numbers and then try to find something different.

 Kate Ross, Middlesex, VT

Sorting It Out

Materials

Shoe storage bag • paper clips • cards • marker • pictures or small objects

What to do

1. Write a number or letter of the alphabet on separate cards. Make as many cards as there are spaces on the shoe storage bag.
2. Clip one of the cards to each space on the storage bag.

(continued on the next page)

3. Put out items for the children to sort and put into the correct spaces in the storage bag. For example, if using numbers, put out number cards or small objects. If using letters, draw pictures that start with the letters on the shoe storage bag.
4. Demonstrate how to sort the items and put them into the correct space on the bag.

 Sandra L. Nagel, White Lake, MI

Fun With Sorting

Materials

Two large hula hoops or two chalk circles on the floor

What to do

1. Explain that the class will be sorting children or things in different ways.
2. Create the first few sorting tasks yourself. When the children have become familiar with the activity, they will have turns creating their own sorting task.
3. Choose six children. Ask three to stand in one circle and three in the other.
4. The challenge is for them to guess the sorting rule used. Some suggestions are: three girls and three boys, three wearing sneakers and three wearing shoes, three who have short sleeves and three who have long.
5. Now demonstrate sorting things in the classroom such as trucks and cars, things that are red and blue, or things that are round and square.
6. Ask the children to think of sorting ideas.
7. Choose a child and arrange his task. The child then asks the children to guess the rule.
8. The child who guesses correctly has the next turn.

 Iris Rothstein, New Hyde Park, NY

One Leaf, Two Leaf, Red Leaf, Green Leaf

Materials

Large, clear plastic zipper-closure bags • collected leaves • assorted leaf paper punches (found at craft store) • brown, green, yellow, orange, and red construction paper • butcher paper • glue stick

What to do

1. Take the children outside for a walk in the park or around the neighborhood. This is a good activity to do in the fall.
2. Give each child a large zipper-closure bag. Ask them to collect 20 leaves each and put them in the bags.
3. Upon return, encourage the children to take out their leaves and sort them by color.
4. Then let the children use leaf paper punches and construction paper to punch out the types and color of leaves found.
5. Construct a class graph using a large sheet of butcher paper.
6. Glue the paper leaves made by the children in the appropriate column.
7. Discuss how many types and colors of leaves were found.

 Quazonia J. Quarles, Newark, DE

Grab a Handful!

Materials

4' x 6' craft paper or oilcloth • marker • individual plastic containers • various items such as cotton balls, rocks, plastic eggs, blocks, buttons, crayons, and shells

What to do

1. Create a Graph Map by drawing columns on a 4' x 6' piece of craft paper or oilcloth. Place the mat on the floor.

(continued on the next page)

2. Fill each container with different items. Start with large items, changing to smaller items as the children become more proficient in counting.
3. Let each child take a turn grabbing one handful of materials.
4. The child then lines up the objects on the graph map while everyone in the small group counts.
5. Children may count the same object to see who can grab the most, or various objects may be compared.

   Tip: Children enjoy this group activity longer if new items with different textures are introduced often.

 Susan R. Forbes, Daytona Beach, FL

Guess My Number

Materials

Pencil • paper

What to do

1. Select one child and ask him to write a number between 1 and 100 on a piece of paper. Keep his number secret.
2. The child then tells the class which multiples of ten his chosen number is between. For example, if he chose 34, he would say, "My number is between 30 and 40."
3. The rest of the class then guesses the chosen number.
4. For younger children, tell them the numbers right before and after the chosen number. For example, if the child chooses 34, he tells them the number is between 33 and 35.

 Elizabeth Bezant, Quinn's Rock, WA, Australia

Guessing Jar

Materials

Large jar or plastic see-through container • small treats to place in the jar, such as jellybeans or M&Ms

What to do

1. Put a large quantity of items in the jar.
2. Ask the children to look at the jar and guess how many items are inside.
3. After everyone has had a turn, count the items as a group.
4. Divide the items in the jar for the children to enjoy. How many will each child get?
5. Change items in the guessing jar throughout the year. Use candy corn, peppermints, conversation hearts, or jellybeans to represent each holiday as it is being celebrated. Use items that start with the "letter of the week" as you are studying about each letter (M&Ms for M, kisses for K, bubble gum for B).
6. Vary the size of the jar and the size of the items for interesting observations.
7. Add different kinds of the same item, for example, bubble gum, stick gum, and gumballs. After the children estimate how many are in the jar, ask them to choose their favorite. Let them chew the gum and save the wrapper. Tape or glue the wrappers to a piece of large poster board and chart which one is the favorite.

 Gail Morris, Kemah, TX

How Many Feet?

Materials

Several copies of each child's feet (an actual copy from the copy machine) • clear adhesive paper • scissors • laminator or clear contact paper • chart paper

What to do

1. Take each child to the copy machine. Hold the child up so he can rest his bare feet on the glass. Make sure the child does not stand or press heavily on

(continued on the next page)

the glass. You must fully support the child's weight. (If making actual copies is impossible, use construction paper and trace around each child's feet.)

2. Make several copies of each child's feet.
3. Clean the copier glass thoroughly.
4. Let the children print their name on the copies of their own feet.
5. Ask the children to cut out the copies of their feet. Laminate the cutouts or cover them with clear contact paper for durability.
6. Use the feet to measure many things in your classroom or school by laying them end-to-end. Ask the children the following questions and let them answer them by using the feet cutouts:
    ☆ How many feet to the bathroom?
    ☆ How many feet to the water fountain?
    ☆ How many feet to the office?
    ☆ How many feet wide is the classroom?
    ☆ How many feet long is the classroom?

7. Create a chart to show the answers to the questions. Label the chart: "How Many Feet?" Across the bottom, print the words "bathroom," "water fountain," "office," "width," and "length." Draw a small foot in each square to represent each five feet the children measured. Compare the distances on the chart.

8. You can measure many things with your feet if you use your imagination. Have fun!

 Virginia Jean Herrod, Columbia, SC

These Belong Together

Materials

Picture pairs of objects that belong together • markers • computer-generated bears in two sizes • scissors • glue stick • poster board or tagboard • rubber cement • laminator • learning mat or pocket chart, optional

What to do

1. Cut out picture pairs of items that go together such as shoes and socks, ball and bat, hammer and nail, lock and key, tooth and toothbrush, and so on.
2. Use markers to color the pictures.
3. Using colored clip art from the Internet, print out the desired number of computer-generated bears in two sizes.
4. Glue one object from each pair to each of the large bears.
5. Glue the corresponding mate of each picture pair to a small bear.
6. Mount the bears on poster board or tagboard using rubber cement (adult only).
7. Cut out the shapes.
8. Label the names of each object on the front or back.
9. Laminate the bear shapes for durability.
10. At circle time, give each child a small bear.
11. Place the large bears on a learning mat or in a pocket chart. Encourage each child, in turn, to place his bear next to the large bear with the corresponding object.
12. Put the activity in a center for individual use during free choice time.

LARGE
BEAR SHAPE
(LAMINATED)

SMALL
BEAR SHAPE
(LAMINATED)

toothbrush

tooth

☆ Jackie Wright, Enid, OK

Woodland Animals

Materials

Pictures of woodland animals from old books or workbooks • tagboard or poster board • scissors • glue stick • laminator, optional • felt • rubber cement • flannel board

(continued on the next page)

What to do

1. Look through old books or workbooks for 13 brightly colored pictures of sets of woodland animals. For example, find one bear, two foxes, three raccoons, four owls, five skunks, and so on to thirteen.
2. Cut tagboard or poster board to make 13 set cards approximately 3 ½" x 4 ¾".
3. Cut tagboard or poster board to make 26 number cards approximately 1 ½" x 4 ¾" (for 13 numeral cards and 13 number name cards).
4. Cut out the sets of animals and glue each set to a separate 3 ½" x 4 ¾" card using a glue stick.
5. Cut out or print your own numerals and number names on the 1 ½" x 3 ¾" cards.
6. Laminate all three sets of cards for durability, if desired.
7. Prepare for flannel board use by gluing felt to the back of the cards using rubber cement.
8. To do the activity, the child first sequences the numeral cards and, if able, the number name cards on the flannel board.
9. Then the child matches each woodland animal set card to the corresponding numeral and number name card on the flannel board.

 Jackie Wright, Enid, OK

Mitten Matching

Materials

Stencil of a mitten • wallpaper books • marker • scissors • clothespin • rope

What to do

1. Cut out several pairs of matching mittens from wallpaper books.
2. For each pair, add a number to the back of one mitten and the appropriate number of dots to its match.
3. Lay all the mittens on the floor. Encourage the children to match them according to their pattern or by looking at the numbers
4. Hang the matching pairs from the rope using the clothespins

 Sandy L. Scott, Vancouver, WA

AB Patterning Using Wallpaper

Materials

Sample wallpaper books • paper cutter • quart-size zipper-closure bags • shoeboxes • construction paper

What to do

1. To make one set of pattern squares, use a paper cutter to cut out a large selection of 1 ½″ squares from six different wallpaper pattern pages. (Wallpaper is pretty durable, so a set of pattern squares should last at least a school year with normal use.)

2. Make a variety of sets of pattern squares so many children can work on the same activity.

3. Store each set in a zipper-closure bag.

4. Have each child dump the contents of the bag into a shoebox. This will keep the pieces contained, yet will allow the child to search for the desired wallpaper square.

5. Give each child a piece of construction paper. Help the child start by putting a designated AB pattern on the left-hand side of the construction paper.

6. Encourage the children to finish the pattern. The child is done when he reaches the other side of the paper.

7. The child can repeat the process with another set of pattern squares, or can try an ABC pattern in the next row.

 Mary Volkman, Ottawa, IL

Wallpaper Shape Match

Materials

Templates of shapes (basic shapes and others such as trapezoid, hexagon, and pentagon) • sample wallpaper books, preferably the largest size available • scissors • markers • ruler • gallon-size zipper-closure bags

(continued on the next page)

What to do

1. Cut out two identical shapes (about 10" x 10") from each wallpaper page using templates. If you don't have templates, use a ruler or freehand.

2. Place two or more sets of each shape in the zipper-closure bags. These bags will hold at least 30 to 40 shapes.

3. Encourage the children to match or sort them by shape or pattern.

4. If desired, cut out a variety of sizes of shapes and have the children sort them from smallest to largest.

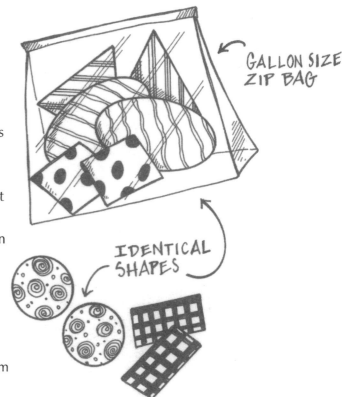

GALLON SIZE ZIP BAG

IDENTICAL SHAPES

⭐ Mary Volkman, Ottawa, IL

Fingerpaint Math Chart

Materials

Large chart paper • paint • paintbrushes • paint smocks • newspaper • markers

What to do

1. Ahead of time, prepare two large charts with the numerals 0-10 in a vertical line down the left side of each paper. Space them widely enough for the correct number of handprints to be placed to the right of each numeral.

2. Hang the charts on the wall near the floor, placing newspaper underneath. Ask the children to put on paint smocks. Discuss how many handprints should be next to each numeral.

3. Paint one child's hand at a time, carefully guiding the child's arm in placing the handprint next to the correct numeral. Repeat until both charts have one print for numeral one, two prints for numeral two, and so on. Let them dry.

4. Cut one dry chart into numeral strips with the corresponding number of handprints. Display the uncut chart on the wall, low enough so that the children can match the strips to the uncut numeral chart.

 Susan Oldham Hill, Lakeland, FL

Graphing Apples

Materials

Variety of apples, such as Granny Smith, Gala, Golden Delicious, and Macintosh • knife • small bowls • pictures of each apple variety • small unit blocks

What to do

1. Cut each apple into bite-size pieces and put them into separate bowls by type.
2. Arrange the bowls in a row on a table.
3. Place a corresponding apple picture next to each bowl.
4. Explain to the children that there are different types of graphs and that they will be making a bar graph.
5. Let them take turns tasting each apple variety. After tasting, ask them to put a unit block on the picture of their favorite apple. The children can stack the blocks on top of each other.
6. When they are finished, they will have a three-dimensional bar graph showing which variety was liked most and which was liked least.

 Christine Maiorano, Duxbury, MA

Our Favorite Apple

Materials

Red, green, and yellow apples • knife (adult only) • white, red, green, and yellow chalk

What to do

1. Ahead of time, cut up small pieces of different kinds of apples.
2. Draw a graph on the chalkboard and write each child's name.
3. Encourage the children to taste each type of apple and decide which one they like best.
4. Let them use colored chalk to draw their favorite apple next to their name on the graph (for example, if a child liked the red apple best, he would use red chalk).

 Liz Thomas, Hobart, IN

Question Charting

Materials

3" x 5" cards • marker • self-adhesive magnetic strips • sentence strips • chalkboard or magnetic board

What to do

1. Make a name card for each child by writing the child's name on a 3" x 5" card. Attach a magnetic strip to the back of each one. Display them on a table.
2. Print a simple question on a sentence strip, and answer choices on smaller pieces of sentence strips. (Which apple do you like the best? Red, green, yellow. How do you get to school? Walk, bus, car.)
3. Place the sentence strip at the top of the chalkboard or magnetic board. Make a column for each answer choice underneath the question.
4. Read the question and different choices to the children.
5. Ask them to place their name card in the column that represents their choice.

6. For variety, chart in different directions (top to bottom, left to right).

7. When discussing the results, talk about different comparison words, such as more, less, most, least, and so on.

 Sandra L. Nagel, White Lake, MI

What's a Minute?

Materials

Items that tell time, such as clocks, stopwatches, hourglasses, and timers

What to do

1. Ask children how long they think a minute is. What could they do in one minute?

2. Explain how long a minute is and ask then count together to 60 to demonstrate.

3. Ask again what they could do in a minute.

4. Have the children watch the clock for one minute. Point out how the second hand has to travel all the way around one time.

5. Set the timer for one minute. Ask the children to sit without making a sound until the timer rings.

6. Ask again, "What else can you do in one minute?" Challenge them to come up with other things they can get done in one minute.

7. Have the children try different movements, starting when you say, "Go," and stopping after one minute, when you say "Stop." (For example, clapping hands, jumping up and down, patting their heads, and so on).

8. Ask the children if a minute would be the same amount of time if you counted to 60 fast or slow.

9. Show the children the various items that tell time. Demonstrate how each works.

 Sandra Suffoletto Ryan, Buffalo, NY

Attendance Garden

Materials

Several colors of construction paper • markers • scissors • photo of each child, optional • 12" dowel rods, one for each child • glue • clear tape • 2 plastic rectangular flower boxes in contrasting colors • rectanglular Styrofoam (enough to fill flower boxes)

What to do

1. Explain to the children that they are going to help you create an Attendance Garden, which will be used to keep track of who is present and who is absent.

2. Let the children choose their favorite color of construction paper and ask them to draw and cut out a flower shape.

3. Help the children write their names in the middle of the flower shape.

4. If desired, take a photo of each child and ask her to glue it to the center of the flower above her name.

5. Encourage the children to cut out flower petals from green construction paper.

6. Demonstrate how to glue and tape the flower and petals to a dowel rod.

7. Label one flower box "Absent" and the other flower box "Present." Put some Styrofoam into each flower box.

8. Ask the children to put their flowers in the box labeled "Present" by pushing the dowel rod down into the Styrofoam. Explain to them that when you see their flowers in the "Present" flower box, you will know that they are in school that day.

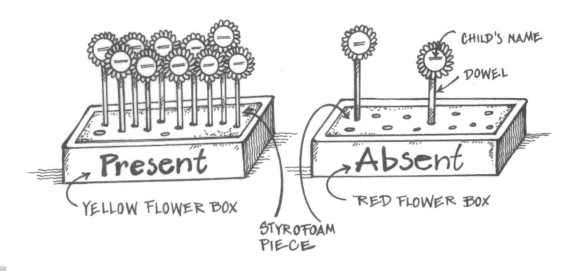

9. At the end of the day, ask the children to put their flowers in the "Absent" flower box. Explain to them that since they are going home they will be absent from school.

10. The next morning, remind the children to move their flowers from the "Absent" to the "Present" flower box as they come to school.

11. Throughout the day, encourage the children to notice the Attendance Garden. Ask them to tell you who is present and who is absent.

Related books

Arthur's Back to School Day by Lillian Hoban
Billy and the Big New School by Laurence Anholt
David Goes to School by David Shannon
Dustin's Big School Day by Alden R. Carter
Fox at School by Edward Marshall
Off to School, Baby Duck by Amy Hest
Vera's First Day of School by Vera Rosenberry

 Virginia Jean Herrod, Columbia, SC

Roll Call Responses

Materials

Roll sheet

What to do

1. Add a little zip to your daily roll call! Instead of having children respond with "Here," encourage them to answer with words or phrases associated with the skills or themes they are studying.

2. Following are some examples of responses:
   ☆ Names of dinosaurs during a dinosaur unit
   ☆ Favorite book title, author, or character
   ☆ Type of fruit, vegetable, tree, or flower
   ☆ A safety rule for home or school

 Jackie Wright, Enid, OK

Greeting Rap

Materials

None

What to do

1. Greet each child with the following rhyme.

   Hi, (child's name), what do you say?
   It's going to be a great day!
   Just clap your hands and boogie on down
   Say "Hi" to another friend in town!

2. If using the rhyme with the whole group, say "friends" instead of the child's name.
3. Ask for other ways to use your hands when greeting someone; for example, shaking hands, hugging each other, and giving a high five.

 Kaethe Lewandowski, Centreville, VA

Waving Song

Materials

None

What to do

1. This is both a hello and a good-bye song. The best part of the song is the waving. Encourage the children to wave a different way each time another verse is sung. It invites participation and stimulates creativity.

Oh, It's Time to Say Hello to My Friends
(Tune: "She'll Be Comin' Round the Mountain")
   Oh, it's time to say hello to my friends. Hi there!
   Oh, it's time to say hello to my friends. Hi there!
   Oh, it's time to say hello, it's time to say hello,
   It's time to say hello to my friends. Hi there!

2. Some examples of wave variations are to wave with an elbow, one finger, an ear, a foot, eyelashes, and two hands. They can wave their hands like windshield wipers, like they are shy, or like a baby.

3. There is no limit to the kinds of waves that the children will demonstrate. Just ask them, "What's your idea?"

 Judy Fujawa, The Villages, FL

Welcome Song

Materials

None

What to do

1. Sing the following song to the tune of "The More We Get Together" as a morning greeting. Repeat until you have acknowledged each child.

   We're glad we're here together, together, together.
   We're glad we're here together,
   We're here at our school!
   There's Jamie and Ashly and Colton and Ryan
   We're glad we're here together,
   We're here at our school.

 Sandy L. Scott, Vancouver, WA

Welcome Song

Materials

None

What to do

1. Sing the following welcome song to the children.

   Welcome to our classroom,
   I'm so glad you're here today.
   We'll have fun here in our classroom
   So lets begin our day.
   Welcome, welcome
   Ryan and John are here.
   Welcome, welcome,
   Jason and Sandy are here.

2. Continue singing until each child is acknowledged.

   ⭐ Sandy L. Scott, Vancouver, WA

Can You Do This?

Materials

Blank flash cards • markers

What to do

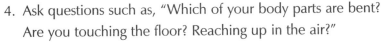

1. Prior to doing this activity, make flash cards of stick figures in a variety of positions.
2. Assemble a small group of children.
3. Invite them to make their bodies look like the stick figure on the card.
4. Ask questions such as, "Which of your body parts are bent? Are you touching the floor? Reaching up in the air?"
5. Ask them what they think they would be doing in a particular position (exercising, playing a game, running, hopping).

 Margery A. Kranyik Fermino, Hyde Park, MD

Character Tags

Materials

Coloring books or workbooks with pictures of the characters in the song "The Farmer in the Dell" • scissors • markers • poster board or oak tag • glue stick • laminator, optional • hole punch • ribbon or yarn

What to do

1. Use coloring books and workbooks for pictures depicting the characters in the song, "The Farmer in the Dell": the farmer, his wife, child, nurse, dog, cat, rat, and cheese.
2. Photocopy the pictures and color them, if needed.
3. Cut them out and glue them to oak tag or poster board.

(continued on the next page)

4. Cut out the pictures and laminate, if desired.

5. Punch holes in the top of each character with a hole punch.

6. Insert ribbon or yarn through the holes and tie the ends together to make a necklace.

7. Assign each child to be a character in the song. The child wears his character necklace and acts out that part of the song as it is sung.

 Jackie Wright, Enid, OK

Container Shaker-Wands

Materials

Two half-pint water bottles with lids, labels removed, per shaker • rolls of brightly colored curling ribbon or shredded gift basket filling • duct tape • small pebbles, optional

What to do

1. Stuff ribbon or basket filling into each bottle. Add small pebbles, if desired.

2. Cap each bottle tightly and place against each other, end-to-end.

3. Attach the bottles together by winding duct tape around both caps until sturdy, forming a "wand."

4. Give each child two shakers. Invite them to hold the shakers as one would hold exercise dumbbells.

5. Provide instructions such as, "Raise your shakers up high; bring them down low; hold one up and one down; bring them together in front of you; put them behind you; shake them high, shake them low."

6. Play recorded music and invite the children to march using shakers as batons.

PEBBLES and FILLING INSIDE BOTH BOTTLES

BASKET FILLING

DUCT TAPE

 PEBBLES

 Margery A. Kranyik Fermino, Hyde Park, MD

Creative Ideas for Carpet Squares Everywhere

Materials

Carpet squares, one for each child

What to do

1. Provide each child with a carpet square and lots of space for creative movement.

2. Ask the children to sit on their carpet squares and scoot around the floor singing, "Row, Row, Row Your Boat." (Make sure the carpet squares can slide along on the floor.)

3. Ask them to suggest some ways to move with the carpet squares and encourage them to participate in the different ideas that are suggested. Here are some wonderful movement ideas:

   ☆ dance on it, kneel on it, stand on it, and so on
   ☆ place it between your legs
   ☆ balance it on your head
   ☆ hold it between your knees
   ☆ stand on it like it was a surfboard/scooter/skateboard
   ☆ lay the squares out like a hopscotch board
   ☆ fly it like a flag
   ☆ hold it like an umbrella
   ☆ twirl around on it like a top
   ☆ attach it to your back like a cape
   ☆ push it around like a toy truck
   ☆ place it under your arm like a package
   ☆ toss it like a horseshoe
   ☆ hold it like a plate
   ☆ use it like a shovel
   ☆ place one under each foot and shuffle along
   ☆ pile them up like blocks

4. These handy squares can provide lots of active and creative fun. Just keep asking the children, "What's your idea?" The ongoing list will amaze you. (It's important to be encouraging and accepting of each child's suggestion.)

 Judy Fujawa, The Villages, FL

Cylinder Band

Materials

Cylinders of all sizes and materials (oatmeal containers, large and small coffee cans, Pringles cans, empty plastic toy containers, soup cans, and other empty food cans) • Phillips head screwdriver • hammer • yarn • the CD "Rhythm Basket" or other percussion music

What to do

1. Make sure the cylinders are clean and that all the edges of the cans are safe. Poke two holes in the tops of some of the cylinders using a screwdriver and hammer. String yarn through the holes so that the item can be easily carried.

2. If available, listen to the CD "Rhythm Basket" (familiar children's songs played completely with percussion instruments). If you don't have a copy of this CD, play other percussion music.

3. Have a discussion about the songs, focusing on the beat, tempo, patterns in the song, and so on.

4. Add the cylinders to your music area and encourage the children to explore the sounds that the different materials make.

5. Challenge the children to keep the beat to their favorite songs. Encourage them to work with a friend and make music together.

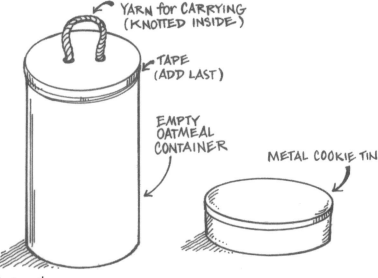

YARN for CARRYING (KNOTTED INSIDE)

TAPE (ADD LAST)

EMPTY OATMEAL CONTAINER

METAL COOKIE TIN

 Ann Kelly, Johnstown, PA

Dance-a-Word

Materials

Chart paper • marker • music, optional

What to do

1. Discuss words that describe body motions with the children, such as stretch, wiggle, slide, and leap.
2. Write the words on chart paper.
3. Invite the children to demonstrate each word with motions.
4. Ask the children to create a "dance" by linking several motions together, such as a stretch, a turn, and a jump. Ask them to explain what they did.
5. Encourage "soloists" to demonstrate their word dance for others to guess.

 Margery A. Kranyik Fermino, Hyde Park, MD

Foot Dance T-Shirt

Materials

Newspaper • pie tins • Perma paint or fabric paint • T-shirt for each child

What to do

1. Spread newspaper on the floor.
2. Fill pie tins with fabric paint.
3. Place each child's T-shirt on the paper.
4. Encourage the child to step into the paint and dance to music across the T-shirt, creating his own foot art tee!

 Lisa Chichester, Parkersburg, WV

Balloon Dance

Materials

Balloons • yarn • favorite song of your class

What to do

1. Blow up several balloons. There should be at least two balloons for each child.
2. Tie a piece of yarn to half of the balloons. The lengths of the pieces of yarn should vary. Put all the balloons in the center of your group time area.
3. Invite the children to come and do a balloon dance.
4. Explain to the children that you are going to play their favorite song and they may use the balloons as they move to the rhythm of the song.
5. Use the activity several times, changing the type of music you use. Try it with classical, jazz, or maybe the blues. Discuss with the children how and why they moved differently to each of the styles of music.
6. Ask them which style they prefer and chart the results.

ONE HALF of the BALLOONS HAVE YARN

YARN (LENGTH SHOULD VARY)

CD of FAVORITE SONG

 Ann Kelly, Johnstown, PA

Colorful Scarf Dancing

Materials

Colored scarves • "The Freeze Song" by Greg and Steve

What to do

1. Let each child pick out a colored scarf.
2. Explain that they will be dancing to music and moving their scarves and bodies any way they want.
3. Ask them to listen to the song for directions. When the music stops, they must freeze.
4. If desired, play freeze all day long. Whenever you call out "freeze," they must freeze, no matter what they are doing.

 Susan M. Myhre, Bremerton, WA

Waving, Wrapping, and Folding Fabric Pieces... For the Fun of It!

Materials

Fabric pieces, about 3' x 3', one for each child (ask home decorator stores to donate fabric from their discontinued samples)

What to do

1. Provide each child with a piece of fabric. The children will need lots of space for this movement activity.
2. Begin with simple movement directions and then add to the variety of movements by asking the children, "What's your idea?"
3. Here are some ideas:
   ☆ shake, roll, or lay it out
   ☆ lay it flat on the ground with no wrinkles

(continued on the next page)

☆ fold it in half, quarters, and so on

☆ sit on it, roll in it, hide under it, cover up with it

☆ roll two sides to the middle

☆ roll it up starting at one corner like a carpet

☆ "scrunch" it up

☆ fold it into a triangle

☆ hold it like a matador

☆ wave it like a flag

☆ hang it on your shoulders like a cape

☆ wrap it around your head, shoulders, waist, and so on

☆ use it to carry something from one place to another

☆ wrap something in it or hide something under it

☆ stuff it into a bag, sock, shirt, and so on

☆ tie it in a knot

☆ use it to toss something into the air

 Judy Fujawa, The Villages, FL

Freely Fluttering

Materials

A variety of fabric ribbons, all colors and widths • scissors • needle and thread • music

What to do

1. Cut the ribbons into pieces large enough to fit over a child's hand and around the wrist.
2. Sew the ends of each ribbon piece together to form wristbands.
3. Cut the rest of the ribbons into 3' long pieces. Sew different numbers of ribbons to the wristbands. One, two, or three pieces to each band will be fine. Make enough for the whole class and any adults.
4. At large group time, each child and adult chooses a wristband.
5. Play some music and encourage the children to flutter freely.
6. If desired, call different sets of children to dance by the color of their ribbons, shirt, shoes, and so on.

 Ann Kelly, Johnstown, PA

Hula-Hooping

Materials

One hula hoop per child

What to do

1. Give each child a hula hoop. Encourage them to try to use it. Demonstrate how they should move their hips to keep the hula hoop from falling.

2. Have a hula hoop countdown. Everyone begins hula-hooping together. Count backwards from ten and try to keep hula-hooping until the countdown finishes.

3. Use the hula hoops with different types of music. Is one type of music easier to hula-hoop to than another? Chart the results.

 Virginia Jean Herrod, Columbia, SC

Movin' and Groovin' and Goin' Down the Aisle

Materials

Aisle (see activity)

What to do

1. Create an aisle in the classroom. Some suggestions are: a chalk-drawn aisle, rug, runner, piece of fabric, sheet, rope, lined-up chairs, children lined up, wooden blocks, or balance beams.

2. This is an opportunity for each child to be highlighted. Encourage each child to move down the aisle in his own way. You will want to assist in the activity by calling out the child's name and asking him to identify the movement he has in mind. This can be sung to the tune of "Shortenin' Bread" or any other tune.

(continued on the next page)

3. For example:
    ☆ Here comes Mary, walking down the aisle; here comes Mary, walking down the aisle.
    ☆ Here comes Johnny, crawling down the aisle; here comes Johnny crawling down the aisle.
    ☆ Here comes Sally, flying down the aisle; here comes Sally, flying down the aisle.

4. Other movements might include galloping, slithering, twirling, sliding, waddling, walking backwards, swimming, crab walking, and walking with eyes closed or hands on hips.

5. Encourage the children to attach creative names to their movements. For example, Jumpin' Jasper, Boing Boing, Tigger Bounce, Skipple, Cherry Picking, or Chocolate Hipple Dance.

☆ Judy Fujawa, The Villages, FL

Music! Music! Music!

Materials

CDs or tapes of several different types of musical styles • portable CD or tape player • outdoor source of electricity or plenty of batteries • large outdoor area • chart paper • markers

What to do

1. Head to the local library and borrow several different genres of music. There are many child-oriented CDs and tapes to be found. Make sure you acquire a wide variety of musical styles.

2. At school, show the children the CDs or tapes and explain that you are interested in what type of music they like.

3. Take the CD or tape player outdoors. Ask the children to choose what type of music they want to try out first.

4. Put on the music and dance, dance, dance!

5. Pay attention to how the children react to the music. Does it hold their interest or do they drift away to play? Do they dance to the music or simply listen to it? Do they attempt to sing along?

6. Create a chart to keep track of the children's reaction to the music. On a large piece of paper, draw one column for each type of music you are exploring. Divide that column in half. Label one half "Yes" and the other half "No."

7. Print the genre names of the music across the bottom of the chart in the columns (for example, country, blues, classical, opera, jazz, reggae, and so on).

8. At the end of the first day, ask the children if they liked the type of music they listened to that day. Record their answers in the "yes" and "no" columns on the chart.

9. The next day, play a different genre of music outdoors. Again, watch their reaction and chart the results.

10. Continue until you have explored all the genres of music you originally chose from the library. This may take several days or even a couple of weeks.

11. After you have explored all the types of music, ask the children to tell you what type of music they liked the best and why. Record their answers on lined paper and let them draw a picture of themselves dancing to the music.

 Virginia Jean Herrod, Columbia, SC

Musical Parents

Materials

One chair for each participating adult • CD, record, or tape player • fun music

What to do

1. This is a great activity to do when parents are in the room for a party (Parents Day, Mother's Day, or Father's Day).

2. Arrange the chairs in a large circle.

3. Ask one parent of each child to sit in a chair.

4. Instruct the children to stand in front of their own parent.

5. Start the music. Have the parents walk in one direction (clockwise or counter-clockwise) while the children walk in the opposite direction. Both groups will walk inside the circle of chairs instead of behind them. If needed, have one teacher lead the group of children. They will instinctively want to follow their parents instead of walking in the other direction.

6. Remove one chair.

(continued on the next page)

7. When you stop the music, the parents try to find a chair.

8. Encourage the children to find their parents and jump into their laps.

9. The parent/child pair that does not find a chair is "out." Give them a sticker or other small reward and let them join the audience.

10. Continue play until one parent/child pair wins the game.

11. Encourage cooperation as game play continues. Provide alternate activities for children who are done with the game.

 Virginia Jean Herrod, Columbia, SC

Musical Walk of Colors

Materials

Construction paper in a variety of basic colors • walking-tempo music

What to do

1. Hold up different construction paper colors and ask the children to name the colors.

2. Place the colored papers on the floor with space between each one.

3. Ask the children to walk among the colors without stepping on them as the music is playing.

4. When the music stops, the children sit down by the nearest color.

5. Ask, "Who is sitting next to the color blue?" (or whatever colors you use). Then say, "Please stand up if it is you!"

6. Continue the game until you have called out all the different colors.

 Liz Thomas, Hobart, IN

Rhythm Band

Materials

Materials to make a variety of instruments: Lumi sticks (dowels cut into 1' lengths, sandpaper, paint and brushes) • drums (round oatmeal boxes, sticky-sided decorative paper,) • shakers (empty film canisters, dry rice or pebbles, tape) • sand blocks (sandpaper, glue, small blocks of wood) • CD of marching music • CD player

What to do

1. Hold a music night or afternoon and invite parents and children to come to school to make instruments. Set up tables so that each parent and child can make instruments.
2. To make Lumi Sticks, sand the ends of dowels and paint them.
3. To make drums, turn the oatmeal boxes upside down and cover the outside with sticky paper. Use dowels for drumsticks.
4. Make shakers by putting rice or pebbles into film canisters and taping them shut.
5. Use wood glue to attach sandpaper to wooden blocks.
6. Let the children figure out how to play the instruments. They will need two of the dowels, shakers, and sand blocks.
7. Demonstrate how to keep rhythm. Put on some brisk music and have a parade around your room.

 Barbara Saul, Eureka, CA

Rhythm Sticks

Materials

Several 3'-long ⅝" dowel rods • saw • fine sandpaper

What to do

1. Saw the dowels every 12". This makes three rhythm sticks out of each length. If you buy 14 lengths, you will saw enough for two sticks for 21 people. Sand the sawed edges lightly.
2. Give two rhythm sticks to each child. Encourage them to play the rhythm of songs such as "Yankee Doodle" and "Twinkle, Twinkle, Little Star" as they sing.
3. March to a record or tape while playing rhythm sticks.
4. Vary directions for playing the sticks, such as high and low, loudly and softly, under one leg, behind the back, tapping the floor, and so on.
5. Use sticks to dramatize the rhyme, "One, Two, Buckle My Shoe." Encourage the children to tap the rhythm of nursery rhymes and say them.
6. Challenge the children to balance one stick on the back of each hand. See how far they can walk before a stick falls.

 Mary Brehm, Aurora, OH

Rhythm Train

Materials

Musical instruments

What to do

1. Let each child choose a musical instrument. If you don't have enough for everyone, use blocks to slide or tap together.
2. At group time, have the children practice repeating a simple rhythm pattern that you play on an instrument or clap using your hands.
3. When they are able to repeat the rhythm, begin your rhythm train!
4. Start by leading and asking a few children to jump on your train. Go around the room playing a simple rhythm pattern with your instrument and have the children repeat after you as your train chugs along. Gradually invite more and more children to hop on the rhythm train until everyone is aboard and repeating your simple rhythms.
5. Give each child a turn leading the train and creating a rhythm to be repeated.
6. As the group gets better at repeating the rhythms, let the train move to the rhythm as well. Do this by having the children stomp their feet to the beat as they go.

☆ Ann Kelly, Johnstown, PA

Singing "Bingo" and Beyond

Materials

Felt in a variety of colors • 3" letter stencils and 3" closed hand pattern, optional • scissors • flannel board

What to do

1. Cut out 3" letters (B-I-N-G-O) in a variety of colors and five 3" closed (clapping together) hands.
2. Put the letters B-I-N-G-O on the flannel board. Sing the first verse of "Bingo."
3. Explain to the children that as they continue to sing each verse of the song, one child will remove the letter you indicate, and another child will put a felt hand in its place. Each time they sing the song, the children will substitute a clap for a letter when they see the hand.

4. Encourage the correct response by asking the class, "How many hands do you see?" (One.) "How many times will we clap?" (Once.)

5. To help the children, clap in a slightly exaggerated manner each time a hand appears and count the claps aloud. ("One-two-N-G-O.")

Tip: This activity lets many children participate at the flannel board. If a few children do not get an opportunity to use the flannel board, they can stand next to you during the last verse and help lead the clapping.

 Christina Chilcote, New Freedom, PA

Sound Magic

Materials

Glasses of water with different amounts • tops for spinning • simple musical instruments • tape of sounds around the house

What to do

1. Talk about sound. Ask the children to sit perfectly still and listen carefully to the sounds around them. Discuss the sounds they hear (e.g., noise from outside, noises from other classrooms, slight sounds of movement in the room).

2. Listen to walking sounds. Ask different children to walk as the rest of the children listen. Do they hear any sound? Do different children make different sounds? After three or four children have walked, ask the rest of the children to close their eyes and see if they can identify which child is walking.

3. Explore making sounds. Pour a different amount of water into several glasses. Tap each one and encourage the children to notice the differences in the sounds.

4. Spin tops and ask the children to listen to the sounds.

5. Show and use musical instruments and ask the children to identify how the sound was made: through blowing, striking, or rubbing across.

6. Play a tape of household sounds. Challenge the children to identify what each sound is (e.g., dishwasher, refrigerator, vacuum cleaner, and so on).

7. Play a game of animal sounds. Ask a child to make an animal sound and ask the others to guess what it is. The first to guess gives the next sound.

 Lucy Fuchs, Brandon, FL

Clapping Patterns

Materials

None

What to do

1. Clap your hands in a pattern and encourage the children to try to follow the pattern. For example, clap two times fast and two times slow.
2. You can extend the pattern by stamping your feet, snapping your fingers, or clapping on other parts of your body such as your head or knees.
3. After the children are familiar with the activity, let them take turns leading the pattern.

 Sandy L. Scott, Vancouver, WA

Syncopated Names

Materials

None

What to do

1. Introduce the idea of syllables by clapping out each child's name as you call them for a transition. For example, Re-be-cca (three claps), Ja-son (two claps).
2. Speed up, slow down, or sing the names as you clap to keep the children interested.
3. Ask the children how many sound sets are in their names.
4. Add middle and last names for more of a challenge.

 Ann Kelly, Johnstown, PA

Rubber Bands Can Be Instrumental

Materials

A piece of wood (possibly a 2″ x 4″, about 18″ long) • 2″ nails • hammer • rubber bands in a variety of sizes

What to do

1. Hammer nails into the piece of wood in a number of locations at a variety of distances.
2. Add the piece of wood to your music area or set it up in a center along with rubber bands of various sizes.
3. Encourage the children to explore the materials. Ask them to listen to and describe the different sounds they can make by attaching the rubber bands to nails in different locations and plucking the rubber bands with their fingers.

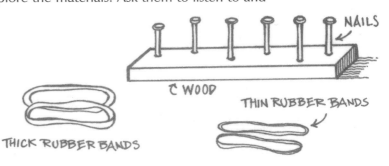

☆ Ann Kelly, Johnstown, PA

Funky One-String Fiddle

Materials

Coffee can or similar-sized can • hammer • nails • string • scissors pencils or sticks • art supplies

What to do

1. Give each child a coffee can, empty and open at one end.
2. Help each child punch a hole in the middle of the bottom of the can using a hammer and nail. (You may want to do this step for them.)

(continued on the next page)

3. Cut string in lengths from the floor to the middle of the child's thigh.

4. Thread the string through the hole, tie a knot inside the can, and tie the other end to a pencil.

5. Demonstrate how to place one foot on the can and hold the pencil so the string is taut. The fiddle works by plucking the string.

6. Let the children decorate their instruments with pompoms, paint, and so on.

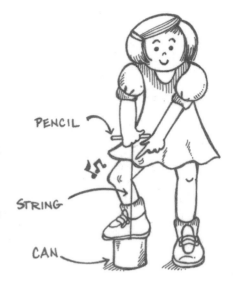

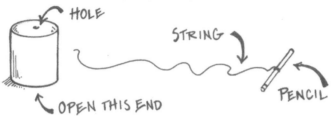

⭐ Lisa Chichester, Parkersburg, WV

You Can Make Music

Materials

Clean, empty cans of different sizes (coffee, soup, vegetable) • rubber bands in a variety of sizes (the bands found on leaf lettuce work great on the coffee cans)

What to do

1. Put the cans and rubber bands in your music area. Encourage the children to experiment with the materials.

2. If necessary, guide them to stretch the bands completely around the can so that they stretch over the opening. Let the children find out what happens when they pull and release the rubber bands.

3. Tell them that if they hold the cans under their arms like a small drum, the sound is much louder.

4. Ask the children to sequence the cans according to pitch.

⭐ Ann Kelly, Johnstown, PA

100 Days Activity: Outside

Materials

Large outdoor area • jump ropes

What to do

1. During outdoor time, practice different ways of counting to 100.
2. Ask the children to line up and hold hands. Together, walk 100 steps, counting aloud as you do it.
3. Line up jump ropes on the ground and ask the children to jump over them 100 times.
4. Gather the children in a circle and count to 100, each child saying a number until you reach 100.
5. Ask the children to spread their hands so they can clearly see ten fingers, then use them to count by tens to 100.
6. Do the "100 Cheer" by loudly counting by tens to 100. With every count, have the children flash all ten fingers.
7. Count by ones and with each decade, have the children move their bodies different ways:

    ☆ 1-10: lean forward with each number
    ☆ 11-20: lean sideways with each number
    ☆ 21-30: clap for each number
    ☆ 31-40: stamp feet for each number

    Continue in this manner until reaching 100.
8. Repeat and let the children take turns demonstrating how to move their bodies with the counting.

Related book

Mrs. Bindergarten Celebrates the 100 Days of Kindergarten by Joseph Slate

 Barbara Saul, Eureka, CA

ABC Hopscotch

Materials

Sidewalk chalk • sidewalk or large outdoor surface • beanbag

What to do

1. Help the children draw a standard hopscotch board on the sidewalk.
2. Fill the spaces in the hopscotch design with random letters instead of numbers.
3. Give each child a beanbag or small token.
4. Let the children take turns playing hopscotch. Encourage them to identify the letter upon which their tokens land.
5. Challenge the children to state two or three words that begin with the letter upon which the token lands.

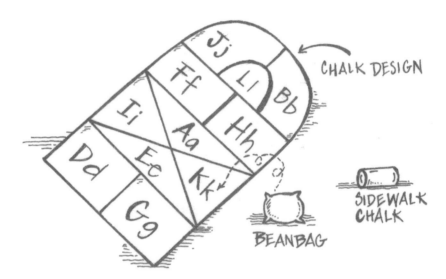

CHALK DESIGN

BEANBAG

SIDEWALK CHALK

6. For an extra challenge, fill the spaces of the hopscotch diagram with letters that, when put together, spell simple words such as "he," "she," "cat," "dog," and so on. Challenge the children to jump on the letters that spell out words in the correct order.

 Virginia Jean Herrod, Columbia, SC

Outdoor Sharing House

Materials

Large appliance box (or handmade playhouse, if possible) • paint • paintbrushes

What to do

1. At the beginning of the year, obtain a large box. If you know someone who is good at carpentry, ask him or her to create a simple house.
2. Ask each child to bring in something special from home for their special sharing playhouse; for example, a small rug, pillow, chair, toy, and so on.
3. Put the box or house outside. Work with the children to create your own special playground playhouse!

 Lisa Chichester, Parkersburg, WV

Blowing Bubbles

Materials

Plastic straws • scissors • mild dish detergent and water or commercial bubble mixture • plastic container

What to do

1. Although this activity seems too simple to be interesting, the children love it. It is a great outdoor activity, especially on a sunny, breezy day. It helps develop fine muscle coordination and breath control.
2. Ahead of time, prepare straws by cutting them in half and cutting 1/2" slits in one end. (This helps hold the liquid and identifies which end goes into the liquid.) Prepare bubble mixture by mixing mild dish detergent with water (about 2 tablespoons soap to 1 cup of water). Or you can use commercial bubble mixture.
3. Check to make sure that children understand how to blow instead of suck through the straw. Explain that the uncut end goes between the lips. Ask them to blow (without bubbles) and feel the air as it escapes.
4. Ask them to dip the cut end into the liquid and blow. (Several children can share one plastic container if you use margarine tubs.)

(continued on the next page)

5. Encourage them to blow gently and watch the bubble form.
6. What happens if they blow harder?
7. Challenge them to try to make a very big bubble by blowing as gently as they can.

 Mary Jo Shannon, Roanoke, VA

Box Kites

Materials

Brown paper lunch bags • scissors • markers • crayons • glitter • sequins • glue • streamers cut into 12" to 15" lengths • stapler • string • tape

What to do

1. Place the materials in the middle of a low table. Gather a group of about four to six children to sit at the table.
2. Explain the directions first, while preparing a demonstration kite, if desired.
3. Ask the children to cut off the bottom of the paper bag, and then open the bag.
4. At this point, the children may wish to decorate their bags using crayons, markers, sequins, glitter, and so on.
5. Let them choose six streamers and staple them around one open end of the bag.
6. For each child, cut a piece of string about 3-5 feet long or longer, if desired. Help the children tape or staple their string to the end of the paper bag opposite from the streamers.
7. Let the children take the kites outside and fly them.

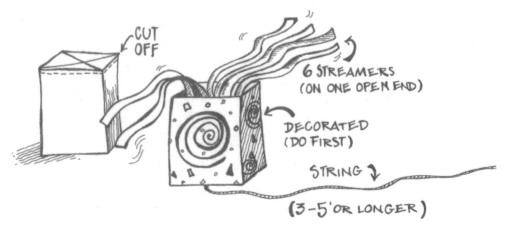

CUT OFF

6 STREAMERS (ON ONE OPEN END)

DECORATED (DO FIRST)

STRING

(3-5' OR LONGER)

 Kate Ross, Middlesex, VT

ExerDice

Materials

Two large Styrofoam blocks • paper • markers • glue or tape

What to do

1. Use the two Styrofoam blocks to create two dice.
2. Cut paper to fit the sides of the Styrofoam blocks. Print various ways to move on six of the pieces of paper and let the children draw pictures to depict the actions below the words. For example, run, walk, crawl, hop, spider-walk (on hands and feet), and tiptoe. Glue or tape these to six sides of one die.
3. Cover the second die with blank paper. On each side, print the number one, two, or three so that you have two of each number on the die. Ask the children to draw circles to represent each number under the number.
4. Gather the children together on the playground.
5. Ask a child to roll the dice.
6. Race around a designated area as directed by the way the dice land. For example, if the movement die lands with "hop" on top and the number die lands with "three" on top, the children should race around the designated area three times while hopping.
7. The goal of the game is not winning the race, but rather to follow the directions indicated on the dice. Encourage the children to cooperate and help each other.
8. Let each child take a turn rolling the dice. Continue play until the children lose interest or become tired.

   Tip: In place of one of the movements on the movement die, print the word "rest" and draw a picture of a child lying down. If the ExerDice lands with the word "rest" on top, all should lie down and rest while they count to the number indicated on the number die.

MOVEMENT   NUMBER

 Viriginia Jean Herrod, Columbia, SC

Washing Chairs

Materials

Buckets filled with soapy water • sponges • plastic chairs

What to do

1. When the weather gets warm, tell the children it's time for spring cleaning.
2. Take your plastic chairs outside along with buckets filled with soapy water and sponges.
3. The children will have a ball washing and scrubbing the chairs! Rinse with clean water from the buckets or hose them off.
4. Leave them in the sun to dry.
5. The children feel a great sense of accomplishment and pride in being able to help, and have fun in the process.

 Tracie O'Hara, Charlotte, NC

Mud Party

Materials

Mud • old clothes and change of clothes • towels • plastic bags • garden hose and lawn sprinkler • related snacks (see below)

What to do

1. Plan a mud party after a rainy day, or make your own mud. It is best to do this on a warm day.
   Tip: Do this activity with a small group of children—too many children can be overwhelming.
2. Instruct the children to come to school in very old clothes. Ask them to bring a towel and a change of clothes. (Children who do not like to get dirty should not be expected to participate.)
3. Let the children slide in the mud, jump in the mud, make mud pies, and so on.
4. After a set amount of time, turn on the lawn sprinkler (away from the mud) and let the children play until relatively clean. Finish by spraying each child with the hose.

5. Provide a changing place for each sex and ask them to change into their spare clothes. Put their dirty clothes into plastic bags.

6. Create a calming transition by serving a related snack, such as chocolate pudding, "dirt" sundaes (ice cream with cookie crumbles), fudge bars, or "mud pies" (chocolate pie).

 Wanda Pelton, Lafayette, IN

Soaring Birds

Materials

Construction paper • scissors • small to medium Frisbees • feathers •wiggly eyes • glue • thick black marker • 4 water bottles

What to do

1. Cut out triangular beaks from the construction paper. Glue the beaks, feathers, and eyes on the Frisbees. Let dry.

2. Wrap construction paper around four full water bottles and glue in place. Use a thick, black marker to mark the four bottles: 3 feet, 6 feet, 9 feet, and 12 feet.

(continued on the next page)

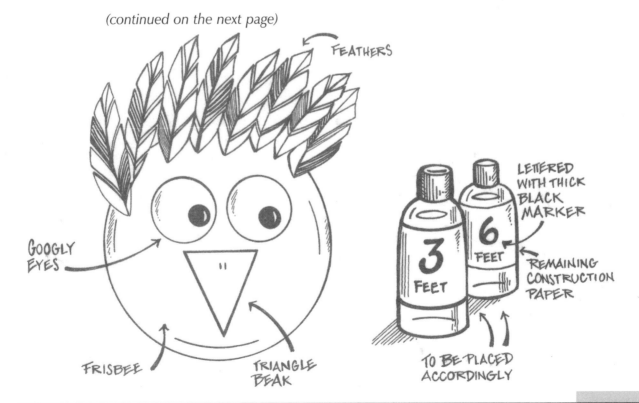

3. Place the bottles accordingly outside.
4. Bring the dry Frisbee birds outside and let the children watch their birds soar.

 Maralien Orantes, New Orleans, LA

Outdoor Animal Safari

Materials

Stuffed "safari" animals, one for each child • carpet squares • "safari" animal books

What to do

1. On a nice dry day, without the children's knowledge, hide the stuffed safari animals on the playground.
2. Ask each child to take her carpet square outside and place it in a semi-circle for a group story time.
3. Read an age-appropriate book about a "safari" animal.
4. Talk about a safari hunt and explain that each child may find one hidden animal on the playground.
5. Dismiss the children from the group one by one to go on their hunt to locate a hidden animal.

 Barb Lindsay, Mason City, IA

Ice Castle, A Winter Activity: Study of Russia

Materials

Books on Russia • 2-liter bottles • sieves in a variety of sizes • plastic trash bags • square cake pans • sandbox toys • food coloring • playdough • freezer • spray bottle filled with water

What to do

1. This is a great activity to do in the winter, in conjunction with a unit on the country of Russia.
2. Read books about Russia to the children. Talk about the country and show pictures. Read Russian folk tales, taste Russian food, and play Russian games.
3. Tell them about the tradition of ice sculpture, which takes place in Red Square in the winter.
4. Explain that they are going to help design an ice castle. Collect a variety of containers to make ice shapes, such as 2-liter bottles, cake pans, and sandbox toys and buckets.
5. Fill the containers with water. Put food coloring in the water to give a rainbow effect to the ice castle.
6. After filling the two-liter bottles, screw on the caps or plug with playdough. Use playdough or plastic trash bags to plug sieves to make domes for the castle towers.
7. Place all the filled containers in the freezer.
8. When frozen, pop out the ice shapes using warm water.
9. Place the frozen shapes outside on a flat surface and "glue" pieces together using a spray bottle filled with water.
10. Demonstrate how to spray pieces, and then hold the two pieces together for a few seconds.
11. If you keep the structure in a shaded place, it will remain for days as long as the temperature remains cold enough.
12. Try making other types of ice sculptures and display them where parents and visitors can see them when coming to your school.

Related books

Count Your Way Through Russia by Jim Haskins
Let's Go Fishing on the Ice by George Travis
Look What Came From Russia by Miles Harvey

 Cookie Zingarelli, Columbus, OH

Painting in the Snow

Materials

Snowy day • empty spray bottles • water • food coloring

What to do

1. Ask the children what color snow is.
2. After everyone yells white, ask if they have ever seen blue snow. What about red snow, or green?
3. Provide each child with an empty spray bottle. (Or, ask them to bring one in from home.)
4. Let each child choose what color she wants her snow to be. Mix water and food coloring for each bottle.
5. Have the children bundle up and go out to "paint" the snow. Challenge them to spray a circle, a square, or their names.

 Sandra Hutchins Lucas, Cox's Creek, KY

Red String Maze

Materials

Ball of red string • playground equipment • *The Red String* by Margot Blair • 1' lengths of red string, one per child • box

What to do

1. Prepare the playground ahead of the activity by winding the red string over, under, and around the equipment. Place a box filled with pieces of red string at the end of the obstacle course.
2. Read the story to the children.
3. Invite the children to begin the obstacle course one at a time. Tell the children to keep one hand on the string at all times until they reach the "treasure box."
4. Stand by the treasure box and tie the "prize" (the red string) on each child's right wrist.
5. After all the children have finished the course, enjoy a game of Simon Says. Emphasize the concept of right and left.

6. If desired, create an indoor obstacle course. Construct a 4' x 4' x 6' cube from PVC pipe and connectors. Wind the string spider-web style throughout the box. Each child may either crawl through the box without the string touching her, or may unravel the string with coaching from a team of three friends.

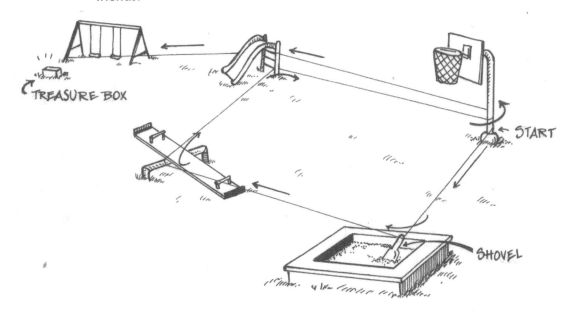

 Susan R. Forbes, Daytona Beach, FL

Good Luck Pet Rocks

Materials

Rocks • paint • paintbrushes • moveable eyes, feathers, rickrack, and other decorating items • glue

What to do

1. Take the children on a walk outdoors. Encourage them to collect rocks to bring back to the classroom.
2. Let them paint their rocks any color.
3. Encourage them to decorate their rocks by gluing on feathers, rickrack, and eyes.
4. Place them in the classroom garden for good luck.

 Lisa Chichester, Parkersburg, WV

Rock Garden

Materials

Books on landscaping and gardens • big and small rocks • garden tools • plants

What to do

1. Help the children design a garden. Bring in landscaping and gardening books for them to look at for ideas.
2. Try making an outdoor rock garden on the playground.
3. Ask the children to find rocks by their homes and bring them in. Buy some plants from your local garden store, or ask parents to donate them.
4. On a nice day, bring in gardening tools and let the children plant and set up the garden.
5. Look for big rocks on the playground or in the ground while digging up your flowerbed.
6. If you wish to keep your rock garden year after year, try planting plants that will come back each year.

 Cookie Zingarelli, Columbus, OH

Shadow Chasers

Materials

Sunny day • sidewalk or cement play area • sidewalk chalk

What to do

1. This is a great activity to do outside on a sunny day. Discuss shadows and how they are made.
2. Let the children experiment with their shadows.
3. Challenge them to make their shadows tall, short, fat, thin, or into a letter or number. They can even combine their shadows with another child to do the same commands.
4. Ask the children to work in pairs to trace around each other's shadows, and then they can color them with sidewalk chalk.

Related book

Gregory's Shadow by Don Freeman

 Barbara Saul, Eureka, CA

Koosh Ball Painting

Materials

Large outdoor space • old clothes • several colors of tempera paint • tin pie pans, one for each color of paint • several Koosh balls • one flat white sheet (twin or full size) • spring-type clothespins • large bucket of warm soapy water • permanent markers

What to do

1. Make sure the children wear old clothes and paint smocks or shirts for this messy activity, and do it outdoors only!
2. Pour several colors of tempera paint in the pie pans.
3. Place a Koosh ball in each pie pan.
4. Use clothespins to attach the sheet to a fence or other outdoor structure. Keep in mind that whatever you attach the sheet to will also be splattered with paint. Cover any exposed wall or fence with old newspapers, if you wish.
5. Place the pie pans several feet from the sheet.
6. Let the children take turns throwing a paint-soaked Koosh ball at the sheet.
7. Put the used Koosh balls back in the pie pans for other children to use.
8. Continue until the sheet is satisfactorily covered in paint splotches.
9. After the sheet dries, the children can use a permanent marker to sign their names to their creation. Children can also use markers to create pictures from the paint splotches.
10. Inspect the sheet with the children. Point out where two colors blended together to make a third color. Point out how three colors combined make yet another color. Name all the colors on the sheet.
11. Display for all to see.

More to do

Instead of Koosh balls, use sponges. This makes the activity much messier but provides a more satisfying splatter on the sheet.

 Virginia Jean Herrod, Columbia, SC

Sheet Spray Painting

Materials

Large, old white sheet • clothesline • clothespins • spray bottles • water • food coloring

What to do

1. Hang a sheet on a clothesline outside.
2. Give each child a plastic spray bottle filled with food-colored water.
3. Encourage them to spray the sheet to create a beautiful watercolor masterpiece!
4. If desired, play music to inspire them while they work.

 Lisa Chichester, Parkersburg, WV

Color Races

Materials

Large outdoor area • six hula hoops in the following colors: red, blue, yellow, green, purple, and orange

What to do

1. Place the hula hoops around a large outdoor area, making sure there is at least 3' between each one. (If necessary, this activity can also be done in a large indoor area.)
2. Choose several points around the area as starting points. For example, you might use a fence post or trees, or you could place chairs around the playground to designate starting points. The starting points should be equal distances from all of the hula hoops.
3. Choose two or three children to gather at each starting point.
4. Ask the children to look closely at the clothing they are wearing. Remind them to notice what color their shirts, pants, shorts, dresses, socks, and shoes are.
5. Explain that you are going to call out an article of clothing ("Ready! Set! Shirts!"). The children then run to the hula hoop that matches the main color

of that article of clothing they are wearing. For example, if you call out "shirts," all the children with red (or mostly red) shirts run to the red hula hoop, the children with blue shirts run to the blue hula hoop, and so on.

6. Encourage the children to cooperate as they run to the hula hoops. When all the children have gathered in the hoops, count the number of children in each one. Compare the numbers and ask the children questions such as, "Which hula hoop has the most children in it?"

7. Have the children return to their starting positions. Repeat the game by calling out, "Ready! Set!" and then the article of clothing of your choice.

8. Continue the game for a predetermined number of turns or until interest wanes.

9. Not all children will run on each turn. For example, when you call dresses, only girls wearing dresses should run.

10. If desired, add in other characteristics. For example, ask everyone with blond hair to run to the yellow hoop, brown hair to the purple hoop, and so on.

 Virginia Jean Herrod, Columbia, SC

Slide Races

Materials

Playground slide • masking tape • black marker • yardstick or carpenter's tape measure • small plastic cars • large balloons • clothespins • chart paper

What to do

1. Help the children measure the length of the playground slide from the bottom to the top. Use masking tape and a marker to mark the slide in 5" increments.

2. Tape a balloon to the back of the small plastic car.

3. Blow up the balloon. Clip the opening shut with the clothespin.

4. Place the car at the bottom of the slide with the front of the car facing up the slide. The children count down (5, 4, 3, 2, 1). Then a child unclips the clothespin from the balloon.

5. The force of the air leaving the balloon will propel the car up the slide. Mark the spot where the car stops with another piece of tape. Help the children measure how far the car traveled. Keep track of each car's results. Continue using different sizes and types of cars.

(continued on the next page)

6. Create a chart to show the results of the races. Brainstorm about why one car travels father than the others. Make notes about the children's ideas. Post the chart and the children's ideas for their parents to see.

7. Use two cars and balloons and have races on the slides.
   Tip: If the angle of the slide is too great and the cars can't move up it, try the activity on a flat surface of the sidewalk. Measure and mark out a 5' or 6' track and proceed as described in the activity.

☆ Virginia Jean Herrod, Columbia, SC

Tricycle, Bicycle, or Wagon License Plates

Materials

Cardboard or poster board • scissors • stencils or alphabet stickers • markers • clear contact paper • string or yarn • hole punch • tricycles

What to do

1. Cut out rectangles from cardboard or poster board. Cut out alphabet letters using stencils, or purchase alphabet stickers.
2. Give each child a rectangle to make a license plate. Encourage them to use the pre-cut letters or alphabet stickers to write the state, month, or whatever they desire.
3. Cover the license plates with clear contact paper.

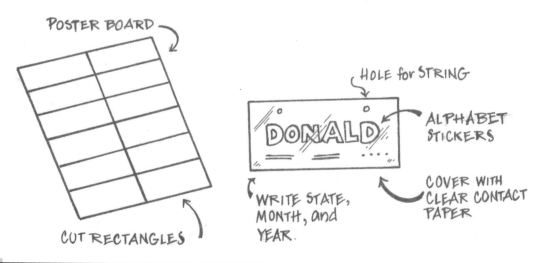

POSTER BOARD

CUT RECTANGLES

HOLE for STRING

DONALD

ALPHABET STICKERS

WRITE STATE, MONTH, and YEAR.

COVER WITH CLEAR CONTACT PAPER

4. Punch holes in each side and tie string through them.

5. Outside, when it is the child's turn to ride the tricycle, attach her license plate to the front or back. Remove it when her turn is over.

 Penni Smith, Riverside, CA

Playground Sculptures

Materials

PVC pipes in curves, joints, and straight pieces (number purchased depends on the size of the sculpture desired) • 2 or 3 old tires • several large cardboard boxes • paint in several colors • large paintbrushes

What to do

1. Place the pipes, tires, and boxes on the playground. Give the children time to express interest and explore the materials.

2. Show the children how the PVC curves and joints fit together with the straight pieces. Let them experiment with the available materials. Soon the children will begin joining the smaller pieces to form larger structures. Encourage them to work together and cooperate as they share the materials. Do not take charge of the emerging sculpture. Let the children lead the way. Offer encouragement and a steadying hand when needed.

3. At some point, comment to the children that their work looks like a large sculpture (see illlustrations on the following page). Explain that when an artist puts a variety of materials together to create a work of art, it is usually called a sculpture. Encourage the children to continue to work together to make the large sculpture.

4. If the children focus on one set of materials, such as the PVC pipes, point out the other materials and encourage them to use them also. Ask questions such as, "I wonder what would happen if you put the cardboard box over the pipes?" or, "These tires look interesting, I wonder if you can use them anywhere on your sculpture." Again, do not take charge of the construction; simply offer small suggestions and comments.

5. Continue to work with children as they add more and more pieces to their large sculpture. Continue until all the pieces are used or the children feel they are finished.

(continued on the next page)

6. Bring out the paint and brushes. Let the children paint the sculpture as desired. When they are finished and the sculpture is dry, have them gather around the sculpture for a group photo. Invite the parents, other children, and staff to come and see the sculpture.

7. Have fun with the sculpture until the children feel like tearing it apart. Then clean the PVC pipe, get some more cardboard, and begin again.

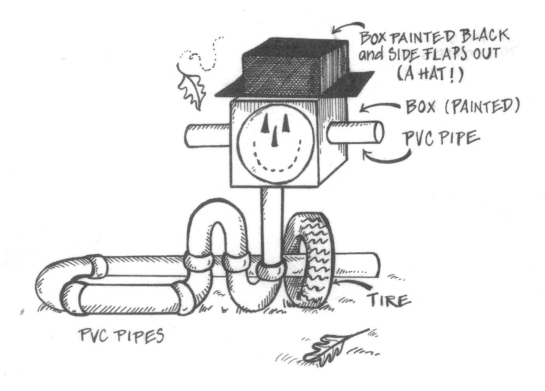

BOX PAINTED BLACK and SIDE FLAPS OUT (A HAT!)

BOX (PAINTED)

PVC PIPE

TIRE

PVC PIPES

More to do

Art: Encourage the children to use straws and clay to create mini sculptures in the classroom.

 Virginia Jean Herrod, Columbia, SC

Playground Excavations

Materials

Old utensils • old pots and pans • old pottery • old dishes • old cups • sand shovels • old paintbrushes • cardboard boxes • play pith helmets

What to do

1. While learning about prehistoric times, create this fun surprise on the playground.
2. When the children are not present, bury old utensils, pots, pans, pottery, dishes, and cups in the sandbox. These items are just a guide. You can also try to find items to bury that might not be familiar to the children such as old mortars and pestles or old tools such as levels, t-squares, and wrenches. Use any safe material that does not have sharp edges.
3. Explain to the children that one way scientists find out about how people lived in prehistoric times is to excavate an area where people used to live. Explain that excavate means to dig up or unearth.
4. Ask them if they think they might find anything from prehistoric times if they decided to excavate the sandbox area.
5. Give each child a sand shovel, an old paintbrush, and a pith helmet.
6. Encourage the children to carefully dig in the sand. Soon they will begin to unearth the items you planted there. Act surprised!

(continued on the next page)

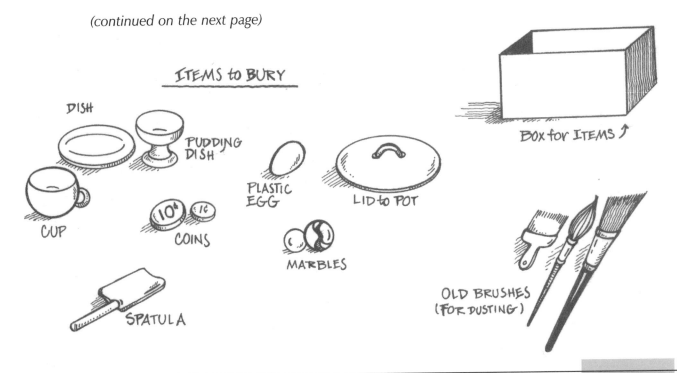

ITEMS to BURY

DISH

PUDDING DISH

CUP

COINS

PLASTIC EGG

MARBLES

LID to POT

SPATULA

BOX for ITEMS ↑

OLD BRUSHES (FOR DUSTING)

7. Encourage them to use the old paintbrushes to carefully remove sand from the items they find.

8. Let the children continue to dig until they have found all the items you buried. Ask them to place their items in the cardboard box.

9. Head back indoors to explore your findings.

10. Examine each found item carefully. Ask leading questions such as, "How do you think a prehistoric person would have used this?" or "What do you think this item is?" Record the children's answers for later use.

11. After they have examined each item, create a display of the things they found on their excavation. Place the items on a display table. Next to each item place a note stating what the children thought the item was and how they thought it was used.

 Virginia Jean Herrod, Columbia, SC

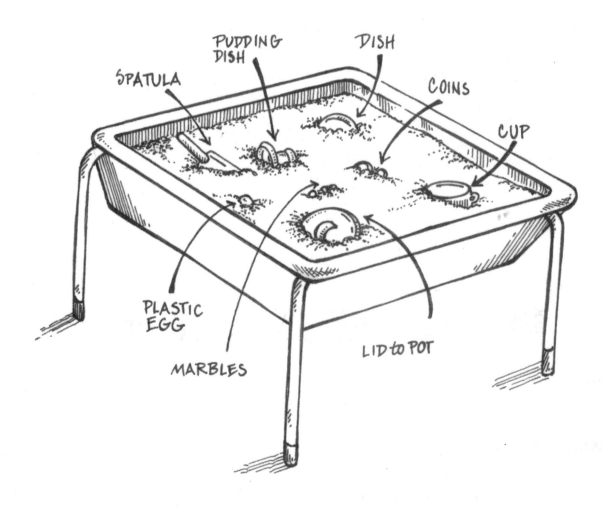

Learning to Relax

Materials

Resting mats

What to do

1. Even small children feel the stress of modern life. A few minutes at the beginning of rest time can teach them relaxation techniques and counteract the effects of stress. As they contract and relax muscles, they begin to sense when they are growing tense and can consciously relax.

2. First, ask the children to stretch out on their backs, close their eyes, and take several deep breaths.

3. Then say, "You are lying on the beach, and the warm sun is shining on your body…take another deep breath…now tighten your legs…tighten your stomach…tighten your arms and your chest…tighten your neck and your face…squinch your eyes, tighter. Now slowly, make your body soft again…first your feet and legs…then your stomach…your arms and chest…your neck and face…. Now open your eyes."

4. Another relaxation technique is to play "rag doll." Tell the children to pretend they are rag dolls without bones. Their heads flop and they can't sit or stand. Now move among the resting children and lift a child's arm, another child's leg, and so on, to see if they are limp.

☆ Mary Jo Shannon, Roanoke, VA

My Favorite Musician

Materials

Teddy bear • Velcro • CD jacket

What to do

1. Attach Velcro to the teddy bear's hands. Attach pieces of Velcro to the backs of either CD jackets of the music you play at rest time or to photocopied sheets of the jackets.

(continued on the next page)

2. Every day before rest time, introduce the musician to whom the children will be listening.
3. Ask a child to come up and attach the picture to the bear.
4. You can display various artists weekly or daily.

 Lisa Chichester, Parkersburg, WV

Nap Buddies

Materials

Fabric • scissors • needle and thread • stuffing • yarn and felt • glue • markers

What to do

1. Cut fabric into 12" x 24" rectangles, one for each child.
2. Fold the fabric in half, and sew the bottom and side of the fabric, leaving the top open for filling.

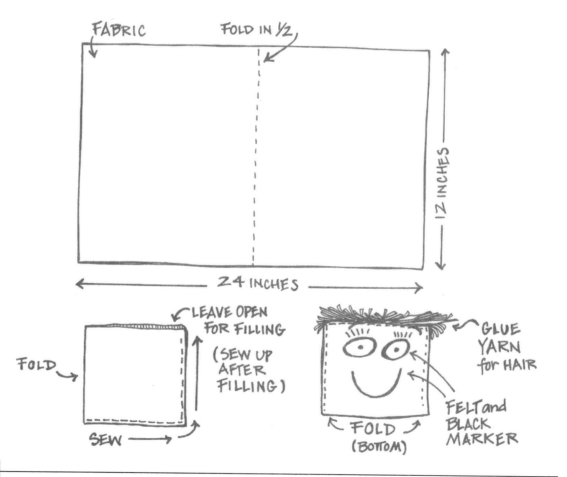

3. Give one to each child. Let them fill their pillows with stuffing.

4. Sew the opening closed for each child.

5. Encourage the children to decorate their nap buddies as desired. They can glue on yarn for hair and felt for eyes, and use permanent markers for added features.

6. The children can sleep with their nap buddies at rest time.

 Lisa Chichester, Parkersburg, WV

Naptime Activity Bags

Materials

Fabric bags or large plastic resealable bags

What to do

1. For the children who do not fall asleep, provide quiet activities for them to do while the others sleep.

2. Fill fabric or plastic bags with quiet activities, such as dominoes, playing cards, magnetic alphabet letters, magnetic numbers, 24-piece puzzles, and "I Spy" books.

 Melissa Browning, Milwaukee, WI

My Naptime Sheet

Materials

One junior-sized fitted sheet for each child • newspaper • variety of fabric paints • sponges • small paintbrushes • fabric pens

What to do

1. Ask the parents to send in a junior-sized fitted sheet for their child. If these sheets will not fit the naptime mats, then ask each child to bring in a junior-size flat sheet instead.

(continued on the next page)

2. Cover several mats with newspaper, and put the sheets on the mats. Encourage the children to use fabric paints, sponges, paintbrushes, and fabric pens to decorate their own sheet.

3. Ask the children to use a fabric pen to print their names on their sheet.

4. Remove the sheets from the mats. Let them dry thoroughly.

5. Wash the sheets as you normally would to remove excess paint and to soften them.

6. Let the children use their Naptime Sheet during regular naptime. They will be more enthusiastic about putting their sheets on their mats when they get to use their own colorful creations.

    Tip: If possible, let the children use alphabet sponges to write their names on their sheets.

Related books

The Napping House by Audrey Wood
Piggies by Audrey Wood and Don Wood
Sleep Book by Dr. Seuss
Time to Sleep by Denise Fleming
Treasure Nap by Juanita Havill

 Virginia Jean Herrod, Columbia, SC

Rest Time

Materials

None

What to do

1. By the time they are five years old, most children are outgrowing their naps. However, they still need time to relax. Here are some ideas to calm things down.

2. Turn out all the lights, leaving a small reading light on. Play quiet music or environmental sounds tapes.

3. Gather for story time with pillows and blankets; as the children get sleepy and want to lie down, they can leave on their own to go to their rest spot.

4. Learn some yoga deep breathing and relaxation exercises (check your library for books or look on the Internet). Lead the children in these exercises,

encouraging them to notice how their bodies feel. If they want to rest, they can go to their mats.

5. Let the children do a quiet activity on their mats, such as writing in a journal, coloring, reading, or just thinking.

6. If children can remain quiet, they can sit together and whisper, share a book, or work a puzzle.

 Tracie O'Hara, Charlotte, NC

Nifty Nap Mats

Materials

Fabric • scissors • needle and thread • polyfiber fill • paint pens • ribbon and scrap material • hot glue gun (adult only)

What to do

1. Cut fabric to fit the naptime mats, one for each child.

2. Fold each piece of fabric in half, and sew them as shown (see illustration). Leave a small opening for stuffing.

3. Encourage the children to fill their fabric with polyfiber fill. Sew the hole closed.

4. Each child can decorate his own mat with paint pens and scrap material. (An adult should glue the scrap material in place.)

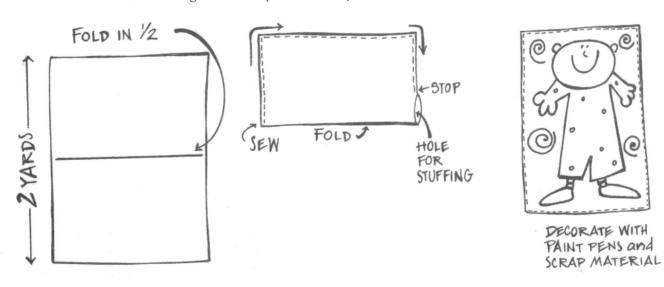

FOLD IN ½

2 YARDS

SEW   FOLD

← STOP

HOLE FOR STUFFING

DECORATE WITH PAINT PENS and SCRAP MATERIAL

 Lisa Chichester, Parkersburg, WV

Rest Time Buddies

Materials

Quiet activities

What to do

1. If some of the children don't sleep during naptime, allow them to play quietly with a child that they usually don't play with (for example, an outgoing child with a very quiet child).
2. Let them sit on a mat with a small box of Legos, puzzles, or markers.
3. This is a great way to encourage new friendships.

 Audrey F. Kanoff, Allentown, PA

Someone to Watch Over Me

Materials

Butcher or newspaper end roll paper • markers, crayons, paint, or any coloring medium • scissors • collage materials and glue, optional • mirrors

What to do

1. Many children this age are no longer taking naps, but their bodies still need quiet time to rest. This activity may help them to relax and get the rest they need.
2. Place unrolled paper on the floor. Ask a child to lie down on the paper.
3. Trace the outside of the child's body and cut the piece off the roll. Do this for each child.
4. Help the children cut out their body shapes.
5. Encourage each child to decorate his body shape to look like his "twin." Have mirrors available to help.

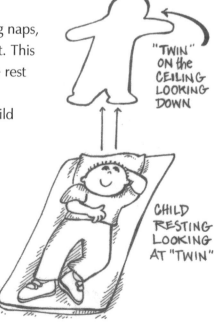

"TWIN" ON the CEILING LOOKING DOWN

CHILD RESTING LOOKING AT "TWIN"

6. When the "twins" are completed, mount them flat on the ceiling in the space above where the children will be resting. During rest time, each child can look up and see himself looking back down from above.

7. Suggest that they imagine going on a trip or to the beach with their twins.

 Amanda Barche Lindberg, Lafayette, IN

Winter Has Come
(poem for rest period)

Materials

None

What to do

1. Recite the following poem.
2. At the end of the poem, the children put their heads in the folds of their elbows.

Winter Has Come

From the heavens above
A million snowflakes came down.
Each snowflake was dressed
In a shimmering gown.
They softly had fallen
During the night.
Had covered the earth
With a blanket of white.
Winter had come
And all was asleep.
Even the flowers
In the ground down deep.

 Ingelore Mix, Gainesville, VA

What Can Be Found Under the Leaves?

Materials

Leaves • nature items (rocks, pinecones, acorns, pebbles, twigs, grass) • plastic bugs • sand and water table • plastic tweezers

What to do

1. In advance, gather a lot of leaves, nature items, and plastic bugs. Place them in the sand and water table.
2. Hide grass, pinecones, rocks, plastic bugs, acorns, pebbles, and twigs among the leaves.
3. Encourage the children to use tweezers to lift up the leaves and find the nature items underneath.
4. After every child has used the area, discuss what they found hidden under the leaves.
5. To extend the activity, go to a park for a leaf walk. Give the children magnifiers and encourage them to look under leaves and find out what is hidden.

 Quazonia J. Quarles, Newark, DE

Finding ABCs

Materials

Sand and water table • sand or small rocks • plastic alphabet letters

What to do

1. Before the children arrive, hide the alphabet letters in the sand.
2. Let each child take a turn finding a letter.
3. Ask the children to hold up their letters and tell what it is.
4. Challenge them to feel around to find the letter their name starts with—without looking.
5. If desired, place 26 objects in the sand, one for each letter. Ask each child to find an object and tell what letter it starts with.

 Sandra Hutchins Lucas, Cox's Creek, KY

Fruit Sorting

Materials

Plastic containers • labels • fruit counters • sand and water table • serving tongs

What to do

1. In advance, collect six plastic containers and make a separate label (word and picture) for each fruit.
2. Place the containers and the fruit counters in the sand and water table.
3. Encourage the children to pick up the fruit with tongs.
4. Ask them to match fruit counters with the correct fruit container by putting the fruit in the container.

More to do

Math: Provide real fruit and a balance scale for weighing. Compare the following: Which pieces of fruit are heavier or lighter? How many pieces of this fruit does it take to equal in weight this other piece of fruit?

☆ Quazonia J. Quarles, Newark, DE

Ice Cube Hockey

Materials

Pipe cleaners • playdough or clay • sand and water table • ice cubes • Popsicle sticks

What to do

1. Bend two pipe cleaners into a "U" shape and push the ends into small balls of clay.
2. Place each of the pipe cleaners (goal posts) at opposite ends of the sand and water table.

(continued on the next page)

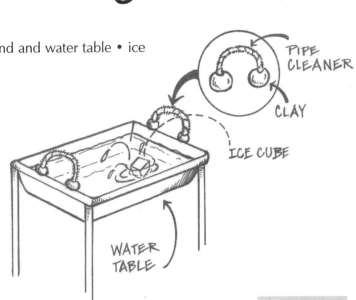

PIPE CLEANER

CLAY

ICE CUBE

WATER TABLE

3. Let two children use Popsicle sticks to try and shoot an ice cube through their goal.
4. Ask them to count how many times they are able to score.

☆ Christine Maiorano, Duxbury, MA

More Than Sand and Water

Materials

Cork bits • birdseed • Styrofoam pieces • shredded paper • crushed ice and ice cubes • rock salt • colored salt • colored water • toy trucks, cars, people, animals, and dinosaurs • plastic eggs • tongs • spoons • sponges • washcloths • scrubbers • play dishes (for washing) • baby dolls • water pumps • water wheels

What to do

1. Include some of the above materials in the sand and water table.
2. For even more fun, take it outside!

☆ Susan M. Myhre, Bremerton, WA

Recycled Materials

Materials

See activity below

What to do

1. Here is a list of some great things to put in the sand or water table that are cheap or free!
    ☆ Recycled materials: film canisters, scoops from detergent or dry formula, lids from liquid detergent bottles, plastic cups from fast food restaurants
    ☆ Inexpensive items: colored plastic rocks or objects for aquariums, about the size of a quarter (not gravel), smooth rocks (usually used in floral arrangements)

☆ plastic Happy Meal toys, Mardi Gras necklaces, rubber fishing lures, marbles, Ping-Pong balls

2. Check your local dollar store for many of these items, as well as your own ideas.

☆ Tracie O'Hara, Charlotte, NC

Seasonal "Sand"

Materials

Sand and water table or large plastic bins • newspaper • cotton balls • non-toxic Styrofoam pieces • shredded wrapping paper • colored aquarium gravel • birdseed • leaves, grass, and twigs • small buckets or cups • shovels and scoops • small dump trucks and cars • plastic figures

What to do

1. Each month or whenever you wish, vary the children's sand and water play by switching the contents. Use classroom themes or seasonal topics to help determine what to use. For example:

   ☆ September: Fill the table with fall leaves and add forest critters to hide in the leaves. The children can use small toy garden rakes, scoops, dump trucks, and so on to move the leaves around.

   ☆ October: Fill the table with spiders and pieces of yarn (webs). Again the children can use the shovels, scoops, buckets, and small boxes to move the spiders around.

   ☆ November: Put in non-toxic Styrofoam and buckets. Add small toy fruit and vegetables for children to gather for Thanksgiving.

   ☆ December: Shredded, colorful wrapping paper is fun. The children can use cars, people, and small toys to scoop and fill cups, trucks, and buckets. Cars can be driven through the cardboard tube "tunnels."

   ☆ January: Cotton balls are great. When finished using them in the table, bring them to the art table and encourage the children to make snow or cloud pictures.

   ☆ February: Fill the table with foam hearts. These can be purchased in large bags or cut from sheets of foam.

   ☆ March: Add green aquarium gravel. Hide "gold" pieces in the gravel and encourage the children to hunt for "leprechaun gold."

(continued on the next page)

☆ April: Fill the table with water and water animals, fish, and ducks. Add squeeze bottles, measuring cups, and wide plastic tubes for fish to "swim" through.

☆ May: Fill the table with potting soil that is free of fertilizer/chemicals. Add toy worms and insects. Let the children use magnifying glasses to look for bugs. When finished, use soil for planting.

☆ June: Fill the table with beach sand; add shells, beach critters, buckets, and shovels.

2. Additional ideas include using crushed ice (use with waterproof mittens); adding space figures and spaceships to sand (to make a "moon" surface); and adding small boxes with lids for children to fill.

Author's Note: All of the above ideas are non-food items. It is my personal preference not to use food to "play with," if possible.

 Maxine Della Fave, Raleigh, NC

Sink or Float– With a Dash of Salt

Materials

Small buckets or tubs • water • salt • variety of objects that may sink or float

What to do

1. This water play activity teaches an important science lesson: salt water is denser ("heavier" or "thicker" are the words children may use) and can suspend a greater weight.

2. Pour plain water in the bucket.

3. Encourage the children to drop in provided objects. Record which float and which sink.

4. Now remove the objects and add one cup of salt.

5. Ask the children to drop in one object at a time. Remember to take time before each item is added to let the children predict what will happen based on the previous trial.

6. After all the items have been dropped in, add more salt and repeat.

7. As an extension to this activity, read a book or discuss going to the beach. This same principle applies to people in water as well—it is easier to swim in the ocean than in a swimming pool because of the salt in the water!

⭐ Amanda Barche Lindberg, Lafayette, IN

Water Day

Materials

See activity below (each station requires different materials)

What to do

1. Have Water Day! Ask parents to send their children to school wearing bathing suits and sunscreen, and to bring towels.
2. Set up the following stations around the room for children to explore.
3. Station A: Have a bucket of assorted objects that sink or float, a deep pan of water, and two trays labeled "sink" and "float." Encourage the children to make predictions about whether an object will sink or float. They test their guess by putting the object in the water and then they place it on the appropriate tray. Ask them to look for trends (wood and wax float, metal and stone sink, and so on).
4. Station B: Place toy sailboats at one end of the sand and water table or a long (under the bed storage) plastic container. Encourage the children to blow through drinking straws to propel the boats to the other end. Have races.
5. Station C: Put a deep pan of water, a plastic single-section microwave dinner dish, and some small stones in this station. Encourage the children to make predictions about how many stones the dish will hold before sinking. Test the hypothesis. "Does the placement of the stones affect the outcome?" "What about the size of the stones?"
6. Station D: Have a large container of water, assorted cups, funnels, sieves, colanders, and scoops for the children to play with at this station. Encourage them to measure, pour, and fill. "Can different shaped containers hold the same amount of water?" "Does a funnel help when filling small openings?" "Can you make the water stay in a sieve?"

(continued on the next page)

7. Station E: Provide buckets of water and large paintbrushes. Let the children paint the walls, sidewalks, and blacktop with water. "Does it look different?" "Do areas in the sun dry at a different rate than areas in the shade?"

8. Station F: Fill clean, empty dishwashing soap bottles with water and replace lids. Line up empty, plastic bottles on a low table or bench. Show the children how to use the soap bottles to squirt water at the objects to knock them off the table. "How far away can you stand and still reach the targets?"

9. Station G: Soak some chalk in water and keep some dry. Encourage the children to draw with wet and dry chalk on black construction paper. Note the appearance of the colors and how the chalks glide or drag. "Which is easier?" "What happens to the drawing when it dries?"

Related books

Bubble, Bubble by Mercer Mayer
Puddles by Jonathan London

 Sandra Gratias, Perkasie, PA

UNDER the BED STORAGE CONTAINER

Science Kits

Materials

Medium-sized plastic totes or buckets • various items for each science kit

What to do

1. Decide on the types of science kits that you would like to make. Purchase that many boxes.
2. Collect various science lesson plans that you have enjoyed using and laminate them or place them in a binder.
3. Label the boxes with the focus for that container (for example, colors, plants, trees, seeds, water, sky, rocks and sand, critters, and so on).
4. Place the lesson plans in the box and make a list of items that are needed for the activities. Ask parents to contribute some of the needed items.
5. Also place books that relate to the theme in the box.
6. These boxes make changing the Science Area easy.

 Melissa Browning, Milwaukee, WI

3-D Deep Sea Porthole

Materials

Lightweight paper plates, 2 per porthole • scissors • construction paper • glue • jumbo paper clips • pictures of tropical fish • 4" squares of white construction paper • markers • blue plastic wrap or cellophane • stapler

What to do

1. Ahead of time, cut out a 5 ½" circle from one of each pair of paper plates (you need two paper plates to make one porthole), leaving the outer rim intact. Cut construction paper into 1" x 4" strips, roll the strips into circles, and glue them to make an "O" shape, securing with jumbo clips until dry. Make three or four of these circles for each porthole scene (to attach the fish to the background).

(continued on the next page)

2. Show the children the tropical fish pictures, calling attention to the

distinguishing features of the colorful fish: stripes, shapes, dots, colors, and fins.

3. Give the children 4" squares of white construction paper and encourage them to create their own colorful fish, drawing one fish per square. Ask them to cut out the fish and glue the flat side of a loop to the back of each fish. Secure with paper clips until dry.

4. Distribute the whole uncut paper plates to the children, face up. When the fish and connecting loops are dry, ask them to glue the underside of each loop to the paper plate, placing the fish inside the 5 ½" circle indented in the plate. This gives the fish a 3-dimensional look.

5. Cut blue cellophane into 6 ½" squares. Give each child a cellophane square and a plate with the center circle cut out. Demonstrate how to glue the cellophane on the plate to cover the hole and make a window.

6. Teacher step: Invert the window plate over the whole plate and staple together so that the blue window reveals the underwater scene.

⭐ Susan Oldham Hill, Lakeland, FL

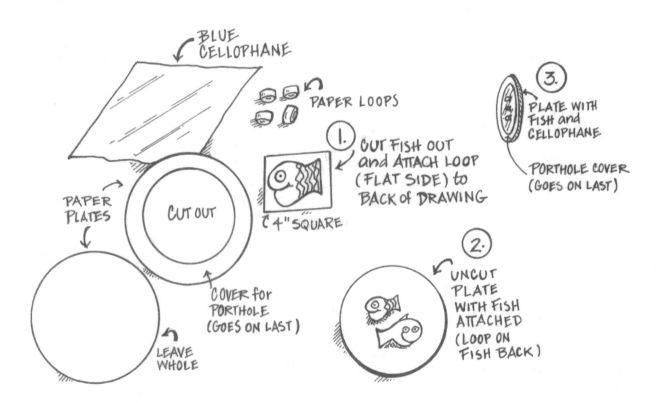

Shark Hat

Materials

Books and pictures of sharks • cardboard or oak tag • pencil • scissors • 12" x 18" white and blue construction paper • white glue • light gray tempera paint • paintbrushes • medium-point black marker • 15mm wiggly eyes • paper cutter • stapler

What to do

1. Have a discussion about sharks. Show the children pictures and books about different types of sharks, such as the great white, the hammerhead, the leopard, and the nurse shark.
2. Discuss how sharks have a keen sense of smell and how they help to clean the ocean by eating dead fish and animals. If possible, show the class shark teeth.
3. Make shark and fin patterns out of cardboard or oak tag.
4. Help the children trace the shark and fins on white paper and cut them out.
5. Demonstrate where to glue the fins on the shark. Allow the glue to dry, then ask them to paint their sharks gray.
6. After the paint has dried, encourage the children to draw a mouth, teeth, and gills with a black marker, then let them glue on a wiggle eye.
7. Use a paper cutter to cut blue paper into 3" x 18" strips (adult only).
8. Give a strip to each child and demonstrate how to cut waves.
9. Help the children staple the water strip to their shark to form a blue headband the size of the child's head. The middle of the shark becomes part of the headband with the head and tail of the shark sticking out.

☆ Mary Brehm, Aurora, OH

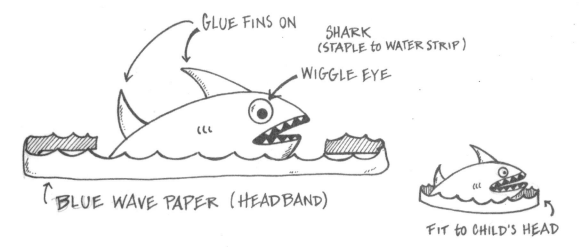

GLUE FINS ON

SHARK (STAPLE to WATER STRIP)

WIGGLE EYE

BLUE WAVE PAPER (HEADBAND)

FIT to CHILD'S HEAD

Tropical Fish Striper

Materials

Pictures of striped fish • construction paper in assorted colors, including black and white • scissors • markers and crayons • glue • wiggly eyes, optional

What to do

1. Show the children pictures of fish with colorful stripes, such as the clown fish. Point out the different appearance of the fish with narrow or wide stripe patterns.
2. Ask the children to draw just the outline of a large fish and cut it out. Encourage them to create a wide outline rather than a thin, narrow fish.
3. After another look at the fish pictures with their stripe patterns, show the children how to draw three or four wavy vertical lines on the widest part of their fish.
4. Distribute another sheet of construction paper in a contrasting color. Ask the children to cut along the lines they drew, beginning at one end. Show them how to cut off just one piece at a time and reconstruct the fish on the whole sheet of paper. As they cut off the second stripe, ask them to put it next to the first piece, leaving a space for the contrasting color to show through. This space will create the stripe.
5. After all the lines have been cut apart, invite the children to reassemble the fish on the other sheet. Ask them to glue the pieces on one at a time, leaving a space between every piece for the contrasting color to show through and make a stripe. Let dry.
6. When the fish are dry, show the children how to draw a line around the edge of the entire fish to create a new outline that includes the striped areas. Ask them to cut around the lines they have drawn. Provide markers to add features such as scales, mouths, and eyes (if desired, use wiggly eyes).
7. For visual interest, mount the fish cutouts on a third piece of construction paper.

 Susan Oldham Hill, Lakeland, FL

Seal Show

Materials

Cardboard • scissors • white construction paper • markers • glue • 10mm wiggle eyes • 1" long white or silver paper clips

What to do

1. Make a cardboard pattern for the seal, ball, and ring (see illustration).
2. Help the children trace all the patterns on white construction paper. Ask them to trace the seal twice.
3. Let them color the ball as desired.
4. Ask them to cut out all the pieces, including the center of the ring.
5. Demonstrate how to glue two seals together at the top of the head and back of the tail.
6. Explain that seals are various colors, including tan, gray, spotted, or dark gray. Encourage them to color their seals as desired, color the nose black, draw whiskers, and glue on wiggle eyes.
7. Ask them to glue the ball behind the seal's nose.
8. Show them how to spread the two seal sides apart and add a paper clip to the back of the tail on the reverse side so the seal will stand up. Then, finish by slipping the ring over the seal's head.
9. Learn about various seals and sea lions. Locate the areas on a map or globe where they live.

(continued on the next page)

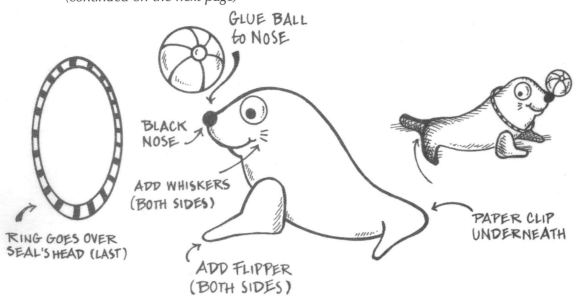

GLUE BALL to NOSE

BLACK NOSE

ADD WHISKERS (BOTH SIDES)

RING GOES OVER SEAL'S HEAD (LAST)

ADD FLIPPER (BOTH SIDES)

PAPER CLIP UNDERNEATH

More to do

Gross Motor: Encourage the children to walk like seals with their knees together and calves and feet spread apart. Encourage them to bark like seals and point their noses upward.

 Mary Brehm, Aurora, OH

Animal Alphabet Parade: Little Lobster

Materials

Picture of lobster pot • real lobster shell or plush toy • box • seashells • small plastic fish or other sea animals

What to do

1. Have a discussion about lobsters. Explain that lobsters are *crustaceans*. Name other crustaceans, such as a crab.
2. Show a plastic model, plush toy, or real shell of a lobster. Also show a model or picture of a lobster pot or trap. Tell the children that lobsters are greenish-black when alive in the water, but turn red when cooked.
3. Discuss other kinds of sea life, and show pictures.
4. Talk about the food lobsters eat such as starfish, mollusks, or dead sea creatures.
5. Make a sea life surprise box. Put seashells and small plastic models (or pictures) of fish, lobster, crab, and jellyfish into a box. Let the children take turns reaching into the box to get something and then show it. Count the objects when finished.
6. Make or purchase felt sea life shapes.
7. Make math problems for the children to solve, such as 2 seashells + 1 lobster = _____.
8. If possible, take the children to an aquarium to see a live lobster.

 Mary Brehm, Aurora, OH

Frog Eatery

Materials

Square tissue box • green paint • paintbrush • scissors • red and green construction paper • glue • black marker • pictures of things frogs eat (spiders, insects, earthworms, tiny fish) and pictures of things they don't eat (hamburger, pizza, a lollipop) • laminate, optional

What to do

1. Explain how frogs eat tiny animals with their long sticky tongues.
2. In advance, make a frog using an empty tissue box. Paint the tissue box green.
3. Cut out eyes, arms, and legs from green construction paper.
4. Cut out a 12"-long tongue from red paper. Use scissors to curl the tongue.
5. Glue the arms onto each side of the box and legs in the front.
6. Glue the eyes on top of box (above the tissue box opening).
7. Using the black marker, draw black eyeballs on the green circles.
8. Glue one end of the tongue to the inside of the tissue box opening (the mouth).
9. Draw or find pictures of things frogs eat and don't eat. Laminate the pictures for longevity, if desired.
10. Ask the children to place the pictures of things a frog will eat into its mouth.

⭐ Quazonia J. Quarles, Newark, DE

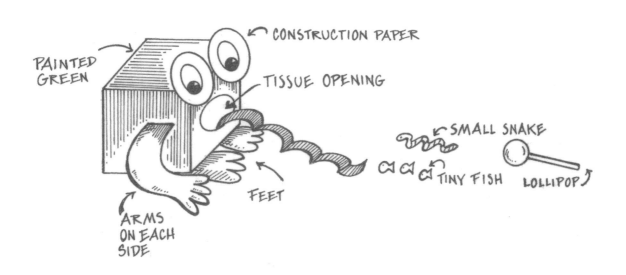

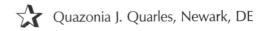

Animal Alphabet Parade: Pretty Peacock

Materials

Tagboard • scissors • construction paper (yellow for legs, white for beak, and blue or blue-green for body) • 6mm wiggly eyes • white glue • white paper plates cut in half • crayons (white, yellow, blue-green, yellow-green, red-orange, purple) • glitter • green feathers

What to do

1. Discuss peafowl with the children. Explain that the *peacock* is male and is bright in color, and the *peahen* is female and is dull in color. A baby peafowl is called a *chick*, which hatches from an egg. They belong to the pheasant fowl family. Peafowl eat berries, seeds, insects, snakes, and mice. Peacocks are kept as pets in China and India.

2. Show pictures and real peacock feathers (feathers can be bought at a craft store).

3. Demonstrate how feathers usually trail behind a peacock, then up behind him to make a fan.

4. Make peacocks with the children. Beforehand, make a tagboard pattern of the body, legs, and beak.

5. Encourage the children to use the pattern to cut out the body, beak, and two legs. Show them where to glue the beak, eyes, and legs on the body.

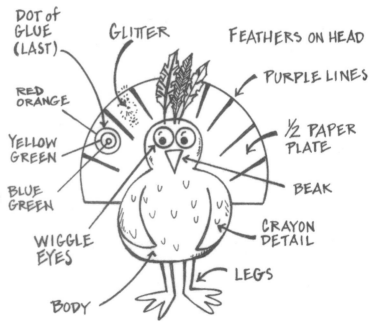

DOT of GLUE (LAST)

GLITTER

FEATHERS ON HEAD

PURPLE LINES

RED ORANGE

½ PAPER PLATE

YELLOW GREEN

BEAK

BLUE GREEN

CRAYON DETAIL

WIGGLE EYES

LEGS

BODY

6. Encourage them to draw details on the body.
7. Give each child a paper plate half. Ask them to draw purple fan lines on the raised side. Then, demonstrate how to draw a series of circles on the fan line, beginning with red-orange, followed by yellow-green and blue-green.
8. Ask the children to put glue dots in the center of each circle. Sprinkle with glitter.
9. The children finish by gluing feathers on the head and the fan on the body.

 Mary Brehm, Aurora, OH

Bird Silhouettes

Materials

Worksheet featuring matching birds and shadows • tagboard • copy machine • markers • scissors • laminator • felt • rubber cement • flannel board

What to do

1. In your teacher resource materials, locate a worksheet with outlines of birds to color and their matching shadow outlines (silhouettes).
2. Using a copy machine, enlarge and copy it onto tagboard.
3. Color the bird pictures using markers.
4. Cut out the colored pictures and the silhouettes.
5. Laminate for durability.
6. Prepare for flannel board use by backing them with felt using rubber cement.
7. To do the activity, the child matches each bird to its shadow.

 Jackie Wright, Enid, OK

Birdfeeding Garlands

Materials

Blunt needles and thread • popcorn, cranberries, and raisins

What to do

1. Give each child a pre-threaded blunt needle.
2. Place a bag of popcorn, cranberries, and raisins in front of the children.
3. Show the children how to make a birdfeeding garland by threading the food onto the needle.
4. Have a "feed the birds" party. Hang the garland on trees and serve bird snacks, such as sunflower seeds, raisins, popcorn, and bird-shaped cookies.

 Lisa Chichester, Parkersburg, WV

Animal Habitat Game

Materials

Small pictures of animal habitats (such as forest, water, desert, arctic) • card stock • glue • laminator • small pictures or drawings of animals • basket

What to do

1. Draw or glue pictures of different habitats on card stock. Laminate all items for durability.
2. Collect about three or four pictures of animals that belong in each habitat. Glue them on card stock and laminate.
3. Place the items in a basket and let the children match the animals to the correct habitats.

 Melissa Browning, Milwaukee, WI

Animal Habitats Interactive Bulletin Board

Materials

Classroom bulletin board • tape • clip art or cut-out magazine pictures of zoo, rainforest, arctic, and jungle animals • laminator • Velcro • small tub • construction paper

What to do

1. Divide the bulletin board into four sections using tape. Place a picture of a different animal habitat (zoo, rainforest, arctic, and jungle) in each section.
2. Stick several pieces of Velcro on the bulletin board in each category.
3. Laminate a variety of animal clip art or magazine pictures and put small pieces of Velcro on the back of each one.
4. Put all of the pictures into one tub and mix them up.
5. The children take turns pulling an animal picture out of the tub and putting it in the correct habitat.
6. This is a great way to encourage discussion, because some animals belong in several groups.

 Wanda Guidroz, Santa Fe, TX

Making Fossils

Materials

16-oz. box baking soda • 1 cup cornstarch • 1 ¼ cup cold water • hot plate or stove • mixing spoon • container • variety of small seashells

What to do

1. Make soda clay beforehand. Mix together the box of baking soda and 1 cup of cornstarch. Add 1 ¼ cup of cold water. Stir over moderate heat until mixture thickens and resembles mashed potatoes. Scrape onto a plate and cover with

(continued on the next page)

a damp cloth. When cool enough to handle, knead until smooth. Keep in a tightly covered container.

2. Read a book about fossils and discuss.
3. Give each child a lump of soda clay to make a "fossil."
4. Demonstrate how to press shells into the clay to leave a print.
5. Carefully remove the shells from the clay.
6. Allow the "fossils" to dry thoroughly.
7. Ask the children to count the number of imprints in the hardened clay. Compare the sizes of the shells. Can they find the shells that match the prints?

 Mary Jo Shannon, Roanoke, VA

Apple Star

Materials

Apple • knife (adult only) • Popsicle stick

What to do

1. Read the "Apple Star" poem to the children.
2. Encourage the children to predict what they will find inside the apple. A star? A worm? Seeds?
3. Slice the apple through the middle, dividing the top and bottom halves.
4. Remove the seeds using a Popsicle stick.
5. Find the star shape at the core.
6. Count the seeds, and name the parts of the apple (pulp, core, seeds, stem, peel or skin).

Apple Star by Beverly Cornish

One October night a billion stars came out to play.
They danced and twinkled in the sky until the light of day.
The smallest star could not keep up so it lost its way.
It tumbled down upon the earth to see what it could see.
It found a lonely orchard with one apple on a tree.
"Come here," whispered the apple, "You've come from far away,
But if you grant a single wish you'll find a place to stay."
"A wish," said the tiny star. "How could I help someone like you?
I am so very little and I've lost my stardust, too."

"You're just right," said the apple, "You're the very star I need
To make the finest cradle for my baby seeds."
The star began to sparkle. Then it agreed to stay.
Now there's a star in every apple 'til this very day.
Next time you have an apple, slice it round and open wide
Still cradling the baby seeds, a star is there inside.

☆ Beverly Cornish, Philadelphia, PA

Apples and Pumpkins

Materials

Poster board • marker • laminator • Velcro • construction paper • scissors • *Apples* and *The Pumpkin Book* by Gail Gibbons • apple • pumpkin

What to do

1. This activity will take a couple of days to complete.
2. Make a chart on a piece of poster board and write the words Apple and Pumpkin at the top. On the left-hand side, write the words *seed, growth, root, flower, leaf, sprout,* and *fruit.* Laminate the poster board and add Velcro to each column.
3. In advance, use construction paper to make seeds, inside of fruit, leaf, flower, stem, root, and tree of an apple. Laminate the parts and place Velcro on the back of each one.
4. Read the book *Apples* by Gail Gibbons and, if possible, visit an orchard.
5. Discuss with the children the parts of an apple and how they grow.
6. Place the construction paper parts of an apple in the apple column. Place each part next to the correct word on the left side of the chart.
7. Prepare in advance the parts of a pumpkin (seed, inside fruit, stem, vine, leaf, flower, and root). Laminate the parts and place Velcro on the back.
8. Read *The Pumpkin Book* by Gail Gibbons and, if possible, visit a pumpkin patch.
9. Discuss with the children the parts of a pumpkin and how they grow.
10. Place the parts of the pumpkin in the pumpkin column of the chart.
11. Display and discuss the chart with the children, pointing out the similarities and differences with the cycle of growth and the parts of each fruit.
12. Leave out the chart, pumpkin, apple, books, and construction paper pieces for the children to observe, touch, and read in the Science Area.

(continued on the next page)

13. Encourage the children to compare the textures of the outside and inside of the fruit. Also, ask them to describe the textures of the inside and outside of a pumpkin and an apple. Write down their observations.

 Quazonia J. Quarles, Newark, DE

Food Facts

Materials

Pictures of a variety of foods

What to do

1. Introduce this activity after a discussion on where the food we eat actually comes from. Make sure the children know that most of the things we eat come from plants and animals.

2. Ask the children to make a list of the things they ate for one meal. (This can be done as a homework assignment or a class discussion.)

3. Brainstorm where the foods came from. Did they grow? Did they come from an animal? In some cases this is an easy question, while others require more thought. Some foods come from both plants and animals, such as pizza (cheese from a cow's milk, crust from wheat, pepperoni from a pig, and so on).

4. After the children become aware of the origin of many foods, distribute cut-out pictures of a variety of foods, one to each child.

5. Explain that they are going to form two "food trains:" a plant train and an animal train. Choose an engineer for each train.

6. Each child tells the name of his food and which train it belongs to. For example, "Milk; the animal train." Then the child "boards" the appropriate train.

7. When everyone has boarded the trains, ask them to put their hands on each other's waists. Play some "train music" while the engineers very carefully steer their trains through the classroom. Rules for engineers: don't bump into people or furniture, and stop whenever the music stops.

More to do

Extend the activity by discussing other ways to classify foods: vegetables, meat, grain, fruit, and milk products. Label a sorting tray for each classification. The children use the pictures to sort the foods by placing them in the appropriate tray.

 Iris Rothstein, New Hyde Park, NY

Color Nappers

Materials

Paint color strips (from the local paint or hardware store) or a large box of crayons • 3" x 5" index cards • access to the outdoors or to a nature trail

What to do

1. This activity focuses on color recognition, alphabet recognition, and word awareness.

2. Beforehand, make alphabet cards by writing a letter (A through Z) on each index card. Make a set for each child.

3. Distribute as many different color strip cards to the children as possible. If you don't have color strips, distribute a box of crayons to each child (look for boxes that have the most creative colors). Try to give each child the same number of cards as well as the same colors. This will eliminate fighting over colors.

4. Give each child a set of alphabet cards.

5. Tell the children that they will be going on a nature safari hike to search for the missing colors that "Color Nappers" have hidden along the trail! It will be their job to find as many of the missing colors as possible. Also explain that these are not common colors and will be difficult to find.

6. Demonstrate how to locate a missing color. Each child will be looking for a color that is on one of his color cards or one that starts with a letter on his alphabet cards. For example, a child may find a mushroom that matches one of the brownish colors on his brown color card. Or, another child may find a leaf, which starts with the letter "L."

7. For more advanced children, ask them to find something that starts with the same letter as its color. For example, a child might come across something that is "Grape Green" or "Yucky Yellow."

8. When a child finds a missing color, ask him to point it out to the entire class.

 Mike Krestar, White Oak, PA

Dancing Colors

Materials

Water • 3 or 4 glasses • colored markers

What to do

1. Place three or four 8-oz. glasses of water on a table. Ask the children to sit at the table.
2. Gently dip the tip of one or two markers into the water.
3. Watch as the colors swirl around and slowly settle at the bottom to form a design.

   Tip: This is also a good way to temporarily restore old markers that have become too dried out to use.

 Ingelore Mix, Gainesville, VA

Roy G. Biv

Materials

Prism • white paper • hose, optional • paper plates, one for every two children • scissors • colored sand: red, orange, yellow, blue, indigo, and violet • white glue • small paintbrushes • rainbow-colored streamers, optional

What to do

1. Take the children outside on a sunny day and hold up a prism so that it makes a rainbow on a sheet of paper. Encourage the children to examine the colors. Explain that the colors of a rainbow are always in the same order: red, orange, yellow, green, blue, indigo, and violet. The first letters of the colors make the name Roy G. Biv. See what happens if you block the sun. Point out that the colors are in the light. If you have access to a hose and can make a fine spray, you can create a rainbow the way that it happens in the sky.
2. Make rainbows to hang in the room. Cut out the flat circle centers of the paper plates. Cut each circle in half.
3. Draw arches on the half circles to create seven spaces in a rainbow shape.
4. Punch a hole at the top of the curve. Give one of the half circles to each child.

5. Pour a different color of sand onto separate paper plates.

6. Encourage the children to paint glue on the outside arch of the half circle. Then, ask the children to turn the plate over and press the glued space into red sand.

7. Encourage the children to paint the second arch with glue and press it into orange sand. Continue gluing and pressing into sand in this order: yellow, green, blue, indigo, and violet.

8. Thread yarn through the hole and hang.

9. If desired, save the discarded outer rims and attach rainbow-colored streamers to them. Tie a long string to each one and let the children run around the playground while holding the string.

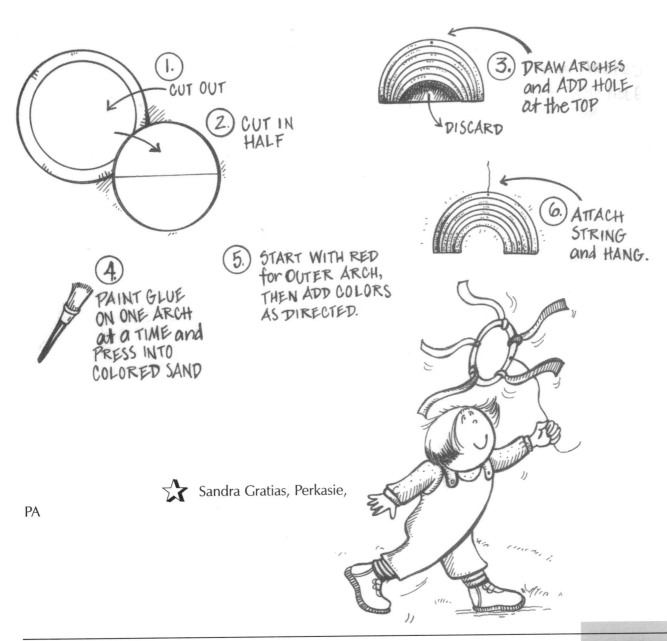

☆ Sandra Gratias, Perkasie, PA

Double Celery Color

Materials

Celery • knife (adult only) • 2 glasses • 2 colors of food coloring

What to do

1. Cut a stalk of celery into two sections at the bottom, leaving the top intact.
2. Fill one glass with colored water.
3. Fill the other glass with another color of water.
4. Place half the stalk of celery in each of the glasses.
5. Observe the color change!

 Jean Potter, Charleston, WV

Glycerin Leaves

Materials

Branch of leaves • newspaper • hammer • glycerin • large jar

What to do

1. Lay the branch of leaves on several layers of newspapers.
2. Using a hammer, tap the end of the stem until it is slightly crushed.
3. Mix one part glycerin to two parts water in a jar.
4. Place the pounded end of the branch into the glycerin mixture and let it set for two weeks. The leaves will be thicker and their color will have changed, but they will not disintegrate or fade.

 Jean Potter, Charleston, WV

Leaf Rubbings and Categorizing

Materials

Assorted leaves • thin paper • unwrapped old crayons • leaf identification book

What to do

1. Ask the children to each bring in five different leaves.
2. Show them how to place thin paper over a leaf. Demonstrate how to rub back and forth using the side of a crayon. This will leave an impression of the leaf shape and its veins.
3. Encourage the children to sort the leaf impressions by their outer shape, toothed or smooth edges, and vein structure.
4. Help them use the leaf identification book to identify the various groupings.

 Sandra L. Nagel, White Lake, MI

Leaf Skeleton

Materials

8" x 10" piece of wood • carpet scrap • tacks or nails • leaf • shoe brush or hairbrush with animal bristles • plastic wrap • newspaper • iron (adult only)

What to do

1. Five-year-olds are fascinated by science and nature, and enjoy doing experiments. Making a leaf skeleton helps the curious five-year-old investigate and study the structure of a leaf.
2. Tack a scrap of carpet to the flat piece of wood.
3. Place a leaf on the carpet, top side up.
4. Holding the leaf with one hand, gently tap the leaf with the bristle end of the brush held with the other hand. Do this until the fleshy parts of the leaf are worn away.

(continued on the next page)

5. Turn the leaf over, and tap the other side of the leaf. A lacy skeleton of the leaf will remain.

6. To save the skeletons for study and investigation (and to enjoy), place it between two sheets of plastic wrap. Cover with a sheet of newspaper and iron over the leaf quickly with a warm iron. The plastic will melt slightly and stick to the leaf, forming a clear holder—great for viewing and display.

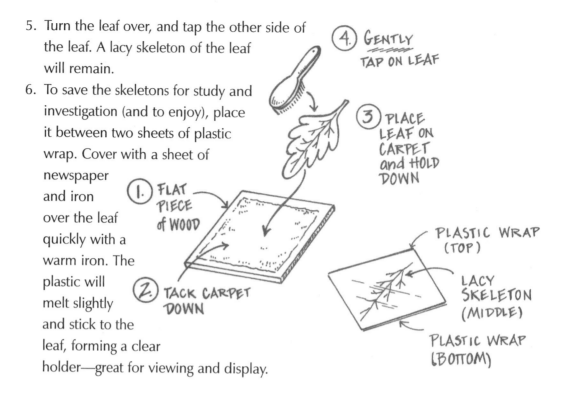

Related books

Fall Leaves Fall! by Zoe Hall

Trees, Leaves, and Bark (Take-Along Guide) by Diane L. Burns

 MaryAnn Kohl, Bellingham, WA

Adopt a Tree

Materials

Large sheet of bulletin board paper • paper in the following colors: different shades of brown, light and dark green, orange, and yellow • scissors • glue • outside tree • watering can • rake

What to do

1. Cover your entire bulletin board with background paper.

2. Cut out a large rectangle from brown paper (tree trunk). Then cut out smaller rectangles (branches). Glue these to the bulletin board.

3. Help the children cut out a generous amount of small leaves from light green paper (spring), larger leavers from dark green paper (summer), and any size leaves from yellow and orange paper (fall). The leaves can be any shape.

4. Take care of an outside tree. Water it, weed around it, and rake leaves away from it. You can even play circle games around it!

5. As the children watch the tree outside, they decorate the tree on the bulletin board to match. As the tree changes colors, write the corresponding season on the bulletin board.

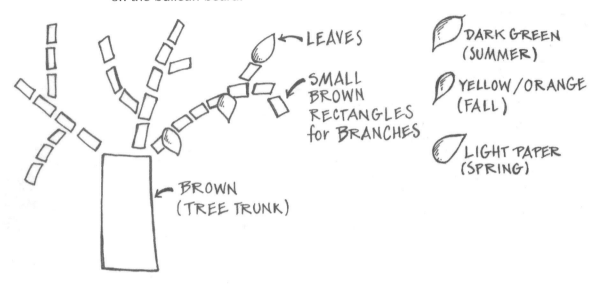

 Ingelore Mix, Gainesville, VA

Designer Insects

Materials

Books about insects • self-hardening clay or playdough • beads • toothpicks • pieces of pipe cleaners

What to do

1. Show the children books and pictures of various insects. Note the characteristics, such as six legs, two antennae, three body parts, wings or no wings, and so on.

2. Make a list of all the observable facts about insects.

3. Let the children make their own insects, using clay for the three body parts, pipe cleaners for the six legs and two antennae, and beads for the eyes.

 Sandra L. Nagel, White Lake, MI

Worms

Materials

Dirt • coffee grounds • large glass jar with lid • hammer and nail • night crawlers • black construction paper • tape

What to do

1. Make your own Worm Farm in the classroom.
2. Mix dirt and coffee grounds together.
3. Fill the jar about ¾ full with the dirt and coffee mixture.
4. Punch holes in the lid using a hammer and nail. The holes will allow the worms air and keep them from becoming too hot.
5. Purchase night crawlers from a local bait store. Night crawlers are bigger and easier to handle.
6. Put the worms in the jar, and replace the lid.
7. Cover the outside of the jar with black construction paper and tape it in place.
8. Place in a cool place or in the refrigerator.
9. Remove the paper the next day and observe how the worms tunneled into the soil.
10. Try placing different types of food on the soil to see what food the worms like; for example, cereal, rice, bread, fruits, lettuce, and so on.
11. Make sure to replace the construction paper after observing.

Related books

Earthworms Underground Burrowers by Adelle D. Richardson
Inch by Inch by Leo Lionni
Inch Worm and a Half by
     Elinor Pinczes
Worms Wiggle by David Pelham
Wormy Worm by
     Christopher Raschka

 Cookie Zingarelli, Columbus, OH

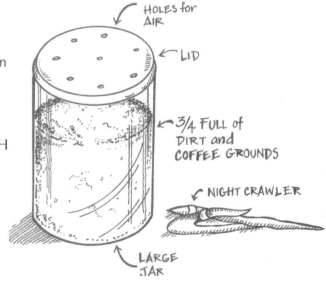

Ladybug Life Cycle

Materials

Picture of each stage of the ladybug's life cycle • computer and printer or paper and felt-tip pen • scissors • glue stick • laminator • stapler

What to do

1. Construct your own five-page book about the life cycle of a ladybug.
2. Print a brief description of each stage on a separate page. Use a large font on your computer or a felt-tip pen.
3. Under each description, glue a picture showing each stage: egg, larvae, pupa, and ladybug.
4. Put a full-color picture of a ladybug on the cover.
5. Laminate the pages and covers.
6. Assemble the pages in order and staple together.
7. After reading the book aloud, leave it in your reading area for the children to enjoy.

 Jackie Wright, Enid, OK

Circle of Life

Materials

Paper plates, one for each child • colored pencils

What to do

1. Give each child a paper plate. Demonstrate how to draw two straight lines (one vertical and one horizontal) across the center of the plate to divide it into four equal quarters.
2. In the top left section, ask the children to draw a picture of the first few leaves of a plant growing through the ground.
3. In the top right quarter, have the children draw a picture of the same plant as it would look when the first flower buds start to appear.
4. In the bottom right sections, ask the children to draw a picture of the plant with the flower in full bloom.

(continued on the next page)

5. In the final section, have the children draw a picture of the flower dying and its seeds falling to the ground.

6. Using a pencil, the children poke a hole in the center of the plate and push the pencil through the hole, so that the plate can spin on it.

7. Encourage the children to spin their own plates and see how the "circle of life" is never-ending.

8. If possible, visit a flower garden to see the circle of life in action.

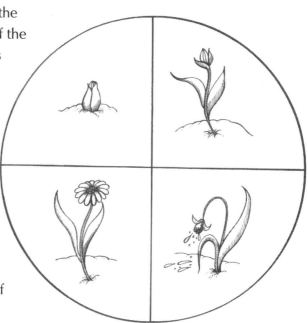

 Elizabeth Bezant, Quinn's Rock, WA, Australia

Big, Medium, and Small

Materials

Drawing paper • colored pencils • scissors

What to do

1. Give each child a piece of paper. Help them trace around their bare feet on the paper.

2. Let the children color their foot shapes, then cut out the feet.

3. Encourage the children to place the "feet" in order from smallest to largest and compare the different sizes.

4. Suggest the children draw around the hands and feet of their family members to see the differences in size.

 Elizabeth Bezant, Quinn's Rock, WA, Australia

Light and Darkness

Materials

Lamps • small flashlight • construction paper • scissors

What to do

1. Start by talking about the light of the sun. It is day when the sun shines, night when it does not.
2. Close the blinds or block the light of the sun. Talk about what you can't do without light.
3. Turn on lamps or lights. Talk about the differences with the lights on and off.
4. Make the room as dark as possible. Then using a very small flashlight, talk about how even a little light is enough to spoil the darkness.
5. Cut out shapes, such as hearts or circles. Lay these on colored construction paper on a table where there is always sunlight. Leave them there for a few days.
6. Ask the children to pick up the shapes and see how the construction paper has faded in the sunlight around the shapes.
7. Try the same thing with the lamps. See if there is any difference. Talk about the power of the sun compared to that of the lamps.

 Lucy Fuchs, Brandon, FL

Guess Drop

Materials

Objects to drop (feathers, marbles, Styrofoam packaging, small blocks, sponges, cotton, and rocks)

What to do

1. Experiment with dropping two objects at the same time and seeing which hits the ground first.
2. Encourage the children to look at two objects (before dropping them) and guess which would hit the ground first.
3. Test the assumptions.

 Jean Potter, Charleston, WV

Marble Raceway

Materials

Clear tubes (light covers, can be purchased in a home improvement center) • cardboard • masking tape • empty margarine tub • large marbles

What to do

1. Cut tubes into a variety of lengths as well as in half lengthwise. Tape these sections to a board or piece of sturdy cardboard in configurations that create a raceway for the marbles.
2. Attach a margarine tub at the bottom to catch marbles.
3. Let the children experiment with placement of the tubes.
4. Experiment with other materials that roll, such as pompoms, small balls, miniature cars, and so on. Why do these roll faster or slower? Ask them to predict which will roll faster.
5. Remove the margarine tub and predict how far the marbles will roll. Measure outcomes.

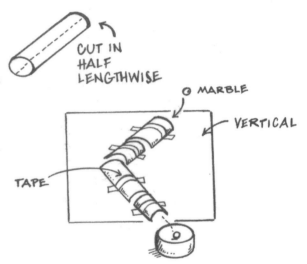

☆ Sharon Dempsey, Mays Landing, NJ

Balance Bears

Materials

Two-basket scale • small objects such as teddy bear counters, dominoes, small tiles, or poker chips

What to do

1. Add the scale and small objects to your Science Area.
2. Encourage the children to add the objects to each basket.

3. Discuss *heavy* and *light, heavier* and *lighter, more* and *less,* and so on.
4. Ask the children to count the number of items in each basket.

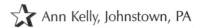 Ann Kelly, Johnstown, PA

The Mirror and Me

Materials

Large mirror on wall • name cards for each child • small unbreakable mirrors

What to do

1. Let the children take turns looking at themselves in the large mirror.
2. Ask each child to hold up his name card to the mirror; the children will see that the mirror reverses the image.
3. Show the children how to see the back of their heads by looking into the small mirrors while they stand with their backs to the large mirror.

 Lucy Fuchs, Brandon, FL

The Recycling Game

Materials

Recycling bin or large containers

What to do

1. Bring in a real recycling bin or some containers that have been labeled with the recycling symbol.
2. Label the containers glass, plastic, paper, and aluminum.
3. Have on hand some clean examples of each.
4. Encourage the children to "read" the labels and place each piece in the appropriate container.

 Tracie O'Hara, Charlotte, NC

Shadow Guessing Game

Materials

Overhead projector • sheet • several small objects, such as a crayon, key, comb, paintbrush, and puzzle pieces

What to do

1. Hang the sheet in the doorway with the children on one side and the overhead projector on the other side.
2. One by one, put a variety of objects on the overhead projector and let the children guess what they are. It is important to use objects that the children are familiar with.
3. Make sure every child gets a chance to guess.
4. For added fun, let the children take turns making hand shadows. Encourage the rest of the children to guess what kind of animal it is.

☆ Sandy L. Scott, Vancouver, WA

Colored Ice Cubes

Materials

Red, yellow, and blue food coloring • water • ice cube trays • zipper-closure plastic bags

What to do

1. Beforehand, prepare red, yellow, and blue ice cubes using water and food coloring.
2. Ask the children to place one red and one yellow ice cube in a bag, one yellow and one blue ice cube in another bag, and one red and one blue ice cube in a third bag.
3. Encourage the children to observe the colored ice cubes melting and creating new colors.

 Liz Thomas, Hobart, IN

Icy Picture

Materials

Dark construction paper • crayons • water • Epsom salt • paintbrush • blender • ice cubes

What to do

1. Talk to the children about ice and how it forms.
2. Ask each child to draw a picture on dark construction paper.
3. Let them help mix together an equal part of Epsom salt and water.
4. Encourage them to dip paintbrushes in the mixture and paint over their picture.
5. As the paper dries, their picture becomes "icy." Ask the children how they think ice feels, and how the "ice" on their pictures is different.
6. Ask them how they think ice tastes. Show them how to crush ice in a blender. Let each child taste the ice. If desired, serve snow cones for snack (crushed ice and Kool-Aid).

 Sandra Hutchins Lucas, Cox's Creek, KY

Frost Formations

Materials

20 ice cubes • tin can • 1 teaspoon of salt • spoon

What to do

1. Place the ice cubes into the tin can.
2. Add a teaspoon of salt and mix rapidly.
3. Encourage the children to watch the frost form on the outside of the can.

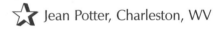 Jean Potter, Charleston, WV

Snowflake Exam

Materials

Cardboard • black felt • glue • snowy day • magnifying glass

What to do

1. Cover a piece of cardboard with black felt and glue in place.
2. Place it in the freezer overnight to keep cold.
3. Bring the cardboard outside to catch some snowflakes on the felt.
4. Encourage the children to examine the snowflakes with a magnifying glass.
5. Explain that snowflakes are frozen water crystals and each flake is unique with its own design.

 Jean Potter, Charleston, WV

Snowman Soup

Materials

Cardboard • marker • blender • ice • water • packages of hot chocolate mix • bowls • spoons • individual thermometers

What to do

1. Draw a large thermometer on a piece of cardboard.
2. Discuss how a thermometer works. Show the children where 32° is and explain what the freezing point means.
3. Place ice in a blender, about ¾ full. Add water, about ½ full.
4. Add half of a package of cocoa mix.
5. Chop and crush the ice mixture until smooth.
6. Pour into soup bowls.
7. Encourage the children to place a clean thermometer in their bowl of snowman soup. Tell them they may eat it when their soup reaches the freezing point!

☆ Vera M. Peters, Elizabethton, TN

Physical Science Experience: Oobleck, Liquid, or Solid?

Materials

For each group of children: 1 box of cornstarch • pitcher of water • green food coloring or liquid watercolor • large mixing bowl • mixing spoon • smock for each child

What to do

1. Read Dr. Seuss's *Bartholomew and the Oobleck* to the children.
2. After reading the book, tell the children that they are going to become scientists and create the substance "oobleck."

(continued on the next page)

3. Divide the children into groups of four.

4. Give each group smocks, a mixing spoon, a bowl, a pitcher of water, a box of cornstarch, and food coloring.

5. Ask the children to pour a box of cornstarch into the bowl, then mix in just enough water to make it pasty.

6. Add green food coloring or liquid watercolor.

7. Ask the children to slowly dip their finger into the mixture. Does it feel runny?

8. Have them put the oobleck into the palm of their hand and try to roll it into a small ball. What happens when they stop rolling?

9. Try tapping it hard with the mixing spoon. What happens?

10. Let them experiment on their own with the substance. Is it a liquid or a solid?

 Kimberly H. Puff, Allentown, PA

A Sticky Experiment

Materials

Newspaper • bowls • glue • liquid starch • water • spoons • measuring spoons and cups • zipper-closure plastic bags • meat trays • paper • marker

What to do

1. Cover a table with newspaper.

2. Fill a bowl with glue, a bowl with liquid starch, and a bowl with water and put them on the table.

3. Put out the spoons, cups, meat trays, and extra empty bowls.

4. Encourage the children to mix the three ingredients in different combinations and watch the results. For example, mixing starch and glue first, and then water makes a stringy linguini-type mixture, while mixing glue and water first, and then starch makes a kind of putty material.

5. Have an adult supervise the experiments and record the recipes and outcomes so that the "good" ones can be repeated.

 Ann Kelly, Johnstown, PA

Balloon Greenhouse

Materials

Clear balloon • funnel • ½ cup dirt • water • radish seeds • string or cup

What to do

1. Put the funnel in the neck of the balloon.
2. Pour ½ cup of dirt into the balloon.
3. Keep holding the balloon by the neck. Add about ¼ cup of water through the funnel. Be sure the soil in the balloon is wet, but not soggy.
4. Use the funnel to drop the radish seeds into the balloon.
5. If the balloon is dirty, wipe it carefully with a washcloth.
6. While holding it gently by the neck, carefully blow air downward into the balloon. Hold the balloon carefully to keep it from tipping.
7. Tie a knot in the neck to keep the air in the balloon, then tie a ribbon around the knot.
8. Tie the balloon to a hook or other place near a window. Or, place the balloon in a cup with the neck at the top.
9. Watch the plant in the balloon begin to grow.

3. RADISH SEED
2. ¼ CUP WATER
FUNNEL
KEEP HAND AROUND the NECK of BALLOON
CLEAR BALLOON
½ CUP DIRT
1.

TIE a KNOT FIRST
TIE a RIBBON and HANG NEAR a WINDOW

WATCH the PLANT GROW

☆ Jean Potter, Charleston, WV

Get Growing

Materials

Lima beans • bowl • two wide-mouth jars • blotting paper (long enough to line the inside of the jars) • paper towels

What to do

1. Soak the beans overnight in a bowl of water.
2. Place the blotting paper to fit tightly against the walls of each jar.
3. Crumple two paper towels.
4. Put a paper towel in the middle of each jar.
5. Fill the jars with water and wait until the paper towel absorbs as much of the water as it can.
6. Pour off the excess water.
7. Push a few of the beans in different positions (horizontal, diagonal, vertical) between the blotting paper and the glass in each jar. Be sure they are spaced apart and near the top of the jars.
8. Keep the jars out of direct sunlight and wait and watch the seeds grow.
9. Water the paper towels every other day so the seeds will keep moist, but not soggy.
10. Once the seedlings have reached about an inch over the jars (about a week), lay one of the jars on its side. In which direction will the seeds grow? Observe for a few days. Tell the children that the growth hormones in a plant respond to the Earth's gravitational pull, which causes roots to always grow down and stems to always grow up (*geotropism*).

 Jean Potter, Charleston, WV

Watch Us Grow

Materials

School or classroom garden plot • sunflower seeds • notebooks for journals • pens • camera or digital camera • yardstick or measuring tape

What to do

1. Tell the children that they will be planting a sunflower garden.

2. Let each child plant a sunflower seed. Encourage them to use their journals to write about the planting and guess what is going to happen.

3. Each week, check the plot and see what is happening with the seeds. Have the children continue to write and draw pictures about it in their journals.

4. When the plants are about a foot tall, take pictures of each student standing next to a sunflower. Measure the plant and the child and ask them to write the measurements in their journals.

5. Continue in this fashion, measuring and taking pictures every week. (The photos may be used in their journals or on a bulletin board.)

6. Encourage the children to check their original estimations and compare them to what actually happened.

7. Encourage the children to write stories about their sunflowers.

   Tip: Use a digital camera and put the photos on a website. Parents can look at the photos and download them, if desired. For safety reasons, do not use children's names on the internet.

Related book

The Garden in the City by Gerda Muller

☆ Barbara Saul, Eureka, CA

Water, Water, Everywhere

Materials

Dish of water for each child • glass with ice for each child • pot of hot water

What to do

1. Talk about water. What do we do with water? (Drink, wash, water plants, cook, and so on.)

2. Explain the three ways water is found:
   - ☆ Liquid: Give each child a dish of water. Encourage them to look at, feel, and slosh it.
   - ☆ Solid: Give each child a glass with ice in it. Encourage them to look at and feel the ice. Point out that the ice will melt and become a liquid.

(continued on the next page)

☆ Gas (or steam): Boil water on a stove or hot plate (adult only). Encourage the children to watch the steam, but to be very careful not to burn themselves on it. Encourage them to notice that as the water cools down, the steam turns to liquid.

3. Ask the children if there is anything else they notice about water, perhaps calling their attention to the condensation that appears on the outside of the glass of ice water. Explain how this is not the water from the inside of the glass, but water that is being taken from the air.

4. Talk about where water is found (in rain, rivers, the ocean, and so on).

5. Tell the children about snow, icicles, sleet, and hail.

More to do

More Science and Nature: If there is a lake nearby, ask the children what color the water is (blue or green, for example). Collect a cup of the lake water and bring it to school. Show the children that the water is colorless. Talk about why it reflects the sky's color and appears blue (or other color) in nature.

Related books

Splish, Splash, Splosh by Mick Manning and Brita Granstrom
Water by Frank Asch

 Lucy Fuchs, Brandon, FL

Dry Finger Surprise

Materials

Glass • water • baby powder

What to do

1. Fill a glass halfway with water and sprinkle a thick layer of baby powder on top of the water.

2. Slowly stick a finger down into the water.

3. Lift the finger straight up out of the glass. What happens? (The finger is dry!)

4. Explain that the powder sticks to the oil on skin and acts as a glove.

 Jean Potter, Charleston, WV

The Surprising Wet Finger

Materials

Glass • water • pepper • liquid detergent

What to do

1. Fill a glass with water and sprinkle some pepper in it.
2. Dip a finger into liquid detergent and then stick the finger in the middle of the glass. What happens? (The pepper shoots away.)
3. Explain that water behaves as if it has a clear elastic skin on it. The soap breaks the "skin," which pulls the pepper away.

 Jean Potter, Charleston, WV

Oil and Ice

Materials

Small glass • vegetable oil • ice cube

What to do

1. Fill the glass with oil.
2. Place an ice cube in the glass. Notice that the ice floats near the top.
3. As the ice melts, water droplets sink to the bottom.
4. Explain that as water freezes, it expands and takes up more room. This makes it less dense and, therefore, it floats on the oil. Once it has melted, the water is heavier than the oil and it falls to the bottom.

 Jean Potter, Charleston, WV

Raisin Elevators

Materials

Clear carbonated water • clear glass • several raisins

What to do

1. Pour clear carbonated water into the glass.
2. Drop four or five raisins into the glass. Observe the raisins moving up and down in the glass. The air bubbles cause the upward movement.
3. Observe the glass later in the day when the water is flat.

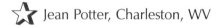 Jean Potter, Charleston, WV

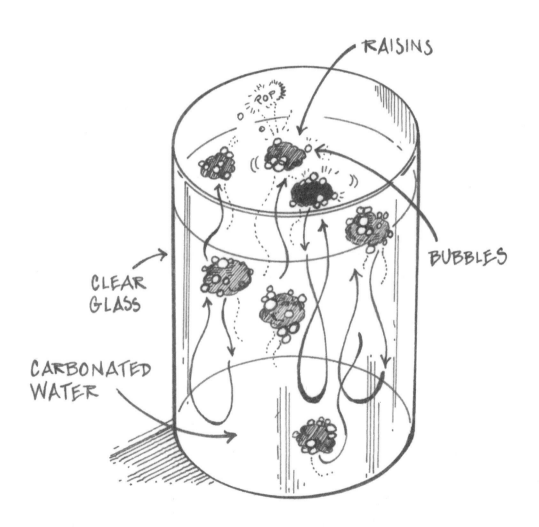

Cooking Aprons

Materials

Inexpensive craft aprons for each child • fabric paint • paintbrushes • fork and spoon stencils • wooden fork and spoon for each child • ribbons

What to do

1. Give each child an apron. Explain that they are going to make their own aprons to wear when cooking.
2. Encourage them to paint their aprons as desired. Ask them to decorate the pockets with fork and spoon stencils.
3. Stencil each child's name on her apron, or write something cute like "Kiss the Cook."
4. Let the children wear their aprons whenever they help prepare food in the classroom.

 Lisa Chichester, Parkersburg, WV

My Tea Party

Materials

Books about tea parties • teacups • 1 or more teapots • small pretty plates • napkins • mild (decaf) tea • tea ball or strainer • small cakes or cookies • tablecloth, doilies, flowers, optional

What to do

1. Read stories about tea parties to the children.
2. Encourage the children to pretend to have tea parties.
3. Bring in real tea items, such as teapots, teacups, plates, and so on. Explore them at group time.
4. Practice good manners during play and real snack breaks.
5. Use the real tea party items to make tea and have a proper "tea party."
6. If desired, have a tea party for parents, grandparents, or school staff.

 Sandra L. Nagel, White Lake, MI

Stargazing Party

Materials

"Star" snacks, such as Moon Pies, star-shaped cookie, star-shaped ice cubes, and Tang

What to do

1. After a visit to the planetarium, plan a stargazing party.
2. Invite the children and their parents to school at night.
3. Ask everyone to bring a lawn chair and wear a bathing suit—for moon bathing!
4. Serve Moon Pies, star-shaped cookies, and Tang with star-shaped ice cubes (you can buy star-shaped trays).
5. Sit back in your lawn chairs and enjoy the night sky!

 Lisa Chichester, Parkersburg, WV

100 Day Celebration

Materials

Small snack items • big bowl • mixing spoon • small containers or plastic bags for each child

What to do

1. Send home a note to parents asking them to send in a snack item to celebrate the 100th day of school.
2. Each child should bring 100 small snack items such as raisins, mini-marshmallows, cereal, M&M's, goldfish crackers, dried fruit, and so on.
3. Let children add their snack item to the big bowl and help mix.
4. Once all the items have been added, divide up the mixture so that everyone has some for snack. There will probably be enough to send some home.

 Sandy L. Scott, Vancouver, WA

Eat a Letter

Materials

Can of refrigerated biscuits • sugar-cinnamon mixture • melted butter • paper plates

What to do

1. After discussing letters, tell the children they can make and eat their favorite letter.
2. Give every child a plate and a biscuit (uncooked).
3. Ask them to roll out their biscuit, like with playdough.
4. Ask them how the dough feels. After rolling out a long snake shape, help them form their letters.
5. Let each child brush her shaped letter with butter, and then sprinkle with the sugar mixture.
6. Bake according to the directions on the package.

 Sandra Hutchins Lucas, Cox's Creek, KY

Alphabet Soup

Materials

Variety of vegetables • cutting boards and plastic knives • crock pot • 2 large cans of chicken broth • 1 large can of diced tomatoes • 1 box of alphabet-shaped pasta

What to do

1. This activity helps children reinforce their letter recognition skills through cooking.
2. Send home a note asking parents to send in different vegetables (corn, peas, beans, onions, carrots, and potatoes).
3. Under supervision, let the children clean and cut up vegetables and put them in the crock pot.
4. Add broth, diced tomatoes, and salt and pepper to taste.

(continued on the next page)

5. Add the noodles in the last few minutes of cooking.

6. Encourage the children to notice the letters as they eat the soup.

Related books

Alphabet Soup by Kate Banks

Eating the Alphabet: Fruits and Vegetables From A-Z by Lois Ehlert

Growing Vegetable Soup by Lois Ehlert

 Janice Bodenstedt, Jackson, MI

Bag Ice Cream

Materials

½ cup milk • 1 tablespoon sugar • ¾ tablespoon vanilla • 1 small freezer bag • ice • 6 tablespoons salt • 1 large freezer bag

What to do

1. Put milk, sugar, and vanilla into the small bag. (This makes one serving.)

2. Close the bag.

3. Put ice into the large bag until the bag is half full.

4. Add salt to the ice.

5. Put the small bag into the large bag, and seal the large bag.

6. Shake the bags for five minutes.

7. Put the bag in the freezer for a few minutes.

8. Serve the ice cream!

 Jean Potter, Charleston, WV

MILK, SUGAR and VANILLA

ICE and SALT

Brown Leafy Toast

Materials

Paper plates • one slice of bread per child • assorted leaf-shaped cookie cutters • 1 pat of butter per child • cinnamon • plastic knives • oven

What to do

1. Ask the children to wash their hands.
2. Give each child a paper plate and a slice of bread.
3. Show the children how to use a cookie cutter to cut out a leaf shape from the bread.
4. Encourage the children to spread the pat of butter and sprinkle cinnamon evenly on top of the butter.
5. Put the leafy shapes into the oven.
6. Warm in the oven until the butter melts and the bread turns a golden brown.
7. Let the children munch and crunch their leaves!

 Quazonia J. Quarles, Newark, DE

Cheerio Necklaces

Materials

Cheerios Counting Book by Barbara Barbieri McGrath • string or shoelaces • scissors • tape • Cheerios or any circle-shaped cereal

What to do

1. Read the book to the children.
2. Cut pieces of string to fit around each child's neck as a necklace.
3. Tape one end of each piece of string and tie a knot in the other.
4. Encourage the children to string the cereal onto the cord.
5. Tie the ends together to make edible necklaces.
6. Eat it for snack.

 Barbara Saul, Eureka, CA

Chummy Chive

Materials

Chive plants in pots • scissors • cream cheese or plain yogurt

What to do

1. Grow chives with the children.
2. Encourage them to snip the chives and save the pieces.
3. Mix chives into a bowl of softened cream cheese or plain yogurt. Spread on crackers, or dip vegetables into the mixture.

Jill Putnam, Wellfleet, MA

Cinnamon Hearts

Materials

Bread • paper plates • heart-shaped cookie cutters • soft butter • butter knife • shaker with cinnamon • shaker with red decorative sugar • cookie sheet • oven

What to do

1. Give each child a slice of bread on a paper plate.
2. Let the children use cookie cutters to cut out a heart shape.
3. Ask them to spread butter evenly over the heart.
4. They can sprinkle with sugar and cinnamon.
5. Place the hearts on a cookie sheet and broil in the oven for about three to four minutes.
6. Eat and enjoy!

Sandy L. Scott, Vancouver, WA

Edible Quilt Squares

Materials

Graham cracker squares • plastic knives and spoons • paper plates and bowls • tub of white frosting • food coloring • mini M&Ms, colored sprinkles, and mini-marshmallows • black or red licorice strings • scissors

What to do

1. Distribute two or four graham cracker squares along with a paper plate, bowl, knives, and spoons to each child.
2. Place enough frosting in each child's bowl to spread on the graham crackers. Let the children color their frosting by adding a drop or two of food coloring and mixing with a spoon. They can share the different frosting colors with each other.
   Note: Remind them not to lick their spoons.
3. Ask the children to spread colored frosting on their graham crackers, with each square a different color if they choose. Make sure it is thick enough to act as a glue for decorative items to stick to.

FROSTING

DECORATED SQUARE
(SPRINKLES, M&M'S,
and MINI MARSHMALLOWS)

4. Encourage them to decorate their "quilt squares" with sprinkles, M&Ms, and mini-marshmallows.
5. When they are done with their squares, ask them to arrange all of the squares together on a paper plate.

SHORT LICORICE PIECES

QUILT SQUARES

6. Let the children use clean scissors to snip short pieces of licorice strings to act as stitches of thread. Demonstrate how to lay the strings across the seam of graham crackers to join them together, like a quilt.
7. Eat the quilt for snack!

⭐ Diane Leschak, Chisholm, MN

Edible Rocks

Materials

2 to 2 ½ cups mini-marshmallows • 1 to 1 ½ cups chocolate chips • mixing bowl and spoon • smooth peanut butter • wax paper • hot plate or stove • saucepan

What to do

1. Mix mini-marshmallows and chocolate chips in a bowl.
2. Add just enough peanut butter so the mixture clumps together.
3. Ask the children to wash their hands.
4. Let each child grab a handful of the mixture and make a rock. Tell the children the rocks resemble sedimentary rocks. The marshmallows and the chocolate chips resemble sediments and the peanut butter represents a mineral that sticks the sediments together.
5. Place "rocks" on wax paper. Place a few of the "rocks" in the pan and heat them over low heat (adult only).
6. When the marshmallows melt, remove a spoonful of the new "rocks." These resemble metamorphic rocks. Explain that the "sedimentary rock" changed its form and structure because of the heat.
7. Eat the rocks for snack.

☆ Jean Potter, Charleston, WV.

Aquarium Snack

Materials

Sand-colored cookies • bowl and spoon • clear plastic cups • blue gelatin • gummy fish

What to do

1. Crush the cookies into crumbs and place them in a bowl.
2. Give each child a plastic cup. Ask them to put a tablespoon of crumbs into their cup.

3. Let each child pour some liquid blue gelatin over the crumbs.
4. Add some gummy fish.
5. Allow the gelatin to cool in the refrigerator until firm. Eat and enjoy!

 Jean Potter, Charleston, WV

A Fish Mix

Materials

Goldfish graham snacks • goldfish pretzels and crackers • Swedish fish • assorted gummy fish • small plastic scoops • plastic bowls • blue napkins

What to do

1. In advance, empty snacks into individual plastic bowls.
2. Place a plastic scoop in each bowl.
3. Ask the children to wash their hands.
4. Give each child a blue napkin ("water").
5. Encourage children to scoop out whatever kinds of fish snacks they want.

 Quazonia J. Quarles, Newark, DE

Fish in the Ocean

Materials

Softened cream cheese • blue food coloring • graham crackers • Popsicle stick to use as knife • goldfish crackers • parsley

What to do

1. Mix a couple drops of blue food coloring into the cream cheese.
2. Give each child a graham cracker square.
3. Encourage them to spread their graham crackers with blue cream cheese, making "waves" in the cream cheese to resemble the ocean.
4. Add goldfish crackers and parsley ("seaweed").

 Sandy L. Scott, Vancouver, WA

Easy Banana Treat

Materials

Paper plates • 3 whole graham cracker rectangles for each child • 1 medium banana for each child, 1 snack pudding for each child, any flavor • plastic knives • plastic wrap • whipped topping or confectioner's sugar, optional

What to do

1. Place one whole graham cracker on each plate. Give one to each child, along with a banana and snack pudding.
2. Ask the children to slice their bananas into at least 16 slices.
3. Tell them to place eight banana slices on the graham cracker.
4. Ask them to top the bananas with one-half of the pudding, and then place another whole graham cracker on top.
5. Repeat banana and pudding steps, ending with the third graham cracker on top.
6. Cover well with plastic wrap and refrigerate 8 hours or overnight.
7. Serve with whipped topping or confectioner's sugar sprinkled on top, if desired.

 Jean Daigneau, Kent, OH

Sun Fruit Roll-Ups

Materials

Fresh fruit (strawberries, grapes, and so on) • knives • sugar • water • measuring cup • mixer • wax paper • sunny day

What to do

1. Chop fruit with the children.
2. Help each children mix 1 cup fruit with 2 tablespoons sugar and 2 tablespoons water.
3. Give each child a piece of wax paper to spread fruit mixture on.
4. Allow them to dry in the sun for a day.
5. Enjoy homemade fruit roll-ups!

 Lisa Chichester, Parkersburg, WV

Fruit Salad Fun

Materials

Plastic containers for each child • paint, paintbrushes, and craft items • whipped cream • food coloring • fruits: strawberries, grapes, pineapple chunks, oranges • mini marshmallows • plastic knives

What to do

1. Ahead of time, ask each child to bring a plastic container from home.
2. Encourage them to decorate their containers with paint or craft items.
3. Place uncut fruit, whipped cream, food coloring, mini marshmallows, and plastic knives on a table.
4. Encourage the children to cut up fruit and put it in their containers.
5. They can add in marshmallows and whipped cream, and then stir in food coloring for fun.
6. Enjoy your funky fruit salad!

 Lisa Chichester, Parkersburg, WV

Fun Ice Cubes

Materials

Ice cube trays • water • food coloring • gummy bears or other tiny candy

What to do

1. Let the children help mix a cup of food-colored water.
2. Ask them to pour the water into an ice cube tray.
3. Let each child place a gummy bear or other candy in each cube.
4. Allow to freeze.
5. Enjoy in cold drinks!

 Lisa Chichester, Parkersburg, WV

"Gingerbread" Houses

Materials

½-gallon milk or juice cartons, one for each child • heavy cardboard, larger than the base of the carton for each child • hot glue gun (adult only) • royal icing mix (from cake decorating supply or craft store) • graham crackers • hard candies, gumdrops, small candy canes, and so on • confectioner's sugar • sugar ice cream cones (optional)

What to do

1. In advance, cut off the bottom 5" of each carton all the way around and discard. Remove the pouring spout.
2. Glue the carton to the cardboard base.
3. Show the children pictures of gingerbread houses in magazines and cookbooks. Read about the Gingerbread Man.
4. Tell the children they will be making their own gingerbread houses.
5. Give each child an undecorated plastic "house." Put out graham crackers, bowls of candies, margarine tubs of royal icing, and confectioner's sugar.

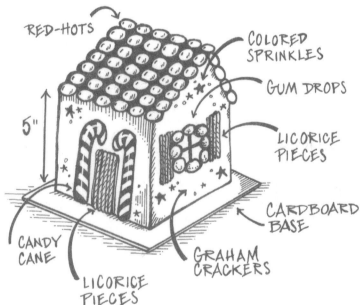

6. Give each child a plastic knife. Ask them to begin by spreading icing all over their house and attaching graham cracker squares.
7. They can then decorate their houses as desired, using the candies to make roof tiles, doors, Christmas lights, flowers, and so on.
8. Use leftover icing as snow on the cardboard base.

 Sandra Gratias, Perkasie, PA

Hot Dog Butterflies

Materials

Hot dogs • buns • paper plates • mustard • ketchup • food coloring • eyedroppers

What to do

1. Cook the hot dogs.
2. Place each hot dog and bun on a plate as shown. Give one to each child
3. Encourage the children to use eyedroppers to drop food coloring on the bun to make butterfly wings.
4. They can use ketchup or mustard to make a face and antennae on the hot dog.

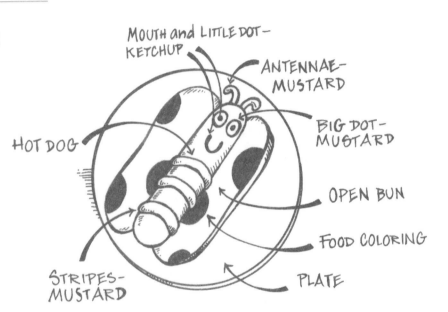

MOUTH and LITTLE DOT- KETCHUP

ANTENNAE- MUSTARD

BIG DOT- MUSTARD

HOT DOG

OPEN BUN

FOOD COLORING

PLATE

STRIPES- MUSTARD

 Lisa Chichester, Parkersburg, WV

Making Lavender Smoothies

Materials

1 cup orange juice • 1 cup strawberries • 2 scoops ice cream • blender • flowers from lavender plant, about ½ cup

What to do

1. Mix all the ingredients together in a blender.
2. Sprinkle lavender flowers on top.
3. Serve and enjoy!

(continued on the next page)

Safety Note: Explain to the children that not all flowers are edible. Tell them that although lavender flowers are not poisonous, many other flowers and plants are. Therefore, they should never eat any flowers or plants unless a trusted adult tells them it's okay.

☆ Lisa Chichester, Parkersburg, WV

Pizza Crackers

Materials

Paper plates • round crackers • pizza or spaghetti sauce • any kind of shredded cheese • pizza toppings

What to do

1. This is a great way to make bite-sized pizzas in just a few minutes.
2. Give each child a few crackers on a paper plate.
3. Ask the children to put about a teaspoon of sauce in the middle of each cracker.
4. They can sprinkle each with a little cheese, and add other pizza toppings as desired.
5. Microwave for 15 to 20 seconds. Let them cool before eating.

☆ Angela R. Trusty, Dayton, OH

Apple Pizza

Materials

Apples, 1 per 4 children • apple corer/peeler/slicer • refrigerated rolls • cookie sheet • oven • butter • sugar-cinnamon mixture

What to do

1. Let each child have a turn preparing the apples using the apple corer/peeler/slicer. Supervise closely.
2. Ask them to spread butter on the apple slices.

3. Place the refrigerated rolls on a cookie sheet.

4. Ask the children to put several slices of apple on top of each roll.

5. Bake according to the directions on the can.

6. Add butter and cinnamon sugar to the top of the apples.

7. Eat and enjoy!

☆ Sandy L. Scott, Vancouver, WA

Mini Apple Pies

Materials

Butter • cinnamon • brown sugar • large mixing bowl and spoon • mini apple pie crusts for each child • apples • knife • food coloring • colored sugar • baking sheet • oven

What to do

1. Let each child help mix cinnamon, sugar, and butter in a bowl.

2. Give each child a small pie shell.

3. Ask them to help peel and cut apples and add them to the sugar mixture. For even more fun, add in food coloring.

4. Let the children spoon some of the mixture into their pie shells.

5. Sprinkle cinnamon and the colored sugar on top.

6. Bake and enjoy!

☆ Lisa Chichester, Parkersburg, WV

Pumpkin Pie

Materials

Pumpkin pie filling ingredients (see recipe below) • mixing bowl • wooden spoon, measuring cups and spoons • wax paper • eggbeater • small bowl • 2 frozen pie shells • oven

Pumpkin Pie Filling

2 cups mashed pumpkin
1 teaspoon cinnamon
¼ teaspoon cloves
2 eggs
2 tablespoons melted butter

¾ cup sugar
¼ teaspoon ginger
¼ teaspoon nutmeg
1 can evaporated milk

What to do

1. Let the children do most of the measuring and preparation for the pie. Work in small groups, letting children take turns with your supervision. Be sure to emphasize washing hands, not putting hands in mouth, and other health precautions.

2. Help the children measure 2 cups of pumpkin and add it to the mixing bowl. **Author Note:** For a richer learning experience, cut up your classroom jack-o-lantern, wrap it in foil, and bake at 350° until it is soft enough to scrape out with spoons. When it cools, the children scoop it out. You can also use canned pumpkin, one can per pie.

3. Ask the children to measure ¾ cup of sugar, leveling with a knife, and add to the pumpkin. Let them take turns stirring the mixture.

4. Let them measure spices on a piece of wax paper. Encourage the children to compare the colors and smells. Add spices to pumpkin and stir again.

5. Crack the eggs into a small bowl. Let the children take turns beating. Add to pumpkin and mix.

6. Add milk and stir.

7. Add melted butter and stir.

8. Pour into the mixture into pie shells. (An adult should do this!)

9. Bake at 350° until knife blade inserted in the center comes out clean.

10. Let cool. Cut into slices and enjoy!

 Mary Jo Shannon, Roanoke, VA

Quesadillas

Materials

Electric skillet (adult only) • tortillas • shredded cheese • spatula • sour cream • guacamole • knife

What to do

1. Place one tortilla on the skillet, top with cheese, and place a second tortilla on top.
2. Turn over to cook both sides.
3. Cut into eighths so each child can try some.
4. Serve with sour cream and guacamole.
5. This is a great early cooking activity for children.

 Sandy L. Scott, Vancouver, WA

Shape Pancakes

Materials

Pancake mix • mixing bowl and spoons • food coloring • electric skillet (adult only) • spatula • cookie cutters • whipped topping

What to do

1. Help the children mix pancake batter.
2. Let them add food coloring of their choice.
3. Make pancakes as you normally would.
4. Let the pancakes cool, and give one or two to each child.
5. Show them how to cut out shapes using cookie cutters.
6. Encourage them to spread whipped cream on a pancake shape and then put another pancake on top to make a shape sandwich!

 Lisa Chichester, Parkersburg, WV

Shape Snacks

Materials

Crackers in various shapes • paper plates • cheese slices • pepperoni or other meats • mini cookie cutters or blunt knives • olives

What to do

1. Ask the children to wash their hands.
2. Let them choose a few crackers and put them on a plate.
3. Demonstrate how to cut out shapes from cheese and meat using mini cookie cutters or knives.
4. Encourage the children to make their own shape snacks by putting various shaped items together.

   Tip: For added fun, use serving dishes in a variety of shapes, such as a round plate, rectangular tray, and so on.

CRACKER
CHEESE SLICE
PEPPERONI
(CUT WITH A COOKIE CUTTER)
BOLOGNA
CHEESE
(BOTH CUT WITH COOKIE CUTTERS)

Related books

The Shape of Me and Other Stuff by Dr. Seuss
There's a Square: A Book About Shapes by Mary Serfozo

⭐ Andrea Clapper, Cobleskill, NY

Stoplight Snack

Materials

Rectangle-shaped crackers • cheese • pickles • knife • pepperoni slices • butter • napkins • Popsicle sticks

What to do

1. In advance, cut cheese and pickles into circles to fit on ⅓ of the cracker.
2. Give each child one cracker, a napkin and butter on a Popsicle stick to spread on the cracker.
3. Give each child a slice of pepperoni, cheese, and pickle to add to the cracker in the form of a stoplight.
4. Eat the snack!

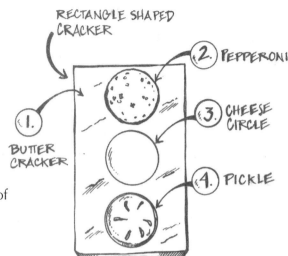

☆ Sandy L. Scott, Vancouver, WA

Tooth Candy

Materials

Chart paper • marker • trail mix ingredients • measuring cups • mixing bowl and spoon • paper plates

What to do

1. While discussing dental health, make this healthy and tooth-friendly recipe.
2. Brainstorm with the children and decide what kinds of foods are good for your teeth. Create a chart showing their good food choices.
3. Choose some foods from the chart that can be combined easily to make a trail mix-type mixture. Some foods you might want to include are rice and wheat Chex-type cereals, raisins, pretzels, Ritz Bits, grapes, and goldfish crackers.

(continued on the next page)

4. Ask the children to volunteer to bring in an ingredient for the Tooth Candy recipe and send a note home to parents. A sample note is:

Dear Parents,
This week we are learning about dental health. We have been discussing what foods are good or bad for our teeth. We have decided to work together to create a tasty, yet tooth-friendly, snack that we are calling Tooth Candy. The children have decided that one of the tooth-friendly ingredients for the recipe is (name food item). Please allow (child's name) to bring in one package of (name food item) to add to our Tooth Candy recipe.

5. When the children bring the ingredients to school, help them decide how much of each ingredient should go into the Tooth Candy. Provide measuring cups and let the children measure out the agreed-upon amount of each ingredient. Make sure you keep track of how much of each ingredient is used.
6. After mixing all the ingredients together, look at the notes you made and create a recipe from them.
7. Enjoy the Tooth Candy at snack time. While eating, remind the children that they are eating a healthy snack that is good for their teeth.

⭐ Virginia Jean Herrod, Columbia, SC

Vegetables in a Pan Pocket

Materials

White construction paper • pencil • vegetable catalogs • scissors • crayons or watercolor paints and brushes • glue • stapler

What to do

1. Beforehand, trace various vegetables on white paper (see illustration).
2. Trace the pan pattern (see illustration) on a piece of long paper or on two papers, adding an extra strip for gluing together.
3. Tear out vegetable pages from catalogs for the children to use.
4. Before doing the activity, discuss parts of various vegetables that we eat such as: corn (seeds), beets (root), celery (stalk), and tomato (fruit of plant). Discuss

how vegetables are grown by a farmer, then transported to canning or freezing plants, and then trucked to a store. Show pictures or posters of vegetables.

5. Ask each child to choose at least four vegetables. Younger children can cut out catalog pictures of vegetables; older children can cut out vegetable patterns.

6. Let them color the vegetables with crayons or paint with watercolors.

7. Cut out a pan for each child and fold. If desired, the children can color their pans.

8. Ask the children to glue together the handles and three sides to form a pocket. Make sure they do not glue the top of the pan. Staple the fold.

9. Encourage them to place their vegetables into their pans.

10. Ask each child to bring in a vegetable. Cut them up and make vegetable soup for lunch or snack.

⭐ Mary Brehm, Aurora, OH

HANDLE

CARROT

FOLD

STAPLE AFTER FOLDED

TOMATO

Cooperation Puzzle

Materials

Puzzles, 24 pieces or more

What to do

1. Pair up the children or put them in teams.
2. Tell the groups they will be putting together puzzles.
3. It may help to start with the children taking turns removing a puzzle piece from the box until the pieces have been evenly sorted among the teams.
4. When the pieces have been sorted, let the children begin putting pieces together. Tell them that they can only use the pieces in their own stack. They must ask the other teams to help find pieces that fit theirs.
5. This can be practiced on a regular basis by changing the teams and rotating the puzzles.

☆ Sandra L. Nagel, White Lake, MI

Ka-Choo Bulletin Board

Materials

Paper • pencils • crayons • scissors • glue • box of tissues • tape

What to do

1. This is a nice activity as part of a "good health" project. Discuss what to do if you have a cold. For example, drink a lot of water or juice, rest, stay warm, and so on. Talk about the importance of covering one's mouth and nose when sneezing (so germs cannot spread).

2. Give each child a piece of drawing paper. Ask him to draw a self-portrait of his face while sneezing.

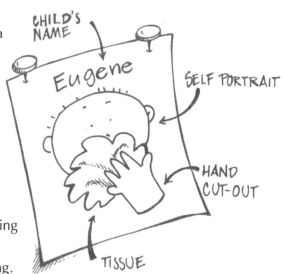

CHILD'S NAME

Eugene

SELF PORTRAIT

HAND CUT-OUT

TISSUE

3. Let the children color their pictures. Make sure to offer crayons in a variety of skin colors and tones.

4. Give the children another sheet of paper. Ask them to trace one of their hands, cut it out, and color it.

5. Demonstrate how to use a dab of glue to attach a tissue to the back of the hand. Ask them to tape the hand to the face.

6. Help the children write their names on their self-portraits. Hang them on a bulletin board.

 Elaine Commins, Athens, GA

My House

Materials

Paper • crayons or markers

What to do

1. Discuss the types of housing in your community. Show the children books of different houses.

2. Give each child a piece of paper. Ask him to draw a picture of his house.

3. Encourage the children to color their houses to match their real homes.

4. Help the children write their names and addresses underneath their pictures.

5. Display the homes on a bulletin board with roads.

Related book

Houses and Homes by Ann Morris

 Sandra L. Nagel, White Lake, MI

Dragon's Rules

Materials

Dragon puppet with a tail (handmade or purchased) • 1 paper lunch bag per child • markers • colored tissue paper and construction paper scraps • scissors • glue • large wiggly eyes or buttons, two per child • 1 knee-high stocking per child • newspaper • stapler

What to do

1. Talk about ways to get along with others and the use of good manners. Make a list of rules and manners for the classroom.
2. Introduce the dragon puppet. Have him talk to the children and read the list of rules. Explain to the children that the dragon wags his tail when he sees good manners in the classroom, and he opens his mouth and growls when he sees unkindness.
3. Let the children make their own dragon puppets to take home to remind their families to remember their manners.
4. Give each child a paper lunch bag. Ask them to make "scales" all over the bag with the markers.
5. Cut out arms and legs from tissue paper or construction paper for the children to glue on the bag.
6. Tell the children that the folded flap of the bag is the head. Help them cut out and glue on ears and horns.

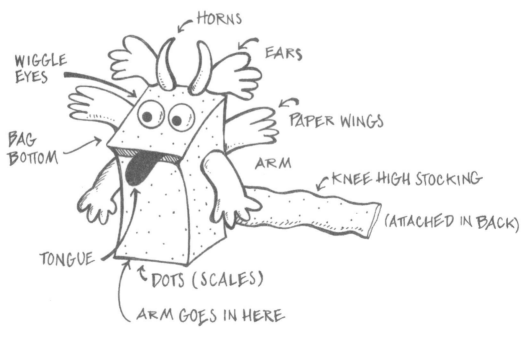

7. Demonstrate how to glue a tongue inside the flap. Glue on button or wiggle eyes.

8. On the back of the bag, the children can glue gathered tissue paper wings.

9. To make a tail to wag, the children stuff a knee-high stocking with torn crumpled newspaper, and then use a marker to make scales on the tail. Help them staple the bottom edge of the "tail" to the bag.

10. Show the children how to put their hand inside the bag to open and close the flap to make the dragon growl or talk. They can wiggle their arm to make the tail wag.

Related books

Big Black Bear by Wong Herbert Yee
Grover's Guide to Good Manners by Constance Allen
Joshua's Book of Manners by Alona Frankel

 Sandra Gratias, Perkasie, PA

Problem-Solving Puppet

Materials

A puppet that looks like a boy or girl • empty coffee can • index cards

What to do

1. On each index card, write different problems that five-year-olds often encounter. Place the ideas in the coffee can.

2. Let the children take turns choosing a card.

3. Have the puppet read the problem to the class.

4. The children can help the puppet come up with ideas to solve the problem. This helps children increase their ability to solve their own problems.

 Melissa Browning, Milwaukee, WI

All About Me Flowers

Materials

A wooden kitchen spoon for each child • green, yellow, red, and blue tempera paints • small paintbrushes • petal-shaped woodsies or other small woodcraft pieces • small plastic or wood beads • glue • plastic flower tray • Styrofoam

What to do

1. Give each child a wooden kitchen spoon. Ask them to paint it green to represent the stem of a flower. Let dry.

2. Give each child eight petal-shaped woodsies or woodcraft pieces. Let them paint them any color they choose. Let dry.

3. While the pieces are drying, ask each child to tell you something nice about each of his classmates. This should be done in private, since children often copy each other's answers when interviewed in a group setting. If the class is large, you can ask each child to tell about certain other children instead of the whole class, making sure you have at least six nice statements about each child.

4. Using the interview results, print the nice words about each child on his flower petal pieces. Don't print sentences, instead pick out key words from the children's interviews. For example, if a child says, "Heidi is nice," then print "nice" on the petal. Continue until each of the six petals has a word written on it.

5. Help the children glue their flower petals to the back of the bowl of the spoon. This will be the bloom of the flower.

6. Ask the children to glue four to six small plastic or wood beads to the center of the spoon bowl to represent the center of the flower.

7. Ask them to glue two of the petal shapes to the handle of the spoon to represent leaves on the flower. Let dry.

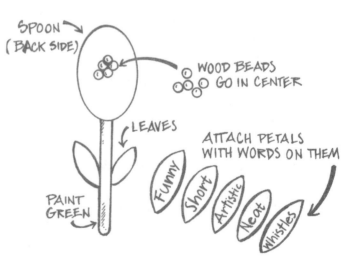

8. Use the flowers to create a "Garden of Good Thoughts" by placing all the flowers together in a plastic flower tray. Use large pieces of Styrofoam to hold them up.

   Tip: If wooden spoons and other craft items are out of your budget, you can use craft sticks for the stem and cupcake liners for the flowers. Glue these to a paper plate and print the nice words about the child around the edge of the plate. Create a "Garden of Good Thoughts" bulletin board to showcase these pretty flowers.

   Author's Note: Be a "good thoughts" example for the children. Notice when children are nice or kind to one another or demonstrate other positive behaviors. Comment on these behaviors. For example, when a child willingly shares a toy, say, "I noticed you shared your toys with Marilyn. You are being nice to Marilyn."

 Virginia Jean Herrod, Columbia, SC

An Evening at Home

Materials

Three-ring binder • construction paper • markers • Polaroid or digital camera • tote bag • *My Special Family* by Emily McCully

What to do

1. Create a cover for the binder with a title page, such as "An Evening at Home."
2. Assemble your "An Evening at Home" bag. Put the three-ring binder, *My Special Family*, and a digital or Polaroid camera in a tote bag, along with a letter of instruction to the parents (see below).
3. Let the children take turns taking the "An Evening at Home" bag home for one night.
4. The child may take up to four photographs of his family at home with the camera. Suggested photos might be one of the front of his home, his family at dinner, his bedroom, or the family involved in an activity together.

(continued on the next page)

5. When the child brings the camera bag back, mount the photographs on construction paper. Let the child dictate a descriptive statement about the activity depicted in each photo. Print these statements on the construction paper and insert it into the three-ring binder. Laminate for durability or insert in protective plastic sleeves.

6. Remind the children to look at each other's photos and read each other's stories when they take the bag home.

7. Sample parent letter:

Dear Parents,

Welcome to our "An Evening at Home" program. In this bag, you will find a three-ring binder, a camera, and a copy of My Special Family by Emily McCully. Please allow your child to take up to four photos of your family at home. You might want a photo of the front of your home, your family at dinner, your child's bedroom or personal space, and your entire family involved in an activity together.

Take time to look at the other children's pages in the three-ring binder and read their stories with your child. Also, please read the enclosed book with your child and take the time to talk with your child about your own special family.

Return this bag and all the contents tomorrow. We will help your child dictate a story about your photographs and add them to the binder. Thank you for participating in our program.

Related books

I Got a Family by Melrose Cooper
The Mud Family by Betsy James
Poinsettia and Her Family by Felicia Bond
Snow Family by Daniel Kirk

 Virginia Jean Herrod, Columbia, SC

Bulletin Board Children

Materials

Tagboard • scissors or die-cut machine • variety of art supplies

What to do

1. Precut or die cut gingerbread figures using tagboard.
2. Give each child two figures—one for the child to decorate in any way he chooses and one for the parents to decorate to represent their child.
3. Encourage the parents to be creative and use pictures, stickers, markers, sequins, and so on.
4. On the bulletin board, hang the gingerbread children so they are hand-in-hand.
5. Above the children, write a title such as "Joined in love and learning," or "We are learning hand-in-hand with our friends."

 Sandy L. Scott, Vancouver, WA

Hand Wreath

Materials

Construction paper in a variety of colors • scissors • paper plates • glue

What to do

1. Give each child a few pieces of construction paper to bring home. If possible, give each child a different color.
2. Make sure to send home enough paper so that the parent can trace and cut out the child's hand six or eight times (depending on what you want).
3. After the children bring back their cut-out hands, have a discussion about the differences between people, the value of sharing, and how people can work together to make wonderful things.
4. Ask the children to trade their hands with the other children, keeping one of their own.
5. Help each child glue his six or eight hands to a paper plate (with the center cut out) to form a wreath.
6. Add a paper bow that says something like "Coming Together as One" or "Hand in Hand Through Time."

 Sandy L. Scott, Vancouver, WA

Moving Day

Materials

2 dollhouses, 1 empty and 1 with furniture • a doll family • toy truck that can be loaded • toy car to hold doll family

What to do

1. This is a great activity to do when a child in your class will be moving soon. It will help the class and the child who will be moving to prepare for the transition.
2. Talk to the children about moving. Ask if any of them have moved to a new house or neighborhood. Explain that the child who is moving will be leaving soon.
3. Set up one dollhouse with the furniture on one side of the rug or play area.
4. Set up an empty dollhouse (or build one with boxes and blocks) in another area.
5. Encourage the children to pack the furniture into the truck and the family into the car.
6. Let them move everything to the empty house and set up the new household.
7. Allow time to play this over and over, as children desire.

Related books

The Berenstain Bears' Moving Day by Stan and Jan Berenstain
The Good-Bye Day by Leone Castell Anderson
The Good-Day Bunnies: Moving Day by Harriet Margolin & Carol Nicklaus

 Sandra Gratias, Perkasie, PA

The People in My School

Materials

Large butcher paper • markers • photos of people that are a part of the child's school experience (teachers, principal, secretary, custodian, librarian, teaching assistants, bus drivers) • copies of the photos • tape or glue sticks

What to do

1. This is a good activity to do the first week of school to introduce the children to the school and the people in it.
2. Take the children on a walk around the school, introducing them to the staff that they will be in contact with.
3. Back in your classroom, help the children draw a map of the school.
4. Ask them to label the rooms and glue or tape the pictures of the people where their rooms or offices are. You may want to pre-print places in the building (such as the cafeteria, gym, music room, library, and so on) on the computer and let the children cut out the words and glue on the map.
   Tip: Copies of photos can be made at most office supply stores, in black and white on the school copy machine, or printed from a scanner.

 Sandra L. Nagel, White Lake, MI

Tricycling for Cancer

Materials

Envelopes • tricycle for each child • photos from home

What to do

1. Ahead of time, set aside a "Fight Cancer" tricycle-a-thon at your school. Explain that the class is going to ride tricycles to raise money to donate for cancer research.
2. Send home envelopes for the children to obtain sponsors.
3. On the designated day, ask each child to bring a picture from home of anyone they know who has or had cancer. If they do not know anyone personally, they can bring in a photo of someone famous with cancer or who survived cancer.
4. Make copies of the photos and line them up in the tricycle area.
5. Have the children ride the specified amount of laps to raise money.
6. Take the children with you to donate the funds you raised, or let them help you send the donations to the organization you chose to support.

 Lisa Chichester, Parkersburg, WV

Voting and Ballots

Materials

Posters of the chosen candidates • shoebox • white paper • glue • red, white, and blue paint • star sponge • red, white, and blue streamers and balloons • small slips of paper

What to do

1. Have a real election in your classroom. Ask the children to come up with two favorite characters from books and stories to run for president.
2. Hang up posters of the two characters and explain to the children that they will vote for which character they would like to elect the class president.
3. Help the children make a voting box by covering a shoebox with white paper and sponge painting it red, white, and blue.
4. Hang streamers and balloons around the room.
5. Make ballot slips with the children by writing each character's name on different slips of paper and drawing pictures underneath.
6. Ask the children to come to the table, one at a time, and place a ballot slip with their favorite character on it in the ballot box.
7. Tally up the votes, announce the winner, and have a president's inaugural party with red, white, and blue cupcakes.

 Lisa Chichester, Parkersburg, WV

You Have Two Hands

Materials

Construction paper • photos of the children • glue • markers • stapler

What to do

1. Five-year-olds tend to have difficulty playing in groups of three. The words, "You're not my friend" are uttered frequently by children of this age.

2. If children want to play very dissimilar things, it's important to realize that sometimes "working things out" or compromising is just not a viable option.

3. As children grow up, they need to understand that although friends may be involved in other activities that they aren't fond of, they can still be friends.

4. Teaching children to use the phrase, "I'm not playing with you right now, but maybe later" results in fewer arguments and less upset feelings.

5. If there seems to be a chance to reconcile the activities, try telling the children, "You have two hands, so you can have two friends."

6. Make a class book of things the children like to do at school. Take pictures of the children involved in these activities. Ask, "Who likes to do puzzles?" and take a picture of all of the children who like to do puzzles working on puzzles. "Who likes to read?" "Who lies to write?" When children are looking for someone to play with, direct them to the book so they can find someone who enjoys the same activity.

Related books

How to Be a Friend by Laurie Krasny Brown and Marc Brown
I Want to Play by Elizabeth Crary

 Linda Ford, Sacramento, CA

Cinco Vaqueros Circle Time

Materials

None

What to do

1. Count backwards in Spanish from 10 to 1 (diez, nueve, ocho, siete, seis, cinco, cuatro, tres, dos, uno).
2. Tell the children that this will be the prompt for them to come to Circle Time.
3. When you start counting, they should already be cleaning up and preparing to come to Circle Time.
4. When they hear "Diez!" they are to begin heading towards the carpet.
5. Everyone should be sitting cross-legged in the designated area by the time you reach "Uno!"

 Stacy Edwards, Jermyn, PA

Play That Tune!

Materials

CD or cassette player • favorite fingerplays or songs on CD or cassette

What to do

1. Play a familiar song or tape at the beginning of cleanup time. Lower the tape after five minutes, so that the children will know to take their places at their seats as soon as possible.
2. While children are at their seats, they can sing along.
3. When all the children are seated, turn off the music. If it is a favorite song or fingerplay, finish it with them.

 Susan R. Forbes, Daytona Beach, FL

Train Whistle Station

Materials

One wooden train whistle

What to do

1. Tell the children that when you blow the whistle, it is time to line up.
2. Blow the train whistle. Say, "Come on! Join the train! Everyone make a line and put your hands on the shoulders of the child in front of you! Here we go! Toot toot!"
3. This is an easy and fun way to move from one activity to another.

 Susan M. Myhre, Bremerton, WA

Transition Time

Materials

Books and puzzles • shelf

What to do

1. Keep a few books and puzzles on a shelf near a large rug area.
2. When children finish projects and you are waiting for the rest of the group to finish, they may go to the rug and choose books to look at or puzzles to play with while they wait for the rest of the group.
3. This makes it easier for the class to move onto the next activity.

 Melissa Browning, Milwaukee, WI

Wild Cards

Materials

4" x 6" index cards • markers • shoebox • spray paint

What to do

1. Away from the children, spray paint a shoebox in wild colors.
2. Make name cards for each child and place them in the shoebox.
3. When it is time to leave group time or line up to leave the classroom, reach into the Wild Cards box and choose one card at a time.
4. The child whose name appears on the card is dismissed from the group.
5. Another method is to use 4" x 6" construction paper rectangles. Hold up a color card and children wearing that particular color are dismissed.

☆ Susan R. Forbes, Daytona Beach, FL

Animal Movements

Materials

None

What to do

BIRD LANDING

1. When moving as a group from one place to another, suggest an animal that the children can move like.
2. For example, they could slither like a snake, buzz like a flying bee, hop like a rabbit, and so on.
3. You could also suggest that they move like transportation items, such as cars, trains, or planes.

☆ Sandy L. Scott, Vancouver, WA

HOPPING RABBIT

SLITHERING SNAKE

Funny Bone Ticklers

Materials

None

What to do

1. If you and the children are stuck waiting somewhere with no toys or books, tell knock-knock jokes! Five-year-olds love jokes, and can tell some pretty silly ones.
2. Another great game is to use silly names. Use silly names to call children to line up, or just as a guessing game.
3. For example, "Whose name sounds like Farol?" "Carol!" They never get tired of it, and often ask to play it to line up.

 Tracie O'Hara, Charlotte, NC

Language Lineup

Materials

None

What to do

1. Turn lining up into a language experience with this simple activity.
2. As each child lines up, ask her to say a word relating to a particular category or holiday. For example, winter: snow, boots, snowman, cold, and so on.
3. Other ideas include:
   ☆ Line up if you have one tooth missing (two, three, and so on).
   ☆ Line up if you are wearing sneakers (boots, sandals, and so on).
   ☆ Line up if you have blue eyes (brown, hazel, and so on).
   ☆ Line up if you have a birthday in January (February, March, and so on).
   ☆ Line up if you have a "z" in your name (a, b, and so on).
   ☆ Line up if you are wearing "r-e-d" (spell out a color).

 Jackie Wright, Enid, OK

The Quiet Game

Materials

None

What to do

1. This is a great chant to use when you are trying to quiet the children or get their attention during Circle Time.
2. As you chant the words below in a soft voice, do a movement with your body quietly.

   Let's all play the quiet game,
   The quiet game, the quiet game.
   Let's all play the quiet game,
   The quiet game, shh, shh, shh.

3. As the children see you do this and chant, they will quiet down and do the movement with you.
4. Eventually the children will quiet down as soon as you start this. They will even come up with their own movements to do quietly as they chant.
5. As a last movement, put your hands in your lap. You now have their attention.

 Darleen Schaible, Stroudsburg, PA

Shapes and Colors

Materials

Tagboard in different colors • scissors • black marker • contact paper

What to do

1. Cut out large shapes from tagboard. Each shape should be a different color and approximately 15" in diameter.
2. Cut out matching smaller shapes in the same color, approximately 4" in diameter. Make a few smaller shapes for each large shape. For example, red squares, white circles, blue triangles, yellow diamonds, and so on.

3. On each shape write the name of the color on one side and the name of the shape on the other side.

4. When it is time for snack, place one of the large shapes at each table.

5. Call each child by name, hand her a smaller shape, and ask her to name the color or shape. Ask the children to go to the table with the matching shape.

   Tip: You can also use the shapes to determine the helpers for the day. For example, whoever has the large square is the cup helper, the large circle is the napkin helper, and so on.

☆ Sandy L. Scott, Vancouver, WA

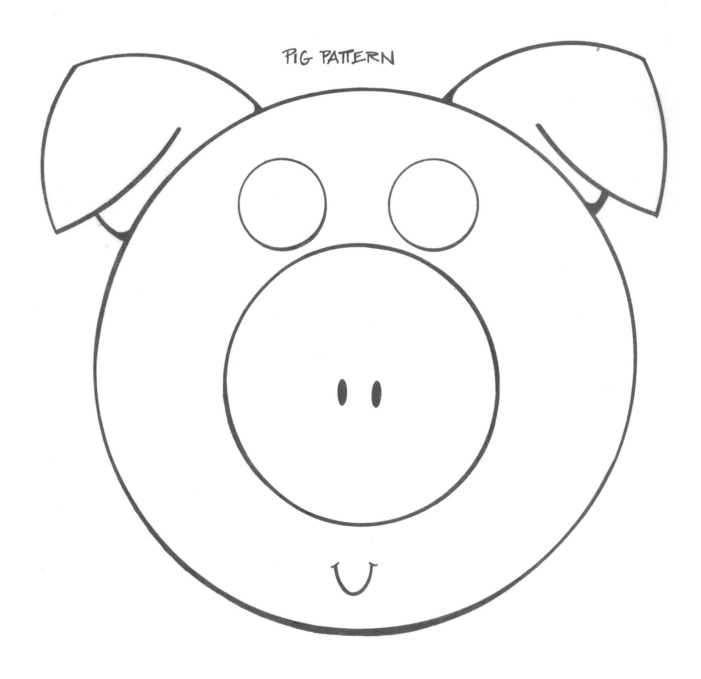

PIG PATTERN

WOLF PATTERN

INDEX

Children's Book Index

1 Is One by Tasha Tudor, 239

1, 2, 3 to the Zoo by Eric Carle, 239

12 Ways to Get to 11 by Eve Merriam, 239, 369

26 Letters and 99 Cents by Tana Hoban, 211, 239, 357

A

A Apple Pie and Traditional Nursery Rhymes by Kate Greenaway, 239

A My Name Is Alice by Jane Bayer, 239

Abe Lincoln's Hat by Martha Brenner, 240

Abiyoyo by Pete Seeger, 240

Across the Stream by Mirra Ginsburg, 240

The Adventures of Spider: West African Folktales by Joyce Arkhurst, 240

The Adventures of Taxi Dog by Debra & Sal Barracca, 240

Ahoy There, Little Polar Bear by Hans de Beer, 240

Alejandro's Gift by Richard Albert, 240

Alexander and the Terrible, Horrible, No Good, Very Bad Day by Judith Viorst, 240

Alexander the Wind-Up Mouse by Leo Lionni, 236, 240

Alexander, Who Used to Be Rich Last Sunday by Judith Viorst, 240

All About Owls by Jim Aronsky, 97

All By Myself by Mercer Mayer, 240

All Fall Down by Brian Wildsmith, 240

All I See by Cynthia Rylant, 310

All Kinds of Children by Norma Simon, 108

Alligators All Around by Maurice Sendak, 357

Alpha Bugs by David A. Carter, 178

Alphabears by Kathleen Hague, 240

The Alphabet Book by P.D. Eastman, 240

Alphabet Soup by Kate Banks, 486

The Alphabet Tree by Leo Lionni, 240

Alphabetics by Suse MacDonald, 178

Amazing Grace by Mary Hoffman, 240

Amelia Bedelia Goes Camping by Peggy Parish, 240

Amelia Bedelia's Family Album by Peggy Parish, 89

Amelia's Nine Lives by Lorna Balian, 240

American Tall Tales by Mary Pope Osborne, 240

Amos and Boris by William Steig, 240

Anansi and the Talking Melon by Eric Kimmel, 240

Anansi the Spider: A Tale From the Ashanti by Gerald McDermott, 240

Angel Child, Dragon Child by Michele Maria Surat, 240

Angry Arthur by Haiwyn Oram, 240

Angus and the Ducks by Marjorie Flack, 240

The Animal Atlas by Barbara Taylor, 241

Animal Homes by Brian Wildsmith, 241

The Animal by Lorna Balian, 240

Animalia by Graeme Base, 241

Animals in Danger by Marcus Schenck, 241

Anna's Art Adventure by Bjorn Sortland, 20, 28

Annie and the Wild Animals by Jan Brett, 241

Annie Bananie by Leah Komaiko, 241

Anno's Alphabet by Mitsumasa Anno, 241

Anno's U.S.A. by Mitsumasa Anno, 241

Antarctica by Helen Cowcher, 241

Appelemando's Dreams by Patricia Polacco, 241

Apples and Pumpkins by Anne Rockwell, 241

Apples by Gail Gibbons, 457

April Fools by Fernando Krahn, 241

Arctic Dreams by Carole Gerber, 132

Are You My Mother? by P.D. Eastman, 88, 241

The Armadillo From Amarillo by Lynne Cherry, 241

Armadillo Rodeo by Jan Brett, 241

Art Dog by Thacher Hurd, 20

Art Lesson (La Clase de Dibujo) by Tomie dePaola, 20

The Art Lesson by Tomie dePaola, 241, 310

Arthur's Back to School Day by Lillian Hoban, 389

Arthur's Eyes by Marc Brown, 241

Arthur's Pet Business by Marc Brown, 116

As the Crow Flies by Gail Hartman, 241

Ask Mr. Bear by Marjorie Flack, 67

At Daddy's on Saturdays by Linda Walvoord Girard, 241

Aunt Chip and the Great Triple Creek Dam Affair by Patricia Polacco, 241

B

Baby Animals by Karen Rissing, 241

Baby Farm Animals by Garth Williams, 241

Back Home by Gloria Jean Pinkney, 241

A Bad, Bad Day by Kirsten Hall, 239

The Balancing Act—A Counting Song by Merle Peek, 241

Balloons and Other Poems by Deborah Chandra, 62

A Bargain for Frances by Russell Hoban, 236

Barn Dance! by Bill Martin Jr., 241

The Barn Owls by Tony Johnston, 97

Barnyard Banter by Denise Fleming, 241

Bartholomew and the Oobleck by Dr. Seuss, 241, 475

Bartholomew the Bossy by Marjorie Weinman Sharmat, 241

Batter Up! by Andrew Gutelle, 241

Be Nice to Spiders by Margaret Bloy Graham, 241

Beady Bear by Don Freeman, 241

The Bear's Cave by Regine Schindler, 241

Bears on Wheels: A Bright and Early Counting Book by Stan & Jan Berenstain, 241

Bedtime for Frances by Russell Hoban, 94

Bee My Valentine! by Miriam Cohen, 241

The Bee-Man of Orn by Frank Stockton, 241

Benny's Pennies by Pat Brisson, 241

Bentley & Egg by William Joyce, 241

The Berenstain Bears Go to School by Stan & Jan Berenstain, 241

The Berenstain Bears' Moving Day by Stan & Jan Berenstain, 512

Berlioz the Bear by Jan Brett, 241

Best Friends by Steven Kellogg, 241

The Best Nest by P.D. Eastman, 241

Big Black Bear by Wong Herbert Yee, 507

Big Blue Engine by Ken Wilson-Max, 206

The Big Bunny and the Magic Show by Steven Kroll, 242

The Big Fat Enormous Lie by Marjorie Weinman, 242

Big Fat Hen by Keith Baker, 242

Big Old Bones—A Dinosaur Tale by Carol Carrick, 242

The Big Sneeze by Ruth Brown, 242

The Big Snow by Berta & Elmer Hader, 242

The Biggest House in the World by Leo Lionni, 242

Biggest Machines by Dennis Kiley, 242

The Biggest Nose by Kathy Caple, 242

The Biggest Pumpkin Ever by Steve Kroll, 242

The Biggest Snowball of All by Jane Belk Moncure, 131

The Biggest, Best Snowman by Margery Cuyler, 131

Billy and the Big New School by Laurence Anholt, 389

The Black Snowman by Phil Mendez, 242

Block City by Robert Louis Stevenson, 62

Blue Sea by Robert Kalan, 242

Boat Book by Gail Gibbons, 242

Book by George Ella Lyon, 64

Books by Gail Gibbons, 348

Borreguita and the Coyote by Verna Aardema, 242

The Boy Who Would Be a Helicopter by Vivian Guzzin Paley, 242

Brave as a Mountain Lion by Ann Herbert Scott, 242

The Brave Cowboy by Joan Walsh Anglund, 242

Brave Irene by William Steig, 242, 236

Bread and Jam for Frances by Russell Hoban, 242

Bread Bread Bread by Ann Morris, 242

Bremen Town Musicians by Jacob Grimm, 242

The Bremen-Town Musicians by Ruth Belov Gross, 236

Brian Wildsmith's ABC by Brian Wildsmith, 242

Brian Wildsmith's Birds by Brian Wildsmith, 242

Bringing the Rain to Kapita Plain by Verna Aardema, 242

Brother Eagle, Sister Sky by Susan Jeffers, 242

Brown Bear, Brown Bear, What Do You See? by Bill Martin Jr., 74

Bubble Bubble by Mercer Mayer, 242, 444

The Bug Book by William Dugan, 242

Bugs by Joan Richards Wright, 97

Building a House by Byron Barton, 242

Building an Igloo by Lilli Steltzer, 132

Bumper to Bumper: A Traffic Jam by Jakki Wood, 242

The Button Box by Margaret S. Reid, 242

C

Camille and the Sunflowers by Laurence Anholt, 50

Caps for Sale by Esphyr Slobodkina, 119, 185, 242

Caps, Hats, Socks, and Mittens by Louise Borden, 242

Career Day by Anne Rockwell, 348

Caribou Girl by Rudolf Murphy, 132

Carl Goes Shopping by Alexandra Day, 242

The Carousel by Liz Rosenberg, 242

The Carrot Seed by Ruth Krauss, 126, 236, 242

Cat Goes Fiddle-I-Fee by Paul Galdone, 242

The Cat in the Hat by Dr. Seuss, 242

The Cat in the Hat/El Gato Ensombrerado by Dr. Seuss, 153

A Chair for My Mother by Vera B. Williams, 236, 239

Changes, Changes by Pat Hutchins, 243

Charlie Needs a Cloak by Tomie dePaola, 243

Check It Out! The Book About Libraries by Gail Gibbons, 243

Cheerios Counting Book by Barbara Barbieri McGrath, 487

Cherries and Cherry Pits by Vera B. Williams, 243

Chicka Chicka Boom Boom by Bill Martin Jr., 83, 117, 357

Chicka Chicka Sticka Sticka: An ABC Sticker Book by Bill Martin Jr. & John Archambault, 83, 243

The Chicken Book by Garth Williams, 236

Chicken Soup With Rice by Maurice Sendak, 84

Chickens Aren't the Only Ones by Ruth Heller, 243

Child's Book of Art by Lucy Micklethwait, 243

Choo Choo: The Story of a Little Engine Who Ran Away by Virginia Lee Burton, 243

Christina Katerina and the Time She Quit the Family by Patricia Lee Gauch, 89

Christopher Columbus by Stephen Krensky, 243

Cinderella Penguin by Janet Perlman, 70

Circles, Triangles, and Squares by Tana Hoban, 62

Circus by Lois Ehlert, 243

City Green by Dyanne DiSalvo-Ryan, 243

City in the Winter by Eleanor Schick, 243

Clara and the Bookwagon by Nancy Smiler Levinson, 65

The Cloud Book by Tomie dePaola, 243

Cloudy With a Chance of Meatballs by Judi Barrett, 243

Cock-a-Doodle Dudley by Bill Peet, 243

Color Dance by Ann Jonas, 243

Colors Are Nice by Adelaide Holl, 243

Colors Everywhere by Tana Hogan, 243

Come a Tide by George Ella Lyon, 243

Come to Our House: Meet Our Family by Ulises Wensell, 83

The Complete Story of the Three Blind Mice by Paul Galdone, 243

Construction Workers by Tami Deedrick, 348

Cornelius by Leo Lionni, 243

Count and See by Tana Hoban, 243

Count Your Way Through Russia by Jim Haskins, 419

Counting Rhymes by Sharon Kane, 243

Courtney by John Burningham, 236

Cowboy Dreams by Dayal Kaur Khalsa, 243

Coyote Steals the Blanket by Janet Stevens, 243

Creak, Thump, Bonk! A Very Spooky Mystery by Susan L. Roth, 243

Creepy, Crawly Caterpillars by Margery Facklam, 243

Crictor by Tomi Ungerer, 243

Crinkleroot's Guide to Knowing the Trees by Jim Aronsky, 243

Crow Boy by Taro Yashima, 236, 243

Curious George by H.A. and Margret Rey, 76, 243

Cyrus the Unsinkable Sea Serpent by Bill Peet, 243

D

Dad and Me in the Morning by Patricia Lakin, 243

Daddy Makes the Best Spaghetti by Anna Grossnickle Hines, 89, 243

Daisy-Head Maysie by Dr. Seuss, 243

Dandelion by Don Freeman, 70, 244

Dandelions by Eve Bunting, 244

Danny and the Dinosaur by Syd Hoff, 244

David Goes to School by David Shannon, 389

The Day Jimmy's Boa Ate the Wash by Reeve Lindbergh, 244

The Day the Teacher Went Bananas by James Howe, 244

De Colores and Other Latin-American Folk Songs by Jose-Luis Orozco, 244

Dear Benjamin Banneker by Andrea Davis Pinkney, 244

Deep in the Forest by Brinton Turkle, 71

Digging Up Dinosaurs by Aliki, 244

The Dinosaur Alphabet Book by Jerry Pallotta, 244

Dinosaur Bones by Aliki, 244

The Dinosaur Who Lived in My Backyard by B.G. Hennessy, 70

Dinosaurs Are Different by Aliki, 244

Dinosaurs to the Rescue! by Laurene Krasny Brown, 244

Dinosaurs, Dinosaurs by Byron Barton, 244

Discovering Seashells by Douglas Florian, 244

Do You Want to Be My Friend? by Eric Carle, 244

Doctor De Soto by William Steig, 244

A Dog Named Sam by Janice Boland, 239

The Dog Who Had Kittens by Polly M. Robertus, 244

Dogs by Gail Gibbons, 244

The Doorbell Rang by Pat Hutchins, 244

Dragon ABC Hunt by Loreen Leedy, 244

Draw Me a Star by Eric Carle, 244, 310

Dreams by Ezra Jack Keats, 244

Drylongso by Virginia Hamilton, 244

Ducks Don't Get Wet by Augusta Goldin Water, 244

Dustin's Big School Day by Alden R. Carter, 389

E

Each Peach Pear Plum by Janet & Allan Ahlberg, 244

The Earth and I by Frank Asch, 244

Earthdance by Joanne Ryder, 96

Earthworms: Underground Burrowers by Adelle D. Richardson, 466

Eating the Alphabet: Fruits and Vegetables From A to Z by Lois Ehlert, 244, 486

Edward the Emu by Sheena Knowles, 244

The Eensy Weensy Spider by Mary Ann Hoberman, 53

Eggbert, the Slightly Cracked Egg by Tom Ross, 236, 244

The Eggs: A Greek Folk Tale by Aliki, 244

Eight Animals on the Town (Ocho Animales) by Susan Middleton Elya, 153

Elbert's Bad Word by Audrey Wood, 244

The Elephant's Child by Rudyard Kipling, 244

Elephants Aloft by Kathi Appelt, 244

Emergency! by Gail Gibbons, 244

The Empty Pot by Demi, 244

Eric Carle's Animals by Eric Carle, 244

Everybody Needs a Rock by Byrd Baylor, 244

Everyday Mysteries by Jerome Wexler, 244

Exploring the Night Sky by Terrence Dickinson, 244

An Extraordinary Egg by Leo Lionni, 240

F

Fables by Arnold Lobel, 244

Fall Leaves Fall! by Zoe Hall, 464

The Fall of Freddie the Leaf by Leo Buscaglia, 245

Fanny's Dream by Caralyn Buehner, 245

Fantastic Frogs by Fay Robinson, 139

The Farm Alphabet Book by Jane Miller, 245

Farmer Duck by Martin Waddell, 245

Farming by Gail Gibbons, 245

Fathers, Mothers, Sisters, Brothers: A Collection of Family Poems by Mary Ann Hoberman, 245

Feathers for Lunch by Lois Ehlert, 245

Feelings by Aliki, 245

Fiddle-I-Fee by Melissa Sweet, 245

Finders Keepers by William Lipkind, 236

Finger Rhymes by Marc Brown, 245

The Fire Engine Book by Jesse Younger, 245

Fire Engines by Anne Rockwell, 245

Fire Fighters by Norma Simon, 348

Fire on the Mountain by Jane Kurtz, 245

Fire! Fire! by Gail Gibbons, 245

Fireflies in the Night by Judy Hawes, 245

A First Atlas by Scholastic First Encyclopedia, 108

The First Snowfall by Anne & Harlow Rockwell, 245

Fish Is Fish by Leo Lionni, 245

Flap Your Wings by P.D. Eastman, 245

Flashy Fantastic Rainforest Frogs by Dorothy Hinshaw Patent, 139

Flossie and the Fox by Patricia McKissack, 245

The Flower Alphabet Book by Jerry Pallotta, 245

Flower Garden by Eve Bunting, 245

Flying in a Hot Air Balloon by Cheryl Walsh Bellville, 245

Fortunately by Remy Charlip, 245

Fossils Tell of Long Ago by Aliki, 245

Four Valentines in a Rainstorm by Felicia Bond, 54, 245

Fox at School by Edward Marshall, 389

Fraction Action by Loreen Leedy, 245

Franklin in the Dark by Paulette Bourgeois, 245

Frederick by Leo Lionni, 245

Freight Train by Donald Crews, 245

Friday Night Is Papa Night by Ruth A. Sonneborn, 245

Friends by Helme Heine, 245

The Frog Alphabet Book by Jerry Pallotta, 245

Frog and Toad Are Friends by Arnold Lobel, 237

The Frog Prince by Edith H. Tarcov, 245

Frog Went A-Courtin' by John Langstaff, 245

Froggy Gets Dressed by Jonathan London, 245

From Pictures to Words: A Book About Making a Book by Janet Stevens, 245

From Tadpole to Frog by Wendy Pfeffer, 99, 138–139

The Furry Alphabet Book by Jerry Pallotta, 245

G

The Gadget War by Betsy Duffey, 245

The Garden in the City by Gerda Muller, 479

The Garden of Happiness by Erika Tamar, 246

George and Martha by James Marshall, 238, 246

George Washington's Breakfast by Jean Fritz, 246

Geraldine's Blanket by Holly Keller, 246

The Giant Jam Sandwich by John Vernon Lord, 246

Gila Monsters Meet You at the Airport by Marjorie Weinman Sharmat, 246

Gilberto and the Wind by Marie Hall Ets, 246

The Gingerbread Boy by Paul Galdone, 86, 246

The Gingerbread Man by John A. Rowe, 246

The Girl Who Loved Wild Horses by Paul Goble, 246

Give Me Half! by Stuart J. Murphy, 246

The Giving Tree by Shel Silverstein, 246

Glad Monster Sad Monster: A Book About Feelings by Ed Emberley, 246

Go Away, Big Green Monster! by Ed Emberley, 246

Go, Dog, Go! by P.D. Eastman, 316

The Goat in the Rug by Charles L. Blood, 246

Goggles! by Ezra Jack Keats, 246

The Golden Christmas Tree by Jan Wahl, 246

The Golden Egg Book by Margaret Wise Brown, 104

Goldilocks and the Three Bears by Jan Brett, 246

Goldilocks and the Three Bears by various authors, 94

Good Dog, Carl by Alexandra Day, 246

Good Morning, Chick by Mirra Ginsburg, 246

Good Night, Gorilla by Peggy Rathmann, 246

The Good, the Bad, and the Goofy by Jon Scieszka, 246

The Good-Bye Day by Leone Castell Anderson, 512

Goodbye Geese by Nancy White Carlstrom, 246

The Good-Day Bunnies: Moving Day by Harriet Margolin & Carol Nicklaus, 512

Good-Night Owl! by Pat Hutchins, 97, 246

Gooseberry Park by Cynthia Rylant, 246

Grandfather Twilight by Barbara Berger, 246

Grandmother's Pigeon by Louise Erdrich, 246

The Grasshopper and the Ant by Aesop, 246

Gray Rabbit's Odd One Out by Alan Baker, 316

The Great Kapok Tree: A Tale of the Amazon Rainforest by Lynne Cherry, 246

The Great Pumpkin Switch by Megan McDonald, 246

The Greedy Python by Richard Buckley, 246

The Greedy Zebra by Mwenye Hadithi, 246

Green Eggs and Ham by Dr. Seuss, 246

Gregory, the Terrible Eater by Mitchell Sharmat, 246

Gregory's Shadow by Don Freeman, 423

The Grey Lady and the Strawberry Snatcher by Molly Bang, 246

The Grouchy Ladybug by Eric Carle, 246

Grover's Guide to Good Manners by Constance Allen, 507

Growing Colors by Bruce McMillan, 126

Growing Vegetable Soup by Lois Ehlert, 246, 486

Guess Who? by Anne W. Ball, 246

Guess Who? by Margaret Miller, 246

H

Hailstones and Halibut Bones by Mary O'Neill, 247

Hand Rhymes by Marc Brown, 247

Hands Off! by Mario Mariotti, 247

Hansel and Gretel by the Brothers Grimm, 247

Happy Birthday, Dear Duck by Eve Bunting, 247

Happy Birthday, Sam by Pat Hutchins, 247

The Happy Day by Ruth Krauss, 247

Happy Easter, Little Critter by Mercer Mayer, 247

Harbor by Donald Crews, 247

Harriet and the Promised Land by Jacob Lawrence, 247

Harry and the Terrible Whatzit by Dick Gackenbach, 247

Harvey Potter's Balloon Farm by Jerdine Harold, 62

Hattie and the Fox by Mem Fox, 247

Have You Seen Birds? by Joanne Oppenheim, 247

Have You Seen My Cat? by Eric Carle, 247

Have You Seen My Duckling? by Nancy Tafuri, 247

Hear Your Heart by Paul Showers, 247

A Helpful Alphabet of Friendly Objects by John Updike, 72

Her Seven Brothers by Paul Goble, 247

Here Are My Hands by Bill Martin Jr., 247

Hi Mom, I'm Home! by Kees Moerbeek, 247

Hi, Cat! by Ezra Jack Keats, 247

Hide and Seek Fog by Alvin Tresselt, 247

A Holiday for Mister Muster by Arnold Lobel, 239

Home for a Bunny by Margaret Wise Brown, 247

Hooray for Me by Remy Charlip, 247

Hooray for Mother's Day! by Marjorie Weinman Sharmat, 247

Hopper by Marcus Pfister, 247

Horton Hatches the Egg by Dr. Seuss, 247

Horton Hears a Who by Dr. Seuss, 88

Hosie's Alphabet by Leonard Baskin, 247

A House for Hermit Crab by Eric Carle, 239

A House Is a House for Me by Mary Ann Hoberman, 239

The House That Jack Built by Tony Brice, 247

Houses and Homes by Ann Morris, 247, 505

How a Book Is Made by Gail Gibbons, 247

How a House Is Built by Gail Gibbons, 62, 247

How Droofus the Dragon Lost His Head by Bill Peet, 247

How I Named the Baby by Linda Shute, 21

How Many Days to America? A Thanksgiving Story by Eve Bunting, 247

How Much Is a Million? by David M. Schwartz, 247

How Teddy Bears Are Made by Ann Morris, 247

How the Grinch Stole Christmas by Dr. Seuss, 247

How the Guinea Fowl Got Her Spots by Barbara Knutson, 248

How the Ostrich Got Its Long Neck by Verna Aardema, 248

How the Sun Was Brought Back to the Sky by Mirra Ginsburg, 248

How to Be a Friend by Laurene & Marc Brown, 515

Huge Harold by Bill Peet, 248

The Hungry Thing by Jan Slepian & Ann Seidler, 248

Hurry Up, Franklin by Paulette Bourgeois, 248

I

I Got a Family by Melrose Cooper, 510

I Have a Pet! by Shari Halpern, 248

I Know a Lady by Charlotte Zolotow, 237, 248

I Like Me by Nancy Carlstrom, 248

I Like the Library by Anne Rockwell, 248

I Love Animals by Flora McDonnell, 248

I Love Going Through This Book by

Robert Burleigh, 64

I See Animals Hiding by Jim Aronsky, 248

I Spy books by Jean Marzollo & Walter Wick, 433

I Spy Two Eyes: Numbers in Art by Lucy Micklethwait, 248

I Took My Frog to the Library by Eric Kimmel, 77

I Want to Be a Vet by Dan Liebman, 348

I Want to Be an Astronaut by Byron Barton, 248, 348

I Want to Play by Elizabeth Crary, 515

I Was So Mad! by Norma Simon, 248

I Wish I Were a Butterfly by James Howe, 248

I'll Always Love You by Hans Wilhelm, 248

I'm a Little Teapot by Iza Trapani, 68, 248

I'm in Charge of Celebrations by Byrd Baylor, 248

I'm Not Sleepy by Denys Cazet, 248

The Icky Bug Alphabet Book by Jerry Pallotta, 248

If Anything Ever Goes Wrong at the Zoo by Mary Jean Hendrick, 248

If I Ran the Circus by Dr. Seuss, 248

If I Were a Penguin by Heidi Goennel, 248

If I Were in Charge of the World and Other Worries by Judith Viorst, 248

If the Dinosaurs Came Back by Bernard Most, 248

If You Give a Moose a Muffin by Laura Joffe Numeroff, 248

If You Give a Mouse a Cookie by Laura Joffe Numeroff, 94, 237, 248

If You Give a Pig a Pancake by Laura Joffe Numeroff, 248

If You Take a Mouse to the Movies by Laura Joffe Numeroff, 28

Iktomi and the Boulder by Paul Goble, 248

The Important Book by Margaret Wise Brown, 248

In a Scary Old House by Harriet Ziefert, 248

In the Night Kitchen by Maurice Sendak, 248

In the Rain With Baby Duck by Amy Hest, 248

In the Small, Small Pond by Denise Fleming, 95

In the Tall, Tall Grass by Denise Fleming, 95, 249

Inch by Inch by Leo Lionni, 237, 249, 466

Inch Worm and a Half by Elinor Pinczes, 466

Insects in the Garden by Dorothy M. Souza, 249

Inside a Barn in the Country by Alyssa Satin Capucilli, 249

Ira Sleeps Over by Bernard Waber, 94, 237, 249

Is It Larger? Is It Smaller? by Tana Hoban, 249

Is It Red? Is It Yellow? Is It Blue? by Tana Hoban, 249

Is Your Storytale Dragging? by Jean Stagl, 287

The Island of the Skog by Steven Kellogg, 249

It Begins With A by Stephanie Calmenson, 360

It Could Always Be Worse by Margot Zemach, 249

It Goes Eeeeeee! by Jamie Gilson, 249

It Looked Like Spilt Milk by Charles G. Shaw, 100–101

It's Halloween by Jack Prelutsky, 249

It's Pumpkin Time! by Zoe Hall, 249

It's Raining, It's Pouring by Kin Eagle, 249

It's Thanksgiving by Jack Prelutsky, 249

The Itsy Bitsy Spider by Iza Trapani, 53, 249

J

Jack and the Beanstalk by various authors, 90

The Jack Tales by Richard Chase, 249

The Jacket I Wear in the Snow by Shirley Neitzel, 249

Jamaica's Find by Juanita Havill, 249

Jamie O'Rourke and the Big Potato by Tomie dePaola, 249

A January Fog Will Freeze a Hog by Hubert Davis, 239

Jasmine by Roger Duvoisin, 249

Jelly Beans for Sale by Bruce McMillan, 249

Jemima Puddle-Duck by Beatrix Potter, 249

Jennie's Hat by Ezra Jack Keats, 249

Jesse Bear, What Will You Wear? by Nancy White Carlstrom, 249

The Jester Has Lost His Jingle by David Saltzman, 120

Jimmy, the Pickpocket of the Palace by Donna Jo Napoli, 249

John Henry: An American Legend by Ezra Jack Keats, 249

Johnny Appleseed by Steven Kellogg, 249

The Jolly Postman or Other People's Letters by Janet & Allan Ahlberg, 249

Joseph's Other Red Sock by Niki Daly, 249

Joshua's Book of Manners by Alona Frankel, 507

Jump! The New Jump Rope Book by Susan Kalbfleisch, 249

Jump, Frog, Jump! by Robert Kalan, 249

June 29, 1999 by David Wiesner, 249

The Jungle by Carroll Norden, 249

Just a Dream by Chris Van Allsburg, 249

Just for You by Mercer Mayer, 237, 249

Just Go to Bed by Mercer Mayer, 250

Just Like Home/Como En Mi Tierra by Elizabeth I. Miller, 153

Just Me and My Little Sister by Mercer Mayer, 250

Just Me and My Mom by Mercer Mayer, 68

K

Katy No-Pocket by Emmy Payne, 250

Keep Looking by Millicent Selsam & Joyce Hunt, 250

The Keepers of the Earth by Michael J. Caduto & Joseph Bruchac, 250

Kitaq Goes Ice Fishing by Margaret Nicolai, 132

Kitten Can … by Bruce McMillan, 250

Kittens Are Like That by Jan Pfloog, 250

Knights of the Kitchen Table by Jon Scieszka, 250

Knots on a Counting Rope by Bill Martin Jr., 237, 250

Koala Lou by Mem Fox, 250

L

The Lady and the Spider by Faith McNulty, 250

The Lady With the Alligator Purse by Nadine Bernard Westcott, 78, 250

Ladybug, Ladybug by Ruth Brown, 250

The Last Dragon by Susan Miho Nunes, 292

The Last Puppy by Frank Asch, 250

The Last Tales of Uncle Remus by Julius Lester, 250

Latkes and Applesauce: A Hanukkah Story by Fran Manushkin, 250

Legend of Earth, Air, Fire, and Water by Eric & Tessa Hadley, 250

The Legend of the Blue Bonnet by Tomie dePaola, 250

The Legend of the Indian Paintbrush by Tomie dePaola, 237

The Legend of the Poinsettia by Tomie dePaola, 250

Lentil by Robert McCloskey, 250

Let's Go Fishing on the Ice by George Travis, 419

Let's Go to the Library by Lisl Weil, 250

Let's Make Rabbits by Leo Lionni, 250

A Letter to Amy by Ezra Jack Keats, 239

Liar, Liar, Pants on Fire! by Miriam Cohen, 250

The Library Card by Jerry Spinelli, 64

Library Dragon by Carmen Deedy, 78

Library Lil by Suzanne Williams, 78

The Library by Sarah Stewart, 250

The Life and Times of the Honeybee by Charles Micucci, 250

Linnea in Monet's Garden by Christina Bjork & Lena Anderson, 250

The Lion and the Little Red Bird by Elisa Kleven, 28

The Lion and the Mouse by Gail Herman, 250

Lion Dancer: Ernie Wan's Chinese New Year by Kate Waters, 250

The Listening Walk by Paul Showers, 250

Little Bear by Else Holmelund Minarik, 70

Little Beaver and the Echo by Amy MacDonald, 250

The Little Black Truck by Libba Moore Gray, 237

Little Blue and Little Yellow by Leo Lionni, 237

Little Cloud by Eric Carle, 250

The Little Drummer Boy by Ezra Jack Keats, 250

The Little Engine That Could by Watty Piper, 119, 237

Little Grunt and the Big Egg by Tomie dePaola, 250

The Little House by Virginia Lee Burton, 61, 237

The Little Match Girl by Hans Christian Andersen, 251

The Little Mouse, The Red Ripe Strawberry, and the Big Hungry Bear by Don & Audrey Wood, 237, 251

Little Mouse's Big Valentine by Thacher Hurd, 251

The Little Old Lady Who Was Not Afraid of Anything by Linda Williams, 237

Little One Inch and Other Japanese Children's Favorite Stories by Florence Sadake, 251

The Little Painter of Sabana Grande by Patricia Maloney Markun, 28

Little Penguin's Tale by Audrey Wood, 70, 251

Little Polar Bear by Hans de Beer, 251

Little Rabbit's Loose Tooth by Lucy Bates, 251

The Little Red Hen by Paul Galdone, 251

Little Toot by Hardie Gramatsky, 237

Lon Po Po by Ed Young, 251

London Bridge Is Falling Down by Peter Spier, 251

Long Train by Sam Williams, 206

Look What Came From Russia by Miles Harvey, 419

The Lorax by Dr. Seuss, 251

Lost at the White House: A 1909 Easter Story by Lisa Griest, 251

Lost by Paul Brett Johnson, 251

The Lotus Seed by Sherry Garland, 251

Loudmouth George and the Big Race by Nancy Carlson, 237, 251

Louise's Search by Ezra Jack Keats, 251

Lovable Lyle by Bernard Waber, 251

Love You Forever by Robert Munsch, 251

Loving by Ann Morris, 251

Lunch by Denise Fleming, 251

M

Ma Dear's Aprons by Patricia C. McKissack, 20

Madeleine by Ludwig Bemelmans, 251

The Maestro Plays by Bill Martin Jr., 251

The Magic Dreidels by Eric A. Kimmel, 251

The Magic Fish by Freya Littledale, 251

The Magic School Bus on the Ocean Floor by Joanna Cole, 102

The Magic School Bus series by Joanna Cole, 251

The Magic String by Francene Sabin, 251

Maisy Drives the Bus by Lucy Cousins, 206

Make Way for Ducklings by Robert McCloskey, 70

Mama Went Walking by Christine Berry, 251

Mama Zooms by Jane Cowen-Fletcher, 251

Mama, Do You Love Me? by Barbara M. Joosse, 251

Maps: Getting From Here to There by Harvey Weiss, 251

Market Day by Eve Bunting, 251

Martin Luther King Day by Linda Lowery, 251

Marvin the Mouse—Opposites Book by Jane Harvey, 251

Mary Had a Little Lamb by Colin & Moira Maclean, 251

Mary Wore Her Red Dress & Henry Wore His Green Sneakers by Merle Peek, 251

Math Curse by Jon Scieszka, 252

Matthew's Dream by Leo Lionni, 20

Max by Rachel Isadora, 252

Max Found Two Sticks by Brian Pinkney, 252

Me and My Family by Paul Showers, 346

Me on the Map by Joan Sweeney, 105

Mean Soup by Betsy Everitt, 252

Meeting Trees by Scott Russell Sanders, 127

Merry Christmas, Strega Nona by Tomie dePaola, 252

Mice Twice by Joseph Low, 252

Mighty Tree by Dick Gackenbach, 252

Mike Fink: A Tall Tale by Steven Kellogg, 252

Mike Mulligan and His Steam Shovel by Virginia Lee Burton, 237, 252

The Milk Makers by Gail Gibbons, 102, 252

Milton the Early Riser by Robert Kraus, 252

Ming Lo Moves the Mountain by Arnold Lobel, 252

Mirandy and Brother Wind by Patricia M. McKissack, 252

Mirette on the Highwire by Emily Arnold McCully, 252

Miss Bindergarten Gets Ready for Kindergarten by Joseph Slate, 69, 252

Miss Mary Mack by Mary Ann Hoberman, 252

Miss Nelson Is Back by Harry Allard, 252

Miss Nelson Is Missing by Harry Allard, 237

Miss Rumphius by Barbara Cooney, 252, 237

Miss Spider's Tea Party by David Kirk, 53, 69, 252

Mister Momboo's Hat by Ralph Leemis, 252

The Mitten by Jan Brett, 252

The Mixed-Up Chameleon by Eric Carle, 252

Mojave by Diane Siebert, 252

Molly's Pilgrim by Barbara Cohen, 252

Mommy Doesn't Know My Name by Suzanne Williams, 21

Monarch Butterfly by Gail Gibbons,

252

The Monkey and the Crocodile by Paul Galdone, 252

Moon Lake by Ivan Gantschev, 252

Moon Rope by Lois Ehlert, 252

Moongame by Frank Asch, 252

More Than Anything Else by Marie Bradby, 252

The Most Wonderful Egg in the World by Helme Heine, 252

Mother Hubbard's Cupboard by Laura Rader, 302

The Mother's Day Mice by Eve Bunting, 237, 252

Mouse Paint by Ellen Stoll Walsh, 28, 95, 252

Mr. Gumpy's Outing by John Burningham, 252

Mr. Rabbit and the Lovely Present by Charlotte Zolotow, 252

Mrs. Bindergarten Celebrates 100 Days of Kindergarten by Joseph Slate, 411

Mrs. Gigglebelly Is Coming for Tea by Donna Guthrie, 68

Mrs. Merriwether's Musical Cat by Carol Purdy, 252

The Mud Family by Betsy James, 510

Mud Puddle by Robert N. Munsch, 252

Mufaro's Beautiful Daughters: An African Tale by John Steptoe, 253

Mushroom in the Rain by Mirra Ginsburg, 253

My Barber by Anne & Harlow Rockwell, 253

My Brother, Ant by Betsy Cromer Byars, 253

My Father's Hand by Joanne Ryder, 253

My First Book of Sign Language by Joan Holub, 363

My First Book of Time by Claire Llewellyn, 253

My First Kwanzaa Book by Deborah M. Newton, 253

My Five Senses by Aliki, 253

My Friend John by Charlotte Zolotow, 253

My Friends by Taro Gomi, 237, 253

My Hands Can by Jean Holzenthaler, 253

My House/Mi Casa by Rebecca Emberley, 253

My Mama Had a Dancing Heart by Libba Moore Gray, 253

My Mama Says There Aren't Any Zombies, Ghosts, Vampires, Creatures, Demons, Monsters, Fiends, Goblins, or Things by Judith Viorst, 253

My Map Book by Sara Fanelli, 108

My Red Umbrella by Robert Bright, 237

My Special Family by Emily McCully, 509

My Spring Robin by Anne Rockwell, 253

My Teacher Sleeps in School by Leatie Weiss, 253

My Very First Mother Goose by Iona Opie, 253, 302

The Mysterious Rays of Dr. Rontgen by Beverly Gherman, 253

The Mysterious Tadpole by Steven Kellogg, 253

N

A Name for Kitty by Marcia Trimble, 116

Nana Upstairs & Nana Downstairs by Tomie dePaola, 253

The Napping House by Audrey Wood, 434

The Napping House Wakes Up by Audrey Wood, 253

Nate the Great and the Boring Beach Bag by Marjorie Weinman Sharmat, 253

Nature's Green Umbrella: Tropical Rain Forest by Gail Gibbons, 253

Never Spit on Your Shoes by Denys Cazet, 253

The New Puppy by Anne Civardi, 116

Night Creatures by Susan Santoro Whayne, 253

Night in the Country by Cynthia Rylant, 253

Night of the Gargoyles by Eve Bunting, 253

Night, Circus by Mark Corcoran, 253

Nine Days to Christmas: A Story of Mexico by Marie Hall Ets & Aurora Labastida, 253

No Good in Art by Miriam Cohen, 310

No Jumping on the Bed by Tedd Arnold, 253

No Moon, No Milk by Chris Babcock, 253

No Nap by Eve Bunting, 253

Noah's Ark by Peter Spier, 253

Nobody Asked Me If I Wanted a Baby Sister by Martha Alexander, 89

Nora's Surprise by Satomi Ichikawa, 253

Norma Jean, Jumping Bean by Joanna Cole, 254

Norman the Doorman by Don Freeman, 254

The Not-So-Jolly Roger by Jon Scieszka, 254

Now I Know Birds by Susan Kuchalla, 254

Now One Foot, Now the Other by Tomie dePaola, 254

O

The Ocean Alphabet Books by Jerry Pallotta, 254

Of Colors and Things by Tana Hoban, 254

Off to School, Baby Duck by Amy Hest, 389

Officer Buckle and Gloria by Peggy Rathmann, 254

Old Bear by Jane Hissey, 254

Old Black Fly by Jim Aylesworth, 254

Old MacDonald Had a Farm by Carol Jones, 254

The Old Woman and Her Pig by Paul Galdone, 254

Oliver Pig at School by Jean Van Leeuwen, 254

Oliver's Milk Shake by Vivian French, 102

On Market Street by Arnold Lobel, 254

On Monday When It Rained by Cherr Kachenmeister, 254

On Mother's Lap by Ann Herbert Scott, 254

On the Day You Were Born by Debra Frasier, 254

On the Go by Ann Morris, 254

Once a Mouse by Marcia Brown, 254

The One and Only Me by Marilyn Singer, 346

One Bear in the Hospital by Caroline Bucknall, 254

One Fish, Two Fish, Red Fish, Blue Fish by Dr. Seuss, 254

One Hundred Hungry Ants by Elinor J. Pinczes, 254

One Hungry Monster by Susan Heyboer O'Keefe, 254

One Is Good, But Two Are Better by Louis Slobodkin, 254

One Small Candle by Thomas J. Fleming, 254

One Snowy Day by Jeffrey Scherer, 131

One Stuck Duck by Phyllis Root, 91

One Sun: A Book of Terse Verse by Bruce McMillan, 254

One Tough Turkey: A Thanksgiving Story by Steven Kroll, 254

Ooops! by Suzy Kline, 254

Opposites by John Burningham, 254

Opposites by Rosalinda Kightley, 254

The Opposites by Monique Felix, 34

The Orchard Book of Nursery Rhymes by Zena Sutherland, 254

Out and About by Shirley Hughes, 254

Outside and Inside Birds by Sandra Markle, 254

Over and Over by Charlotte Zolotow, 254

Over in the Meadow by John Langstaff, 237

Over in the Meadow by Olive A. Wadsworth, 254

Over the River and Through the Woods by Brinton Turkle, 254

Owl Babies by Martin Waddell, 97

Owl Moon by Jane Yolen, 96, 254

Owly by Mike Thaler, 97

The Ox-Cart Man by Donald Hall, 254

P

Painted Dreams by Karen Lynn Williams, 28

Painting the Wind by Michelle Dionetti, 50

A Pair of Red Clogs by Masako Matsuno, 239

A Pair of Socks by Stuart J. Murphy, 239

Pancakes, Crackers, and Pizza: A Book of Shapes by Marjorie Eberts et al., 255

Pancakes, Pancakes by Eric Carle, 255

Panda by Caroline Arnold, 255

Papa, Please Get the Moon for Me by Eric Carle, 255

Parade by Donald Crews, 255

The Patchwork Quilt by Valerie Flournoy, 255

Paul Bunyan by Steven Kellogg, 255

Peace at Last by Jill Murphy, 255

Peanut Butter and Jelly by Nadine Bernard Westcott, 255

Pelle's New Suite by Elsa Beskow, 255

Perfect Father's Day by Eve Bunting, 255

Perfect Pigs: An Introduction to Manners by Marc Brown, 255

Perfect the Pig by Susan Jesch, 255

The Perky Little Pumpkins by Margaret Friskey, 255

Pet Show by Ezra Jack Keats, 116, 255

Peter Rabbit by Beatrix Potter, 76

Peter's Chair by Ezra Jack Keats, 255

Petunia by Rober Duvoisin, 238, 255

Picnic by Emily Arnold McCully, 255

A Picture Book of Abraham Lincoln by David Adler, 239

A Piece of Cake by Jill Murphy, 240

The Pied Piper by Alan Benjamin, 238

Pig Pig Gets a Job by David McPhail, 255

Piggies by Audrey & Don Wood, 255, 434

Pigs Ahoy! by David McPhail, 255

Pigs Aplenty, Pigs Galore! by David McPhail, 255

Pigs by Peter Brady, 255

Pigsty by Mark Teague, 238, 255

Pink and Say by Patricia Polacco, 255

Pinkerton, Behave! by Steven Kellogg, 255

Pirates by Brenda Thompson & Rosemary Giesen, 255

Planes by Anne Rockwell, 255

The Planets by Gail Gibbons, 255

Planting a Rainbow by Lois Ehlert, 126, 255

Play Ball, Amelia Bedelia by Peggy Parish, 255

Play Rhymes by Marc Brown, 255

Play With Me by Marie Hall Ets, 255

The Pledge of Allegiance by Francis Bellamy, 255

A Pocket for Corduroy by Don Freeman, 85, 238

A Pocketful of Seasons by Doris Van Liew Foster, 240

Poinsettia and Her Family by Felicia Bond, 510

The Poky Little Puppy by Janette Lowrey, 255

Polar Bear, Polar Bear, What Do You Hear? by Bill Martin Jr., 255

The Polar Express by Chris Van Allsburg, 100, 255

The Post Office Book: Mail and How It Moves by Gail Gibbons, 256

Pretend You're a Cat by Jean Marzollo, 256

Puddles by Jonathan London, 444

The Puffins Are Back! by Gail Gibbons, 256

Puffins Climb, Penguins Rhyme by Bruce McMillan, 256

The Pumpkin Book by Gail Gibbons, 457

Pumpkin Pumpkin by Jeanne Titherington, 256

The Puppy Who Wanted a Boy by Jane Thayer, 256

The Purse by Kathy Caple, 256

Puss in Boots by Charles Perrault, 256

Q

Quacky Duck by Paul & Emma Rogers, 256

The Quarreling Book by Charlotte Zolotow, 238, 256

Quick as a Cricket by Audrey Wood, 256

The Quilt Story Tony Johnston, 256

The Quilt by Ann Jonas, 256

R

Raccoons and Ripe Corn by Jim Aronsky, 256

Rachel Carson by William Accorsi, 256

Rachel Fister's Blister by Amy MacDonald, 256

The Rag Coat by Lauren A. Mills, 256

Raggedy Ann's Tea Party Book by Elizabeth Silbaugh, 69

Rain Forest by Helen Cowcher, 256

Rain Makes Applesauce by Julian Scheer, 256

The Rainbow Bridge by Audrey Wood, 256

The Rainbow Fish by Marcus Pfister, 256

Rainbow Fish and the Big Blue Whale by Marcus Pfister, 256

Rainbow Fish to the Rescue! by Marcus Pfister, 256

Rapunzel by the Brothers Grimm, 256

The Rattlebang Picnic by Margaret Mahy, 256

Raven: A Trickster Tale From the Pacific North by Gerald McDermott, 256

Red Bear by Bodel Rikys, 85

Red-Eyed Tree Frog by Joy Cowley, 139

Red Is Best by Kathy Stinson, 256

Red Light, Green Light by Golden MacDonald, 256

The Red String by Margot Blair, 420

Regards to the Man in the Moon by Ezra Jack Keats, 256

Regina's Big Mistake by Marissa Moss, 256

The Relatives Came by Cynthia Rylant, 256

Richard Scarry's Busy Town by Richard Scarry, 61

Richard Scarry's Chipmunk's ABC by Roberta Miller, 256

The Right Number of Elephants by Jeff Sheppard, 256

River Day by Jane B. Mason, 256

Roll-Over: A Counting Song by Merle Peek, 256

Rosie's Walk by Pat Hutchins, 257

Roxaboxen by Alice McLerran, 257

The Runaway Bunny by Margaret Wise Brown, 238, 257

The Runaway Chick by Robin Ravilious, 257

S

Sadako by Eleanor Coerr, 257

The Salamander Room by Anne Mazer, 257

Sam and the Tigers by Julius Lester, 257

Sam Who Never Forgets by Eve Rice, 257

Sam's Sandwich by David Pelham, 257

Say Hola to Spanish by Susan Middleton Elya, 153

Say It! by Charlotte Zolotow, 257

Scary, Scary Halloween by Eve Bunting, 257

School Bus by Donald Crews, 257

School by Emily Arnold McCully, 257

Screech Owl at Midnight Hollow by Drew Lamm, 97

Seashore Story by Taro Yashima, 257

The Seasons of Arnold's Apple Tree by Gail Gibbons, 257

The Secret Birthday Message by Eric Carle, 82

Secret Valentine by Laura Damon, 257

Seven Blind Mice by Ed Young, 257

The Shape of Me and Other Stuff by Dr. Seuss, 500

Shapes by Guy Smalley, 257

Shapes, Shapes, Shapes by Tana Hoban, 257

Sheep in a Shop by Nancy Shaw, 257

The Sheepish Book of Opposites by George Mendoza, 257

The Shoemaker and the Elves by Adrienne Adams, 257

Shoes by Elizabeth Winthrop, 257

Shy Charles by Rosemary Wells, 257

The Sign Book by William Dugan, 257

Signing at School by S. Harold Collins, 363

Silly Tilly's Thanksgiving Dinner by Lillian Hoban, 257

Simple Signs by Cindy Wheeler, 363

Sing a Song of Popcorn: Every Child's Book of Poems by Beatrice Shenk de Regniers, 257

Six Foolish Fishermen by Benjamin Elkin, 257

The Skeleton Inside You by Philip Balestrino, 257

Sleep Book by Dr. Seuss, 434

Sleepy Bear by Lydia Dabcovich, 70, 257

Sleepy Heads by Aileen Fisher, 257

The Sleepy Owl by Marcus Pfister, 97

Small Green Snake by Libba Moore Gray, 257

Small Pig by Arnold Lobel, 257

The Smallest Cow in the World by Katherine Paterson, 257

Smokey by Bill Peet, 257

Snakes by Seymour Simon, 257

Snap! by Marcia Vaughan, 257

Snow by Roy McKie & P.D. Eastman, 131

Snow Dance by Lezlie Evans, 131

Snow Family by Daniel Kirk, 510

Snow Is Falling by Franklyn M. Branley, 131

Snowballs by Lois Ehlert, 131, 257

The Snowman by Raymond Briggs, 131, 258

The Snowy Day by Ezra Jack Keats, 131, 258

So Many Circles, So Many Squares by Tana Hoban, 62

So You Want to Be President? by Judith St. George, 89

Some Things Go Together by Charlotte Zolotow, 258

Something Big Has Been Here by Jack Prelutsky, 258

Something Special for Me by Vera B. Williams, 258

Somewhere in the World Right Now by Stacy Schuett, 258

Song and Dance Man by Karen Ackerman, 238, 258

Soup Should Be Seen, Not Heard by Beth Brainard & Sheila Behr, 258

Space Case by Edward Marshall, 258

Spider on the Floor by Raffi, 258

Splish, Splash! by Joan Bransfield Graham, 258

Splish, Splash, Splosh by Mick Manning & Brita Granstrom, 480

A Spoon for Every Bite by Joe Hayes, 240

Spots, Feathers, and Curly Tails by Nancy Tafuri, 258

Squirrel Nutkin by Beatrix Potter, 258

St. Patrick's Day in the Morning by Eve Bunting, 258

Stand Back, Said the Elephant, I'm Going to Sneeze! by Patricia Thomas, 258

Stanley by Syd Hoff, 258

The Star Spangled Banner by Peter Spier, 258

Stellaluna by Jannell Cannon, 238, 258

Stevie by John Steptoe, 258

The Stinky Cheese Man and Other Fairly Stupid Tales by Jon Scieszka, 258

Stone Soup by Marcia Brown, 258

The Storm Book by Charlotte Zolotow, 258

Storms by Seymour Simon, 258

Storms in the Night by Mary Stoltz, 258

The Story of Ferdinand by Munro Leaf, 238

The Story of Ruby Bridges by Robert Coles, 258

The Story of the Pilgrims by Katharine Ross, 258

A Story, a Story by Gail E. Haley, 240

The Stranger by Chris Van Allsburg, 258

Stringbean's Trip to the Shining Sea by Vera B. & Jennifer Williams, 258

Suddenly! by Colin McNaughton, 28

Sukey and the Mermaid by Robert D. San Souci, 258

The Summer Snowman by Gene Zion, 258

The Sun's Asleep Behind the Hill by Mirra Ginsburg, 258

Sunflower House by Eve Bunting, 126

Sunshine by Jan Ormerod, 258

Sunshine Makes the Seasons by Franklyn Mansfield Branley, 258

Supermarket by Anne & Harlow Rockwell, 258

Swamp Angel by Anne Isaacs, 258

Swapping Boy by John Langstaff, 259

Swimmy by Leo Lionni, 102, 128, 238, 259

Sylvester, the Mouse With the Musical Ear by Adelaide Holl, 259

T

Tacky the Penguin by Helen Lester, 70, 259

Tail Twisters by Aileen Fisher, 259

The Tale of Benjamin Bunny With Peter Rabbit by Beatrix Potter, 259

The Tale of Peter Rabbit by Beatrix Potter, 259

The Tale of Two Bad Mice by Beatrix Potter, 259

Tales of Oliver Pig by Jean Van Leeuwen, 259

The Talking Eggs by Robert D. San Souci, 259

Tea Party Today: Poems to Sip and Savor by Eileen Spinelli, 69

Teatime With Emma Buttersnap by

Lindsay Tate, 69

The Teddy Bears' Picnic by Jimmy Kennedy, 259

The Teeny Tiny Woman by Jane O'Connor, 259

Ten Apples Up on Top! by Theo LeSieg, 259

Ten Black Dots by Donald Crews, 259

Ten Little Ladybugs by Melanie Gerth, 259

Ten, Nine, Eight by Molly Bang, 259

Thanksgiving Day by Gail Gibbons, 259

That's Good, That's Bad by Margery Cuylen, 34

That's What a Friend Is by P.K. Hallinan, 259

There Was an Old Lady Who Lived in a Shoe by various authors, 80

There's a Nightmare in My Closet by Mercer Mayer, 259

There's a Square: A Book About Shapes by Mary Serfozo, 500

There's an Alligator Under My Bed by Mercer Mayer, 94

There's No Such Thing as a Dragon by Jack Kent, 259

Thidwich, the Big-Hearted Moose by Dr. Seuss, 259

The Third Planet: Exploring the Earth From Space by Sally Ride, 259

This Is My House by Arthur Dorros, 105

This Is the Bear and the Scary Night by Sarah Hayes, 259

This Is the Farmer by Nancy Tafuri, 259

This Is the Way We Go to School by Edith Baer, 259

This Next New Year by Janet S. Wong, 292

This Old Man by Robin Michal Koontz, 259

This Year's Garden by Cynthia Rylant, 259

The Three Bears by Paul Galdone, 94, 259

Three Billy Goats Gruff by various authors, 119

Three by the Sea by Edward Marshall, 259

Three Cheers for Tacky by Helen Lester, 259

Three Ducks Went Wandering by Ron Roy, 259

Three Little Indians by Gene S. Stuart, 259

Three Little Kittens by Paul Galdone, 238

The Three Little Pigs by James Marshall, 259

The Three Little Pigs by various authors, 92–93

The Three Little Wolves and the Big Bad Pig by Eugene Trivizas, 259

Through Grandpa's Eyes by Patricia MacLachian, 259

Through Moon and Stars and Night Skies by Ann Warren Turner, 259

Thumbelina by Hans Christian Andersen, 260

Tico and the Golden Wings by Leo Lionni, 260

Tidy Titch by Pat Hutchins, 260

A Tiger Called Thomas by Charlotte Zolotow, 240

Tigress by Helen Cowcher, 260

Tilabel by Patricia Coombs, 260

Tim O'Toole and the Wee Folk by Gerald McDermott, 260

Time Flies by Eric Rohmann, 260

Time for Bed by Mem Fox, 260

Time to Sleep by Denise Fleming, 434

Timothy Goes to School by Rosemary Wells, 260

The Tiny Seed by Eric Carle, 126, 260

Titch by Pat Hutchins, 260

To Space and Back by Sally Ride & Susan Okie, 260

To Think I Saw It on Mulberry Street by Dr. Seuss, 260

Toad for Tuesday by Russell E. Erickson, 260

Today Is Monday by Eric Carle, 260

Tomie dePaola's Mother Goose by Tomie dePaola, 260

Tomorrow's Alphabet by George Shannon, 360

The Tomten by Astrid Lindgren, 260

Too Many Books by Caroline Feller Bauer, 78

Tops and Bottoms by Janet Stevens, 34, 260

The Tortilla Factory by Gary Paulsen, 260

The Tortoise and the Hare by Janet Stevens, 260

The Town Mouse and the Country Mouse by Lorinda Bryan Cauley, 260

Train Song by Diane Siebert, 260

Trains by Anne F. Rockwell, 260

Treasure Nap by Juanita Havill, 434

A Tree Is Nice by Janice May Udry, 238, 240

Trees, Leaves, and Bark (Take-Along Guide) by Diane L. Burns, 464

The Trek by Ann Jonas, 260

The Trip by Ezra Jack Keats, 260

The True Story of the Three Little Pigs by Jack Prelutsky, 260

The Tub People by Pam Conrad, 260

A Turkey for Thanksgiving by Eve Bunting, 240

Tyrannosaurus Was a Beast by Jack Prelutsky, 260

U

Umbrella by Taro Yashima, 260

Under the Moon by Dyan Sheldon, 260

The Underwater Alphabet Book by Jerry Pallotta, 102

Uno, Dos, Tres: One, Two, Three by Pat Mora, 260

V

Valentine's Day by Gail Gibbons, 260

The Vanishing Pumpkin by Tony Johnston, 260

The Velveteen Rabbit by Margery Williams, 238

Vera's First Day of School by Vera Rosenberry, 389

The Very Busy Spider by Eric Carle, 260, 53

The Very Hungry Caterpillar by Eric Carle, 81, 260

The Very Lonely Firefly by Eric Carle, 260

The Very Quiet Cricket by Eric Carle, 260

A Very Special House by Ruth Krauss, 240

The Village of Round and Square Houses Ann Grifalconi, 260

The Village Tree by Taro Yashima, 260

A Visit to Grandma's by Nancy A. Carlson, 240

W

Wake Up, Little Children: A Rise-and-Shine Rhyme by Jim Aylesworth, 260

Walter the Baker by Eric Carle, 261

Water by Frank Asch, 480

We Are Best Friends by Aliki, 261

The Wednesday Surprise by Eve Bunting, 261

Weird Parents by Audrey Wood, 261

The Whale's Song by Dyan Sheldon, 70, 261

What About Ladybugs by Celia Godkin, 261

What Comes in 2's, 3's, and 4's? by Suzanne Aker, 369

What Does Word Bird See? by Jane Belk Moncure, 261

What Happened to Patrick's Dinosaurs? by Carol Carrick, 261

What Makes a Bird a Bird? by Mary Garelick, 261

What Sank the Boat? by Pamela Allen, 261

What Would You Do If You Lived at the Zoo? by Nancy White Carlstrom, 261

What's Under the Ocean? by Janet Craig, 70

What's Your Name? by Eve Sanders, 21

The Wheels on the Bus by Paul Zelinsky, 261

When Autumn Comes by Robert Maass, 261

When I Am Old With You by Angela Johnson, 261

When I Was Five by Arthur Howard, 261

When the Wind Stops by Charlotte Zolotow, 261

Where Do They Go? Insects in Winter by Millicent E. Selsam, 261

Where Does the Sun Go at Night? by Mirra Ginsburg, 261

Where Is Spot? by Eric Hill, 261

Where the Bald Eagles Gather by Dorothy Hinshaw Patent, 261

Where the River Begins by Thomas Locker, 127

Where the Sidewalk Ends by Shel Silverstein, 261

Where the Wild Things Are by Maurice Sendak, 238, 261

Where's My Teddy? by Jez Alborough, 70, 261

Whistle for Willie by Ezra Jack Keats, 261

White Snow, Bright Snow by Alvin Tresselt, 261

Who Said Red? by Mary Serfozo, 261

Who Says That? by Arnold L. Shapiro, 261

Who Uses This? by Margaret Miller, 261

Who Will Be My Friends? by Syd Hoff, 261

Who's in Rabbit's House? A Masai Tale by Verna Aardema, 261

Whose Mouse Are You? by Robert Kraus, 261

Whose Shoe? by Margaret Miller, 261

Why Do Leaves Change Color? by Betsy Maestro, 90

Why the Chicken Crossed the Road by David Macaulay, 261

Why the Sun and the Moon Live in the Sky by Elphinstone Dayrell, 261

The Wild Christmas Reindeer by Jan Brett, 238, 262

Wild Wild Sunflower Child Anna by Nancy White Carlstrom, 126

Will I Have a Friend? by Miriam Cohen, 261

William the Backwards Skunk by Chuck Jones, 261

William's Doll by Charlotte Zolotow, 238

Willy's Pictures by Anthony Brown, 20, 28

The Wind Blew by Pat Hutchins, 262

Window by Jeannie Baker, 262

Worms Wiggle by David Pelham, 466

Wormy Worm by Christopher Raschka, 466

The Worst Person's Christmas by James Stevenson, 238

The Wump World by Bill Peet, 262

Wynken, Blynken, and Nod by Eugene Field, 262

Y

Yankee Doodle by Edward Bangs, 262

The Year at Maple Hill Farm by Alice & Martin Provensen, 262

Young Martin Luther King Jr. by Joanne Mattern, 262

The Young People's Atlas of the United States by James Harrison, 108

Your Mother Was a Neanderthal by Jon Scieszka, 262

Your Skin and Mine by Paul Showers, 262

The Yucky Reptile Alphabet Book by Jerry Palotta, 262

Yummers! by James Marshall, 262

Z

Zin! Zin! Zin! A Violin by Lloyd Moss, 262

Zinnia and Dot by Lisa Ernst Campbell, 262

Zomo the Rabbit: A Trickster Tale From the West by Gerald McDermott, 262

The Zoo Book by Jan Pfloog, 262

Zoo Dreams by Cor Hazelaar, 262

INDEX

Index

100 days activities, 372, 411, 484

A

Acceptance
  books about, 241, 256
Acorns, 181, 277, 367, 438
Acrylic paint, 101
Action rhymes
  "Summer Sun," 173
  "Weather Moves," 175
Adding, 373–374
Adding boxes, 267
Adhesive paper. See Contact paper
Adjectives, 331
Aisles, 401–402
Alligators
  books about, 243, 245
  purses, 78
Alphabet charts, 332
  Egyptian, 336–337
  signing, 362
Aluminum foil, 27, 61, 67, 119–120, 142, 358
American flags, 277, 305–306
American Indians
  books about, 237, 250, 254, 259
  clothes, 111
American Sign Language, 153, 362–363
Animals, 115–116, 340, 381–382
  books about, 239, 241–242, 244–245–247, 249, 251, 253–254, 257, 260–262
  habitats, 454–455
  plastic, 264, 440
  water, 238, 242, 247, 249–251, 254, 256, 259, 261, 442, 447, 451
Apples, 111, 456–458, 496–497
  books about, 239, 249, 256
  stars, 456
  various kinds, 385–386
Appliance boxes, 52, 132, 270, 291, 315, 413, 427
April Fools Day
  books about, 241
Aprons, 27, 29, 102, 114, 134, 384, 483
  homemade, 19–20, 483
Aquariums, 99
  accessories, 440
  gravel, 441
Arbor Day
  books about, 238, 240
Art prints, 41

Andy Warhol's "Campbell's Cans," 309
Frank Lloyd Wright's "Fallingwater," 309
Leonardo Da Vinci's "Mona Lisa," 309
Norman Rockwell paintings, 309
Van Gogh's Sunflowers, 49
Art
  activities, 19–57, 193–194, 309–310, 428, 452
  books about, 241, 243–244
  setting up, 223–225
Art smocks, 27, 29, 475
Attendance, 388–389
Autumn
  activities, 44–48, 90, 280–281, 342, 377, 438, 441, 456–458
  books about, 241–242, 245–246, 254, 257–258, 261
  hats, 277

B

Baby powder, 480
Baby-wipe boxes, 264
Bags, 91, 114, 288, 310, 325
  canvas, 112, 211
  drawstring, 121
  fabric, 433
  freezer, 486
  fruit, 267
  gift, 24
  grocery, 122, 124, 135, 186, 289, 341
  laundry, 234
  lunch, 40, 77, 142, 179, 278, 301, 337, 338, 414, 506
  mail, 121, 356
  monthly, 221
  paper, 24, 40, 77, 124, 209
  plastic, 130, 140–141, 416, 484
  sandwich, 368
  shoe, 375
  shopping, 221
  tote, 112, 211, 445, 509
  trash, 131, 273, 418
  zippered plastic, 23, 85, 121, 176, 218, 234, 342, 377, 383, 433, 473, 476
Baking
  books about, 248
Balance beams, 88, 274, 401
Balloons, 62, 124, 266, 275, 398, 425, 514
  clear, 477
Balls, 52, 187, 270, 310
  bouncing, 52

cotton, 91, 104, 126, 276, 277, 284, 285, 348, 377, 441, 469
  koosh, 80, 423
  ping-pong, 178, 441
  Styrofoam, 291
  tea, 483
Bananas, 76, 492
Baskets, 65, 91, 182, 197, 204, 217, 221, 223, 301, 337, 454
  Easter, 300–301
  laundry, 495
  May Day, 303
  Mother Goose, 302
  plastic, 224
Batons, 119, 394
Bats, 310
  books about, 238, 258
Beach props, 59
Beads, 27, 138, 264, 465
  homemade, 49
  plastic, 366, 508
  wooden, 54, 508
Beanbags, 187, 196, 270, 271, 273, 412
  making, 271
Bears, 310–311, 380
  books about, 240, 255, 257, 259
  flocked, 85
  gummy, 493
Beds, 291
Bells, 100, 286
Belts, 114, 186
Benches, 235
Bethune, Mary McLeod, 308
Bibs, 114, 186
Binding machines, 71, 225–228, 232, 351–353, 445
Binoculars, 205
Birdfeeders, 454
Birdhouse kits, 205
Birds, 453–454
  books about, 242, 245, 247, 254, 260–261
  Frisbee, 417–418
  paper bag, 40–41
  silhouettes, 453
Birdseed, 440–441
Birthdays
  books about, 247–248, 251–252, 254, 258
Blankets, 124, 291, 434
Blenders, 473, 475, 495
Blindfolds, 262, 359
Blocks, 34, 93
  activities, 58–63
  cardboard, 61, 266, 317
  character cubes, 317

labeling, 58
large, 62
Legos, 34, 436
pattern, 212
sand, 404
small, 469
unit, 385
wood, 58
Board games, 118, 190
Boats, 433
books about, 240, 242, 247, 252, 261
Body awareness, 268
books about, 246–247, 253, 257, 262
Bookmaking center, 343
Bookmarks, 67
Books, 127, 132, 211, 235, 284, 329, 370, 517 (see also Reading lists)
about China, 292
about gardens, 422
about insects, 97, 465
about Russia, 418–419
about safari animals, 418
about sharks, 447
about tea parties, 483
activities, 64–108
alphabet, 72–73, 333
architecture, 296
bear-shaped, 71–72
box, 220
covering, 231
food riddle, 70–71
game, 229
grocery bag, 341–342
heavy, 44
homemade, 74–75, 105–108, 333, 341–352, 344–352, 358–359
leaf baggie, 342
leaf identification, 463
Mother Goose, 302
of 100, 372
picture, 233
poetry, 232–233
recycled, 220–221
song, 228–229, 232
telephone, 43
Bottle brushes, 80
Bottles
2-liter, 270, 418
plastic, 264, 270, 418, 444
soda, 164, 264
spray, 216, 418, 420, 424
squeeze, 26, 442
squirt, 90
water, 31, 222, 394, 417
Bouclé, 358

Bouncing balls, 52
Bow ties, 114
Bowls, 30, 34, 88, 181, 286, 310, 475–476, 478, 488–490
mixing, 23–24, 145, 294, 297, 475, 484, 490, 497–499, 501
paper, 276
plastic, 491
salad, 353
small, 308, 385, 498
Bows, 24, 221
Box kites, 414
Boxes, 52, 186, 218–219, 329, 420, 441, 450
adding, 267
art-sorting, 223
baby wipe, 264
book, 220–221
candy, 294
cereal, 140
corrugated, 220
covered, 219
felt, 309
file folder, 223
gift, 22
large, 52, 132, 270, 291, 315, 413, 427
medium-size, 292
pizza, 142
recipe, 315
shoeboxes, 186, 224, 367, 383, 514, 518
small, 22, 185, 198, 286, 442
story, 329
tissue, 451
treasure, 264
videocassette, 309
Bracelets, 186
Branches, 131
Bread, 279, 466, 487–488
biscuits, 485
buns, 498
rolls, 496
tortillas, 499
Brushes
basting, 20
bottle, 80
kitchen, 80
paint, 19, 21, 34, 38, 40, 42, 45, 48–49, 51, 92, 99, 122, 124, 128, 204, 206, 283–284, 286, 288–292, 384, 404, 413, 421, 427, 429, 433, 444, 447, 451, 460, 472–473, 483, 493, 502, 508
roller, 80
scrub, 80, 440
shoe, 463
tooth, 264

vegetable, 304
Bubble machines, 269
Bubble wrap, 80, 358
Bubbles, 269, 413
books about, 242
recipe, 263
Buckets, 53, 59, 204, 416, 423, 441–445
5-gallon, 132
Bulletin board paper, 117, 126, 464
Bulletin boards, 41
animal habitats, 455
children, 510–511
ka-choo, 504
storing, 225
trees, 464–465
Bunny ears, 337
Burlap, 40, 274, 358
Butcher paper, 24, 321, 377, 436, 512
Butter, 485, 487–488, 496–498
Butterflies, 267
books about, 252
Button-making kits, 207
Buttons, 53, 137, 181, 193, 224, 273, 367, 506

C

Cake pans, 418
Cakes, 483
Calculator paper, 371
Calendars, 148–149, 196, 330
books about, 239
Cameras, 72, 192, 209, 225, 478, 509
Camping, 126
books about, 240
Cancer Tricycle-a-thon, 513
Candles, 27, 279
Candy, 196–197, 279, 295, 377–378, 484, 489–490, 493, 501
canes, 295, 494
gumdrops, 494
gummy bears, 493
gummy fish, 490–491
hard, 494
hearts, 196
jellybeans, 378
licorice, 489
lollipops, 477
M&Ms, 196, 298, 378, 484, 489
making, 294
molds, 294
wrapped, 284
Cans, 401
coffee, 396, 409–410, 507
food, 396

potato chip, 396

soup, 396, 410

tin, 474

vegetable, 410

watering, 464

Canvas bags, 112, 211

Capes, 119

Carbon paper, 33

Carbonated water, 482

Cardboard, 19, 33, 42, 53, 57, 61, 67, 104, 119, 178, 181, 185, 207, 270, 306, 310, 336, 426, 373, 447, 449, 470, 475, 494

blocks, 266

boxes, 429

corrugated, 80, 358

egg cartons, 129

fish, 132

shiny, 170

tubes, 125, 441

tubes, 22, 63, 284, 338

Cards, 198, 375

color, 192

file, 174, 375

gift, 25

greeting, 224, 276, 286, 343, 353

index, 70, 141, 192, 203, 229, 232, 315, 332, 340, 342, 367, 386, 459, 507, 518

lacing, 276

name, 214, 471

note, 27, 354–355, 367

number, 192

Old Maid, 189

picture, 212

playing, 364, 433

poem, 232

song, 232

wild, 518

word, 315

Cardstock, 21, 49, 80, 141, 144, 183, 217, 223, 370, 454

Caring

books about, 249

Carle, Eric, 66, 80–81

Carpentry nails. See nails

Carpet squares, 21, 109, 418

ideas for, 395

remnants, 463

Cars. See Toy cars

Carver, George Washington, 288

Cash registers, 126, 134

Cassette tapes, 83

music, 120, 157, 162, 217, 233, 292, 402–405, 407, 516

nature sounds, 434

Catalogs, 357

seed, 280

vegetable, 502

CD jackets, 431

CD players, 292, 402–405, 431, 516

CDs

demo, 364

music, 217, 292, 398, 400, 402–405, 431, 516

"Rhythm Basket," 396

Cellophane, 358

colored, 300, 445

Cereal, 298, 466, 484, 487, 501

boxes, 140

Cheerios, 487

Chex, 501

Chairs, 33, 88, 214, 268, 401

lawn, 484

plastic, 416

Chalk, 376, 386, 401, 444

sidewalk, 22, 412, 422

Chalkboards, 386

Character education, 236–238

Character tags, 393–394

Chart paper, 72, 95, 145, 168, 169, 172, 225, 271, 353, 379, 384, 397, 402, 425, 501

Charting activities, 385–387, 402–403, 425–426, 457

Charts, 168, 373, 384–385

alphabet, 332

pocket, 360, 380

signing, 362

Cheese, 496, 499–501

Chinese New Year, 291–293

Chocolate

chips, 490

kisses, 279

pies, 417

playdough, 294

pudding, 417

Chopsticks, 39

Christmas, 138, 283, 286, 353

books about, 238, 246, 252–254, 255–256, 262

Christmas trees

hand-print, 283

small, 286

tissue, 284

Cinco de Mayo

hats, 277

Circle time activities, 105, 109–118, 209–210, 516

Circus, 122–125

books about, 248, 252–253

Class rules, 506–507

Classroom display index, 225

Classroom visitors

naturalist, 96

park guide, 96

Clay, 48, 263, 439

self-drying, 48, 465

soda, 455–456

ClayPressions, 48–49

Clean-up time, 215–216, 416

books about, 260

Clip art, 343, 455

Clocks, 387

Clothes hangers, 267

Clothesline, 424

Clothespins, 204, 230, 268, 382, 423–425

Clothing, 310–311, 329, 416, 423 (See also Dress-up clothes; T-shirts)

books about, 239, 242, 243, 249, 251, 257, 260

Coffee cans, 396, 409–410, 507

Coffee filters, 51

Cognitive development milestones, 16

Coins, 196, 369, 371, 429

Colanders, 443

Collages, 80–81, 193, 324

Colored pencils, 33, 70, 101, 135, 467–468

Colored salt, 440

Colored sand, 460

Colored sugar, 488, 497

Coloring books, 393

Colors, 26–29, 34, 38–39, 54–55, 95, 115, 192, 209, 214, 264, 268, 352, 377, 400, 404, 420, 423–425, 459–462, 473, 520

books about, 243, 247, 251–252, 254, 256–257, 261

Columbus Day

books about, 243

Combs, 472

Comets, 277

Community helpers, 347

books about, 237, 246, 258

Compassion

books about, 237, 250

Computers, 89, 127, 210, 217, 228, 332, 352–353, 361, 363, 467

Confetti, 27

Construction paper, 25, 29, 32–33, 35, 38, 42, 44–45, 47, 54–55, 58, 61, 64, 72, 74, 77–78, 82–83, 86, 88, 90, 92, 94, 97, 101, 104, 119, 122, 126, 128, 131, 134, 142, 148, 166, 176–177, 179, 192–193, 209, 223, 228, 269, 278, 282, 284–285, 292, 296–298, 300–301, 306, 310, 318, 320, 322, 324, 326, 330–331, 333, 336, 338, 343–344, 346, 348, 351–353, 357, 371–373, 377, 383,

388, 404, 417, 445, 447–449, 451–452, 455, 457, 466, 469, 473, 502, 506, 509, 511, 515

Construction
books about, 242, 261

Contact cement, 293

Contact paper, 46, 166, 176, 193, 220, 222, 317, 318, 404, 520
clear, 58, 83–84, 90, 177, 189, 192, 318, 357, 373, 379, 426

Containers, 52, 182, 200, 218, 284, 288, 361, 455
cylinder-shaped, 176
deli, 26
grocery, 341
holiday treat, 285
margarine tubs, 188, 413, 470
oatmeal, 396, 404
plastic, 23, 26, 268, 377, 413, 439, 443, 493
seasonal, 221
shallow, 24, 102
small, 23, 484
toy, 396

Cookie cutters, 221, 294, 499
Christmas, 286
heart-shaped, 488
leaf-shaped, 487
mini, 500

Cookie sheets, 26, 48, 286, 295, 488, 496–497

Cookies, 304, 483
bird-shaped, 454
crumbled, 417
sand-colored, 490
star-shaped, 484

Cooking activities, 483–503

Cooking oil, 24, 145, 294, 481

Cooking spray, 295

Cooperation, 504
books about, 236–239, 259

Copy paper, 45, 71

Cords, 26

Corduroy, 274, 358

Cornstarch, 24, 455, 475

Corrugated cardboard, 80, 358

Corrugated paper, 119

Corsages, 36

Costumes. See Dress-up clothes

Cotton balls, 91, 104, 126, 276, 277, 284, 285, 348, 377, 441, 469

Cotton, 252, 358

Counters, 211 (See also Teddy bear counters)

Counting
activities, 115, 126, 166, 182, 192–193, 267, 288, 293–294, 364, 368, 372–373, 377–378, 384–385,

456, 487
books about, 239, 241–243, 256, 259
in Spanish, 516

Courage
books about, 236–237, 242, 249–250, 252

Cowboys/cowgirls
books about, 242–243

Cows, 320
books about, 252

Crabs
pictures, 450

Crackers, 484, 488, 491, 500
goldfish, 484, 491, 501
rectangle-shaped, 501
Ritz Bits, 501
round, 496

Craft eyes. See Wiggly eyes

Craft items, 27, 32, 80, 129, 132, 193, 194, 224, 276, 286, 315, 409, 436, 493, 510
storing, 223

Craft knives, 53

Craft paper, 24, 377

Craft sticks, 35, 69, 132-133, 155, 181, 200, 290, 293, 300, 322, 348, 439, 456, 491, 501, 509
jumbo, 129, 365

Crayons, 21, 25, 27, 39, 41, 45, 61, 67, 70–71, 74, 86, 90, 94, 99, 102, 105, 125, 135, 144, 168, 172, 179, 223, 280, 282, 296–297, 315, 320, 323, 330, 343, 346, 348–349, 369, 371, 377, 414, 436, 448, 452, 459, 463, 472–473, 502, 504–505
cleaning up markings, 216

Cream cheese, 488, 491

Cream of tartar, 145, 294

Crepe paper, 128, 306

Crock pots, 485

Cultural diversity, 151–153, 209, 291–293, 327, 336–337, 499
books about, 236, 238–240, 243, 248, 251–254, 257–260, 418–419

Cupcake liners, 509

Cupcakes, 279, 514

Cups, 100, 304, 329, 429, 441, 443, 477, 480
measuring, 23–24, 34, 145, 263, 304, 413, 442, 455, 476, 486, 492, 495, 498, 501
paper, 122
plastic, 211, 440, 490
small, 42, 303
Styrofoam, 287, 290
tea, 479, 483

Curling ribbon, 284, 394

Cutting boards, 485

Cylinders, 396

D

Da Vinci, Leonardo, 309

Dancing activities, 96, 105, 136, 199, 393–410

Decorations, 221, 304 (See also Ornaments)

Deli containers, 26

De-Solve-It citrus solution, 216

Dice, 118, 181, 192, 221, 317, 373
exerdice, 415
fairytale, 318–319

Die-cut machines, 80, 510

Dimes, 369

Dinosaurs, 121–122, 345
books about, 242, 244–245, 248, 250, 260–261
plastic, 440

Dirt, 466, 477
potting, 90, 442

Dishes, 43, 126, 134, 429, 440, 479 (See also Plates)
microwave dinner, 443

Dishpans, 33

Dishwashing liquid, 33, 51, 413, 481
bottles, 444

Doilies, 36, 277, 483

Doll furniture, 512

Dollhouses, 512

Dolls, 440, 512
clown, 124

Dominoes, 433, 470

Double-sided tape, 45

Dowel rods, 35, 109, 132, 388, 404–405

Dragons
books about, 247, 259
Chinese New Year, 291–293
puppet, 506

Dramatic play, 67–68, 72, 93, 286
activities, 119–136

Drawers, 222, 335

Drawstring bags, 121

Dreams
books about, 241

Dress-up clothes, 93, 113–114, 119, 125, 186 (See also Clothing)

Drink mix, 145, 473

Drinking glasses, 407, 460, 462, 479–482

Drinking straws, 49, 86, 298, 428, 443
plastic, 413

Drums, 404

Dry-erase markers, 208

Ducks, 442
   plastic, 164
   puppets, 301–302
Duct tape, 22, 394
Dusters, 215
Dustpans, 215

E

Earth Day
   books about, 239
Easel paper, 24
Easter, 300–302
   books about, 238, 242, 247–248,
      250–251, 257, 259
Easter grass, 270, 300
Egg cartons, 80, 291
   cardboard, 129
Eggbeater, 498
Eggs, 498
   books about, 236, 242, 244, 245,
      252
   plastic, 88, 105, 377, 429, 440
Egyptian alphabet sheets, 336–337
Election Day, 514
Electric skillets, 499
Elephants
   books about, 241, 252, 256, 258
Empathy
   books about, 237, 248, 256, 258
Envelopes, 70, 121, 141, 356, 513
   colored, 361
   laminate, 361
Epsom salt, 473
Erasers, 284
Extracts
   coconut, 145
   vanilla, 486
Eyedroppers, 26, 91, 100, 495
Eye-hand coordination, 146,
   187–188, 199, 268, 270, 272, 276

F

Fabric, 112, 132, 142, 274, 348, 358,
   399, 401, 432, 435
   bags, 433
   glue, 19, 112
   markers, 211, 433
   paint, 19, 57, 109, 397, 433, 483
   scissors, 19
   scraps, 94, 129, 223, 286, 315,
      334, 435
   squares, 271
Face paint, 164
Fairness

books about, 236
Fairytales
   books of, 259–260
   dice, 318–319
Fall. See Autumn
Families, 346–347, 509–510
   books about, 237, 240–241, 250,
      253–256, 259, 261
Family game night, 118
Farms
   books about, 236, 240, 242–247,
      249, 251, 254, 257–259, 262
Father's Day, 304–305
   books about, 255
Feather dusters, 215
Feathers, 20, 274, 276, 278, 286,
   306, 358, 417, 421, 452, 469
Feelings, 323–324
   books about, 238, 240, 245–246,
      249–250, 252–253, 256–257, 261
Felt, 83, 101, 112, 157, 162, 170,
   178, 193, 309, 334, 358, 359, 370,
   381, 406, 432, 453, 474
   adhesive-backed, 309
Felt-tip markers, 28
Felt-tip pens, 293, 299, 467
Field trips
   aquarium, 450
   bus trips, 206
   flower garden, 468
   lake, 480
   library, 363, 402
   McDonald's, 206
   Nature Center, 96–97, 206
   nature trail, 459
   planning, 205–206
File cards, 174, 375
File folders, 183, 222, 227
   boxes, 223
   hanging, 223
   manila, 280
File jackets, 227–228
Film canisters, 404, 440
Fine motor activities, 137–147
Fine motor skills, 19–57, 80–81,
   88–89, 94, 97, 199, 276, 278, 286,
   366, 428, 447–448, 451–452,
   464–465, 487, 494, 502–503
Finger foods, 304
Fingerpaint, 29, 54, 282–283
Fingerplays
   bird-related, 41
   "Cinco Vaqueros," 152–153
   "Five Little Valentines," 293–294
   "Little Bunny," 164–165
   "Mice Are Nice," 166
Fire safety, 266

books about, 245
First day of school, 58, 112
   books about, 207, 237, 241, 249,
      252–253, 255, 257, 259–260
Fish, 35, 442
   cardboard, 132
   crackers, 484, 491, 501
   graham crackers, 491
   gummy, 490–491
   pictures, 450–451
   plastic, 132, 264, 450
   Swedish, 491
   tropical, 445, 448
Fishing line, 28
Fishing lures, 441
Flag Day, 305
Flags, 59
   American, 277, 305–306
   friendship, 109
   making, 306
   Mexican, 277
   numbered, 121
Flannel boards, 83–84, 101, 157, 162,
   170, 234, 334, 370, 381, 406, 453
   storing, 234–235
Flashcards, 95, 364–365
   blank, 393
   letters, 81
   word, 317
Flashlights, 126, 297, 469
Flocked bears, 85
Flour, 24, 145, 294, 304
Flower boxes, 388
Flower trays, 508
Flowerpots, 90
Flowers, 237–238, 483
   all about me, 508–509
   books about, 252
   buttercups, 43
   fresh, 43, 80
   growth, 321
   lavender, 495
   masks, 111
   mock orange blossoms, 43
   pansies, 43
   silk, 49, 80
   sunflowers, 49–50, 478–479
   tissue paper, 303
   violets, 43
Foam hearts, 441
Foil. See Aluminum foil
Folders, 176
Folktales, 239–240, 248–249,
   252–253, 255–256, 260–262
Food, 347
   books about, 237, 242–244, 246,

248, 251, 255, 257, 260, 262, 258

cans, 396
  facts, 458
  magazines, 280
  play, 124, 134, 310
Food coloring, 23–24, 31, 34, 55, 145, 264, 418, 420, 424, 440, 462, 473, 475, 489, 491, 493, 495, 497, 499
Forks, 429
  plastic, 80
  wooden, 483
Fossils, 455–456
Fourth of July. See Independence Day
Freezer bags, 486
Freezers, 418, 474
Friendship, 515
  books about, 236–241, 245–246, 248–254, 256–257, 259, 261
Frisbees, 417
Frogs, 99, 451
  books about, 237, 245, 249
  origami, 138–139
Frost, 474
Frosting
  royal, 494
  vanilla, 489
Fruit, 304, 329, 466, 492–493
  apples, 111, 385–386, 456–458, 496–497
  bananas, 76, 492
  cranberries, 454
  dried, 298, 484
  grapes, 492–493, 501
  maraschino cherries, 196
  oranges, 493
  pears, 310
  pineapple, 493
  plastic, 411
  strawberries, 492–493, 495
  tomatoes, 485
Funnels, 443, 477
Fur, 274, 358

G

Galoshes, 111
Game booklet, 229
Game pieces, 222
Games, 176–198
  action words, 183
  airplane toss, 272
  alphabet hopscotch, 177–178
  animal name, 340
  beanbag toss, 271–273
  board, 118, 190
  bowling, 270

bubble game, 161–162
button math, 181
Candy Land, 118
Chutes and Ladders, 118
clothespin drop, 268
dart balls, 178
Doggie, Doggie, Where Is Your Bone? 179–180, 185
dominoes, 180
fair, 164
Go Fish, 118
guess drop, 469
guessing, 378–379
letter carrier, 356
listening, 182
marble race, 470
matching, 176, 181–182, 184, 190, 192
memory, 191
mystery boxes, 185–187
name and toss, 187–188
nursery rhyme, 188–189
Old Maid, 118, 189
part of the whole, 191
peanut number, 288
quiet, 520
riddle me this, 325–326
scavenger hunt, 98
shadow guessing, 472
Simon Says, 420
spinner board, 195
take-home, 211–212
tic tac toe, 299
Trouble, 118
unscramble, 354
Valentine's hearts, 197
What do you see? 74
Who goes first? 198
Garden hose, 416, 460
Garden rakes, 441
Garden stakes, 90
Garden tools, 125, 422
Gardening
  activities, 90–91, 478–479, 488
  books about, 259–260
  greenhouse, 477
  magazines, 280
  rock, 422
Geese
  books about, 244
Gelatin, 490 (See also Jell-O)
General tips for working with five-year-olds, 199–265
Generosity
  books about, 251, 238, 241, 251
Gift bags

homemade, 24
Gift basket filling, 394
Gift boxes, 22
Gift cards, 25
Gift wrap. See Wrapping paper
Gifts, 304–305
  corsages, 36
  peppermint hearts, 295
  pressed-flower placemats, 43–44
  Valentine's candy, 294
Gingerbread houses, 494
Glitter, 27, 31–32, 40, 42, 51, 90, 145, 193, 223, 264, 282, 306, 414, 452
Globes, 105
Gloves, 113, 186
  clear plastic, 91
Glue, 20, 25, 27, 31–32, 36, 39, 42, 44, 47, 49, 51, 55, 61, 63, 67, 72, 77–78, 81–82, 97, 118, 122, 124, 128–129, 134, 141–142, 144, 155, 179, 181, 193, 194, 223, 224, 230, 247, 267, 270–271, 274, 276–278, 280, 284, 286, 290–292, 296, 300, 306, 315, 320–322, 331, 341, 343–346, 348–349, 358–359, 371, 373, 388, 404, 414–415, 417, 421, 432, 445, 448–449, 451, 454, 464, 474, 476, 502, 504, 506, 508–509, 511, 514–515
  colored, 28
  fabric, 19, 112
  guns, 40, 54, 69, 178, 230, 264, 284, 293, 435, 494
  sticks, 38, 83, 176, 180, 183, 189–190, 195, 223–224, 228, 232, 299, 324, 332, 341, 353, 361–362, 370, 377, 380–381, 393, 467, 512
  white, 23, 28, 30, 35, 119, 148, 276, 285, 301, 303, 324, 338, 447, 452, 460
  wood, 204–205
Glycerin, 263, 462
Goats
  books about, 246
Goldfish crackers, 484, 491, 501
Google eyes. See Wiggly eyes
Graham crackers, 489, 491–492, 494
  goldfish, 491
Grandparents
  books about, 238, 252–253, 258–259, 261
Grapes, 492–493, 501
Graph paper, 288, 343
Graphing activities, 385–386
Grass playdough, 23–24
Grass, 320, 438, 441
  clippings, 23
  Easter, 270

Gravel, 105

Gravity, 478

Greeting cards, 224, 276, 286, 343, 353

Grocery ads, 331

Grocery bags, 122, 125, 135, 186, 289, 341

Grocery containers, 341

Gross motor activities, 266–275

Gross motor skills, 52, 88, 96, 105, 173, 175, 177–178, 187–188, 199, 393–430, 450, 518

Groundhog Day, 196, 289–290
  books about, 242

Gummed reinforcements, 86, 138, 166, 333

Gummy bears, 493

H

Hairbrushes, 463

Halloween, 270
  books about, 237, 240–241, 248–249, 253, 255–260

Hammers, 205, 396, 409, 462, 466

Hand wreaths, 511

Hanukah, 279, 282
  books about, 250–251

Happy notes, 203–204

Hats, 113, 119, 124, 130–131, 185–186, 191, 208, 288
  books about, 249
  brimmed, 273
  feathery, 114
  jester, 120
  leprechaun, 111
  New Year's, 286–287
  party, 276
  pilgrim, 111
  President's Day, 297
  Santa, 111
  shark, 447
  sun visors, 60
  witch, 111
  Yankee Doodle, 306–307

Headbands, 55

Hearts, 277, 293
  candy, 196
  cinnamon, 488
  foam, 441
  peppermint, 295
  stickers, 110
  Valentine's, 197

Helpfulness
  books about, 237–238, 249

History, 135–137, 297
  books about, 239–240

Hole punches, 26, 28, 35, 38–39, 46–47, 67, 70–72, 80–81, 92, 140, 144, 147, 166, 214, 224, 228, 276, 300, 318, 333, 336, 343–344, 348, 350–351, 393, 426

Holidays, 111, 276, 308
  Chinese New Year, 291–293
  Christmas, 138
  Easter, 300–302
  Father's Day, 304–305
  Flag Day, 305
  Groundhog Day, 196, 289–290
  Halloween, 270
  Hanukah, 279, 282
  in February, 196
  Independence Day, 21–22
  May Day, 301–303
  Mother Goose Day, 302
  Mother's Day, 36, 43–44, 304
  New Year, 286–287
  President's Day, 196
  St. Patrick's Day, 277, 298–300
  Thanksgiving, 278, 280–282
  Valentine's Day, 196–197, 277, 293–295, 488

Holidays and special days, 276–308

Homes, 454, 505
  books about, 239–240, 247, 253, 261

Honesty
  books about, 236, 238, 244, 249, 255

Hospitals
  books about, 254

Hot chocolate mix, 100, 475

Hot glue guns, 40, 54, 69, 178, 230, 264, 284, 293, 435, 494

Hot plates, 455, 490

Hourglasses, 387

Housekeeping props, 119

Houses. See Homes

Hula hoops, 122, 266, 272, 376, 401, 424
  stands, 266

Humility
  books about, 238, 255

Humor
  books, 239

I

Independence, 199

Ice cream, 417, 495
  cones, 494
  containers, 268
  recipe, 486

scoops, 495

spoons, 129

Ice cubes, 439–440, 473–474, 481, 493
  star-shaped, 484
  trays, 473, 493

Ice, 133, 475, 479, 486
  castles, 418–419
  crushed, 287, 440, 442, 473

Icing. See Frosting

Imagination
  books about, 256

Index cards, 70, 141, 192, 203, 232, 332, 340, 342, 367, 386, 459, 507, 518
  spiral-bound, 229

Index tabs, 225

Independence Day, 21–22, 305–307
  hats, 277

Individuality
  books about, 236, 244

Insects, 97–98, 465, 457
  books about, 242–243, 245–246, 248–250, 254–255, 257, 259–261
  pictures, 451
  plastic, 438, 442

Irons, 215, 463

Ivory dish detergent, 263

J

Jar lids, 24

Jars, 378
  large, 462, 466
  lidded, 466
  peanut butter, 263
  plastic, 263
  science, 264
  stress, 263
  wide-mouth, 478

Jeans, 39

Jell-O, 31 (See also Gelatin)
  molds, 221

Jellyfish, 450

Jewelry, 186
  homemade, 26, 36, 49, 366

Jewels, 118, 291

Jokes, 519

Joy dishwashing liquid, 51, 263

Juice, 304
  bottles, 264
  cartons, 494
  orange, 495

July 4. See Independence Day

Jump ropes, 88, 411

K

KidStuff: A Treasury of Early Childhood Enrichment Materials, 287
Kindness
   books about, 236–238, 243, 248, 252, 256–258
Kitchen brushes, 80
Kitchen timers, 194, 387
Kites
   box, 414
   homemade, 35, 414
Knee-high stockings, 506
Knives, 291, 292, 385–386, 429, 456, 462, 492, 497, 499, 501
   blunt, 500
   butter, 488
   craft, 53
   plastic, 286, 485, 487, 489, 492–493
Kool-Aid, 145, 473
Koosh balls, 80, 423
Kwanzaa
   books about, 253

L

Labels, 176, 213–214, 217, 220–221, 234, 263, 335, 439, 445, 471
Lace, 285, 293
Lacing cards, 276
Ladybugs, 467
Laminate, 38, 44, 69, 70, 83–84, 90, 176–177, 180–181, 183, 189–192, 195, 197–198, 211, 215, 219–220, 228, 230–231, 271, 299, 334, 352–353, 357, 360, 362, 370, 373, 379, 380–381, 393, 445, 451, 453–455, 457, 467
   scraps, 143, 227
Language activities, 199, 309–329, 519
   milestones, 16
   Spanish, 151–153, 209, 327, 516
Lanterns, 126
Laundry bags, 234
Laundry baskets, 113
Lawn chairs, 484
Lawn sprinklers, 416
Lazy Susans, 194
Leaf patterns, 90
Leaf presses, 44
Learning mats, 176–177, 380
Leaves, 44–48, 90, 465, 277, 310, 342, 377, 438, 441, 462–463
Legos, 34, 436
Leis, 59

Leprechauns, 277
   hats, 111
Lesson plans, 226
Letter recognition, 20–22, 33, 62, 72–73, 81–82, 117–118, 121, 134, 141, 177–178, 211, 214, 264, 331–342, 355–357, 359, 412, 450, 452, 459, 485
   alphabet books, 239–248, 254, 256, 262
Letters
   magnetic, 211, 335, 357, 433
   plastic, 211, 214, 264, 438
   pre-cut, 81
   sandpaper, 359
   stencils, 406
Libraries
   books about, 243, 248
   visiting, 363
Lids, 24, 440
Life cycles, 467–468
Light/dark, 469
Lining up, 206–207
Lions
   books about, 250–251, 255
Liquid soap, 95, 263
Liquid starch, 23, 284, 476
Liquid watercolor, 475
Literacy development, 20–21 (*See also* Letter recognition)
   activities, 330–363
Lollipops, 377
   pictures, 451
Long-reach staplers, 231
Love
   books about, 238, 251, 257, 261
Loyalty
   books about, 258
Lumi sticks, 404
Lunch bags, 40, 77, 142, 179, 278, 301, 337, 338, 414, 506

M

M&Ms, 196, 298, 378, 484
   mini, 489
Magazines, 82, 132, 134–135, 277, 324, 331, 340–341, 343–344, 346, 349, 357, 455
   cooking, 134
   food, 280
   gardening, 280
   home, 134
Magnetic boards, 101, 357, 386
Magnetic letters, 335
Magnetic strips, 386
Magnetic tape, 101

Magnets, 126, 132
Magnifying glasses, 90, 369, 442, 474
Mailbags, 121, 356
Manila file folders, 280
Manila paper, 88, 94, 142, 341
Manipulatives activities, 364–366
Manners, 506–507
   books about, 255
Maps, 105, 135
Marbles, 52, 264, 429, 441, 469
   large, 470
Marching, 403–406
Mardi Gras necklaces, 441
Margarine tubs, 188, 413, 470
Markers, 20–21, 25, 32, 35, 38–39, 44, 55, 58, 61, 64, 67, 70, 72, 74, 78, 80–82, 85–86, 90, 92, 95, 101, 104–105, 116–118, 121, 125–126, 128–129, 134–135, 138, 144, 147–148, 164, 168–169, 172, 174, 177, 179, 185, 192, 195–198, 207, 213, 223, 270, 272–273, 280, 282–283, 292, 296–297, 299, 304–305, 310, 315, 317–318, 321, 323, 325–326, 329, 331–332, 335–338, 341, 343–346, 349–351, 353–356, 358, 360, 365, 367–368, 371–373, 375, 380, 382–384, 388, 393, 397, 414–415, 425–426, 432, 436, 445, 448–449, 451, 453, 457, 460, 475–476, 501, 505–506, 509, 512, 515, 518, 520
   caps, 192
   dry erase, 208
   fabric, 211, 433
   felt-tipped, 28, 195
   fine-tipped, 26
   medium-point, 74, 447
   permanent, 26–27, 109, 137, 157, 188, 193, 204, 216, 264, 423
   restoring, 450
   water-based, 353
   wide-tip, 21, 417
Marshmallows, 279, 484
   mini, 489–490, 493
Martin Luther King Day
   books about, 251, 262
Masking tape, 42, 109, 130, 140, 268, 270–272, 276, 298, 342, 365, 368, 425, 470
   colored, 286
Masks
   flower, 111
   snowflake, 111
Matching games, 176, 181, 184, 190, 192, 340, 365, 370, 373–374, 380–384, 453–456
Materials list, 226
Math

activities, 59, 115, 126, 166, 181–182, 211, 364–387, 439, 450, 456, 487
books about, 239, 247, 252
charts, 384–385
Mats, 214, 436
learning, 176–177, 380
rest, 431, 435–436
May Day, 301–303
Mazes, 146, 420–421
Measuring activities, 59, 321–322, 379–380, 439, 468, 470–471, 478–479, 486–487, 498
Measuring cups, 23–24, 34, 145, 263, 304, 413, 442, 455, 476, 486, 492, 495, 498, 501
Measuring spoons, 52, 145, 263, 413, 474, 476, 486, 498
Measuring tapes, 478
Meat, 500
hot dogs, 495
pepperoni, 500–501
trays, 24, 28, 147
Memory games, 191
Memory shirts, 57
Menorahs, 282
edible, 279
handprint, 282
Metal rings, 70, 72
Metallic paint, 284
Mexico
Cinco de Mayo hats, 277
pictures, 277
Spanish language, 151–153, 209, 327, 516
Mice
books about, 236–237, 240, 244–245, 248–251, 254–255, 257, 259–261
Milk, 486
evaporated, 498
half-gallon cartons, 300, 317, 494
Mini Sorters, 227
Mirrors, 41, 74, 436, 471
Mittens, 113, 130, 186, 288, 442
books about, 238
Mixers, 492
Mobiles, 39
Money, 369–371
books about, 240, 258
learning about, 126, 134, 142, 211
photocopies, 371
Monkeys
books about, 243
Monopoly money. See Play money
Monsters, 323–324

books about, 246, 249, 253–254, 259
Monthly sacks, 221
Months, 110–111, 148–149, 196
Moose
books about, 259
Moral choices, 240
Morning greeting, 388–392
Mosaics, 37
Mother Goose Day, 302
Mother's Day, 304
books about, 236–237, 239–240, 247, 250, 252–254, 259
gifts, 36, 43–44
Moving day, 512
Mural paper, 125
Music, 397, 402, 424
activities, 105
books about, 241, 250–251, 255, 258–259, 262
Chinese, 292
different genres, 402–403
during transitions, 516
lively, 136, 403
marching, 122, 404
quiet, 434
space, 120
walking-tempo, 404
waltzes, 130
Music and movement activities, 393–410
Musical instruments, 406–407
cylinder band, 396
homemade, 105, 396, 404–405, 409
one-string fiddle, 409–410
rhythm band, 404–405
rubber band banjo, 409
Myths, 240

N

Nails, 205, 409, 310, 463, 466
Name cards, 214, 471
Name plates, 21
Name recognition, 21, 214, 332, 357–358, 408, 471
Nap time. See Rest time
Napkins, 297, 304, 483, 501
blue, 491
paper, 43
National Audubon Society Field Guide to North American Trees: Eastern Region Trees: Trees Identified by Leaf, Bark, and Seed (Fandex Family Field Guides) by Stephen M.L.

Aronson, 47
National soup month, 287–288
Nature
activities, 26–27, 35, 43, 90–91, 96–99, 113–114, 125–126, 128–129, 181–182, 442, 443–482
books about, 238, 240–242, 251, 253, 256
items, 438
Necklaces, 441
Cheerio, 487
homemade, 26, 49
Needles, 112, 262, 273, 400, 432, 435
blunt, 454
Net fruit bags, 267
News Year's, 286–287
Chinese, 291–293
Newspaper, 29, 40, 43, 45, 102, 131, 278, 284, 344, 384, 397, 433, 441, 462–463, 476, 506
Newsprint, 45, 286, 372, 436
Nickels, 369
Night crawlers, 466
Nighttime, 469, 484
books about, 244–246, 253–254, 257, 259–262
Note cards, 27, 354–355, 367
Notebooks, 343, 478
Notepads, 362
Notes
observation, 212
Post-It, 93, 212
Numbers
books about, 239, 241–243, 256, 259
in the environment, 375
magnetic, 433
plastic, 214
recognition, 115, 126, 166, 182, 192–193, 211, 267, 288, 293–294, 364–368, 372–373, 377–378, 384–385
Nursery rhymes, 168
games, 188–189
"Little Boy Blue," 119
"Little Miss Muffett," 119
"Solomon Grundy," 360
Nutrition
books about, 244, 246
Nuts, 277, 298

O

Oak tag, 69, 90, 180–181, 195, 223, 231, 334, 356–357, 361, 393, 447

Oatmeal containers, 396, 404

Observation sticky notes, 212

Obstacle courses, 420–421

Occupations, 347
   books about, 241, 243, 246, 253–255, 257, 261

Oceans, 128–129, 264

Opposites, 34, 348–349
   books about, 245, 251, 254, 257, 260

Oranges, 493
   juice, 495

Origami, 138–139

Ornaments, 286
   autumn leaf, 46–47
   candy cane, 138
   homemade, 28
   hooks, 230
   snowflakes, 51

Outdoor activities, 35, 43–48, 130, 263, 267, 269, 272, 402, 411–430, 440, 459–461, 464–465, 478–480, 484, 513

Ovens, 26, 48, 295, 485, 487–488, 496–498
   microwave, 496
   play, 286

Overhead projectors, 472

Owls, 96–97
   books about, 246, 254
   pellets, 97

P

Packing peanuts, 273

Packing tape, 131, 213, 219, 227, 342

Page protectors, 232
   homemade, 227

Paint, 20, 26, 33, 45, 48, 52, 54, 61, 92, 95, 99, 100, 102, 121–122, 124, 128, 204, 206, 276–277, 286, 288–292, 297, 315, 384, 404, 413, 421, 427, 436, 451, 493, 514
   acrylic, 101
   fabric, 19, 57, 109, 397, 433, 483
   face, 164
   fingerpaint, 29, 54, 282–283
   metallic, 284
   oil pastels, 49
   Perma, 397
   permanent, 21
   poster, 24, 49
   spray, 277, 518
   tempera, 22, 24, 29, 52, 54, 101, 179, 277, 283, 423, 447, 508
   washable, 40, 42

watercolor, 25, 38, 277 502

Paint pens, 435

Paint samples
   color chips, 214
   color strips, 459

Paint smocks, 102, 384

Paint trays, 29, 179

Paintbrushes, 19, 21, 34, 38, 40, 42, 45, 48–49, 51, 99, 122, 124, 128, 206, 283–284, 286, 288–292, 384, 404, 413, 421, 427, 429, 433, 444, 447, 451, 472–473, 483, 493, 502
   large, 92
   small, 204, 460, 508

Pancakes
   books about, 248
   mix, 499
   shape, 499

Pans, 304, 429, 443, 490
   cake, 418

Paper, 20, 26, 29, 31, 33–34, 37, 39, 41, 52, 57, 65, 74, 80, 89, 99, 100, 102, 105, 115–116, 118, 121, 126, 129, 138, 142, 148, 164, 172, 193–194, 197, 210–211, 223–224, 226, 268, 280, 282–283, 296, 301, 304–306, 315, 317, 320, 323, 329, 336, 341, 343, 345–346, 351–352, 356, 358, 365, 369, 378, 415, 440, 460, 464, 467–468, 476, 504–505, 514
   bulletin board, 117, 126, 464
   butcher, 24, 321, 377, 436, 512
   calculator, 371
   carbon, 33
   chart, 72, 95, 145, 168, 169, 172, 225, 271, 353, 379, 384, 397, 402, 425, 501
   construction, 25, 29, 32–33, 35, 38, 42, 44–45, 47, 54–55, 58, 61, 64, 72, 74, 77–78, 82–83, 86, 88, 90, 92, 94, 97, 101, 104, 119, 122, 126, 128, 131, 134, 142, 148, 166, 176–177, 179, 192–193, 209, 223, 228, 269, 278, 282, 284–285, 292, 296–298, 300–301, 306, 310, 318, 320, 322, 324, 326, 330–331, 333, 336, 338, 343–344, 346, 348, 351–353, 357, 371–373, 377, 383, 388, 404, 417, 445, 447–449, 451–452, 455, 457, 466, 469, 473, 502, 506, 509, 511, 515
   copy, 45, 71
   corrugated, 119
   craft, 24, 377
   crepe, 128, 306
   easel, 24
   fingerpaint, 29
   graph, 288, 343

manila, 88, 94, 142, 341
   mural, 125
   newspaper, 29, 40, 43, 45, 102, 131, 278, 284, 344, 384, 397, 433, 441, 462–463, 476, 506
   newsprint, 45, 286, 372, 436
   parchment, 48
   poster, 172
   rolled, 343
   ruled, 344
   shiny, 170
   story, 350
   thin, 463
   tissue, 24, 35–36, 86, 267, 270, 276, 284, 303, 506
   typing, 317, 343
   wax, 43, 54, 130, 142, 276, 284, 490, 492, 498
   wrapping, 24, 119, 135, 148, 180, 200, 219, 230, 286, 343, 441
   writing, 349

Paper airplanes, 272

Paper bags, 24, 40, 77, 124, 209

Paper box lids, 222

Paper cups, 122

Paper cutters, 43, 348, 383, 447

Paper fasteners, 344

Paper plates, 33, 47, 57, 66, 81, 122, 124, 276, 293, 303, 321, 445, 452, 460, 467, 485, 487–489, 492, 495–496, 500–501, 509, 511

Paper punches, 377

Paper snowflakes, 277

Paper towels, 35, 55, 216, 478

Paperclips, 33, 42, 126, 230, 375, 449
   jumbo, 445

Parades, 338, 450, 452
   books about, 255

Parchment paper, 48

Parents, 403–404
   notes to, 210–211, 502, 510
   stargazing party, 484
   tea party, 483

Parties
   100-day, 484
   stargazing, 484
   tea, 68–69, 483

Party hats, 276

Pasta
   alphabet-shaped, 485
   macaroni, 333
   noodles, 377

Paste, 25, 72, 88, 94, 99, 224, 371

Patience
   books about, 237, 248

Pattern blocks, 212

Patterning activities, 383, 408

Patterns
  alligator, 79
  animal puppets, 338–339
  bears, 312, 381
  calendar snowman, 149–150
  Christmas tree, 284
  dominoes, 180
  duck puppets, 301
  fair time, 164
  fish kites, 36
  fish, 103
  gingerbread boy, 87
  horn o' plenty, 281
  jester hats, 120
  leaf, 90
  Little White Duck, 158
  May Day baskets, 303
  mobile, 195
  mouse, 167
  overalls, 311
  pocket, 85
  shark hats, 447
  tic tac toe pieces, 299
  veggie pockets, 503
  walrus puppets, 338
  Yankee Doodle hats, 307

Peacemaking
  books about, 238, 255–256

Peanut butter, 279, 490
  jars, 263

Pebbles, 24, 270, 394, 404, 438

Pencils, 20, 35, 41–42, 44, 49, 67, 74,
  77–78, 82, 119, 134, 141, 148,
  164, 176, 197, 212, 223, 226, 284,
  301, 306, 320, 323, 330, 343, 348,
  359, 365, 378, 409, 447, 502, 504
  colored, 33, 70, 101, 135, 467–468

Penguins
  books about, 241, 259

Pennies, 196, 369

Pens, 41, 46, 66, 89, 100, 121, 195,
  210, 212, 284, 310, 344, 478
  felt-tip, 293, 299, 467
  paint, 435
  squiggle, 146
  watercolor, 322

Perma paint, 397

Permanent paints, 21

Perseverance
  books about, 236–237, 239, 242,
  252

Pets
  books about, 236, 239–242, 244,
  247, 250, 253, 255-256, 261

class, 332
  pictures, 325–326
  rocks, 421

Phonemic awareness, 199

Photo albums, 209
  pages, 134

Photocopiers, 74, 90, 101, 164, 180,
  191, 195, 217, 225–226, 229, 319,
  357, 371, 379, 453, 512
  color, 69, 83, 231

Photographs, 141, 224
  cancer survivors, 513
  children, 63, 191, 200, 217, 332,
  357, 345, 388, 515
  school people, 512

Physical development
  fine motor skills, 19–57, 80–81,
  88–89, 94, 97, 137–147, 199, 276,
  278, 286, 366, 428, 447–448,
  451–452, 464–465, 487, 494,
  502–503
  gross motor skills, 52, 88, 96, 105,
  173, 175, 177–178, 187–188, 199,
  266–275, 393–430, 450, 518
  milestones, 15

Picnics
  books about, 243, 247, 255–256,
  259
  winter, 287–288

Picture cards, 212

Pictures, 191, 232, 268, 271, 315,
  331, 361–362, 365, 375
  action words, 183
  alphabet, 334
  animal habitats, 454
  animals, 155, 340, 454–455
  apples, 385
  art prints, 309–310
  city skylines, 61
  crabs, 450
  Egypt, 336
  fish, 448, 450–451
  food, 458
  Great Wall of China, 60
  hamburger, 451
  hieroglyphics, 336
  insects, 181–182, 451
  jellyfish, 450
  ladybugs, 467
  lobster pots, 450
  lollipops, 451
  menorahs, 282
  Mexico, 277
  mosaics, 37
  Mother Goose, 188
  pairs, 380

pets, 115, 325
  pizza, 451
  portraits, 41
  quilts, 140
  sharks, 447
  signs, 344
  spiders, 451
  St. Patrick's Day, 299
  tropical fish, 445
  Van Gogh's Sunflowers, 49
  vegetables, 503
  woodland animals, 381
  worms, 451

Pie tins, 135, 397, 423

Pies
  apple, 497
  chocolate, 417
  crusts, 308, 497–498
  fillings, 308
  pumpkin, 498

Pigs
  books about, 246, 248, 255,
  257–259, 262

Pilgrim hats, 111

Pillowcases, 273

Pillows, 434
  nap buddies, 432

Pinecones, 438

Ping-pong balls, 178, 441

Pipe cleaners, 40, 53, 55, 97, 138,
  286, 300, 366, 439, 465

Pirates, 255

Pith helmets, 429

Pizza
  apple, 496–497
  boxes, 142
  crackers, 496
  pictures, 451
  pretend, 373
  sauce, 496
  toppings, 496

Placemats, 43–44

Plants, 200, 422
  books about, 236–237, 242–244,
  245, 253, 255, 260
  chives, 488
  lavender, 495

Plaster of Paris, 22, 304

Plastic, 31
  animals, 264, 440
  bags, 130, 140–141, 416, 484
  beads, 366, 508
  bins, 441
  bottles, 264, 270, 418, 444
  bowls, 491

bubble wrap, 80, 358

bugs, 438

containers, 26, 268, 413, 439, 443, 493

cups, 211, 440, 490

dinosaurs, 440

ducks, 164

eggs, 88, 105, 377, 429, 440

figures, 93, 264, 440–441

fish, 132, 450

flower boxes, 388

forks, 80

fruit, 441

jars, 263

knives, 286, 485, 487, 489, 492–493

rocks, 440

saws, 275

spoons, 80, 287, 489

straws, 413

tote bags, 445

tubes, 442

vegetables, 441

zippered bags, 23, 85, 121, 176, 218, 234, 342, 377, 383, 433, 473, 476

Plastic wrap, 29, 42, 295, 463, 492

colored, 445

Plates, 52, 304, 500

decorated, 483

name, 21

paper, 33, 47, 57, 66, 81, 122, 124, 276, 293, 303, 321, 445, 452, 460, 467, 485, 487–489, 492, 495–496, 500–501, 509, 511

Play equipment, 266

Play food, 126, 134

Play money, 126, 134, 142, 211, 277

Playdough, 31, 418, 439, 465

chocolate, 294

grass, 23–24

homemade, 23–24, 145, 294

scented, 145

uncolored, 286

Playground equipment, 420

Playground sculptures, 427–428

Playhouses, 413

Playing cards, 364, 433

Old Maid, 189

Pledge of Allegiance, 156

Pocket charts, 360, 380

Poem cards, 232

Poems, 84 (See also Fingerplays; Rhymes)

"Apple Star" by Beverly Cornish, 456–457

books of, 254–255, 257, 261

"Effie Lee Newsome" by Patricia Murchison, 165–166

"Funtime Fair Time," 163–164

"George Washington Carver" by Patricia Murchison, 288–289

"Harriet Tubman" by Patricia Murchison, 298

"Little Crocus" by Mary Brehm, 171–172

"Little Flower," 171

"Mary McLeod Bethune" by Patricia Murchison, 308

"Monster, Monster" by Barbara Saul, 323

"Monthly Holidays" by Mary Brehm, 148–151

"Paul Revere Williams" by Patricia Murchison, 296

"Phyllis Wheatley" by Patricia Murchison," 168

"The Scarecrow," 169

"Sounds at Night," 172–173

"Stephen Square" by Patricia Murchison, 168

"There Was an Old Lady Who Lived in a Shoe, 80

"Visiting the Farm" by Mary Brehm, 174

"Winter Has Come," 437

Pointers, 111, 117

Poker chips, 189, 368, 470

Pompoms, 55, 119, 129, 277, 285, 290, 300, 367

Popcorn, 124, 164, 454

Popsicle sticks. See Craft sticks

Poster board, 38, 116–118, 128, 142, 174, 189–190, 196, 271, 342, 352, 359, 362, 380–381, 393, 426, 457

Poster paint, 24, 49

Poster paper, 172

Posters, 225, 321

political, 514

vegetables, 503

Post-It notes, 93, 212

Pots, 287, 429

Potting soil, 90, 442

Predictions, 469–470

President's Day, 196

books for, 239–240, 246

hats, 297

Pretzels, 164, 491, 501

sticks, 279, 298

Printers, 352, 361, 467

color, 299

Prisms, 460

Problem solving, 344, 507

Pudding

chocolate, 417

snack, 492

Pumpkins, 270, 457–458, 498

canned, 498

Puppet house, 129

Puppet theaters, 315

Puppets, 211, 507

alphabet, 338–340

animal, 155

birds, 417–418

dragon, 506

frog, 451

marionettes, 86

paper bag, 40–41, 77, 278, 301–302, 338–340, 506

paper tube, 338

spoon, 338

stick, 69, 182, 232, 338

Purses, 78

Puzzles, 140–141, 433, 435–436, 504, 517

picket, 365–366

pieces, 472

PVC pipes, 421, 427

Q

Quarters, 369

Quesadillas, 499

Quilts, 38–39, 140

books about, 255–256

edible squares, 489

R

Rabbits, 300–302, 310

books about, 238, 242, 247–248, 250–251, 257, 259, 261

Races, 424–426, 470

Raffia, 24

Rainbows, 460–461

Rainy days, 42–43, 352

books about, 248–249, 253–254, 256, 258

Raisins, 164, 279, 298, 454, 482, 484, 501

Reading lists, 363

character education, 236–238

literature, 239–262

Rebus rhymes, 361

Recipe boxes, 315

Recipes

alphabet soup, 485

apple pizza, 496–497

aquarium snacks, 490–491
bag ice cream, 486
banana treats, 492
bubbles, 263, 413
chocolate playdough, 294
chummy chives, 488
cinnamon hearts, 488
edible letters, 485
edible menorahs, 279
edible quilt squares, 489
edible rocks, 490
evaporating paint, 34–35
fish in the ocean, 491
fish mix, 491
fruit salad, 493
fun ice cubes, 493
"gingerbread" houses, 494
grass playdough, 23
hot dog butterflies, 495
lavender smoothies, 495
leafy toast, 487
mini apple pies, 497
oobleck, 475–476
peppermint hearts, 295
pizza crackers, 496
playdough, 24
pumpkin pie, 498
quesadillas, 499
scented playdough, 145
shape pancakes, 499
shape snacks, 500
sidewalk chalk, 22
silly putty, 23
snow paint, 51
snowman soup, 475
soda clay, 455–456
stoplight snacks, 501
sun fruit roll-ups, 492
tooth candy, 501
trail mix, 298, 501
Recycling bins, 471
Refrigerators, 491–492
Relaxation activities, 431, 434
Respect
books about, 236–238, 243, 245, 249, 252, 256
Responsibility
books about, 236–238, 242
Rest time, 431–437
activity bags, 433
mats, 431, 435–436
Restaurants, 134–135
Rhymes (See also Fingerplays; Poems)
action, 173, 175
rebus, 361

Rhyming activities, 84, 91, 328, 361–362, 393–410
riddles, 326
Rhythm band, 404–405
Rhythm sticks, 405
Rhythm train, 406
Ribbon, 20, 40, 59, 100, 119, 224, 268, 276–277, 285, 303, 393, 400, 435, 483
curling, 284, 394
Rickrack, 119, 421
Riddles, 325–326
Rings, 164, 333, 343
homemade, 366
Rocks, 24, 377, 421–422, 438, 443, 469
books about, 257
edible, 490
Rockwell, Norman, 309
Role playing, 298
Roll sheets, 217–218, 389
Roller brushes, 80
Rolling pins, 48, 286, 294
Rope, 88, 382, 401
Rubber bands, 40, 120, 166, 271, 365, 409–410
Rubber cement, 83, 219–220, 229, 334, 362, 365, 370, 380–381, 453
Rubber date stamps, 210
Rulers, 25, 59, 141, 296, 383
Russia, 418–419

S

Safety, 116
books about, 238, 245, 252–257
fire, 266
peanut allergies, 288
poisonous plants, 496
Sailboats, 443
Salad spinners, 26
Salt, 24, 34, 145, 294, 442, 474, 485–486
colored, 440
Epsom, 473
rock, 440
Sand, 24, 30, 270, 438
colored, 460
Sand and water activities, 438–444
Sand and water table, 133
Sand blocks, 404
Sandboxes, 164
toys, 59, 418, 429
Sandpaper, 300, 358–359, 404–405
Sandwich bags, 368
Sanitizing spray, 129

Santa
beard, 111
hat, 111
toilet roll, 284–285
Saving work samples, 210
Scarves, 130–131, 288, 399
Scented playdough, 145
Science activities, 26–27, 33–35, 43, 55, 90–91, 96–99, 105–108, 113–114, 121–122, 133, 263–264, 275, 407, 442–443, 445–482
Science jars, 264
Scissors, 23–26, 28, 32, 35–40, 42, 45–47, 51–52, 55, 58, 61, 67, 69, 71, 77–78, 81–83, 85–86, 88, 90, 92, 94, 97, 102, 104, 117–119, 122, 124–126, 128–129, 137, 140–143, 148, 157, 162, 166, 176, 178, 180, 183, 188, 190, 195, 219–220, 222–224, 227–230, 268, 270, 276, 278, 280, 282–286, 289–291, 293, 296, 298–302, 303, 306, 309–310, 317–318, 320–322, 324, 331, 334, 336, 338, 340–345, 348, 351, 353, 356–357, 359, 361–362, 367, 370, 373, 379–383, 388, 393, 400, 406, 409, 413–414, 417, 426, 432, 435–436, 445, 447–449, 451, 453, 457, 460, 464, 467–469, 487–489, 502, 504, 506, 510–511, 520
fabric, 19
Scoops, 440–441, 443, 491 (See also Ice cream scoops)
Screwdrivers, Phillips, 396
Scrub brushes, 80, 440
Seashells, 30, 60, 264, 377, 442, 450, 455
Seasons, 464–468 (See also Autumn; Springtime; Summer; Winter)
books about, 237, 240, 242, 245, 257–259, 262
Seating
assigned, 213
breaking up cliques, 214
days-of-the-week, 213
Seed catalogs, 280
Seeds, 244
birdseed, 440–401
green bean, 90
lima bean, 478
radish, 477
Self-adhesive pins, 207
Self-discipline
books about, 237, 240, 251
Self-esteem, 346–348, 508–509
books about, 236, 240, 244, 247–249, 251, 254, 260

Senses, 23–25, 27, 30–31, 33, 80–81, 142, 274, 358–360, 457–458, 475–476
  books about, 246–247, 250, 253, 260
Sentence strips, 72, 101, 141, 330, 332, 360, 386
Sequencing activities, 212, 365–366, 381–382, 410
Sequins, 27, 32, 193, 223, 276, 285–286, 414
Sewing, 144, 262, 271, 432, 435
machines, 262, 334
Shadows, 244, 290, 422, 453, 472
Shakers, 105, 404, 488
Shaker-wands, 394
Shamrocks, 277
  making, 298–300
Shapes, 25, 33, 39, 268, 336, 364, 383–384, 472, 499–500, 520
  books about, 242–244, 255, 257, 261
Sharing
  books about, 236–237, 239, 251–252, 258
Shark hats, 447
Sheep
  books about, 257
Sheet protectors. See Page protectors
Sheets, 92, 124, 128, 132, 135, 287, 292, 401, 423–424, 433, 472
Shells. See Seashells
Shoe bags, 375
Shoe brushes, 463
Shoeboxes, 186, 224, 367, 383, 514, 518
Shoelaces, 80, 144, 146–147, 487
Shoes, 119, 186
  boots, 130
  galoshes, 111
  sandals, 60
Shopping bags, 221
Shovels, 59, 429, 441–442
Sidewalk chalk, 412, 422
  homemade, 22
Sieves, 418, 443
Sign language. See American Sign Language
Sizes, 468
  books about, 242, 257, 261
Sleeping bags, 126
Slides, 425
Smocks. See Aprons; Art smocks
Snack and cooking activities, 483–503
Snack time seating, 213
Snacks

100-day mix, 484
alphabet soup, 485
apple pizza, 496–497
apples, 456
aquarium, 490–491
bag ice cream, 486
banana treats, 492
bird food, 454
  books about, 257
Cheerio necklaces, 487
chocolate pudding, 417
chummy chives, 488
cinnamon hearts, 488
cupcakes, 514
"dirt" sundaes, 417
edible menorahs, 279
edible quilt squares, 489
edible rocks, 490
fish in the ocean, 491
fish mix, 491
fruit salad, 493
fudge bars, 417
fun ice cubes, 493
"gingerbread" houses, 494
hot dog butterflies, 495
individual pies, 308
lavender smoothies, 495
leafy toast, 487
letter biscuits, 485
mini apple pies, 497
Mother's Day tea, 304
"mud pies," 417
peppermint hearts, 295
pizza crackers, 496
pumpkin pie, 498
shape snacks, 500
snow cones, 473
snow soup, 287
snowman soup, 475
space, 120
star, 483
stoplights, 501
sun fruit roll-ups, 492
tea party, 483
tooth candy, 501
trail mix, 297–298, 501
vegetable soup, 503
Snow, 287, 420, 474
  books about, 236, 242–243, 245, 254, 257–258, 260–261
  soup, 287, 475
Soap, 416, 423 (See also Liquid soap)
Social development
activities, 109–110, 112–113, 134–135, 199–200, 504–515

milestones, 16
Soda bottles, 164, 264
  2-liter, 270, 418
Soda clay, 455–456
Song cards, 232
Songbooks, 228
Songs, 398
  "Albuquerque Turkey Song," 278
  "All Around the Circle," 197
  "Alphabet Song," 82
  "B-I-N-G-O," 406–407
  bird-related, 41
  "Blow Air in Our Bubble," 161–162
  "Buenos Dias," 152
  "Call a Friend," 153
  "Craft Stick Count," 155
  "Did You Ever Hear a Tiger?" 156
  "Down By the Bay," 328
  "Dress-Up Song," 114
  "The Farmer in the Dell," 393–394
  "Five Brown Teddies," 162–163
  "Flag Salute Song," 156
  "The Freeze Song" by Greg & Steve, 399
  "Green Frog," 157
  "Greeting Rap," 390
  "Halloween Song" by Penni Smith, 154
  "The Itsy-Bitsy Spider," 52
  "Little White Duck," 157–158
  "My Ears," 158–159
  "My Eyes," 159
  "My Nose," 160
  "My Skin," 160–161
  "My Tongue," 161
  "O Susanna," 136
  "Old Dan Tucker," 136
  "Over in the Meadow," 328
  "Rainbow Bubbles," 162
  "Row, Row, Row Your Boat," 395
  "See Your Dentist" by Penni Smith, 154
  "Sister Sky," 170
  "Spanish Days of the Week," 327
  "Sweet Betsy From Pike," 136
  "This Old Man," 328
  "Twinkle, Twinkle, Little Star," 405
  "Waltz of the Snowflakes" by Peter Ilyich Tchaikovsky, 130
  "Waving Song," 390–391
  "Welcome Song," 391–392
  "When Johnny Comes Marching Home," 136
  "Yankee Doodle Dandy," 136, 405
Sorting

activities, 143, 288, 315–316, 335, 364, 375–378, 439, 458, 463

trays, 194

Soup, 287
  alphabet, 485–486
  cans, 396, 410
  snow, 287
  snowman, 475
  vegetable, 503

Space ships, 277

Space
  books about, 256, 258–261
  hats, 277
  snacks, 120

Spanish language, 151–153, 209, 327, 516
  books, 253, 260

Spelling skills, 20–21, 134, 141

Spices
  cinnamon, 285, 485, 487–488, 496–498
  cloves, 498
  ginger, 498
  nutmeg, 498
  pepper, 481, 485

Spiders, 441
  books about, 241, 242, 249, 252, 258
  pictures, 451
  webs, 52–53

Sponges, 19, 21, 24, 57, 80, 102, 121, 128, 181, 221, 284, 416, 423, 433, 440, 469, 514

Spools, 20, 54, 118

Spoons, 52, 100, 145, 263, 304, 308, 338, 413, 440, 429, 474–476, 486, 490, 498
  metal, 295
  mixing, 23, 145, 287, 297, 455, 475, 484, 490, 497, 499, 501
  plastic, 29, 80, 287, 489
  wooden, 483, 498, 508

Spray bottles, 216, 418, 420, 424

Spray paint, 277, 518

Springtime, 300–304
  activities, 40–44
  books about, 236, 239, 241, 243, 253, 256, 259

Square dancing, 136

Squeeze bottles, 26, 442

Squirt bottles, 90

St. Patrick's Day, 298–300
  books about, 258
  hats, 277

Stamp pads, 343, 372

Stamps, 343

date, 210

insect, 333

paw-print, 179

postage, 121

rubber, 273

Staplers, 17, 35, 55, 74, 82, 104, 109, 119, 278, 284, 289, 292, 297, 306, 332, 341–344, 351, 358, 372, 414, 445, 447, 467, 502, 506, 515
  long-reach, 231

Starfish, 60

Stars, 277, 484
  apples, 456
  stickers, 170, 305–306, 358

Stencils, 57
  alphabet, 333, 359, 406, 426
  fork, 483
  mittens, 382
  spoon, 483

Stethoscopes, 119

Stick puppets, 69, 182, 232, 338

Stickers, 121, 135, 197, 207, 268, 270, 272, 338, 343, 371
  American flags, 277
  animals, 196
  apples, 110, 333
  Christmas trees, 110
  circles, 192
  flowers, 110
  fruits, 280
  ghosts, 110
  groundhogs, 196
  hearts, 110
  Kwanzaa symbols, 110
  letters, 426
  menorahs, 110
  Mother Goose, 188
  pears, 310
  pumpkins, 110
  shamrocks, 110
  smiley faces, 268
  snowmen, 110
  spring, 301
  stars, 170, 305–306, 348
  turkeys, 110
  umbrellas, 110
  vegetables, 280

Sticks, 126, 132, 135, 409

Sticky notes. See Post-It notes

Stockings, 506

Stones, 118

Stopwatches, 387

Storage, 219–230, 234
  alphabet sorting case, 335
  containers, 219

pockets, 190

science kits, 445

Stories
  "Bare Bear," 310–312
  box, 329
  on tape, 233
  recording, 349–351
  "Sad Little Rabbit," 146
  writing, 318–319

Storms
  books about, 258

Storytelling, 327–328

Strawberries, 492–493, 495

Streamers, 122, 414, 460, 514

Stress jars, 263

String, 35, 38–39, 46, 53, 81, 92, 126, 137, 166, 230, 273, 278, 286, 291, 336, 342–343, 409, 414, 420–421, 426, 477, 487

Stringing activities, 26, 49, 138, 487

Stuffed animals, 70, 289
  bats, 310
  bears, 431
  elephants, 88
  lobsters, 450
  monkeys, 76
  rabbits, 310
  safari, 418

Styrofoam, 132, 275, 388, 440–441, 508
  balls, 291
  blocks
  cubes, 193, 318
  cups, 287, 290
  meat trays, 24, 28, 147
  packing peanuts, 273, 469

Substitutes
  helping, 217–218

Subtracting, 373–374

Sugar, 263, 485–486, 492, 496, 498
  brown, 497
  colored, 488, 497
  powdered, 492, 494

Suitcases, 114

Summer activities, 49–50, 173

Sun, 277, 422, 492
  books about, 248, 261

catchers, 26, 38–39, 44–45

visors, 60

Sunflowers, 49
  growing, 478–479
  seeds, 50, 298, 454, 478

Sunglasses, 59, 113, 310

Sunscreen, 443

Swap day, 208

Sweatshirts, 19
Swimsuits, 59, 186, 443–444, 484

T

Tablecloths, 483
  vinyl, 188
Tables, 208, 328
Tagboard, 77, 83, 102, 180, 188, 190, 232, 284, 296, 299–301, 320, 352, 359, 370, 380–381, 452–453, 510, 520
  cards, 325
Tang, 120, 484
Tape, 29, 33, 55, 66, 78, 117–118, 125–126, 128, 132, 143, 148, 166, 223–224, 264, 270, 286, 317–318, 343, 369, 404, 414–415, 455, 466, 487, 504, 512
  colored, 286
  double-sided, 45
  duct, 22, 394
  magnetic, 101
  masking, 42, 109, 130, 140, 268, 270–272, 276, 298, 342, 365, 368, 425, 470
  packing, 131, 213, 219, 227, 342
  transparent, 227, 388
Tape measures, 55, 425
Tape players, 83, 120, 127, 157, 162, 217, 233, 292, 402–405, 407, 516
Tea, 304, 483
Tea parties, 68–69, 483
Teachable moments, 201–202
Teapots, 479, 483
Teddy bears, 431
  books about, 238, 249, 254, 259, 261
  counters, 85, 368, 470
Telephone books, 43
Tempera paint, 22, 24, 29, 54, 101, 179, 277, 283, 423, 447, 508
  powdered, 52
Templates, 25
  shapes, 383
Tents, 126
Textures, 23–25, 27, 30–31, 33, 80–81, 142, 274, 358–360, 457–458, 475–476
Thanksgiving, 278, 280–282
  books about, 240, 252, 254, 257–259
Thermometers, 475
Thread, 26, 112, 262, 273, 400, 432, 435, 454
Three-prong folders, 350
Three-ring binders, 72, 232, 509
Tickets, 214, 315
Ties, 186

Tiles, 49, 470

Time
  books about, 239, 253
  measuring, 387
Timers. See Kitchen timers
Tissue boxes, 451
Tissue paper, 24, 35–36, 86, 267, 270, 276, 284, 303, 506
Tissues, 504
Toilet paper tubes, 22, 63, 284, 338
Tongs, 439–440
Tongue depressors. See Craft sticks
Toothbrushes, 264
Toothpicks, 49, 465
Toppings
  ice cream, 308
  pizza, 496
Tote bags, 112, 211, 445, 509
Towels, 26, 33, 95, 416, 443
  paper, 35, 55, 216, 478
Toy cars, 329, 425, 440–441, 512
Toy containers, 396
Toy trucks, 440–441, 512
Trail mix, 297, 501
  recipe, 298
Trains
  books about, 260
  whistles, 517
Transition activities, 516–521
Transportation
  books about, 237, 242, 245, 247, 252, 255, 257, 260–261
Trash bags, 131, 273, 418
Traveling
  books about, 260
Trays, 91, 134, 222, 443, 500
  meat, 24, 28, 476
  paint, 29, 179
  shallow, 55
  sorting, 194
  star-shaped, 484
Treasure boxes, 264
Trees, 464–465
  books about, 243, 252, 260
  of hands, 283
  tissue, 284
Tricksters
  books about, 240, 256, 262
Tricycles, 426, 513
T-shirts, 57, 121, 397
Tubman, Harriet, 297–298
Tubs
  margarine, 188, 413, 470
  small, 455

washtubs, 95
Tunnels, 88
Turkey puppets, 278
Turtles
  books about, 245, 248
Twigs, 20, 438, 441
Typewriters, 332
Typing paper, 318, 343

U

Umbrellas, 111, 113, 122
Unit blocks, 385

V

Valentine's Day, 196–197, 293–295
  books about, 241, 245, 247, 251, 257–258, 260
  hats, 277
  snacks, 488
Vegetable brushes, 304
Vegetable catalogs, 502
Vegetable oil. See Cooking oil
Vegetables, 287, 485, 488, 502–503
  books about, 244
  carrots, 76, 485
  celery, 279, 462
  chives, 488
  frozen, 287
  lettuce, 466
  onions, 485
  parsley, 491
  peas, 485
  plastic, 441
  potatoes, 485
  pumpkins, 270, 457–458, 498
Velcro, 176, 178, 190, 361, 431, 455, 457
Videocassette boxes, 309
Vinyl tote bags, 112
Voting, 514

W

Wading pools, 164
Wallpaper, 343
  sample books, 25, 140, 382–383
  scraps, 94
Warhol, Andy, 309
Watches, 186
Water, 22, 24, 31, 33–34, 52, 55, 145, 264, 294, 304, 407, 413, 416, 418, 420, 423–424, 440, 442, 455, 460, 473, 475–477, 479–481, 492–493

carbonated, 482

distilled, 263

Water animals, 442, 447, 451

books about, 238, 240, 242, 247, 249–251, 254, 256, 259, 261

Water bottles, 31, 222, 417

half-pint, 394

Water pumps, 440

Water wheels, 440

Watercolors

liquid, 475

paints, 25, 38, 277, 502

pens, 322

Watering cans, 464

Wax paper, 43, 54, 130, 142, 276, 284, 490, 492, 498

Weather, 113–114, 173, 175

books about, 242, 257, 262

Weaving, 53

Weighing, 470–471

Welcome board, 208

Whales

books about, 261

Whipped topping, 492–493, 499

White board, 208

Wiggly eyes, 35, 40, 129, 148, 285, 290, 300–301, 338, 417, 421, 447–449, 452, 506

Wigs, 119

Wild cards, 518

Williams, Paul Revere, 296

Winter

activities, 51, 100, 130–132, 148–149, 287–288, 351, 418–420, 437, 473–475

books about, 242–243, 245, 247, 258, 260–261

hats, 277

Witch's hats, 111

Wood, 132

beads, 54, 508

blocks, 401, 404

boards, 274

craft hobby, 204

dowel rods, 35, 109, 132, 388, 404–405

glue, 204–205

pieces, 358, 409, 463

shapes, 54

skewers, 49

Woodcraft pieces, 508

Wooden forks, 483

Wooden spoons, 483, 498, 508

Wool, 275, 358

Word cards, 315

Workbooks, 393

Worksheets, 453

Worms, 441–442, 466

pictures, 451

Wrapping paper, 119, 148, 180, 200, 219, 230, 286, 343, 441

brown, 135

homemade, 24

Wright, Frank Lloyd, 309

Writing skills, 20–21, 199, 264

X

X-acto knives, 129, 359, 361

Y

Yardsticks, 117, 425, 478

Yarn, 20, 32, 38, 40, 42, 47, 53, 67, 71, 72, 86, 104, 119, 124, 129, 132, 140, 142, 144, 147, 148, 193, 228, 270, 276–277, 285–286, 291, 298, 318, 348, 351, 393, 396, 398, 426, 432, 441, 434

Yogurt, 120, 488

Z

Zippered plastic bags, 23, 85, 121, 176, 218, 234, 342, 377, 383, 433, 473, 476

The GIANT Encyclopedia of Theme Activities for Children 2 to 5

Over 600 Favorite Activities Created by Teachers for Teachers

Edited by Kathy Charner

This popular potpourri of over 600 classroom-tested activities actively engages children's imaginations and provides many months of learning fun. Organized into 48 popular themes, from dinosaurs to the circus to outer space, these favorites are the result of a nationwide competition. 511 pages. 1993.

ISBN 0-87659-166-7

Gryphon House

19216 / Paperback

The GIANT Encyclopedia of Circle Time and Group Activities for Children 3 to 6

Over 600 Favorite Circle Time Activities Created by Teachers for Teachers

Edited by Kathy Charner

Open to any page in this book and you will find an activity for circle or group time written by an experienced teacher. Filled with over 600 activities covering 48 themes, this book is jam-packed with ideas that were tested by teachers in the classroom. 510 pages. 1996.

ISBN 0-87659-181-0

Gryphon House

16413 / Paperback

The GIANT Encyclopedia of Art & Craft Activities for Children 3 to 6

More Than 500 Art & Craft Activities
Written by Teachers for Teachers

Edited by Kathy Charner

A comprehensive collection of the best art and craft activities for young children. Teacher-created, classroom-tested art activities to actively engage children's imaginations! The result of a nationwide competition, these art and craft activities are the best of the best. Just the thing to add pizzazz to your day! 568 pages. 2000.

ISBN 0-87659-209-4

Gryphon House

16854 / Paperback

The GIANT Encyclopedia of Science Activities for Children 3 to 6

More Than 600 Science Activities
Written by Teachers for Teachers

Edited by Kathy Charner

Leave your fears of science behind as our *GIANT Encyclopedia* authors have done. Respond to children's natural curiosity with over 600 teacher-created, classroom-tested activities guaranteed to teach your children about science while they are having fun. 575 pages. 1998.

ISBN 0-87659-193-4

Gryphon House

18325 / Paperback

The GIANT Encyclopedia of Preschool Activities for Three-Year-Olds
Edited by Kathy Charner and Maureen Murphy

Looking for tried and true ways to capture the attention of your three-year-olds? This comprehensive collection of over 600 teacher-created activities provides hours of fun and interesting activities perfectly tailored for this age group. Discover new ways to use everyday items to create fresh, exciting art projects; learn new classroom management techniques from experienced teachers; and find helpful tips for working with three-year-olds. Formerly titled, *It's Great to Be Three*. 576 pages. 2004.
ISBN 0-87659-237-X
Gryphon House
13963 / Paperback

The GIANT Encyclopedia of Preschool Activities for Four-Year-Olds
Edited by Kathy Charner and Maureen Murphy

Written just for four-year-olds, this collection of over 600 teacher-created, classroom-tested activities has everything from songs and books to activities in art, circle time, transitions, science, math, language, music and movement, and more! Helpful classroom management techniques are included. This complete resource of the best selections from a national contest is sure to become a classroom favorite. Formerly titled, *It's Great to Be Four*. 624 pages. 2004.
ISBN 0-87659-238-8
Gryphon House
14964 / Paperback

The Complete Book of Rhymes, Songs, Poems, Fingerplays, and Chants

Over 700 Selections

Jackie Silberg and Pam Schiller

Build a strong foundation in skills such as listening, imagination, coordination, and spatial and body awareness with over 700 favorite rhymes, songs, poems, fingerplays, and chants. 500 pages. 2002.

ISBN 0-87659-267-1

Gryphon House

18264 / Paperback

The Complete Book of Activities, Games, Stories, Props, Recipes, and Dances

For Young Children

Pam Schiller and Jackie Silberg

Are you searching for just the right story to reinforce your theme? Trying to play a game but can't remember the rules? Looking for your favorite no-bake cookie recipe? It's all right here! This book is chock full of over 600 ways to enhance any curriculum. The companion to *The Complete Book of Rhymes, Songs, Poems, Fingerplays, and Chants,* it's a teacher's best friend! 512 pages. 2003.

ISBN 0-87659-280-9

Gryphon House

16284 / Paperback